AMERICAN BATTLEFIE OF WORLD WAR I, CHÂTEAU-THIERRY—THEN AND NOW

A GUIDEBOOK, ANTHOLOGY AND PHOTOGRAPHIC ESSAY

BY DAVID C. HOMSHER

FIRST EDITION
2006
BATTLEGROUND PRODUCTIONS

American Battlefields Of World War I, Château-Thierry—Then And Now
By David C. Homsher

© 2006 David C. Homsher

Battleground Productions, PO Box 624, 85 Tilton Avenue, #4, San Mateo,
California 94401, United States of America.
Tel. (650) 347-6073
daveh@battlegroundpro.com
www.battlegroundpro.com

Permissions: Photographs, maps and illustrations used are from two main
sources and are not separately identified. All historic "artwork" with no attri-
bution are in the public domain from U.S. Official sources. The "Now" photos
are courtesy of the David C. Homsher Collection, as taken by David Homsher.
All others are identified with the source of the photograph, map or illustration.

DISCLAIMER

The purpose of this book is to provide information on the subject matter
covered, to educate, to entertain, and to guide. Neither the editor nor Battleground Productions shall have liability or responsibility to any person or entity
with respect to any loss or damage caused or alleged to be caused directly or
indirectly by the information contained in this book.

First Edition 2006

Designed and Typeset by Katherine de Marne Werner, RSBPress LLC

Printed in the United States of America by Central Plains Book Manufacturing
Printed on New Life recycled paper

ISBN 978-0-9702443-0-7

10 9 8 7 6 5 4 3 2 1

WARNING:

Wartime relics, such as shells, grenades, etc.,
are usually in a *highly dangerous condition
and still cause death and injury*. Any such objects found during visits to the battlefields
should be strictly left alone.

Also much of the land is private property and
must be respected as such.

It is *your* responsibility to heed the above
warning. Battleground Productions cannot
be held responsible for your actions during
the tour.

Homsher, David C.
American battlegrounds of World War I, Chateau-Thierry–then and now / David C.
Homsher. – 1st ed. – San Mateo, CA : Battleground Productions, 2006.

p. ; cm.

Includes bibliographical references and index.
ISBN: 978-0-9702443-0-7

1. World War, 1914 1918–Battlefields–France–Guidebooks.
2. United States. Army. American Expeditionary Forces–History. 3. World War,
1914-1918–Campaigns–France. 4. World War, 1914-1918--United States. 5.
France–Guidebooks. I. Title. II. Chateau-Thierry.

D528 .H66 2004
940.4/1273–dc22   0506

Dedication

This Book Is Dedicated To The One Hundred
And Sixteen Thousand, Seven Hundred And
Eight Americans Who Endured All And Who
Gave All During The First World War That
Honor And Justice Might Prevail And That The
World Might Enjoy Freedom And Inherit Peace

DEDICATION AND REMEMBRANCE

THE DOUGHBOYS

There will be voices whispering down these ways,
The while one wanderer is left to hear,
And the young life and laughter of old days,
Shall make undying echoes

— Geoffrey Young
Stars and Stripes, 1918

Generations of Americans born since 1918 scarcely remember or appreciate what their fathers, grandfathers and great-grandfathers experienced in France during World War I. Knowledge of the battles, the battlegrounds, and the American participation in that war is no longer in our national memory. It is a sad commentary that "the war to end all wars" has been relegated to the dustbin of history less than a century after the final shots were fired. During World War I, almost five million Americans wore the uniform of their country; two million soldiers went overseas, and 116,708 of them gave their lives—53,513 in combat action and another 63,195 from disease and other non-hostile causes.

This volume is dedicated to all of the American soldiers, sailors and marines who fought so valiantly on land and sea and in the air during the greatest struggle for liberty in the history of the world prior to 1914. 'Lest We Forget,' this book is written with a determination that "Time will not dim the glory of their deeds." As such, it is a labor of gratitude and respect for those who served so well.

Photo Credit: David Homsher collection

Dedicated to America's Unknown Soldier

4

SOLDIER COURAGE

The American soldiers were not press-heroes; they were young, idealistic men who fought hard for a cause they felt was right. This book does not seek to highlight the glories of war. But this does not mean there is not room to spotlight the courage inherent in war. There is no greater quality than courage, especially when demonstrated in the process of saving one's fellow soldiers. Such selflessness is an endearing quality often formed in the crucible of combat. This selflessness is genuinely one of most important, albeit, unheralded legacies of war. Certainly it is a heritage worth preserving and perpetuating. It is for this reason that the author constantly kept one eye on the list of citations and decorations of the AEF.

Deeds of valor by units and individuals are picked out for description, but no claim is made that these men were the best or bravest on the battlefield. Rather, these descriptions were chosen only as representative samples. Thus, they owe their inclusion herein to the double chance of being on conspicuous record as well as being pertinent to the story. Medal of Honor citations are freely quoted because they give a vivid picture of the fighting and accurately represent many other acts of supreme courage and sacrifice. Citations and decorations are not the final standard by which to judge the service rendered by individuals. For every man who received the Medal of Honor there were thousands of other men who did as much or more than those who were cited or decorated, who performed similar deeds of heroism and received lesser awards or no reward at all. The Medal of Honor recipients given in this book are merely representative heroes of the AEF, those whose valorous deeds were witnessed and recorded. To recognize all the deeds of heroism performed by members of the AEF, recorded and unrecorded, would be like calling the roll of the stars in the sky. Ninety-four men were awarded the Army Medal of Honor during World War I. As the majority of these men were in the infantry, the branch of service is indicated in the text only in case the soldier was affiliated with some other combat arm or branch of service.

AUTHOR'S NOTE

It is improper and inaccurate to refer to World War I Medals of Honor as the "Congressional" Medal of Honor. Modern Medals of Honor are awarded by the President of the United States and in the name of Congress. During World War I, however, each service issued its own Medals of Honor—the Secretary of War for the Army, and the Secretary of the Navy for the Navy. There were no lower medals for conspicuous bravery at that time.

For the most part, U.S. Marines serving with the AEF were awarded both the Army and Navy Medals of Honor because the Marines were actually part of the U.S. Army in France. No Marine officers of the AEF were awarded Medals of Honor by General Pershing (one, 2d Lt. Talbot got a Navy MOH while flying with the U. S Navy in support of the British Front). Some consider this to have been a blatant slap in the face; at least two marine officers (George Hamilton and Logan Feland) displayed enough mettle to qualify. Ironically, virtually every Navy officer serving in the 4th Brigade at Belleau Wood received the Medal of Honor. Marines of the AEF were not eligible for the Navy MOH because they were under the jurisdiction of the Articles of War; Navy officers attached to Marine units were under Article of the Navy.

After the war, the Medal of Honor was converted to a national (rather than service) award. At that time the word "Congressional" was unofficially added—this was done so all dual (i.e., Army and Navy medals awarded for the same action) Medals of Honor were consolidated into a single award.

PREFACE

World War I, fought between 1914 and 1918, was a significant event in U.S. history because that massive conflict changed our nation forever and set the pattern for America's current dominant role in world affairs. The American Expeditionary Force of almost two million soldiers provided the strategic counterweight that tipped the scales of victory in favor of the Allies. Without American intervention on the battlefield in 1918, no one knows how the "Great War" might have ended or how the course of history might have changed. All we can say for certain is that the "Sammies" (our French allies referred to American soldiers as "Les Amis" [Our Friends], a phrase that the Doughboys mistook to be French slang for "Uncle Sam") went "Over There" and that the Allies emerged victorious within a year and a half of that influx. In 1917 the United States of America entered World War I and left behind forever its role as a bystander in global affairs.

WHY THIS BOOK EXISTS

My goal is to make modern Americans aware of the deeds and sacrifices of their fathers, grandfathers, and great-grandfathers by briefly telling the story of the AEF using their battlefields in Western Europe as a medium. Touring those battlefields while using this guide will help American visitors understand the motives that spurred enthusiasm for a just crusade, explain the driving force behind uncounted acts of collective and individual bravery on the field of battle, and make clear the part America played in the final victory. Readers, young and old alike, can profit from understanding the Doughboys' self-denial and courage almost a century ago. I want to give the younger generations the understanding needed to go to Europe and to visit the fields where their forefathers secured future freedom for themselves and their children. It is also my hope that this book helps them to better appreciate the ravages of war and will urge them to find a way to avoid a repetition of this history.

This book is the first in a planned series of guidebooks by Battleground Productions, each of which will follow a similar "then-and-now" format. The purpose of this series is to provide a retrospective comparison of the AEF battlefields in France and Belgium. This book is the result of many years of arduous effort. The research alone for the first three volumes took almost a decade, and the writing process another ten or so years. My information is based upon hundreds of military unit histories, numerous other books, articles, and periodicals. Unfortunately, obtaining exact citation and acknowledgement permission from the original publishers of hundreds of books and magazine articles, most of which had been published between fifty and eighty-six years ago, presented many difficulties. Every reasonable effort has been made to give full credit to original sources. In too many instances, however, it has proven impossible to trace the genealogies of long defunct publishing houses, some of which have been bought out many times over and have thus undergone many name changes and owners. It has also proven very difficult to identify the present-day holders of copyrights and the literary executors of certain authors. I am, therefore, still actively seeking information to ensure complete acknowledgement of sources. I will be grateful for any information as to their identity and whereabouts.

This book primarily uses U. S. Government official photographs which are in the public domain. In all such instances, the source of the photograph is not indicated. Also, a number of photographs in this book were originally sold in France as postcards after the World War. Most of them have not, to the best of my knowledge, been published elsewhere. Some of the remaining photographs are from my own personal collection while others were copied from military unit histories which are in the public domain.

Maps and line drawings were mostly garnered from long out-of-print military unit histories. The drawings and other art works by AEF combat artists are, of course, in the public domain. As is the case with the text of this book, every reasonable precaution has been exercised to avoid copyright infringement.

ABOUT THIS BOOK

This book is a succession of battle-tableaux, written when the memories, events and incidents of war were still glowing vividly in the minds of the writers. This book is written in a 'tone-of-the-times' format so that the reader will enjoy a fuller appreciation of the accomplishments of the AEF on the Western Front. The personal element gives interest to the events described.

By writing contemporaneous with the event, no problems of memory or distortions due to hindsight arise. Rather, the war unfolds for the reader as it did for the soldier. The writings were chosen so you can appreciate what it must have been like for the officers and men of both armies at the front.

It also identifies the American military cemeteries and monuments located within the battle areas. These books are designed to be "user-friendly" guides, designed to accompany American visitors on their journeys to those foreign landmarks of American history which reside within France's historic Marne Valley.

It is obviously impossible to describe a complicated military engagement using the same manner one would tell of a peaceful walk or a scenic drive as do most travel guides. This account provides more than a brief description of the terrain. It also gives the traveler context and background information necessary to comprehend the importance of the fighting in the Marne salient. Stories of minor incidents are no less authentic than the accounts of the battles because they provide color and add a personal touch.

The history books tell of generals, daring airmen, and feats of individual heroism. This book focuses on the daily heroics of common soldiers, those Doughboys who huddled under fire in muddy trenches or went "Over the Top" at zero hour. The words of the common soldiers tell their own story, and they need no introductory comment.

Battleground Productions' 'then-and-now' comparison photography brings the past to life by matching precisely the wartime photographs with the same areas as they appear today. In addition to being an outstanding historical reference, *American Battlegrounds of World War I* also contains detailed maps and instructions, making it easy for you to locate various historical sites for yourself. This book is a "must have" for any military historian and is a valuable addition to any research library.

Using this book, an interested sojourner will not have to go to numerous different sources for the information needed to journey to the American battlegrounds because this book contains all the necessary information.

A Note on Historical Accuracy and Prose

Those who have a personal acquaintance with war know that military operations are never completely clear and orderly, even under the best of circumstances. War is usually the epitome of confusion, and battles usually do not fit the exact patterns they ascribe to in the history books, no two of which will precisely agree on much of anything. Clausewitz's expression, "the fog of war," is not an idle commentary.

Selections from older writers are often accurate representations of how soldiers thought and acted at the time. Some of their writings contain historical inaccuracies. Where the inaccuracies of historical content are obvious and of notable magnitude, notes are given in the text.

Both primary and secondary historical sources have been used in the writing of this book. Primary sources, the accounts of participants, although usually not too historically accurate, can impart to the reader some of the 'tenor-of-the-times.'

The primary purpose of this book is to entertain and guide. If, secondarily, it also instructs and educates—then so much the better. As to this book being a history, scholars and historians are advised to look elsewhere! This is an anthology of soldier writings on the AEF in battle, not its history.

American Armies and Battlefields in Europe, published in 1938 by the American Battle Monuments Commission is considered to be extremely accurate in its presentation of the placement of various army units in the battlefield at different times. The same is true of their *Summary of Operations in the World War* (by divisions), 28 volumes, Washington, DC., American Battle Monuments Commission, GPO, 1944.

All casualty figures were derived from official records of the War Department and, unless otherwise specified, include only the killed and wounded in action and those who died of wounds received in action. The figures exclude all missing in action, captured and sick. In all cases, casualties are given only for the time periods units actually served in the front line.

For the benefit of those readers who find this book to be absorbing and wish to delve a little deeper into the subject of American participation in World War I, there are innumerable accounts of the war written by various participants and historians. Listed in the bibliography of this book are some unit histories and other writings recommended for reading by those who would like to read more about the American soldier and the fight that he waged in the Marne salient of 1918. In the appendix is a listing of historical organizations which specialize in the study of World War I. There is also a listing of World War I reenactment organizations, museums and companies which conduct battlefield tours, as well as information on the U.S. 3rd Division, which was involved in the fighting at Château-Thierry.

FOREWORD

David Homsher, an amateur historian of the battlefields of the American Expeditionary Forces(AEF) during World War I, has created a series of guidebook specifically intended for travelers interested in touring the American battle-sites in France and Belgium. Prior to this publication there was no up-to-date guidebook to American battlefields readily available. The most recent AEF battlefields guidebook was the American Battle Monuments Commission's (ABMC) verbatim 1992 reprint of American Armies and Battlefields in Europe, a work first published in 1927, and again in 1938.

Mr. Homsher's work is important because locating information about specific battle-sites can be a daunting task for the traveler. The volume of literature about the AEF sent to France in 1917 and 1918 is enormous. Uncounted general histories about World War I line the shelves of almost every library, but while these works devote many pages to general analysis about political and military events and describe in detail the personalities of world leaders and famous generals between 1914 and 1918, they do not give the detail necessary to guide one to the specific battlefields. Military unit histories are invaluable for historians, but they are not readily available to the general public. Additionally, they are written for a sophisticated readership composed of professional historians and military men, thus, they do not reduce the narrative to the simple terms appropriate for a tourist, nor do they acquaint the traveler with French culture.

In general, people hoping to visit the battlefields must devote themselves to strenuous studies of complex campaign histories or hire a professional guide in order to get to the battlefields of their choice. Then they must find places to stay, decide what to look for once they are there, and know how to properly interpret what they see. Needless to say, a tourist should have some appreciation of the French people, their language, and their culture to make the trip more memorable. In short, no suitable guide for touring the American battlegrounds of World War I was available until David Homsher filled this glaring void.

David Homsher first contacted the Michelin Company regarding this project in 1988. His unexpected inquiry caused a mild revelation. Company representatives were surprised by his request for permission to use the contents of long out-of-print Michelin battlefield guidebooks 75 years after they were first written. Michelin representatives wrote: "We were happy to learn that our old battlefield guidebooks might still contribute to a contemporary understanding of the heroism of the long-forgotten 'Sammies' [U.S. soldiers]. The actions of the American Divisions in North-East France in 1918 was at the time decisive, and the sacrifices of the United States Armed Forces are still warmly appreciated by the French population to this very day. Immediately after the Great War, the MICHELIN TIRE COMPANY wrote three Battlefield Guides under the title *The Americans in the Great War*. Mr. Homsher's modern project stays true to our intent to commemorate the hallowed ground where the American Doughboys bled and died to preserve freedom and save Europe from the forces of Imperial Germany. His work describes the monuments, cemeteries, and memorials created in the interim between the publication of our works during the 1920's and the dawn of the 21st century, and we at Michelin feel this is an important project."

Alain Arnaud, External Relations Director,
Michelin Tire Company, France, 1998

ACKNOWLEDGMENTS

Like any written work, this book was a collaborative effort. For those things I got right, I owe many people, but any errors regarding fact or interpretation are mine alone.

I wish to thank many individuals for their assistance. Many good people have edited, advised, guided, praised, criticized, or provided me with research materials: Henry Spall, LtCol Ronald Brown, USMC (Ret), Katherine de Marne Werner, James Nilo, the staffs of the interlibrary loan departments of the Alameda and San Mateo County, California Library Systems, together with the Lancaster County, Pennsylvania Library, all of whom have been unfailingly helpful to me in the long search for books dealing with American participation in World War I; the many libraries nationwide who have loaned me books through the National Interlibrary Loan Program; the respective staffs of the U.S. National Archives Still Photographs, Maps and Textual Reference Divisions for their unstinting help in locating appropriate photographs, maps and textual materials; Hal Barber, Donna Cunningham, Clark Jarrett,

THE LEADERS

KAISER WILHELM
HOHENZOLLERN
EMPEROR OF GERMANY

WOODROW WILSON
PRESIDENT OF THE
UNITED STATES

GEORGES CLEMENCEAU
PREMIER OF FRANCE

Catherine Platt, Sylvia Ward and the Bank of Lancaster County; the staff of the U.S. Military History Institute Reference Division who encouraged me, answered my many questions, and guided me through their photographic and textual archives; the Library of Congress Geography and Maps Division and Prints and Photographs Division; and all of the unnamed military historians of the American Expeditionary Force.

There remain others to whom I must express my gratitude. First, my family—all of them have been fully supportive of and active in the efforts required to bring this book to the American public. Second, Gilles Lagin, a French historian with an extensive knowledge of the American battlefields in the Marne Salient of 1918. He has been kind enough to show me places on the battlefields which, without his assistance, would not have been included in these books.

INTRODUCTION

THE AEF BATTLEFIELDS

The Second Battle of the Marne in 1918 was the result of German operations *Blücher* and *Yorck*, components of the Ludendorff offensive which began on 21 March 1918. The Germans had made tactical gains but no strategic success, and on 27 May, with a fresh, well-trained and well-equipped force of 200,000 men, they attacked the French Sixth Army on the Chemin des Dames, above the Aisne River, driving it back to the Marne at Château-Thierry, capturing 30,000 to 40,000 prisoners and 400 guns. Although General Pershing had decreed that his American Expeditionary Force (AEF) would only fight united, he was prepared to commit formations piecemeal to meet the Allied crisis. The first Americans committed were at Cantigny on 28 May, and, more significantly, at Château-Thierry/Belleau Wood on the Marne and to its north in May and June. Just as the Marne had proved the high water mark of German success in 1914, so it did in 1918.

The Marne Salient was a large triangle of French landscape marked off by Soissons, Reims and Château-Thierry and it is also the setting of a dramatic story. It was there that the United States of America made its dramatic entry into the war when American troops braced to block the German thrust for Paris in May of 1918.

This book relates to some of the Allied and American sites of interest northwest of Château-Thierry and when the AEF was under French operational control.

The battlefields of the U.S. 3rd Division of Regulars cover the Aisne Defensive Operation, 27 May to 5 July, and specifically the defense of Château-Thierry by the 7th Motorized Machine Gun Battalion.

IN THEIR OWN WORDS

History cannot be revised to suit contemporary standards. If one is to accurately judge the actions of those who lived so long ago, those actions must be evaluated in accord with the standards, concepts, beliefs, and societal attitudes prevailing at the time. To do that, I use the actual words of the American soldiers who fought in the Marne salient during 1918.

This book is written in a 'tone-of-the-times' format that presents a "soldiers eye view" and leaves it to others to sort out inaccuracies in the historical record. We sometimes overlook the testimony of ordinary soldiers because they were not scholars and were unaware of the so-called "big picture." They were, in fact, experts by virtue of their presence on the battlefield. They rode the emotional roller-coaster of combat and suffered the privations of the front lines. These first-person accounts frequently correct discrepancies perpetuated by academics whose knowledge of particular events was second-hand. Participants often reveal details that are not commonly known. The soldiers observed people and events from a special viewpoint. Thus they are the primary sources used by this author.

A battlefield might be compared to a theatre. There is a curtain between the actors and the audience. In the theatre, the audience has some idea of what the performance is about but only the players themselves really know all of the details. Similarly, one might say there is a curtain between a battlefield and headquarters. Accepting this metaphor, only the soldiers on the "stage side" of that curtain really know the details. A basic assumption of this book is that since there are roughly ten thousand soldiers to every commanding general, it is the soldiers, not the generals, who really know the details. Therefore, this narrative uses the words of the Doughboys and usually stays away from headquarters staff perspectives; there is little mention of the actions of generals and politicians, and only cursory discussion of strategy. The words and photographs in this narrative were gathered from many histories of the AEF. The written testimony comes from letters, diaries and memoirs. Wartime letters are used as frequently as possible because these contemporary documents are the most vivid accounts of the men in conflict. They best portray the emotions of American soldiers in combat, and they are much better expressions of the humor, quiet fortitude, and rugged courage of American soldiers than are the sanitized memoirs written long after the guns fell silent.

Personal narratives describe the awful trials and unspeakable horrors that befell soldiers on the Western Front. Many of these men, gassed and battle-scarred for life, wrote letters and stories which bring "the shout, the shock, the crash of steel" to life. They wrote in a manner so vital and realistic as to surpass the pen-pictures of the most famous war correspondents or the colorful stories of novelists. After all, the heart of war is to be found in actual combat, and as such it is more monstrous than any other phase of hostile activity.

I have tried to be very selective in the presentation of "In Their Own Words" accounts. Although there are many accounts available, I have limited my presentation to a few of what I consider the best, for each site, town or village. To present them all would be tedious and boring to the reader and would result in a much larger guidebook.

What You Will See and Read in This Book

This book contains an extensive collection of "then-and-now" photographs as well as many carefully selected line-drawings and works of art illustrating the life of the AEF both behind and in the front lines. It aims to preserve the visual presentation of the fields of combat as they were then and as they are now. None of these pictures show what actually happened when men went forward to confront the German forces. They often show the results of the fighting, but words are all anyone has to paint the picture; there are few moving or still pictures of actual combat.

You will see and read about the American battlefields of the second battle of the Marne in 1918, when the Germans were driving hard for Paris and when the U.S. 2nd Division, with its Fourth ("Marine") Brigade, stood across the Paris Road and showed the Germans who was master of the battlefield, not only defying them, but proceeding to clear them out of Belleau Wood in a savage fight lasting twenty days.

At Château-Thierry, you will see where the Yanks held the Germans on the banks of the Marne River, and then threw them back. You will see and read about the banks of the Marne River where the U.S. 3rd Division of Regulars earned its immortal name of "Marne Division" for the heroic defense of the vital bridges over the Marne at Château-Thierry and for repulsing the German assault crossing at the Jaulgonne Bend of the Marne on 15 July 1918.

You will see and read about many unknown shrines located behind the battle lines, places never under any circumstances mentioned in the press dispatches, but nonetheless crowded with the ghosts of old AEF fighters who revisited them in postwar years when they returned to France. Typical of such places were the many division, regiment and battalion headquarters, command posts, and the sites of aid stations and field hospitals.

What This Book Will Show You

This book will enable you to go to the battlefields, to follow the fighting of the American and German soldiers as they fought in the fields and forests of northwestern France. You will be able to accurately retrace the glorious passage of American arms in France, to see the blood-soaked lands where, over eighty years ago and some three generations past, our fathers, grandfathers and great-grandfathers, fought the "war to end all wars."

You will learn how to get to the American battlefields, what to look for while you are there, and how to interpret what you see. You can visualize the battle areas as they were then and as they are now. You will explore sites towns and woods seldom visited today. You will see many farms and dwellings which were aid stations, command posts, and divisional, regimental or battalion headquarters in 1918.

This book is a sentimental journey through one of the most attractive regions of France. It is a journey intended to appeal to experts and novices alike. The tour is carefully planned to place you on the ground and recreate for you the experience of World War I, an experience that molded an entire generation and forever changed our world.

The stops and associated stands in the tour are arranged to present the most important phases of the battles as they developed, while recognizing that we cannot take a strictly chronological approach to all events.

You are encouraged to get out of your car and walk as much as possible. Terrain determines tactics—and it always looks differently from a soldier's point of view than on a two-dimensional map. Go to these hallowed places—touch the earth where heroes fell; put your feet where they struggled, see the terrain from eye-level. Walk the roads and fields and hills that the doughboys of the AEF once walked. Feel the burning in your lungs as you climb Hill 181 at the southern edge of Belleau Wood or imagine the feeling the marines had as they walked through the wheat field outside of Lucy-le-Bocage knowing that death lies somewhere just ahead. Stumble and slip a few times as you walk in "Gob Gully," and among the huge boulders of Belleau Wood.

For many who visit the American battlefields the most productive study period may be after they have stopped at key points, viewed the terrain, and shared the recollections of the participants.

SUGGESTED BATTLEFIELD TRAVELS

The American battlefields in the Marne salient of 1918 stretch from the Chemin des Dames south to the Marne River at Château-Thierry. The battlefields divide themselves naturally into four main regions which can be visited in turn: Château-Thierry; the area northwest of that city; the battlefields east of Château-Thierry; the battlefields extending northward from Château-Thierry to the Ourcq and Vesle Rivers, and the battlefields southwest of Soissons.

The itineraries within this book cover a range of about 50 miles—from the Charles de Gaulle airport to, and including, Château-Thierry. Also listed are many of the military cemeteries, monuments and memorials. Additional short tours to other areas of interest are also included. The tour includes many small villages and towns. Separate descriptions and itineraries are given to these places.

It is suggested that you do the walking tour of Château-Thierry. As far as the American soldiers were concerned, Château-Thierry was the best-known and most-loved town in France. During the fighting in the Marne salient, about 300,000 men of the AEF went into or out of this town between the end of May, 1918 to early September, 1918. To the Doughboys of the AEF their campaigns to clear the Germans from the Marne salient of 1918 were collectively known as "The Battle of Château-Thierry." Many thousands of American soldiers and civilians visited Château-Thierry after the Armistice. For information concerning an escort on the battlefields you are referred to the appropriate section of the appendix.

Having just read about this book, in the next section you will learn about the American battlefields in the Marne salient of 1918.

> "The race is not to the swift, nor the battle to the strong...
> but time and chance happeneth to them all."
>
> Ecclesiastes

> "The smallest detail taken from an actual incident in war is
> more instructive to me, a soldier, than all the Thiers and Jominis
> in the world. They speak for the heads of states and armies, but
> they never show me what I wish to know—a battalion, company
> or platoon in action. The man is the first weapon of battle. Let
> us study the soldier for it is he who brings reality to it."

—Ardant Du Picq, French colonel, pioneer writer on the behavior of men in war
and Crimean War veteran who died in battle in the Franco-Prussian War.

THE GENERALS

General John J. Pershing
American Forces

Generals Foch and Pershing
17 June 1918

TABLE OF CONTENTS

SECTION ONE

THE FIELDS OF THE MARNE

The fields of the Marne are growing green
The river murmurs on and on;
No more the hail of machine-guns
The cannon from the hills are gone.

The herder leads the sheep afield
Where the grasses grow o'er the broken blade;
And toil worn women till the soil
O'er human mold, in sunny glade

The splintered shell and bayonet
Are lost in crumbling village wall;

No sniper scans the rim of hills,
No sentry hears the night bird call

From blood wet soil and sunken trench,
The flowers bloom in summer light;
And farther down the vale beyond,
The peasant smiles are sad, yet bright.

The wounded Marne is growing green
The gash of Hun no longer smarts;
Democracy is born again,
But what about the wounded hearts?

The verses were signed Sergeant Frank Carbaugh, and below his name was this
note: "Written while lying wounded in hospital; died August, 1918."

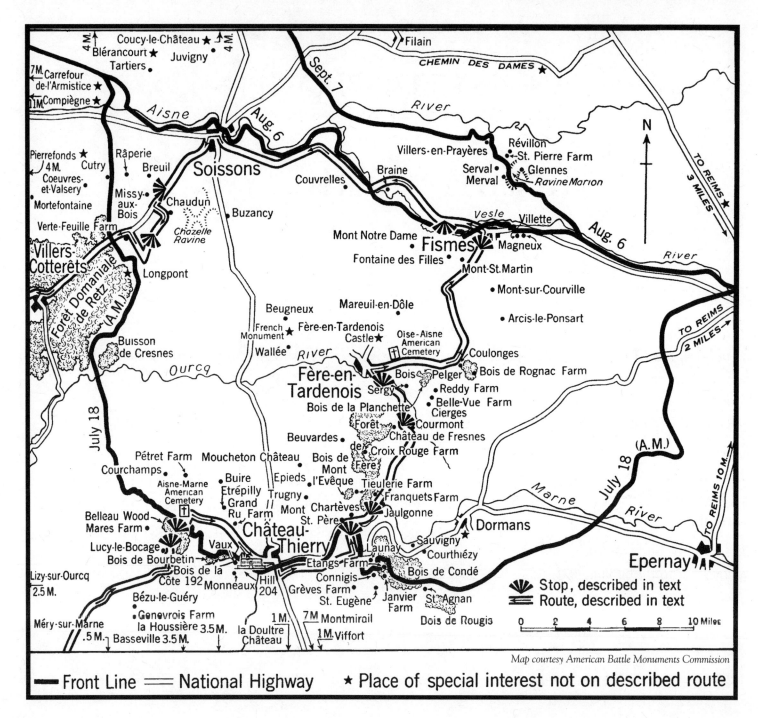

Map courtesy American Battle Monuments Commission

━━━ Front Line ═══ National Highway ★ Place of special interest not on described route

AMERICAN BATTLEFIELDS IN THE MARNE SALIENT

"Everyone felt that the Americans were present at the magical operation of blood transfusion. Life arrived in torrents to revive the mangled body of a France bled white by the countless wounds of four years."

Jean de Pierrefeu
Staff Officer, French Army Headquarters, 1918

INTRODUCTION

American troops played an important part in turning the tide of World War I in favor of the Allies at the Second Battle of the Marne. Château-Thierry saw the first fighting of American forces as a separate unit—and their participation under their own officers was decided upon as a final desperate effort to stop the triumphal entry of the German troops into Paris.

At about the time the Second Battle of the Marne ended, German Field Marshal von Hindenburg, attempted to explain and justify "strategical retreat," declaring that "the decisive victory" of German arms had merely been temporarily postponed. The scales had begun to weigh in favor of the Allies and, however long it might take to bring about the final decision, the second Battle of the Marne was the beginning of the end of World War I. For the third time in its history, the Marne had proved to be the bulwark of the free nations of the world.

The part played by U.S. divisions at Château-Thierry, in what is very properly termed the Second Battle of the Marne, forms a remarkable chapter in the history of the AEF in France. It was an initial effort, and although the American forces at this time were under French control, it saw the first actual functioning of the American Army Corps, it produced the army commanders who controlled American units under General Pershing, and it was essentially the battle of baptism of the American fighting forces.

Eight American divisions took part in the Marne salient battle; four saw real fighting, and one took part in an offensive operation. The other four had either seen no fighting at all, or so little during their training in calm sectors that they had not yet received the classification of fighting units. But they gave so clear a demonstration of the fighting quality of American troops, even though not fully trained, that they had completely restored the morale of the Allied battle line.

AISNE DEFENSIVE OPERATION

MAY 27 – JUNE 5, 1918

Germany's plan for her military campaigns in 1918 called first for the destruction of the British Army in the Spring, then, all forces were to be concentrated to crush France. In furtherance of the strike at the British, attacks were launched in Picardy and Flanders during March and April. These failed in their announced purpose. Meanwhile, German preparations had gone steadily forward for a blow against the French along the Aisne River line.

The Allied High Command realized that a German attack was in the making, but it was considered improbable that it would come against the Aisne front.

On the morning of May 27, German assault troops struck the Aisne front from between Berry-au-Bac and Anizy-le-Chateau. The blow was a complete surprise and the Germans overran the Chemin des-Dames positions and crossed the Aisne River by noon.

AISNE CAMPAIGN

<u>AISNE 27 MAY – 5 JUNE 1918</u>

The next major German attack fell on 27 May on the thinly held but formidable terrain along the Aisne River known as the Chemin des Dames. The original objective of this new offensive was to draw southward the Allied reserve accumulated back of the British sector, in preparation for a final German attempt to destroy the British Army in Flanders.

The French and British defenders were taken completely by surprise, and their positions were overrun rapidly on a 40-mile front. German progress on the first day was so rapid (advances up to 13 miles were made at some points) that Ludendorff altered his plans and decided to make the diversionary attack a main effort. Most of the Aisne bridges were captured intact.

The thrust toward Rheims failed but Soissons was taken, and by 31 May the Germans had reached the outskirts of Château-Thierry on the Marne, less than 40 miles from Paris.

In the next few days the Germans sought to exploit and expand the deep and exposed salient which they had established.

But by 4 June they had been stopped everywhere. Some 27,000 American troops took part in the check of the German advance. The 3ᵈ Division foiled enemy attempts in the period 1-4 June to secure a firm bridgehead across the Marne at Château-Thierry. West of the town the 2ᵈ Division, which included a Marine brigade, defended the road to Paris, and on 6 June successfully counterattacked in Belleau Wood.

Château-Thierry was an emergency; it had no part whatever in the plans prepared by the general staff of the American Expeditionary Forces (AEF) or in the original French scheme for the entry of American forces upon the Western Front.

The result of the German attack on the morning of May 27, 1918, was that in 4 days, or by the evening of May 30, the leading elements of the German troops had driven from the Chemin des Dames and were at Château-Thierry. The following day the German communiqué stated, "We stand along the Marne." No greater measure of self-satisfaction was ever reflected in an announcement than in this. It was a big advance, nearly 40 miles in 4 days. An advance of 40 more miles would see Paris in German hands and end the war in favor of the Germany and the Central Powers.

But on this same fourth day at Château-Thierry the German troops encountered a small American fighting unit, the 7th Motorized Machine Gun Battalion, U.S. 3rd Division. The 7th had traveled a distance of 110 miles in 30 hours in its own motor transport and set up its machine guns to defend Château-Thierry.

For 72 hours the 7th Machine Gun Battalion successfully contested the crossing of the river. The delay occasioned by the French-American resistance at Château-Thierry gave French General Foch and his staff the needed precious time to plan for the organization of the defensive strategy which culminated in the battle of Belleau Wood and the defense of the Marne east of Château-Thierry. Subsequently, American divisions initiated and sustained the counteroffensive that marked the turning point of World War I.

By the second day of June the infantry of the U.S. 3rd Division was in position along the river from Château-Thierry to the east for a distance of about 12 miles. The U.S. 2nd Division, which included the Marine Brigade, arriving from a point north of Paris, was in position from Château-Thierry to the west for a distance of about 8 miles, standing astride the Paris-Metz Road, and the German drive halted at this point.

At this point, the battles northwest of Château-Thierry, and in particular the savage fight for control of Belleau Wood, took on an importance far beyond the strategic or tactical value of the area or of the Wood itself. Belleau Wood took on a new dimension, discounting the limited value of the terrain in question and emphasizing the psychological aspects of winning and losing—and neither side wanted to lose. From having been a formerly valueless little wood, and one having really no strategic or tactical importance, Belleau Wood now became a battle for supremacy of forces. If the Americans were beaten in the battle for the wood, the Germans would publish the news in every world newspaper, thus giving the American and Allied morale a severe drubbing which might change the course of the war. If the Germans lost the battle, it would prove the value of American arms to the world at large, thus giving a great boost to sagging Allied morale. The outcome of the fighting in Belleau Wood and elsewhere in the Marne Salient would decide once and for all who was the master of the battlefield—the Germans or the Americans.

Although most European military historians (and some American ones also) tend to discount the value of American arms in 1918, most will, if pressed, reluctantly concede that American intervention on the battlefield in 1918 changed the course of the war.

Château-Thierry is a small town in the valley of the Marne about 50 miles east of Paris, now once again picturesque, but sadly battered in 1918. To the AEF Château-Thierry signified the whole area over which its divisions contended through ten weeks of bitter fighting. More than all else, it signified the fact that the tide of military fortune had turned at that point, that the AEF had taken the measure of the Germans, and were no longer anxious as to the final result. They were then certain that victory would surely be theirs at sometime in the future, though even the most optimistic did not count it possible in 4 short months.

Just a few miles east of Paris, were enacted the combats of the Second Battle of the Marne. They took place within a picturesque theater of war, a panoramic stage of forested hills and fertile valleys, with vineyards, fields, meadows and woodland in between. It is a rolling terrain intersected by streams and rivers flanked by steep ridges and webbed together by rail and highways, roads and towns. Villages and hamlets nestled in the valleys, perched on the hills or clung to their slopes. Here also an appalling number of young Americans sacrificed their lives to capture and hold the hills and towns. The men of the AEF thought that, for every yard they conquered, it was at the cost of a doughboy's life. It is there that we begin our tour of the battlefields of the AEF in the Marne salient.

Drive the country roads in and around the valley of the Marne in northeastern France, and you will pass by prosperous stone villages flanked on all sides by fields of wheat. The country north of the Marne was a pleasant place in peacetime. The thick greenery of forests rimmed the yellow of the wheat fields. Here and there were the red-tiled roofs of a farm homestead or one of the tiny rural villages so familiar to the traveler in France. A beautiful landscape, indeed, but a bitter place for men to be in when every woodland hid masses of artillery and every innocent tuft of forest shrubbery concealed a machine gun. The terrain along the Marne was mostly woody and the fighting that took place there was mostly from tree to tree and rock to rock. It is said that the Germans, cleverly concealed in the forests and woods, had a machine gun for about every 10 yards of their front.

But in previous days, this area, like the other battle areas of France and Belgium, was besieged by artillery, gashed with trenches and shell craters, and shrouded in the black and foul air of war. The Germans deluged woods and wheat with mustard gas, thrown in liquid form from artillery shells, which hung, an invisible blanket of poison, over the ground which the Americans must cross to reach their foes. The appearance of the American skirmishers always gave a signal for the German artillery and machine guns to open fire. So skillfully were their guns placed to sweep the ground that a soldier could scarcely stand upright and live; to drop flat and crawl forward was hardly better. A

GERMAN HIGH COMMAND

General Erich Ludendorff Quartermaster General German Army

Marshall von Hindenberg

Marshall von Hindenberg, Kaiser Wilhelm and General Ludendorff going over battlefield maps

THE FRENCH

Commander-in-Chief, French Army
General Ferdinand Foch

General H. P. Petain
Commander, French Army

General Jean Degoutte
Commander, French XXI Corps

Official French Photographs

dozen courageous machine gunners could make an assault battalion pay a fearful price for a few hundred yards of ground. Then, if conditions favored, the defenders might withdraw to fresh positions before the oncoming Americans could get to grips with their exasperating foes.

Following each rush there would ensue a period of silence during which none moved except the groaning wounded crawling back, when they could, through the spattered wheat. But for these and the twisted bloody bundles that lay motionless here and there, an observer might fancy, during these deceitful lulls, that he was alone in a deserted countryside. But presently, emerging again from shelter of the woods, the brown steel helmets of the Americans would appear, wave upon wave, the bayonets of the men flashing before them and their heads bent to resist the storm they knew would break. In just an instant the opposing woods would burst into an angry metallic chatter, the wheat suddenly to swarm with vicious invisible insects, and overhead the air was flecked with the countless white and black puffballs of the bursting German shrapnel-shells. Men heard the sickening sound of a bullet against flesh, saw their comrades vanish utterly in a swirl of flame and smoke, and finally, after an eternity of this, the shadow of the woods would fall across their front. From that point until the woods were cleared of the enemy the action would resolve to scores of individual fights. Men, grim of eye, hunted one another like quarreling wolves from copse to copse and from tree trunk to tree trunk, moving with a kaleidoscopic rapidity that made one feel that soon one would emerge from this ghastly nightmare and find oneself in a motion picture theater watching those shadowy characters on the screen. Such was the daily, almost hourly experience of the American soldiers in the Marne salient battles of 1918.

Having read about this book and about the American battlesites in the Marne Salient of 1918, in the next section of this book you will read about and observe some of the Allied and American sites of interest between the Charles de Gaulle airport and Château-Thierry.

SECTION TWO

FROM THE AIRPORT TO CHÂTEAU-THIERRY

"The world must be made safe for democracy. It is a fearful thing to lead this great peaceful people into war, into the most terrible and disastrous of all wars, civilization itself seeming to be in the balance. But the right is more precious than peace. The day has come when America is privileged to spend her blood and her might for the principles that gave her birth and happiness and the peace which she has treasured. God helping her, she can do no other."
—President Woodrow Wilson
in an address before Congress
2 April, 1917

On 6 April 1917, Congress declared that a state of war existed between Imperial Germany and the United States of America.

"The Allies were losing very definitely from March to July, 1918. We have their word for it that their backs were to the wall and that they must have help, quickly and in force, or the best they could hope for—and that highly unlikely—was a draw."
—MajGen Hunter Liggett, AEF

"The French are a broken reed."
—Diary entry of British General Haig

Photo courtesy George Gaadt, The Great War Association

The Germans issued the following announcement to their troops opposing the Americans:

"Should the Americans at our front even temporarily gain the upper hand, it would have a most unfavorable effect for us as regards the morale of the Allies and the duration of the war. In the fighting that now confronts us, we are not concerned about the occupation or non-occupation of this or that unimportant wood or village; but rather with the question as to whether Anglo-American propaganda, that the American Army is equal to or even superior to the Germans, will be successful."
—Unnumbered order by the German
28th Division, dated 8 June 1918

To American General Pershing on the expectation of American aid:
"I hope it isn't too late."
—Pétain

"We not only dashed the cup of victory from the hands of the German, we smashed it into his face."
—Frederick Palmer, AEF Staff officer, 1918

THE GERMAN SOLDIER
A PHOTOGRAPHIC ESSAY

The advance to the Marne. Infantry advancing through their own artillery position

Column carrying bridge material passing a position May 30, 1918

German soldiers in a trench

The advance of the infantry over the Chemin des Dames

This photographic essay on the German soldier is included for two reasons: It represents a fitting tribute to the German soldiers of World War I who fought valiantly and bravely for their Fatherland, and, to the best knowledge of this editor, these photographs have never before been published.

The Chemin des Dames Battle—Regiment crossing the Aillette Canal. 5 June 1918

French prisoners on their way to the rear near Chateau-Thierry

Western Front—German machine-gun firing

Infantry deploying in combat formation over the Chateau-Thierry Road, June 1918

Between the Aisne and the Marne. In the captured French hospital at Mont Notre Dame. Captured British and French soldiers with a captured American ambulance.

The Winterberg Offensive. A machine gun section crossing the Vesle River.

German soldiers running through battle smoke

Building a pontoon bridge

GERMAN OFFENSIVES
BEHIND THE LINES TO CHÂTEAU-THIERRY

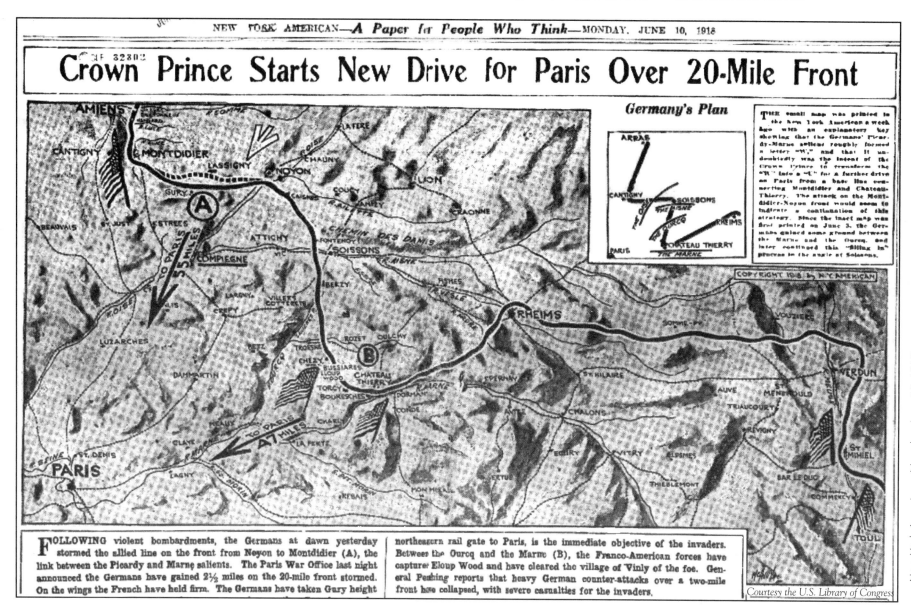

New York American, Monday, June 10, 1918

SITUATION MAPS

JUNE 1918

The central line shows the
German positions on June 2, 1918. the
broken line to the left shows the defensive position as
originally planned, which became the object of the German attack in
this area. The heavy line to the right shows the German position on June
14, 1918 after the attack by the American Second Division.

1

SITUATION MAP
MARNE FRONT
4 JUNE 1918

2

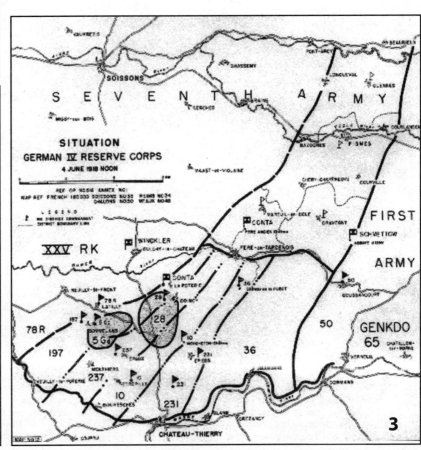

3

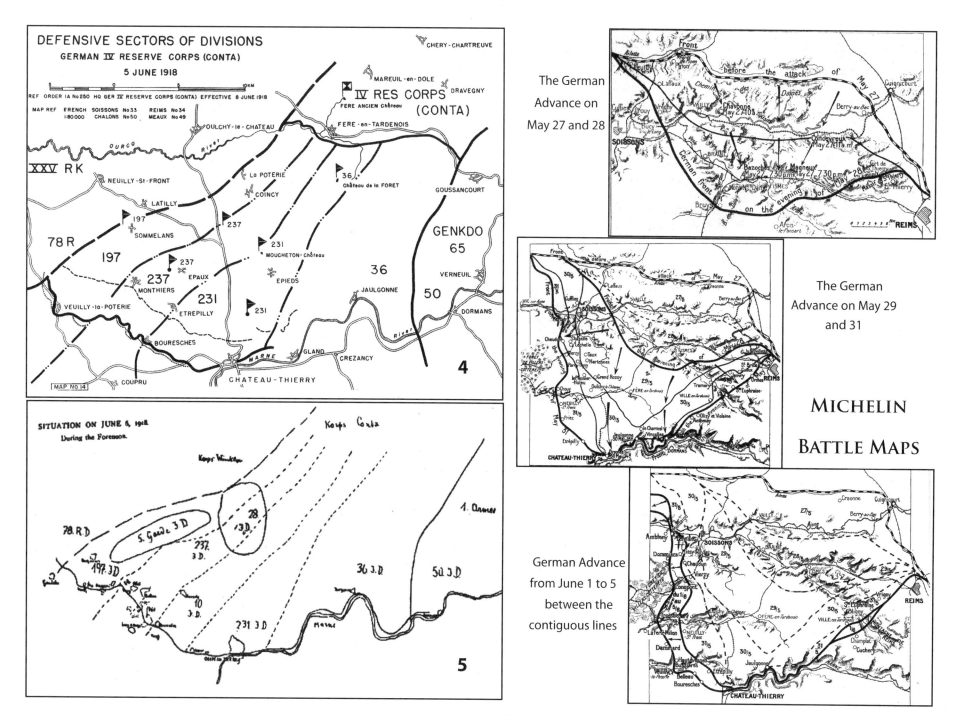

DEFENSIVE SECTORS OF DIVISIONS
GERMAN IV RESERVE CORPS (CONTA)
5 JUNE 1918

The German Advance on May 27 and 28

The German Advance on May 29 and 31

MICHELIN BATTLE MAPS

German Advance from June 1 to 5 between the contiguous lines

SITUATION ON JUNE 6, 1918
During the Forenoon.

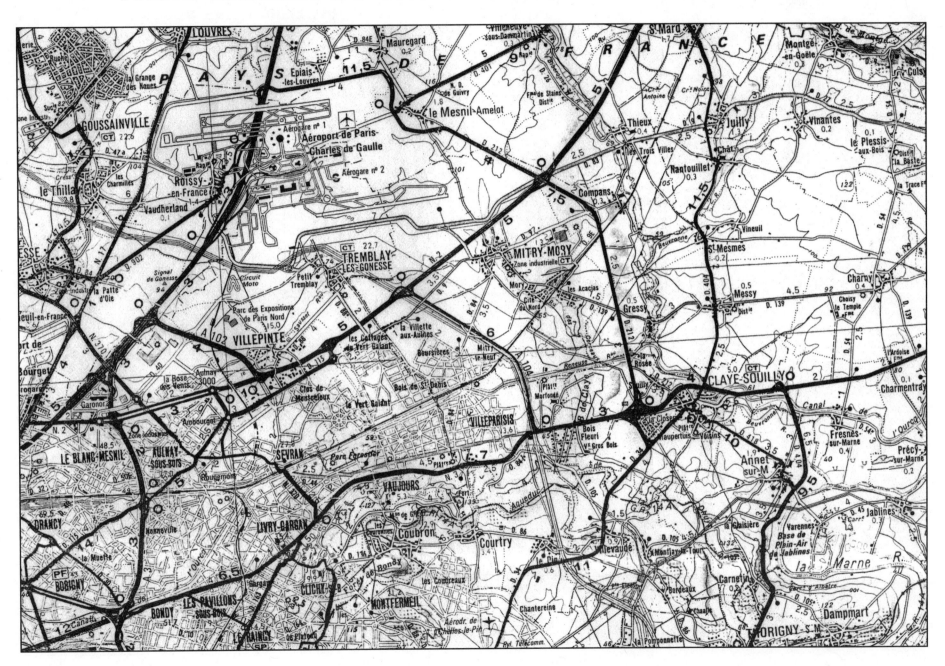

CLAYE-SOUILLY TO MEAUX

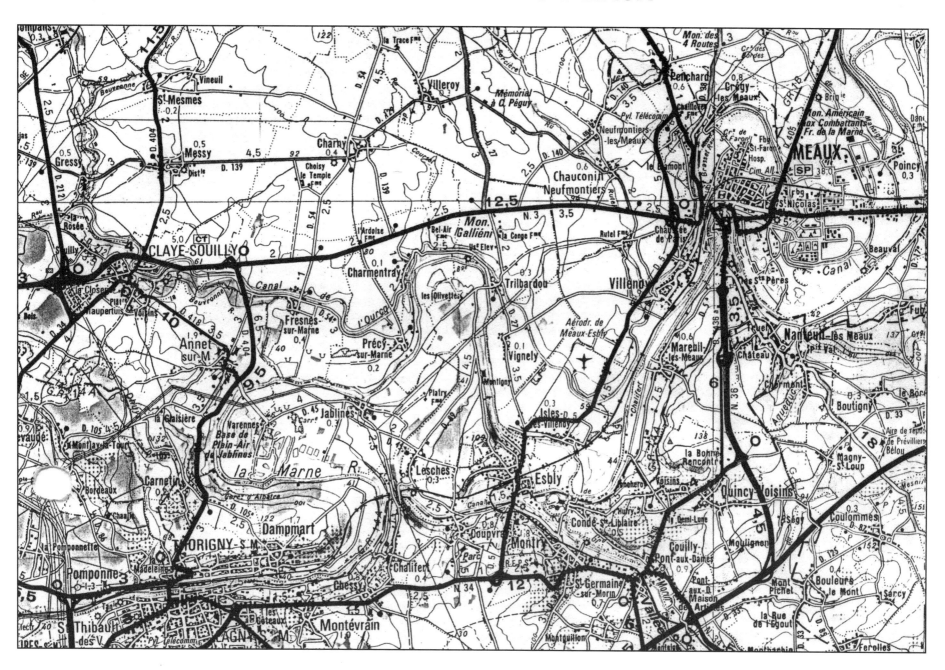

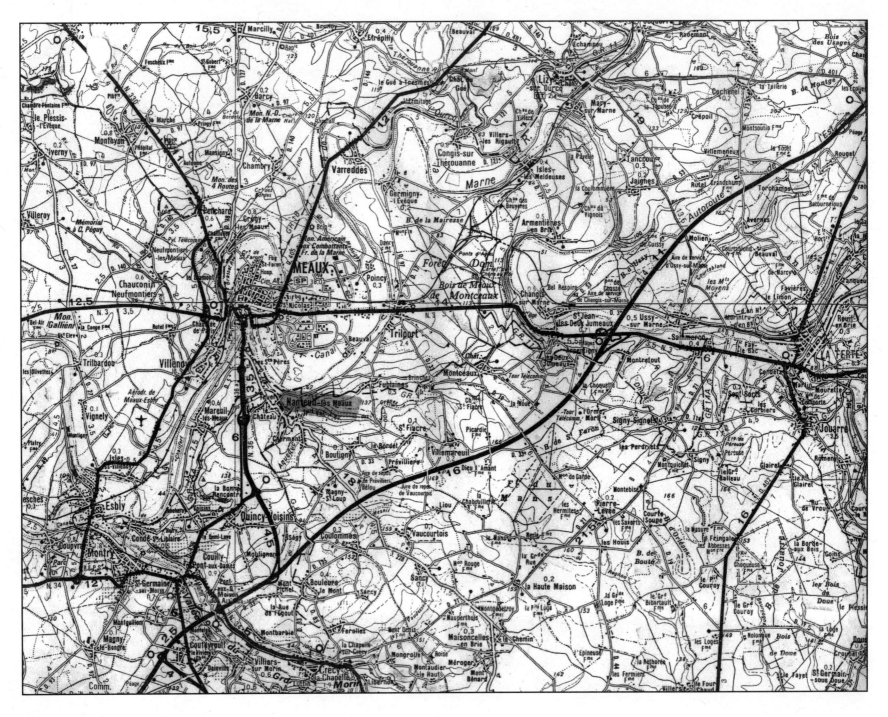

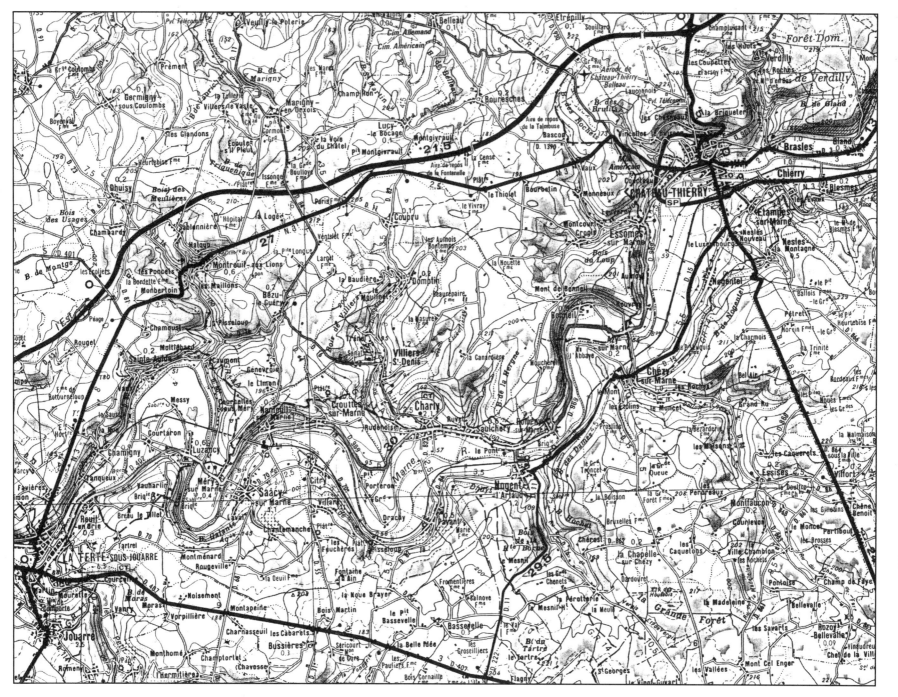

FROM THE AIRPORT TO CHÂTEAU-THIERRY—POINTS OF INTEREST

A DESCRIPTION OF THE TOUR

This tour begins at the Charles de Gaulle International Airport, just northeast of Paris, France and continues eastward to the town of Château-Thierry.

It was in the Marne salient of 1918 that troops of I and III American Army Corps (U.S. 1st, 2nd, 3rd, 4th, 26th, 26th, 28th, 32nd, 42nd and 77th Divisions) distinguished themselves. This, the first volume of the series on the American battlegrounds in the Marne salient of 1918, covers the AEF battlegrounds and sites from the Charles de Gaulle airport to and including Château-Thierry. Although this book relates primarily to the defense of Château-Thierry by the machine gunners of the U. S. 3rd Division, mention is made on the way to Château-Thierry of sites relevant to our allies, the British and the French, and to many other American units and/or divisions moving around in the covered geographical area.

The tour is not a long one, but may be completed rather hurriedly in one day if you take care not spend too much time at interesting points near the beginning of the tour, and if you pass by most of the smaller places given in the tour.

The chapters on military operations in the Marne salient area should be kept in mind and the appropriate maps consulted so that the various operations that took place in the region of this tour will be more clearly understood.

Many of the given optional short tours are on two-lane paved roads which are actually only wide enough for one automobile to stay entirely on the paved surface. When two autos meet on this type of road, one or both vehicles must veer off onto the dirt shoulder of the road in order to pass each other. Extreme caution is urged upon the automobile driver when using these narrow roads, particularly at night.

Beverages, lunch and small snacks should be carried along on the tour, as a restaurant may not be within convenient driving distance when the pangs of hunger begin to strike you.

Although the land in the Aisne-Marne battle area has long since been returned to agricultural uses and the once-ruined villages have been rebuilt, it will perhaps be of benefit to the traveler to realize that after the war deeply-moving traces of the fierce fighting which had passed through this region were visible everywhere and continued to exist for many years thereafter. The destroyed villages were as the shells and bombs had left them. Everywhere were branch-less trees and jagged stumps, shell craters roughly filled in, trenches, barbed wire entanglements, and shelters for men and ammunition. Thousands upon thousands of artillery shells, empty shell casings, rifles, gun limbers, and machine guns lay scattered about. For some years after the war, an occasional corpse could still be seen.

Over all this land, as far up stream as Reuil-sur-Marne and down river to the bends

GERMAN DRIVES MARCH 21–JULY 17, 1918

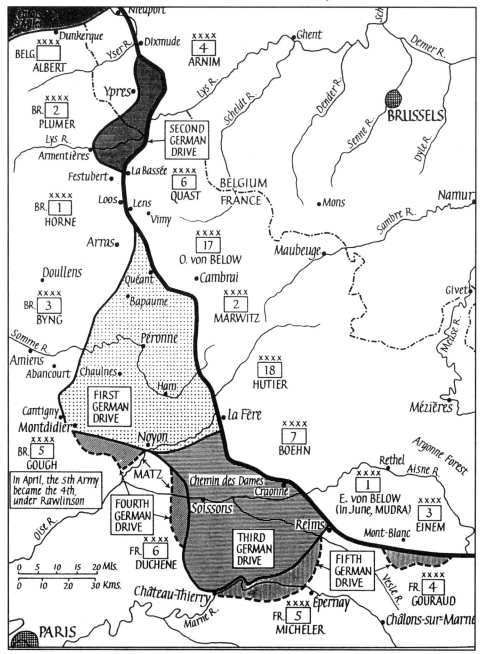

below Château-Thierry and as far north as Fismes, the debris of military occupation was thickly scattered, especially ammunition. Beginning in the summer of 1919 and continuing for many years thereafter, parties of French engineers and German prisoners of war were still busy on all parts of the battlefields, gathering into heaps for salvage hundreds of thousands of empty shell cases and into other heaps untold quantities of "duds" and unexploded Germans shells from their abandoned dumps and battery positions. The German ammunition was assembled in spots remote from buildings and in the center of each heap was placed a detonator, which was then fired electrically from a distance. Nothing was more common on the still, bright summer days of the once-more peaceful countryside than to hear the deep boom of an explosion and to see arise above the treetops beyond some distant, bare hillside, a billowing cloud of smoke, betokening the destruction of one more collection of deadly projectiles.

Before the war this part of the country was one of the prettiest and most interesting in France. Nearly every village had an old church, a castle, or ruins of archaeological interest. Many of these ancient buildings and ruins were totally destroyed during World War I.

Today, almost 90 years after the end of the War, there are few remaining traces of the terrible combats which were fought in the Marne salient. Postwar clean-up, economic progress, and the passage of time have all but eliminated most war-related sites in this area of France. One of the outstanding places where such traces still exist is at Belleau Wood, which is retained in its original condition as a memorial to the Americans who died within its confines.

Major points of interest in the Aisne-Marne battle area, such as Belleau Wood and the American Memorial on Hill 204 at Château-Thierry, can be a little crowded on spring and summer weekends. These places are reminiscent of our own Gettysburg battlefield during the summer months, when one can barely maintain a minimum degree of concentration because of the numbers of people and their attendant noise. If your itinerary permits you to do so, you might prefer to visit these places on weekdays thus avoiding the crowds.

EN ROUTE FROM THE CHARLES DE GAULLE INTERNATIONAL AIRPORT TO CHÂTEAU-THIERRY

GENERAL GUIDANCE

Getting out of Charles de Gaulle airport and onto any local highway is tricky, and the tourist who is unfamiliar with the surrounding area can become lost. When at the airport rental car kiosk be sure to receive motoring directions from the airport to Châ-teau-Thierry. The rental car agent will give you a map of the airport area and show you how to get out of the airport and onto your desired route. Be certain that you write the agent's instructions down explicitly, step by step.

You are advised to take your time and try to figure out every move in advance, particularly if you are a first-time driver in France. If you become lost in the maze of airport interchanges and traffic circles, the basic direction of your travel from the airport is EAST and in the direction of Metz, Nancy, Marne-la-Vallée, Soissons, and Château-Thierry. If going onto the *péage* (toll road) of A-4 to Château-Thierry, take the A-1 (direction Paris), then A-104 (south), and then A-4 East.

This tour will assume that you are new to France and to driving in the country. The tour takes you directly to Château-Thierry and by the most direct route. The reasoning for this is simple; you are probably a little tired by the time your plane arrives at the airport and are anxious to get to your destination and to your hotel for some rest and refreshment before starting out on a walking tour of Château-Thierry and of the battlefields in this area.

If, when trying to find the A-1 or A-104 south, or D-212 south to the N-3, you accidentally enter one of many traffic circles or other roads and become lost, make the best of your error by pulling over at a safe opportunity to do so, or exiting, and consult your highway map. There is always a way to get to your desired location. Remember that your general direction of travel is east, toward the river Marne, and in the direction of (not to) le Mesnil, Dammartin, Mitry-Mory, and Meaux. If you are so fortunate as to be able to speak some of the French language, you will find the French people to be most helpful in getting you back on the right road to your destination. If nothing else works, head in the direction of the French Disneyland!

The most important thing to be constantly conscious of while driving in France is the rule of *prioritié a droit*—of yielding the right of way to the car on the right.

Secondly, is the matter of traffic circles, of which there are many. When you see the sign, *Vous n'avez pas la prioritié*, or *Cédez le Passage*, this means that you do NOT have the right of way when entering a traffic circle, and that traffic already in the circle does have the right of way. If the traffic circle has no such sign, then you have the right of way when entering the circle. Even if you have the right of way, don't push your luck with big trucks or busses!

The time given by Michelin for driving from the airport to Château-Thierry of 1 hour and 2 minutes would be at a speed of over 100 km/hr— some very fast driving. Your routing from the airport to Château-Thierry on either the toll expressway or on N-3 is given below.

OPTIONS

If this is your first visit to France and to the American battlefields, you are advised to proceed directly into Château-Thierry and to use this town as a base for battlefield touring. Other, more experienced travelers may wish to follow the old national road (N-3) and proceed to Château-Thierry on that route. This routing, although more interesting culturally, is more complex, requires more time, and goes through the towns of Claye-Souilly, Trilport, Meaux, La-Ferté-sous-Jouarre, and many confusing traffic circles. You may wish to take highway A-4 to its exit for Meaux and follow the N-3 east from that point. The N-3 routing into Château-Thierry takes you to see some of the sights of interest relevant to the first battle of the Marne in 1914, and to the AEF battles of 1918.

Perhaps the most logical routing is to take the A-1 (direction—Paris) from the airport, then A-104 and A-4 in the direction of Soissons, etc. If you leave A-4 at Montreuil-aux-Lions and go onto N-3, you are entering the edge of the American battle area. In this way, one gets the best of both travel worlds, the fast route on the A-4 to the battle area, then the slower route of N-3 through the American battlefields and into Château-Thierry. The final choice is left up to you.

The town of Meaux is very difficult to get around in by automobile because of its many traffic circles. Particularly difficult to find, and north of Meaux, is the American monument to the first battle of the Marne.

Consider which routing is best for your particular set of conditions. The American battlefield area does not really start until you reach the town of Montreuil-aux-Lions, on N-3. Although sites of military significance and interest are given in the towns of Claye-Souilly, Meaux, La-Ferté-sous-Jouarre, etc., they all relate to either French or British operations during the first battle of the Marne. Seeing these monuments and memorials to the battles of 1914 enable you to remember the heroic sacrifices of our French and British Allies. Viewing these monuments and sites of historic significance also somewhat set the stage for your later scenes of the American battlefields of the second battle of the Marne in 1918.

Château-Thierry
the most direct route:

For those travelers who wish to go to Château-Thierry by the fastest and direct route; follow the blue signs marked *"péage"* out of the airport, leading to the following given directions and towns:

From the Airport follow the sign, "PARIS EST, BOBIGNY, MARNE La VALLÉE, A-1." (You are headed for, but not to, ROISSY-en-FRANCE).

Continue on A-1 (direction of Gonesse) until you see a sign saying BORDEAUX, NANTES, LYON, MARNE LA VALÉE, PARC DES EXPOSITIONS, A-104-FRANCIL-LENNE."

TAKE A-102 to N-2 AND TO A-104 South (in the direction of Marne la Vallée and Torcy).

Continue on A-104 until you see a sign saying, "METZ-NANCY-A-4."

Continue on A-4 (in the direction of METZ and NANCY) for many miles until you see a sign saying "SORTIE 20, CHÂTEAU-THIERRY, SOISSONS, FERE-en-TARDENOIS." TAKE THE EXIT TO CHÂTEAU-THIERRY.

Note:
The toll for automobiles is posted at the toll booth entrance. It is advisable that you have adequate coinage to pay several tolls. It is much easier to use coins than paper money. If you are using paper money, be certain that you pass through the right-hand toll booths where there is a person on duty.

Château-Thierry from route A-4:

For those travelers who are arriving directly in Château-Thierry from the route A-4:

Take the D-1 into CHÂTEAU-THIERRY and follow the signs to the center of the village and to your hotel.

If you are arriving directly in Château-Thierry from the Charles de Gaulle airport, it is suggested you begin your tour of the AEF battlefields by first taking the walking tour of Château-Thierry and then drive out of Château-Thierry on N-3 to Montreuil-aux-Lions. In Montreuil, you can reverse your direction of travel and slowly work your way back to Château-Thierry. Starting with the Mairie (town hall) in Montreuil, the headquarters of the U. S. 2nd Division on 1 June 1918, follow the given directions taking you into Château-Thierry via N-3 while visiting many interesting towns and places associated with the AEF in 1918. This tour uses N-3 as an east-west axis, taking the battlefield visitor progressively eastward while periodically going in north-south excursions which chronologically visit the AEF battle and other sites.

For those travelers who wish to take the longer, more difficult, but also more interesting route of N-3 from the Charles de Gaulle airport: Highway N-3 from Paris is the same road used by Gen Gallieni, commander of the Paris garrison, who moved up his "taxicab army" from Paris at a critical time of that desperate first battle of the Marne.

Take the A-1 NORTH from the AIRPORT (direction of Senlis and Compiegne). Look for the sign saying, D-212-le MESNIL. Follow D-212 SOUTH until it intersects with N-3. Turn LEFT on N-3 east in the direction of CLAYE-SOUILLY, MEAUX and LA FERTÉ-SOUS-JOUARRE.

CLAYE-SOUILLY

Claye-Souilly, due west of Meaux, is the point nearest Paris reached by the Germans in the first battle of the Marne, September, 1914. While reconnoitering the road to Paris, German bicycle patrols encountered French outposts and were beaten back. On the eve of the French counter-attacks of September, 1914, the southern extremity of the French Fourth Army line (Dammartin to Claye) went to Claye. This little town hosted the headquarters of Gen Maunoury, commander of the French Sixth Army, (the so-called "Paris army") in the first Marne battle. At Claye those 600 Paris taxicabs taking the Paris Army to battle, each carrying a minimum of five soldiers and their arms and equipment, turned to the left and went to Nanteuil. The taxis made the round-trip to Paris twice that night, before the Paris army struck German Gen von Kluck's army on the flank.

On 31 May 1918, the U.S. 2nd Division, on its way to Meaux, passed through Claye in French trucks.

The AEF had a big veterinary depot in Claye during the war. This depot, equipped with the most modern appliances, treated all of the diseases of and performed operations on horses and mules.

JUILLY

Thirty miles east of Paris and 7 km north of Claye is the little village of Juilly.

In 1916 the American Ambulance Field Service with the French Army established a second American Ambulance Hospital (the first was at Neuilly-sur-Seine, a suburb of Paris) at Juilly. Through the generosity of a friend of France, the venerable College of Juilly was steam-fitted, electric-lighted and plumbed, and made over into a hospital for about 200 additional wounded, with distinguished American surgeons in charge. In June, 1918 the College had become American Red Cross Hospital No. 6. To visit this hospital site take the D-404 north from Claye. There was also a Red Cross hospital at Neuilly, twin village to Juilly.

IN THEIR OWN WORDS

This description of the village of Juilly was taken from Frederick A. Pottle's book, *Stretchers, The Story of a Hospital Unit on the Western Front:*

JUILLY, a little village in the smiling fields of Seine-et-Marne, seems to derive its name from Julius Caesar. Its Latin name, Juliacum, probably perpetuates the memory of a Roman camp established by the great Roman in the near vicinity. The history of Juilly begins with Saint Geneviève, the maiden who, by persuading the people of Paris not to flee before the Hun Attila, became the patron saint of the grateful city. This was in 451. Geneviève often traveled between Paris and Meaux, passing through the grounds on which the Collège now stands. The spring there is called by her name, and tradition says that she called it into being by a miracle. A wonderful spring it certainly is, for in 1918 we must have been drawing from it upward of fifteen thousand gallons of water a day. It soon became an object of pious veneration, and was visited by throngs of pilgrims during the Middle Ages. One can still descend the worn stone steps and see the bright jet spurting from the wall much as it did then; the old stone walls go back to the 12th century, and the polychrome statue over the fountain to the 13th. It was in the 12th century that the spot became of such importance that a monastery of monks took over its management and administered it for 450 years. The school, which in these latter days has eclipsed the spring, came into existence in the 13th century. Blanche de Castille, mother of France's sainted king, Louis IX, made here a foundation to care for the children of the knights who fell in her son's disastrous crusade. During the hundred years' war with England it suffered much from the English troops which had overrun all this part of the country. On her return from Orléans, Jeanne d'Arc passed through Juilly, winning a great victory at Lagny near by. The Abbaye was then almost in ruins; it was rebuilt in the middle of the 16th century, but in 1637 the monks finally left Juilly, turning their charge over to the order of the Oratory, whom Louis XIII had commissioned to found a seminary for the education of his young nobles. The school was called an "Académie Royale" and was allowed to quarter the lilies of France with the crown of thorns of the Oratory. Many of France's most famous sons have been pupils at the old Collège de Juilly. Montesquieu, La Fontaine, and Jerome Bonaparte were among the number, as were also two of the most famous of England's illegitimate royalties—the Duke of Monmouth and the Duke of Berwick. Bossuet, as Bishop of Meaux, was closely connected with the school, and La Fayette had an estate near by and always showed great fondness for it. In the Library is still preserved a facsimile of the American Declaration of Independence, given by Congress to La Fayette and by him presented to the College. During the Revolution it was nearly extinguished, most of the Oratorians going to the guillotine during the Terror, the direction of which was largely in the hands of certain radicals who had formerly been on its faculty.

The Collège was three times a hospital before the World War: First, during the war with England in 1790, then in 1814, when Napoleon, near the end of his career, was fighting on the Marne, and in 1870 when Juilly was occupied by the Prussians. In 1914 the Germans almost reached Juilly again.

Collège de Juilly

Smithsonian Institution

A battery of French 75's Shelling the Germans on the Ridge to the Left of Chateau-Thierry, W.J. Duncan, June 1918, pencil sketch (Smithsonian Institution)

An American soldier

Photo: Great War Association/George Gaadt

They occupied St. Soupplets, some five miles away, and for a time it looked as though they would advance as far as Juilly itself. The wounded from the first Battle of the Marne were brought to the Collège, many of them being picked up by the superintendent in a furniture van drawn by an old horse which had been rejected as unfit for military service. In January, 1915, the French Government put a part of the buildings at the disposal of Mrs. Harry Payne Whitney, who equipped and maintained there a hospital for the care of French wounded. It was known as American Ambulance No. 2, and was a sister institution to American Ambulance No. 1 (later Army Red Cross Hospital No. 1), at Neuilly, a suburb of Paris, the latter institution being also supported by American charity. The staff—doctors, nurses, and ambulance corps—was mainly composed of American volunteers.

When the Second and Third Divisions were sent in at Belleau Woods and the Marne, there was no American military hospital service back of them at all. It had been agreed that the French Sixth Army, in which they were serving, should provide all the necessary service of hospitalization and evacuation. It developed that they were quite unable to do anything of the sort. During the months previous to the great German advance of the spring of 1918, the stable condition of the line, and the obvious advantages to be gained by early treatment of wounds, lured the French to carry their advanced hospitals nearer and nearer to the front, and to make them constantly larger and less mobile. When the Germans broke through, the French lost at a blow thousands of beds and enormous quantities of hospital stores. Because of these losses they were barely able to care for their own wounded. Furthermore, the French command failed to inform the American Medical Staff of the destination of our divisions, so that they had to discover where they were after casualties had already begun. Had we been earlier advised of the true state of things, it would have been possible to handle the wounded from the June fighting much more effectively. But it is doubtful whether the French knew the true state of affairs any too well themselves. Everything was in confusion; the enemy were advancing rapidly, and were within striking distance of Paris. From the military standpoint only one thing was clear: the enemy must be stopped. In such an emergency the handling of wounded, though of the greatest importance, was a secondary consideration.

On June 2 the French Sixth Army notified our liaison officer (Lieut. Col. A. D. Tuttle) that the French would be largely unable to fulfil their promise of hospitalization, and begged the American command to do what it could to meet the situation. Our troops had already been in action 24 hours or more. A hasty survey showed that the Ambulance at Juilly was the only American institution available for an evacuation hospital. The capacity was then only 250 beds, and the personnel was inadequate to care for even that number. Plans were immediately formed to increase the capacity to 800. There were still some 250 boys (pupils) still left at the Collège, which had continued its work as an educational institution in spite of the partial conversion into a hospital. These were hurriedly sent away, and an appeal made to the Red Cross in Paris for the necessary material, which began to arrive by June 4. There remained the grave difficulty of personnel. The surgical consultant of the Second Division collected such teams as he could find, and frantic telegraphic appeals throughout the AEF brought in several others. The marines have no medical corps, but are cared for by surgeons and corpsmen of the navy. Consequently one of the busiest teams we found when we arrived at Juilly was that of P.A. Surgeon John H. Long from Navy Base Hospital No. 1 at Brest. On the night of June 3 the patients began to arrive, and soon jammed the hospital. It must be remembered that the material for the proposed expansion was only just arriving, and that the surgical teams were coming in one by one. On the morning of June 4, the senior representative of the Medical Department with G-4, G.H.Q. (Col. S. H. Wadhams), visited Juilly in company with the chief surgeon of the A.E.F., General Ireland, now surgeon general. On his return to Paris the same day, General Ireland requested of G.H.Q. that Evacuation Eight, the only evacuation hospital available anywhere in France, be sent at once to Juilly. We had meanwhile been making our pleasant, but useless, trip across France, and had just arrived at Bazoilles. It was hoped that we would reach Juilly on June 5, but the French were unable to provide the necessary railroad transportation. On June 5 the Acting Chief of Staff, G-4, G.H.Q., made an urgent plea to the chief of the French mission to expedite the movement. The cars were made available at Bazoilles on the morning of June 6, but the railroads were so congested that we did not reach Juilly until the morning of the eighth.

Meanwhile the situation had been considerably alleviated by the arrival on June 6 of the 40 army nurses of Replacement Hospital A. This group had been organized by the army in New York City, April, 1918, five nurses being selected from each of eight different cantonments scattered from Massachusetts to Texas. They sailed from New York on May 19, 1918, suffered a submarine attack, but without casualties, and landed at Liverpool on May 31. On June 2 they crossed the channel to Le Havre, remained there two days, and then were rushed to Juilly by way of Paris and Meaux. On June 9, Miss Goodine, the chief nurse, and 10 others were detached and ordered to La Ferté-sous-Jouarre for duty with Field Hospital No. 23. Here they remained until July 19. The hospital

Operating Room of an American field hospital

Wounded but still happy, these soldiers are arriving at the American hospital No. 1, Neuilly, 7 June 1918. The passengers are a bit battered but their exhultation at the beating they have given the Germans at the Marne bolsters up their spirits.

Here are some of the American boys who advanced across a wheat field in the face of a line of machine guns and heavy field pieces. They cleaned up the machine-gun nests and captured the field pieces. It was near the Marne. The Germans insisted it was impossible even after they had done it

Here are some American boys who advanced across a wheat field in the face of a line of machine guns and heavy field pieces. They cleaned up the machine-gun nests and captured the field pieces. It was near the Marne. The Germans insisted it was impossible even after they had done it.

was subjected to air raids, during which two of the nurses, Miss McNamara and Miss Zang, distinguished themselves by unusual bravery, and were later cited.

The heroic quality of those four days before our arrival at Juilly is best communicated, I think, by the terse and restrained words of the Surgeon General's Report. "On June 4 and 5 arrangements were made for evacuations by ambulance from the hospital at Juilly…. The personnel at that time was becoming physically exhausted…. On the morning of June 6 all available ambulances and numerous trucks were evacuating from the front of the 2ᵈ Division into Juilly…. Though the surgical teams there worked day and night, they were insufficient to care for all the wounded received. As a matter of fact, not more than a fourth of the personnel needed by this hospital could be furnished it. The next day [June 7] the first hospital train arrived at Juilly. [Because Juilly was some distance from the railroad, the method of evacuating by train required handling the patients twice, and had to be abandoned because of the small number of men available for carrying litters, and their exhaustion.] On June 6 and 7, by ambulance and train, 1,183 patients, practically all of whom had come from the 2ᵈ Division, were sent from Juilly to Paris. On the dates mentioned the small hospital at Juilly had received about 1,700 patients, and for a period of four days its personnel worked 20 hours a day. The litter bearers—most of whom were French soldiers unfit for front-line service— worked even longer hours. Their labors were supplemented by ambulance drivers. Finally all were too weary to lift a litter to the level of the upper tier of an ambulance. A detachment from the 2ᵈ Division then relieved them until the personnel of Evacuation Hospital No. 8 arrived on June 8."

The number of admissions continued very large after our arrival. From June 4 to June 20 there were admitted in all 3,274 patients; that is, in the 12 days after we took over the hospital, we received about as many as had been admitted in the previous four days. As a matter of fact, immediately after our arrival the admissions were heavier than these figures indicate, for our admissions practically ceased from June 16 to July 15. The reason was that another evacuation hospital had been established at a place more accessible to the front and to the railhead. On June 12 Evacuation Seven reached Château Montanglaust, a mile or so from Coulommiers, and was joined there by Mobile Hospital No. 1. Within a few days these hospitals were ready for work, and the stream of wounded from the Second Division was diverted to them. In the six weeks subsequent to June 13, these two units received and evacuated twenty-seven thousand men.

Because we brought none of our army hospital equipment with us to Juilly, but were operating entirely with Red Cross supplies, the hospital was officially known at first as Army Red Cross Hospital No. 6, though, as an organization, Evacuation Eight never lost its own name. By the first of July or earlier, however, this designation was dropped, and our own substituted."

LtCol Richard Derby, Medical Corps, and Chief Division Surgeon, U.S. 2nd Division, wrote in his book, *"Wade in, Sanitary! The Story of a Division Surgeon in France"*:

I went at once to visit the *Médicin Inspecteur* of the Sixth French Army to obtain instructions as to how the [medical] evacuation was to be carried out. The French said that all wounded must be sent to Paris. They flatly refused permission to establish our hospital for non-transportable wounded upon the north bank of the Marne, stating that the enemy would surely cross the river and we would needlessly sacrifice our wounded, medical personnel, and property.

The problems of the medical department in anticipation of the heavy fighting that was now to be expected were very difficult. There were but few well-organized French hospitals of any size immediately back of the new front created by this last advance of the Huns. In that territory just evacuated by the French some twenty thousand hospital beds were lost. The nearest hospital that was in any way sufficient was at Juilly, about seventy kilometers to the rear. Considering the length of evacuation back to Juilly and the heavy casualties we were suffering, our hospital facilities were utterly inadequate. With the heavily wooded areas just back of our front, in which our support and reserve battalions were concealed, we might expect a gas bombardment as soon as the enemy's guns were brought up in numbers. To handle a large number of gas casualties we were utterly unprepared. Our line was now stabilized and the French could no longer raise their former objection to bringing our hospital up to the Marne.

This hospital [Juilly] occurred to me, as I studied my map on the drive to Meaux, for in 1914 when working in the American hospital in Neuilly, my friend Dr. Walton Martin of New York was in Paris outfitting this hospital established by Mrs. H.P. Whitney. In company with my wife, the three of us, on our afternoons off duty, had brought supplies ranging from pillow-cases to surgical instruments.

I knew this hospital would fill our needs, as largely due to Dr. Martin's great ability and interest, backed by Mrs. Whitney's generosity, it had become one of the best organized and equipped institutions in France. It was in charge of American medical officers and nurses and was capable of expansion to eight hundred beds. Outside of it there was nothing closer than the already overtaxed ones in Paris. In moving to the front we dropped off medical officers and enlisted personnel at Juilly with instructions to enlarge the hospital to its utmost capacity.

Three Allied soldiers during the retreat—An American soldier conversing with a wounded British soldier and a French Soldier. Montmirail, France 31 May 1918

THE MONUMENT TO MARSHAL GALLIENI

Continue EAST on N-3 until you see a sign marked "D-27 TRIBARDOU" to the right. *Do not turn right at the turnoff point.* **Fifty feet past the right hand turnoff to TRIBARDOU, and on your RIGHT, is a clump of trees. Remembering that the N-3 is a high-speed road,** *carefully* **pull over into this area and park.**

This monument was erected by the City of Paris

LtCol Jonathan Jaffin, USA, states in his booklet, *Medical Support for the American Expeditionary Forces in France During the First World War*:

> The biggest problem was to supply hospitalization behind the divisions. The only hospital in the area that could serve as an evacuation hospital in the initial fighting was Army Red Cross Hospital No. 7 at Juilly. This was a 280-bed hospital which had its available beds increased to 800 on 2 June, 1918. Three surgical teams arrived on 3 June, but the wounded swamped the hospital.

THE MONUMENT TO MARSHAL GALLIENI

The monument to General Gallieni is in this clump of trees. Notice that the General is looking northeast in the direction of the German advance on Paris.

Joseph Gallieni was born in Haute Garonne in 1849. He joined the army and served in West Africa and Tonkin and in 1886 was appointed governor of Upper Senegal. This was followed by the position of governor-general of Madagascar (1897–1906). Gallieni retired from the French Army in 1914 but was recalled on the outbreak of the First World War in 1914. He was given the task of organizing the defense of Paris. When Gallieni realized that the German First Army was turning east in early September, he sent his Sixth Army to Maunoury at the Marne in taxicabs. This was the famous 'taxicab army.'

Gallieni was retained as governor of Paris until made Minister of War in on 29 October 1915, where he served until ill health caused his resignation on 16 March 1916. A grateful nation made Gallieni a Marshal of France posthumously on 21 April 1916.

MEAUX

Meaux, the center of the Pays Meldois, is about 80 miles from Paris, and is halfway between the capital and Château-Thierry. Meaux is a cathedral town, provincial capital, and is the principal town of this local region. Above Meaux the waters of the Ourcq flow into the Marne.

The population of Meaux before the war was 14,000 people.

Originally a stronghold of the Meldi, a Gallic tribe, Meaux later became the capital of the Haute-Brie. During the revolt of the Jacquerie (1358), the town was sacked and 9,000 peasants massacred. Besieged twice by the English in the 15th century, occupied by invading German armies in 1814 and again in 1870, Meaux became the center of the famous first battle of the Marne in 1914.

MEAUX DURING THE WAR

The main part of the British Expeditionary Forces (BEF), on the long retreat southward from Mons, reached Meaux on the 2nd and 3rd of September, 1914. The British blew up the famous Market bridge (*Le Pont du Marché*) over the Marne and a footbridge farther upstream. They also sank the famous floating baths.

Some German patrols operating on the right flank of the main army that was pursuing the retreating French and British Armies, passed through the town in August, 1914, but had not much time to do great damage.

German Gen von Kluck reached Meaux and was about to cross the river, when French Gen Maunoury attacked the German right flank. Immediately Sir John French attacked northward, toward Meaux, with his small British Army. The battle lines were very close to the city for several days and it became the high-water mark of the German advance during the first battle of the Marne in 1914.

Desperate fighting took place immediately to the north of Meaux. Gen von Kluck, forced to retire back of the Marne, finally left the line altogether and retired towards Compéigne. In the words of a British soldiers' song, 'We got them on the go at a little place called Meaux.'

In 1918, once again the city became inundated by a flood of soldiers and civilians that poured into it from all directions. The retreating French Army and the fleeing refugees so congested Meaux, before the U.S. 2nd Division arrived, that the town was useless as an assembly point. There would be great confusion if the hundreds of trucks carrying fifteen thousand American infantry went into Meaux. The leading units of the division went instead to the village of May-en-Multien, several miles farther to the northeast.

The re-routing of the Americans out of Meaux and on to other towns and villages nearer the front improved matters somewhat, although the road between Meaux and May-en-Multien became clogged with thousands of refugees who reduced the trucks' progress to a crawl. These refugees were astonished to see troops headed in what appeared to be the wrong direction; to these dazed and battered farmers and shopkeepers anyone with any sense was moving west. "*La guerre est fini!*" [the war is finished!] they called to the men in the trucks, gesturing for them to go back the way they had come. The Americans would yell back "*Pas fini!*" [not finished!]—a reply which gave a name to the part of the lines occupied by the Americans.

Officially, Meaux was never much of a center for the activities of the Americans in olive drab of war times, for the reason that it was far to one side of the duly defined American areas. In point of fact, however, from June until September, 1918, it was thronged with those who were about the business of United States divisions fighting along the upper Marne, on the battle line between Château-Thierry and Soissons, and finally, along the Vesle. It was the headquarters of the American Third Army Corps, under MajGen Robert L. Bullard, before the counter-offensive of July 18, and at Meaux a large number of the troops of the "Yankee Division" celebrated July 4, 1918, with a parade, an athletic meet and a band concert.

Marshall Joseph Gallieni

Carefully return to N-3 and TURN RIGHT, continue on N-3 to MEAUX.

CAUTIONARY NOTE—It is easy to become lost in Meaux because of it's many traffic circles. To visit the American monument to the First Battle of the Marne, follow the green signs marked D-405—Soissons/Vareddes. Your direction is north. Free auto parking in Meaux is very difficult to find. There is ample parking in the pay-lots. If you can find a vacancy, there is a small free-parking lot for tourists at the City Hall. Many pay parking lots have vacant stalls during the French mid-day main meal time of 12 to 2 PM.

British soldiers in Meaux, 1914

Meaux—Pont du Marché and the destroyed public baths

American soldiers in Meaux town square, 1918

Meaux suffered German bombardment several times in 1918, both by aerial bombs and long-range artillery. A few of the shells fell in the town square and on the area of the railroad station but did no material damage.

At first, AEF Field Hospital No. 23 established a relay station at Meaux between Bézu-le-Guery and Juilly and treated sick and slightly wounded. A château in Meaux, at No. 56 rue Ste. Faron, was requisitioned for another of the 2nd Division's field hospitals. It moved forward on 9 June and treated the seriously injured at La Ferté-sous-Jouarre. The horse-drawn Field Hospital, No. 16 reached Meaux on 4 June, 1918, where it assisted Field Hospital No. 23 at Meaux. It moved to Luzancy on 11 June, where it joined Field Hospital No. 15.

Ambulance Company No. 23 began operating an ambulance post at Meaux on June 1, but the next day, leaving four ambulances to serve the 23rd Field Hospital, it moved to Bézu-le-Guery.

Evacuation Hospital No. 6 started operations 20 July at Meaux and began receiving patients from the front immediately. It moved to Chierry, near Château-Thierry, on 29 July.

On 12 June 1918 elements of the U.S. 4th Division of Regulars detrained at Meaux.

In 1918 there was a technical school for American officers at Meaux.

MEAUX NOW

Today, the Brie, of which Meaux is the principal town, is still a country full of charm from early spring to late autumn. It is a region of great forests, most of them belonging to the State. It is an area of ancient market towns and villages, of pleasant chateaux, and of farms which supply the needs of Paris. In the direction of Champagne, there are vineyards covering the hillsides. The peaceful landscape appears today as if it never suffered war and devastation. However, the name of every village and hamlet in this area recalls some important or romantic incident in peace or war.

There is an interesting old cathedral on the left of the road in the center of the town of Meaux. Notice that all the heads are knocked off the statues on the side of the church.

The Germans did not do this damage—the French populace did it during the French Revolution.

There are several notable churches in Meaux, of which the best is the Cathedral of St. Stephen, a flamboyant Gothic edifice of the 12th to 16th centuries. The one finished tower should be climbed to get a splendid view of the battlefield of the Ourcq during the first battle of the Marne in 1914.

The ancient part of Meaux follows the loop of the Marne. On the river banks stood a number of old mills, almost entirely burned down in 1920 and never rebuilt.

Before the war there stood on the terrace of the modern Hôtel de Ville, a venerable antiquity—a mortar, one of the first ever made. The French captured it from the

English, near Meaux, in the Hundred Years War, almost six centuries ago. The mortar is not there now. Presumably it went the same route as did other weaponry in 1940—into the German steel mills for reprocessing into modern guns.

It is in the Brie that the celebrated '*fromage de Brie,*' a cheese which ripens between layers of musty hay is made.

The first battle of the Marne of September, 1914, is celebrated every year since by an official pilgrimage to Meaux, the cemetery of Chambry, and the battlefield. There is no town in the Ile de France more full of historical associations.

IN THEIR OWN WORDS

LtCol Richard Derby, Medical Corps, Division Surgeon, U.S. 2nd Division, wrote in his *Scribner's Magazine* article, *"Wade in Sanitary!"*:

> By sunrise [30 May 1918] the division was moving toward the designated concentration point at Meaux. I went by automobile with my chief, Colonel Morrow, through Pontoise, St. Denis, Sévran, and Claye. As we passed the long line of dust-enveloped busses, from the sounds of singing and joking that came from them one would have supposed this an excursion to a country fair rather than a movement into one of the grimmest battles of the war. We reached Meaux at noon.
>
> All day long successive units of the division passed through Meaux and went out to the northeast. The roads in every direction were very much congested; troops marching toward the north and refugees moving to the south. There was a continuous procession of all sorts and kinds of oxen-drawn vehicles filled with women and children. Flocks of sheep, herds of cattle, and small collections of geese and chickens made up the motley array.
>
> On the night of May 31, the infantry units of the division were on the march or in bivouac along the Meaux-Vincy road. The train was halted just outside of Meaux, and during the night there were many hostile airplanes aloft which bombed the city and attempted to locate the position of the troops.
>
> In the early morning light the world appeared strangely confused—a world that had not gone to sleep, for sleep during the past few nights had been murdered. Propped up against a tree alongside the road with a month-old baby in her arms slept a weary mother. Grouped about her on the ground, in the same position in which they had thrown themselves down, slept the older children. In the background squatted the grandmother preparing breakfast, while a pair of oxen tethered to the heavily laden chariot chewed their cud in melancholy meditation. When these weary pedestrians turned off the road for

Meaux town square now

The charming old town of Meaux

The ancient mills and market town of Meaux

American troops in Meaux

American soldiers in Nanteuil-les-Meaux on the street where they were billeted. July 1918

a halt, they fell in their tracks into a state of unconsciousness from which they arose in an hour or so's time to continue their weary march.

Round the turn, in a huge two-wheeled cart drawn by four oxen and heaped high with hay which served a double purpose as fodder for the animals and as a soft bed for the passengers came another family, already under way. The children slept, while the parents looked back with anxious faces, for above the noise of the column on the road could be heard the deeper note of artillery fire.

In a field on the left, two small boys with the aid of a dog were rounding up a herd of sheep, preparatory to moving on. Down this road came a herd of cattle, kept in column of two by the opposing line of traffic on the one hand, and a deep ditch on the other. They were followed by never-ending string of animal drawn vehicles each loaded to capacity. Where families were too numerous to find a place for each, the mother had fastened a baby carriage to the tail of a cart, and trudged along in the wake. Even wheelbarrows had been pressed into service, and loaded with household goods, followed closely in the path of the family units. Dogs strained at the traces of small four-wheeled carts heaped high with treasures from home. The grotesqueness of the procession was punctuated by its pathos.

William Scanlon, a marine in the 2nd Division, wrote the following account in his book, *God Have Mercy on Us: A Story of 1918*:

By the time we reached Meaux, we were sure something must be doing. The town itself was in confusion. Furniture and bundles of bedclothes were piled in the streets and the people were standing everywhere in bunches gabbing away and waving their arms.

Then, after we left Meaux, we began to meet the refugees. They were moving toward Meaux in every imaginable style. An old man and woman would come trudging along with their belongings tied to their backs. There were people pushing baby carriages and wheelbarrows heaped high with clothes and pots and pans. Some had hayracks with all their stuff piled on an the family perched on top. Some had chickens and geese in crates tied underneath the wagons. There were droves of sheep and hogs. We were held up quite a while in front of a drove of hogs. They would not get off the road. And there were slow-moving oxen-drawn wagons. Most of the women were crying.

Lt Elliot D. Cooke, an army officer serving with the Fourth Marine Brigade in France, wrote in his *Infantry Journal* article, "We Can Take It":

Against that conglomerate current [of refugees] we wound a careful course and by late afternoon rolled into the town of Meaux—rather a large place, seething with refugees of the wealthier class. Unlike those poor unfortunates trudging the highways, they were not all resigned to the state of their affairs. No indeed. They fussed and crowded and pushed their way onto the railway trains provided by the military, all the while demanding their rights and denouncing the war that had left their homes in the path of an advancing German Army. The arrival of American troops on the scene they ignored completely.

Our 2^d Battalion was halted on the side of a road looking down into a railroad yard.

"No one leaves the trucks," Captain Wass called, hearing Becker and me speculating on how far it was to the nearest café.

We had hoped to wash some of the dust out of our throats, but Captain Wass said the halt would be too short. And it was. In a few minutes our camions pulled out of Meaux, heading north. From there on we had the road to ourselves. No civilians, no soldiers—nothing. Just an ominous emptiness that could be felt, like a cold wind.

"Well," Becker shrugged, pulling out the box of food I had brought from the mess, "it's near supper time. Who wants to eat?"

As the cold meat and bread were being passed around another officer spoke up from the front of the bus.

"Captain Murray," he said, "If I don't come out of this, will you send these papers home to my wife?"

A sandwich remained suspended halfway to Becker's mouth. He regarded it blankly while digesting that other officer's remark. Slowly then he lowered the roughly cut hunk of war bread in his hand.

"I'm not as hungry as I thought I was," he admitted.

None of us were. The mention of home, the sudden realization that many of us would never return from that deserted land, left us glum and silent. We shoved the food box back under a seat and gazed out at the passing countryside where lengthening shadows widened into dark pools of warning. Night was closing in on us and we felt lonely.

Editor's note: *Camion* is the French word for a motorized truck.

Elton E. Mackin, a marine who was there in 1918, wrote the following semi-fictional account in his book, *Suddenly We Didn't Want to Die:*

It seemed an age since the evening that had brought sudden orders to entrain for the front. He had a confused memory of forced marches, of a long ride in boxcars jammed with others of his kind. Passenger trains had

HITTING THE HAY
Few and far between were billets as soft as this, at Nanteuil-les-Meaux.

HITTING THE HAY
Few and far between were billets as soft as this, at Nanteuil-les-Meaux

French Civilians giving Members of Company M, 101st United States Infantry, Straw for Fresh, Clean Beds. Nanteuil-les-Meaux, France, July 1, 1918.

Members of Company M, 101st United States Infantry, washing up after a Long Trip. Nanteuil-les-Meaux, France. 1 July 1918

Well discovered and put to use by two Members of Company F, 101st United States Infantry, 26th Division, Nanteuil-les-Meaux, France, 18 July 1918.

been shunted aside to let their troop train through; the cheering populations of the little towns of France had turned out along the way. He had also caught a glimpse of Paris from the railroad yards, where sentries had stood at car doors while the late afternoon had faded into dusk—at which time the ride to the north could be resumed in comparative safety from aerial observation.

Then Meaux, in a sprinkling rain, and a few hours of rest in sodden blankets along an avenue of great trees, while the sky in the north was lighted by a never-ending cannonade whose distant roar and tremble penetrated even to the back areas of the Zone of Advance.

Morning. War waited 'til then to show its awful face. Refugees in endless streams followed the ditches or clung to the roads with pitiful belongings piled high on ancient barrows. Great two-wheeled farm carts, stacked with the possessions of hurried departures, were here and there crowned with little children, singly or in groups of two and three, tucked amid the jumble of featherbeds, poultry coops, and sacks of forage. In all that pitiful column not one laughed, or paused to greet the "soldats" as the French are wont to do. They picked their way to the west—hopeless, fear-stricken, heartsick, and weary, but such is war.

Breasting that stream as best it could in broken formation, Slim's column had taken up its march toward the muttering guns beyond the horizon.

Around the great bend in the road had come cavalcade of Ford ambulances carrying shattered fragments of battle to the rear. At the sight of the green-clad marine column a cheer of frenzied exhortation had risen from the lesser wounded who road seat, running board, and tailgate.

"Gyrenes, gyrenes, you—you goddamn leathernecks, go take 'em!"

You're needed up there bad. The outfit is all shot to hell—go get 'em marines!"

Cries and curses; loving curses from the lips of broken but unbeaten men. Their feverish exhortations were an inspiration, a challenge, a comrade's benediction, almost a prayer.

Then had come a train of trucks into which the marines had been crowded like sheep—the sheep in those cattle cars going through the Pennsy yards back home, headed for Hares Island and slaughter.

Another march. As night closed in they began to pass scattered batteries of barking 75s. Then single file over dim trails that wound through wood and field, drawing ever nearer to the distant rattle of "sho-shos" [Chauchat—a French automatic rifle] and rifle fire.

Lt Peter P. Wood, 6th Machine Gun Battalion, Fourth Marine Brigade, wrote in his diary:

> June 1, 1918-Left at 5 AM. Passed thru Meaux and saw people evacuating the city. Went up road and one side was literally filled with soldiers of all kinds and military equipment while the other side was pretty full. People evacuating the town carrying all their earthly belongings in their arms on wagons, in wheelbarrows, in baby carriages and in bags on their backs. Large flocks of sheep and cattle. Many aged men and women unable to stand it completely exhausted on the road side. A sight I hope to never see again.

Members of Company I, 101st Infantry, washing up after a dusty Hike from the Train to their Billets. Nanteuil-les-Meaux, France. 1 July 1918

NANTEUIL-LES-MEAUX

NANTEUIL-les-MEAUX, 3 km SSE of Meaux, is where the U.S. 26th Division established its headquarters and where the division troops billeted in July, 1918.

THE AMERICAN MONUMENT TO COMMEMORATE THE FIRST BATTLE OF THE MARNE

You are looking at a monument, situated on 40 acres of land and consisting of a colossal statuary group, erected by the American Friends of France to commemorate the first battle of the Marne in 1914. On 6 September 1914, the French Sixth Army, with its back to the gates of Paris, attacked the German First Army in this area. The ensuing Franco-British offensive along the River Marne compelled the German armies between Paris and Verdun to retreat. Their retreat saved Paris, but four long years of suffering lay ahead.

After the Armistice in 1918, an idea of erecting a statue to commemorate the Battle of the Marne in 1914 was realized. A model contest was organized, the winner of which was Frederick MacMonnies. It was fourteen years later in September 1932 that the monument was inaugurated with a solemn ceremony, in the presence of the President of the Republic, Albert Lebrun and of the president of the Council, Edouard Herriot. Also in attendance were the American Friends of France and the Ambulance Corps of the American Field Service. This grandiose memorial, erected by Americans with funds raised in America, bears the inscription, "Here speak again the silent voices of the heroic sons of France who dared all and gave all in the day of deadly peril and turned back the flood of imminent disaster and thrilled the world by their supreme devotion"

The statuary is approximately 20 to 25 meters high on a base 15 meters to a side. The principal unit is composed of a naked woman, *Marianne* [the female symbol of the French Republic], who stands overlooking the Marne Valley. On top of her right leg she carries her son, who died in combat. *Marriane* holds a baby in one arm, a broken sword in the other and dead all about. Steps and hedges surround the monument.

American Memorial to the First Battle of the Marne

Bouillancy—destruction from the battle

Meaux to Chateau-Thierry

In going from Meaux to Chateau-Thierry, follow the signs marked, "Chalons-sur-Marne," "A-4 Metz," "La Ferté-sous-Jouarre," and the yellow, diamond-shaped road sign which indicates that you are on the route which has the "*prioritié*" (priority or right of way).

NANTEUIL-les-MEAUX, 3 km SSE of Meaux

Time required for this side-trip is about one-half hour.

Continue into MEAUX on N-3 until you intersect with D-405 NORTH which goes to VAREDDES and SOISSONS. Continue on D-405 for 1.5 KILOMETERS until you begin climbing a long hill. Almost at the top of the hill and on your right is seen a large, white statuary. Pull over to the right into this area and park.

BOUILLANCY

Bouillancy is about 11 km north of the American monument to the First Battle of the Marne. The town of Bouillancy was used as a rest and training area by the Fourth Marine Brigade, U.S. 2nd Division.

Clarence Richmond, a marine, wrote in his diary:

The next day I allowed myself to be fooled into rolling up my pack on a fake order to pack up. I had my pack nearly rolled before I caught the joke. However, we did move later on in the day, going to another village named Bouillancy. We were billeted on a farm about five hundred yards from the town. The buildings were all grouped in a rectangular shape, and in some places connected with a high wall, making a rectangular fortress, having a courtyard in the center. We entered through a gate, which connected two buildings. The buildings had the appearance of having been there a good many decades, maybe centuries. We had a good hay loft, but not such a good ladder leading up to our beds.

We drilled about three and a half hours in the morning and had instruction on the automatic rifle or Chauchaut (sho-sho). We would take it apart and then put it together again. The idea was to learn as much as possible about the gun.

While there was nothing much in the way of eats in Bouillancy, we could get figs, nuts, and a few other things. A good American grocery store would have been as welcome as a bubbling spring in the heart of the Sahara Desert. The French towns did not have anything that even resembled an American grocery store. There were some ducks running around the place, and two other fellows and myself pooled our resources and bought one for ten francs. This was too much to pay for a duck, but we had the money and were hungry and the woman had the ducks and needed the money, therefore we traded. We had the duck roasted at our galley, and with our regular meal, had a good square meal once. But few of the fellows had any money, or probably all of the ducks would have died while we were there. Such a thing as pay day had not been hinted at since I had been with the company.

Our daily routine here was practically the same. There were two new dugouts in some trenches near. These were specially prepared dugouts, deep down in the ground. Many, like myself, had never seen of been in a dugout of this kind. The entrance was from the trench, and sloped down like a stairway for about ten feet. Wooden bunks were fitted out in the bottom of the dugout.

MAY-EN-MULTIEN

May-en-Multien is 16 km NNW of Meaux on D-405 and west of the Canal de l'Ourcq and the Bois de Gesvres.

The French Sixth Army was to attack between here and Lizy-sur-Ourcq when the Allied offensive of early September 1914 began. The German IV Corps commander had his command post at that time south east of the village at Saint-Féron Farm. Von Linsigen, whose troops had been rushed to this area by forced marches to meet the threat of the French Sixth Army, had his headquarters a few miles away to the south at Beauvoir (Beauval on modern maps), to the east of Trocy. Fierce fighting took place on the Multien plateau on 6 September 1914. The war memorial in May-en-Multien (next to the church) contains 37 names, five seemingly from one family (Bouvranche), three from that of Dumont, three more named Cheron, four called Pettifrére, and three more called Pierre (Julien, Eugene and Léon). Also commemorated is 'Mme. La Forest, Victime Civile'.

On 31 May 1918 the U.S. 2nd Division went to May-en-Multien by truck to avoid the congestion at Meaux. Thousands of refugees clogged the road between Meaux and May-en-Multien reducing the forward progress of the 2nd Division to a crawl. On the night of 31 May 1918 U.S. 2nd Division headquarters was established at May-en-Multien.

On 5 July 1918, the 59th Regiment, U.S. 4th Division marched to May-en-Multien, where it went into shelter camp in the woods near the town and just above the canal. The men found themselves in the midst of the French heavy artillery concealed in the woods, and became accustomed to the noise and reverberation day and night, of the large guns. The 12th Machine Gun Battalion, U.S. 4th Division too, camped in this area.

The U. S. 1st Aero Squadron was stationed at May-en-Multien on 5 August 1918.

On 5 July 1918 the U. S. 4th Division (less the division artillery and the 7th Infantry Brigade) moved to the vicinity of Lizy-sur-Ourcq and May-en-Multien, along the Ourcq Canal, where it occupied a second position in anticipation of a German attack.

In Their Own Words

According to John W. Thomason, Jr., in his manuscript, *The Second Division Northwest of Château-Thierry*:

> There followed some consideration of the map. As far as Meaux, the Paris-Metz highway was the best road, and the camions were now upon it. There was required a place not too far from Meaux, to which they could be diverted, and where they could assemble after debussing. Fifteen kilometers northeast, the town of May-en-Multien stood out on the hachured sheet. The route nationale from Meaux to Soissons passed through it, and the secondary roads provided

Unless you wish to trace the route of the American troops farther NORTH on D-405 to MAY-en-MULTIEN, return to MEAUX and follow the GREEN N-3 road signs to CHÂTEAU-THIERRY.

French and American soldiers

a detour to the highway from the west of Meaux: from May-en-Multien the unloaded camions could circle back on another road from the west. As the contours ran, there was open country around the village where the regiments might form, and the Ourcq River was a short distance to the east. Colonel Brown suggested that the Division infantry be directed upon May-en-Multien, and General Duchesne [sic] acquiesced. Let the 2nd Division go into that area, concentrating on the towns of Lizy-sur-Ourcq, Crouy-sur-Ourcq, and Vendrest with Division Headquarters at Crouy-sur-Ourcq, he said, and orders would be forthcoming. It was apparent that at May-en-Multien, the Division would be astride the Soissons-Meaux highway, along which the enemy might advance.

The 9th Infantry, Colonel Leroy S. Upton, was the first regiment of the 2nd Division to arrive in the Meaux area. At 4:30 PM, the First and Second Battalions were debussing at May-en-Multien, in the midst of a vast traffic congestion of fleeing refugees and disorganized French troops, for May-en-Multien was an important road junction, and the back-wash from the battle zone was ebbing through it.

Here is an excerpt from *Memoirs of an Ambulance Company Officer*, by Harry L. Smith, M. D.:

But some of the 59th Infantry of our Division [U. S. 4th Division] drew a rare plum: a free trip to the French capital. The 59th Regiment was selected as one unit of the American troops who marched down the newly-named Avenue de President Wilson in the parade climaxing the great celebration of the American holiday in Paris that year. Three days later, after dark, came what we all believed would be the first sight of blood and death. Under cover of darkness, with all lights extinguished and no man permitted to smoke, we started in trucks for the little village of May-en-Multien on the River Ourcq, about 15 miles west of Château-Thierry. We passed several trains of French motor trucks, it nettled us to see the French soldiers were smoking whereas we were not.

Our journey was slow, mysterious and fascinating. We worked our way forward very slowly and cautiously. Not until break of dawn did we reach the completely deserted and shell-torn village of May-en-Multien on the Ourcq, in the vicinity of the First Battle of the Marne....

As we rolled into the little shambles of a town we could hear the thunder and roar of massed French artillery. Often we could see the showered flash and glare of a bursting shell over the hillsides, and in the daylight hours, from cover, we occasionally watched an Allied airman soaring about in the skies above us.

Officers were billeted in partially destroyed buildings and cottages, and the men found shelter in nearby barns and sheds. We stayed in this region for ten

Avenue de President Wilson

days, listening to the sullen booming of the French guns and peering up uneasily at night at the skies for the chance sight of a star shell. From this time until the signing of the Armistice we were not out of earshot of the artillery.

The 12th Machine Gun Battalion of the 4th Division was encamped in the woods to one side of us, and the 59th Infantry Regiment (headquarters) was at Lizy-sur-Ourcq.

We found the morale of the French soldiers to be at a surprisingly low ebb. They seemed to have no hope of success for the Allies, despite the stimulating effort of America's entry into the war. "Why did you wait so long to come?" a French officer asked me, "La guerre, c'est fini!"

Yet there was an understanding of their despondency. Not far from where we were a gargantuan "Big Bertha" [the nickname for a large German long-range cannon] from the Krupp works began to hurl huge shells at the housetops of Paris on the morning of July 15, shuffling the affrighted citizens out of their beds in the early light of dawn. A large siege gun mounted on a turntable in the Bois de Châtelet commenced to rain missiles on the villages of Meaux, Coulommiers and La Ferté-sous-Jouarre, all in our immediate neighborhood.

At times we could hear the ominous drone of a German airplane motor, growing louder and louder as the airplane approached the French lines. It was a sound we will never forget. We learned to recognize the sound of the mighty 200-horsepower Hispano-Suiza engine in the British Sopwith Se-5 pursuit planes, the curiously staccato hum of the French Baby Nieuport biplanes, with their 90-horsepower Rhone rotary engines, the powerful roars of the British de Haviland observation planes, and the rumble of Liberty motors in American biplanes, but the sound of German Rumplers, Fokkers with Mercedes engines, Friedrichshafen bombers and Pfaltz scouting planes, seemed to be distinctive. They struck terror into most of us.

Editor's note: An error which has been made many times over, both then and now, is to call any German long-range artillery, "Big Bertha." The name was commonly used at the time for any long-range German artillery. The gun which bombarded Paris was actually the Paris Gun. The excellent book on this topic is *The Paris Gun* by Henry Miller, 1930, reprinted by Naval and Military Press. Big Bertha, the name, was applied to many German guns but, more properly, it was a 42-centimeter howitzer used to demolish fortresses such as those at Liege and Namur. The Paris gun was the long distance gun that fired over 60 miles and actually reached into outer space on its trajectory. It fired much smaller projectiles than did the larger, but shorter-range German guns.

Photo: Great War Association/George Gaadt

A young German Soldier

LtCol Frederic M. Wise, commander of the 2nd Battalion, 5th Marine Regiment, tells of his arrival in May-en-Multien. In his book, *A Marine Tells It to You*:

> It was about six o'clock that evening when we entered May. It was a small village and most of the population had fled.
>
> The minute we got out of the camions, their drivers headed them back the way we had come. Other camion trains were pouring troops into the place. An American officer from Division Headquarters looked me up and gave me orders to go to Gondelu, several miles beyond May. The battalion fell in and we started. About a mile and a half beyond May, a motorcycle courier came tearing up the road and caught me. He handed me a written order. "Return to May at once. The Germans have already taken Gondelu." Back we went. We pitched pup tents in the fields on the outskirts of May. The place was one mass of troops. Every half hour another camion train rolled in with new outfits of the Second Division. Several divisions of French cavalry were there already. Their picket lines seemed to stretch for miles.

According to Willard R. Morrey's book, *The Ninth U.S. Infantry in the World War*:

> On 30 May, during Regimental Review and Ceremonies, Field Order Number 3, Second Division, 1918, was received, directing the Ninth Infantry to proceed to Beauvais-Les-Noncoins. The Regiment stood to, the men sleeping that night in their equipment. A long line of French camions formed up in Laconville. The Regiment was assembled there before daybreak, ready to embuss. The start, however, was not made until well in the forenoon. Through terrific dust and head the train rambled along until the middle of the afternoon, when those elements of this camion train still intact messed into a big jam of traffic in May-en-Multien. The best information obtainable was that the Regiment would bivouac there during the night and take up a defensive position on the heights North and East of town. Billeting parties again started out to nearby villages. The main highway at this point was filled with a solid column of French artillery, cavalry, infantry and thousands of French peasants, carrying their household goods, or driving ox carts filled with children and old people, and all their possessions, going to the rear. The men bivouacked in the wheat. The enemy had undoubtedly seen the approach of the Regiment and his night bombing planes dropped bombs, but no casualties were suffered."

Lt Elliot D. Cooke the army officer serving with the Fourth Marine Brigade, continues his narrative of advancing to the front. From his article, "We Can Take It":

> The wheels of our trucks rumbled over the cobblestoned streets of a silent

The French Poilu

village, pronounced by one of the senior officers to be "May-en-Multien." We left it behind us, followed a long ridge, then dipped down into a heavily wooded valley where the column slowed down and jerked to a sudden halt.

"They're unloading," Jackson shouted, leaning around to look ahead.

Orders came down to debus and we all climbed out, stiff, sore, and thirsty. The Annamese wasted no time getting their vehicles turned around and starting to the rear. The beat of cannon throbbed on the air and the chug-chug-chug of a heavy machine gun could be distinctly heard. The men adjusted packs and looked at their officers inquiringly.

Up ahead Colonel Wise, our battalion commander, was listening to the French liaison officer who had brought orders for us to halt and detruck. We must leave at once, the Frenchman insisted. The town to which we had been ordered was already five kilometers behind the German lines. The Boche were coming fast—he made running motions with his fingers to show how fast they were coming—and there was nothing between us and the advancing Germans.

Colonel Wise shook his head in vehement refusal. We heard him say that he had come thousands of miles, all the way from America, to fight the Boche and this place looked as good as any to start it at. And besides, he, "Fritz" Wise, Lieutenant Colonel of the U.S. Marines, was sick and tired of taking orders from every lieutenant and noncommissioned officer in the French Army. He had come to fight Germans and this was where he intended doing it, and that was that, by God!

The kids in the ranks overhearing that tirade fingered the hundred rounds in their ammunition belts, tilted their helmets at a knowing angle and grinned. That was telling 'em, all right.

Just then and automobile, a long, low, horizon-blue affair, came skittering up, its wheels showering us with gravel. The occupants were Frenchmen, but Colonel Wise and all the rest of us could see that they were neither lieutenants nor noncoms. They were too heavily covered with stars, gold braid, medals, and mean looks. Besides, they did all the talking.

Without any preliminaries they told Colonel Wise to go back. At once! The piece of terrain we were on meant nothing. It was the Paris-Metz highway—the open door to France's capital—which must be blocked. To the west the Boche were already eight kilometers closer to it than we were! We must hurry! Vite! Vite! Allez to beat hell!

We hurried. Up out of the valley we marched, back along the ridge and through the silent streets of May-en-Multien. Behind us the velvet blackness of the horizon flowered into flames, marking the advance of the oncoming Germans. The glow of burning houses, haystacks, and ammunition dumps

Soldiers marching towards a village

Soldiers marching in the rain

Photo: Courtesy of Jacques J. Lesage

Blown bridge at Trilport

Trilport (S.-et-M.) – The bridge destroyed by the French engineers

cast grotesque night shadows which mingled with the column and dogged our steps. The men growled and grumbled, muttering that we should stop and do something about it instead of running away. But the orders remained unchanged. We had to keep going.

About midnight we overtook our 1st Battalion which had bivouacked alongside of the road. We halted and fell out, still fuming at not having been given a chance to fight.

"I would like to see one German, at least," barked Captain Wass. He couldn't have gotten his wish any quicker if he had rubbed a magic lamp. A lone airplane came scouting low over the treetops, banked swiftly and wham! Wham! Wham! Laid a string of eggs right down the road where we were sitting. Wass and I dove for the ditch, but before I landed, a fragment of hot steel smacked against the seat of my pants.

"Pipe down," Captain Wass interrupted my heartfelt cursing while he helped to ascertain the extent of my injury. "You'll get a wound chevron for this."

"And what do I say when people ask where I got hit?" I demanded with all the sarcasm permitted a junior officer.

The captain offered several curt suggestions, all to the point, if a little crude. Fortunately I was not reduced to adopting any of his advice because my nether portions had received but a glancing blow and suffered little more than the loss of a few inches of hide. I told the first-aid man who had appeared to put up his iodine and salts. Just then orders arrived for us to start marching again.

As we moved off down the road some kids in the first platoon broke out with a new version of the "Parley Voo" song.

"The lieutenant, he saw an airplane pass," they caroled, and went on happily to describe in detail just what happened to the lieutenant.

I told Captain Wass that the next time he asked to see a German I hoped he'd leave me out of it. The song didn't bother me. I was glad the men sang while they could, because pretty soon the sun came up and the going got tough. Canteens were empty. There was no place to fill them and we couldn't have stopped if there had been. Demands kept coming for greater speed.

"Hurry," commanded the staff officers.

"Close up," barked the platoon leaders.

"Take the lead out of your pants," growled the noncoms.

On and on, and on. Dirt, heat, thirst and hunger. No sleep and no food for twenty-four hours. But the Boche had nearly reached the Marne. We had to close the gate to Paris. If we didn't get there soon, it would be too late.

And then, all of a sudden, ahead was a road. At regular intervals along its edge were beautifully green and peaceful trees. The Paris-Metz Highway! The head of the column turned left. At the side of the road was a sign post pointing to the right—Paris, 65 kilometers. We had beat the Boche to it. The road was blocked. Heinie would do no spring shopping in Paris that year.

Editor's note: *Boche* was the derogatory French slang word commonly used by the French people and the French and Allied soldiers for the soldiers of the German Army. *Boche* stems from the French *albosche*, meaning "cabbage-head."

TRILPORT

At the western edge of Trilport, as you enter the town, highway N-3 goes over the historic Marne River on a masonry bridge. The French destroyed the bridge in 1814, and again in 1870 to hinder the march toward Paris of the invading armies of Germany.

At 2:30 PM.on 3 September 1914, soldiers of a cavalry regiment of the British Army destroyed the road-bridge at the west-end of town, as they passed through Trilport on their retreat from Mons. The adjacent railroad-bridge at Germiny was blown on 8 September 1914 by retreating German troops.

On 5 September 1914, the right flank of the German Army, skirting along the eastern bank of the river, passed through Trilport in its advance toward Paris.

Trilport was the headquarters of the French Sixth Army in early June of 1918.

On 12 June 1918 elements of the U.S. 4th Division detrained at Trilport.

IN THEIR OWN WORDS

LtCol Richard Derby, Chief Surgeon, U.S. 2nd Division, wrote in his article "*Wade in Sanitary!*":

> "The Marne as it crosses under the La-Ferté-Meaux road at Trilport, was filled with a slow-moving, densely packed column of canal-boats, moving steadily toward the south and safety."

From Joseph M. Hansen's, *The Marne, Historic and Picturesque:*

> "Where the Paris-Metz railway crosses the Marne, Trilport raises its fourteenth-century church spire against the skirts of the Bois de Meaux from the midst of truck gardens and fields of carrots and turnips. Here one begins to sense the proximity of a city, for at Trilport on holidays the surface of the river resembles that near Paris, being gay with canoes and the boats of fishermen, while other pleasure seekers from Meaux resort to the shades of the Bois de Meaux, well quartered by avenues leading to sheltered resting places."

Trilport bridge, repaired and in use

In more modern times. If one looks closely at this photograph, it can be seen where the bridge was reconstructed. There is a different shading to the new brickwork—the repaired section is much lighter in shading.

Photo: Courtesy of Jacques J. Lesage

The Germigny bridge destroyed (above), and rebuilt (below)

The Trilport railroad station

TRILPORT NOW

In the vicinity of the highway-bridge at Trilport, find a safe place to park your automobile. There is a small park area to the right (south) of the highway-bridge. From this park one can see where the two spans of the road and railroad bridges have been rebuilt. Particularly in the area of the center spans of the two bridges, the difference in masonry color can be seen where the new and old constructions join.

Older historical literature says there are small plates on the right hand wall of the road-bridge to record the several dates of its destruction and reconstruction. These plates were not evident in 1988 nor in 1997. Perhaps the Germans stole the plates in 1940 or they were stolen later by vandals.

LIZY-SUR-OURCQ

Lizy-sur-Ourcq is 13 km NE of Meaux and just above the great bends in the Marne, north of the Bois de Meaux.

General Order No. 6 of September, 1914, signed by Joffre, announcing that 'The time [had] come' to concentrate 'all the efforts of the Allied Armies of the extreme left', ordered all available Sixth Army forces north east of the Ourcq to be ready to cross that river between Lizy and May-en-Multien (to the north). They were to attack 'in the direction of Château-Thierry.' Von Kluck rapidly moved up his *II Corps* to the area. Lizy fell when the Germans began their great retreat. It was a scene of a great disaster when a Red Cross train fell into the river. There is a superb picture of the wreck in *The War Illustrated*, 31 October 1914. One of the histories of the war issued during the conflict (edited by H. W. Wilson) said that the train 'with wounded soldiers was blown up by the Germans as it was crossing the...Ourcq...Forty soldiers were drowned.'

Lizy contained an artillery dump where an impressive 1.5 million artillery shells awaited the American units in June of 1918.

Lizy was the U.S. 4th Division headquarters from 5 to 23 July 1918. The headquarters of the 59th Infantry Regiment, U. S. 4th Division was also at Lizy-sur-Ourcq.

IN THEIR OWN WORDS

From *The Marne, Historic and Picturesque*, by Joseph M. Hansen:

"It was at Lizy-sur-Ourcq, tucked into the last bend of the Ourcq River before the latter mingles with the Marne, that there was far greater American activity when General George H. Cameron had there the headquarters of his division, the Fourth, while his troops were fighting under French command at Hautevesnes and Noroy. Therefore, Lizy, like La Ferté, than which it is less than half as large, is a place where Americans are still regarded with more than casual interest. The crowd in the main street, which is narrow and, with its cobbled sidewalks and dingy two-and three-story buildings, rather shabby in general appearance, gave us those sort of glances which need no spoken word to attest that they mean welcome. The place, though old, has few monuments beyond the parish church and a certain quaint stone bridge. The latter, a relic of the 12th century, spans the slender Ourcq with its narrow, round arches, pillared piers, and mossy stone railing, on a little-frequented woodland road just above the town. The church is a 15th-century edifice, having a roof line serrated, like that of St. Crépin's at Château-Thierry, with deep gables, and a square tower much broken by German shells, which may have been fired in 1914, when Maunoury and von Kluck were fighting for the line of the Ourcq, or perhaps in July, 1918.

During the first battle while the Germans remained in possession from September 3 to 9, Lizy suffered severely at the hands of the pillagers. Mr. Toynbee relates [according to the author]

Break Time by Morgan Dennis

> The contents of chemist's shops, ironmonger's shops, bicycle shops were loaded on motor-lorries and horse-wagons and hand-carts. "The most eager pillagers were men wearing the Red Cross badge. If one attempted to stop and watch them at work, then came and thrust their revolvers at one's chest." The Inspector of Gendarmerie at Lizy states that all of the communes in his district were plundered in this thoroughgoing fashion, and the booty carried off in vehicles commandeered from the inhabitants.

> A huge factory of ferro-nickel is about the only industry which Lizy can boast, though in the rich, rolling uplands of the Multien, to the eastward, are some of the largest farms in France, among them the great estates of Beauval and Echampeu, this region furnishing much Brie cheese to the market at Meaux. A sixteenth-century Chateau, solid, but not large, and surrounded by a thickly wooded park, lends a touch of dignity to the environs of the typical country town. But the Chateau was badly shattered during the days of the war and stands in pitiful need of repair in the midst of the park, grown unkempt from neglect.

Editor's note: Arnold Toynbee (1889–1975) was a noted English economic historian.

1stLt Elmer Hess, 15th Field Artillery, 2nd Division, wrote about the march to May-en-Multien on 31 May, 1918, in his book, *The Second Division*:

> June 1st, we marched up the road to Lizy and halted in the evening, tired, dusty and dirty, and bivouacked in the town. On a corner was a lone French woman who had remained to feed the retreating French soldiers with whom

Return to N-3 and turn left in the direction of TRILPORT and LA FERTÉ-sous-JOUARRE and TRILPORT

the town was filled. Stragglers and infantrymen in great confusion, wearing the horizon-blue of the French, dragged themselves to the rear. An entire regiment of French field artillery galloped through the town towards the rear carrying their wounded.

MARY-SUR-MARNE

According to Joseph M. Hansen in his book, *The Marne, Historic and Picturesque*:

Great, wind-swept hills of Orxois look down from the east side of the long Marne bend upon the *presqu'ile* of Armentiérs and Isles-les-Meldeuses, and the white and elegiac church spires of these hamlets, pricking above the treetops are duplicated on the farther shore by those of Jaignes and Tancrou and Mary-sur-Marne. Cozy, smiling bailiwicks of the farmers of the neighborhood, these places in July, 1918, heard the thunders of the Allied advance on Belleau and Bussiares and Hautevesnes roll down the open slopes from the northeast, and a thin trickle of blood so freely spilt there found its way into their quiet precincts.

It was on the hilltop a few hundred feet above the low-roofed cottages of Mary, with the links of the Marne coiling among the trees and grass lands far below, that the writer came, one afternoon, upon the village cemetery. The older portion, wherein "the rude forefathers of the hamlet sleep," is enclosed within a neat stone wall. But the terrible casualties of the first and second battles of the Marne, which had raged all over the surrounding country, had compelled an addition to even this isolated place of the dead, and just outside the wall were a half-dozen rows of graves; all, apparently, at first glance, those of French soldiers. Each mound was neatly rounded and planted with bright flowers and at its head each was marked with a little tricolor flag and the black wooden cross bearing a tricolored rosette which is the last tribute of France to her fallen sons. But a second glance discovered in one of the rows 5 white crosses, scattered between the black headboards of 21 poilus. They indicated the resting places of Lieutenant Arthur T. McAllister of the Fifty-ninth United States Infantry and 4 enlisted men of the Fifty-eighth and Fifty-ninth Infantry and the Tenth Machine-Gun Battalion, all of the Fourth Division. As shown by the legends on the crosses, all of these soldiers, French as well as American, met death on 18 July 1918, when the troops of the Eighth Infantry Brigade, Fourth Division, with those of the One Hundred and Sixty-fourth French Division, to which they were attached, attacked and carried Hautevesnes, Chevillon, and the Sept-Bois.

Laid here by the village cemetery of Mary-sur-Marne, far separated from the

Mary-sur-Marne is 1 km SSE of Lizy-sur-Ourcq

hosts of their fallen comrades who lie in large cemeteries exclusively American, the condition of these graves of Americans revealed as nothing else could the touching tenderness with which the French regard the memories of the New World allies fallen on her soil. On every American grave the flowers planted by the women of Mary seemed, if possible, more carefully tended than those on the French graves adjoining them, and at the head of each mound a small American flag fluttered in the same breeze which stirred the folds of the Tricolors three or four feet away. The caretaker of the cemetery, a white-moustached veteran of the War of 1870, stood reverently with us as we looked down upon the resting places of our dead countrymen, and at his side his little grandson, like the old soldier, straight, clear-eyed, serious, shared our mood with a depth of comprehension which no child could have felt who had not himself lived under the shadow of war. And beyond the crosses, white and black, sparkled in the distance the waters of the Marne, that wondrous, impersonal incarnation of the immortal love of country which united the past of the veteran, the present of ourselves, and the future of the lad, and whose silver thread, by virtue of the mingled graves scattered all along its shores, today knits together in sentiment, let us hope for always, the hearts of France and America.

Both a highway bridge and a bridge of the Chemin de Fer de l'Est, the latter on the line following the Ourcq Valley from Meaux to Reims, cross the Marne in front of Mary. The original stone spans were blown up by the Germans on the eve of their retreat, September 8, 1914, and the superstructures were replaced by steel spans after the war. Lines of trenches and machine-gun pits for a long time marked the river banks above and below the bridges, showing where the enemy vainly prepared to stand against the Franco-British advance.

For a time after the withdrawal of the Twenty-sixth American Division from the Marne counter-offensive, in the summer of 1918, Mary was the headquarters of some of the echelons of the New Englanders.

In the Shadows

"Rough"

L'ANGE GARDIEN (KNOWN AS CHATEAU LA RUE IN 1918)

In a big house some kilometers before La Ferté and on the right side of N-3, AEF Field Hospital No. 15 had its location. In 1918 the house was called Chateau La Rue. Field Hospital No. 15 was located here from 4 to 16 June 1918 and during this time it operated as an auxiliary triage, treating 1112 wounded American soldiers. Today, the place is called L'Ange Gardien. Field Hospital No. 15 moved to Luzancy on 16 June 1918.

Site of the BEF pontoon bridge at La Ferte. The bridge to the right had been blown up. The Royal Engineers, BEF built a pontoon bridge between the two pylons shown on the river banks.

BEF memorial at La Ferté —The sarcophagus holds trophies, ensigns, magazines, bayonets and a steel helmet

IN THEIR OWN WORDS

From the *History of Base Hospital No. 18, AEF (Johns Hopkins Unit), 1919*:

The Hun was finally stopped in his tracks, but it was quite apparent that it was only a question of time before he would launch another onslaught. So thousands upon thousands and tens of thousands of American troops were hurried into the region—and this time the Medical Department came into its own. Hospitals of all sizes and types were got up, equipped, staffed and held in readiness, a little advanced hospital for non-transportables being established at La Ferte-sous-Jouarre, just a few miles back of the line. Indeed, this hospital was started before the first show was over but it did not function properly until later on. We moved up to it on July 5th and were there when the famous offensive started on July 15th. Up until that time things had been very quiet in the line and work was only of an intermittent character. With the Hun thrust, however, and our own counter, things broke loose and from then on it was a constant drive by day and by night. The wounded came in by the hundreds, ambulance trains seemingly never ending. All seriously wounded such as abdomens, sucking chests, the terribly shocked and the bleeding were sorted out, retained and operated on by us, the remainder, and of course, by far the majority, being sent on to the evacuation hospitals in the rear.

The underlying idea of an advanced hospital is not only to afford early and prompt operation to the desperately wounded but to provide a stopping place for them after operation, until their condition improves to such an extent that they may be evacuated. This plan we attempted to follow and did as far as lay in our power. There were four regular operating teams (occasionally two more), and by dint of constant hard work our prospective tents were kept fairly well cleared. But our bed capacity was but a scant two hundred and soon gave out, so in order to make room, certain cases, that under ordinary circumstances should never have been moved, had to be evacuated, and a certain number of lives were lost. Again, however, it must be remembered that these were actual war conditions and such conditions do not permit of a perfect arrangement concerning such matters. As a result, however, of this experience, we recommended that no advanced hospitals in the future should have less than five hundred beds and that if possible the number be one thousand.

The allied counter-offensive was a joyous success from the very start, and, as a consequence our little advanced hospital became less and less advanced. So along about July 24th some casual medical officers came in to care for our patients while we packed up our belongings and went forward ourselves—this probably being the first time a hospital of the AEF had advanced. Chateau-Thierry had already fallen and it had been intended for us to move in there, but conditions were so indescribably chaotic and filthy as to render the shell-ridden city unfit as yet for human habitation. So our tents were pitched at Villiers-sur-Marne, around the chateau made famous by Mrs. Francis Wilson Huard in her well-known book, "My Home in the Field of Honour."

THE COMMONWEALTH MEMORIAL TO THE MISSING OF THE BRITISH EXPEDITIONARY FORCES

The memorial is situated in a small park on the south bank of the River Marne, just off the main road to Paris.

Carefully walk across the traffic circle and to the large white monument seen by the river bank. Constructed of white Massangis stone, the memorial stands in a small park presented by the family of Monsieur Bernard de Jussieu.

This is the Commonwealth Memorial to the Missing and to the Unknown Dead of the British Expeditionary Forces (BEF) who died in August, September and the early part of October, 1914 in the battles of Mons, Le Cateau, the Marne and the Aisne. The panels of the memorial contain the names of 3,888 British Commonwealth soldiers who have no known grave. The Memorial Register is kept at the Town Hall.

The monument consists of a rectangular block of stone, 62 feet by 30 feet and 24 feet high, with the names of the dead engraved on stone panels on all sides of the monument. At the four corners of the terrace pavement are columns supporting urns, carved with the coats of arms of the Empire.

The large, squat memorial is surmounted by a sarcophagus holding trophies, ensigns, magazines, bayonets and a steel helmet. The placement of a steel helmet on the sarcophagus appears to be a 'deliberate error,' as the BEF was not equipped with the steel helmet until 1916.

Four columns stand at the corners of the terrace supporting urns and bearing the arms of the United Kingdom. The memorial, designed by G.H. Goldsmith, had its unveiling on November 4, 1928 by Gen Sir William Pulteney in the presence of Marshal Foch, Field Marshal Milne and Gen Weygand.

La Ferté-sous-Jouarre was on the advance of German Gen von Kluck's First Army; its center thrusted towards La Ferté, its left wing to Château-Thierry.

The BEF destroyed the two bridges over the Marne at La Ferté on 3 September 1914 during their retreat from Mons. The bridge on the Rue des Pelletiers, the chief business thoroughfare of La Ferté, was destroyed during the fighting of 1914 but its stonework has been replaced by not ungraceful steel arches.

Follow N-3 INTO LA FERTÉ-sous-JOUARRE. At the junction of the two river bridges and at the traffic circle, you will see a large, white monument on your left. There is parking on the road going out of the traffic circle across from the monument.

City Hall at La Ferté now

La Ferté, 1918

It was here that the BEF, after its memorable fighting retreat, struck back at the German Army in the first battle of the Marne in 1914. The BEF, which began its counteroffensive on 6 September 1914, arrived at La Ferté on 9 September 1914 to find the Germans well, placed on the northern banks and the bridges still down. The Germans strongly opposed the British crossing here.

The British artillery dealt severely with the enemy guns and the engineers of the 4th Division, BEF, built a floating bridge to enable the left wing of their army to cross and continue its northward advance in September 1914.

On each riverbank, slightly downstream and by the left side of the modern road bridge in back of the monument, is a white, rectangular obelisk. This marks the position of a floating pontoon bridge that was built by the 4th Division Engineers, BEF. On the opposite bank of the river are twin pylon markers, which indicate the other side of the British pontoon bridge. The pylon markers on both riverbanks are crowned with the grenade of the Royal Engineers mounted on a circular paving. This is where the BEF recrossed the river on the temporary bridge while under hostile artillery fire.

The village of La-Ferté-sous-Jouarre is about one kilometer north of the memorial and the two bridges there over the Marne River. In the ancient part of town you can see the old bridge and the marketplace. The descriptions given below refer to the old town of La-Ferté and not to the area where the monument is located.

Ample parking is usually available at the La Ferté railroad station, from which point it is but a short walk down to the center of town and to the river. Mounted on the wall of the railroad station is a metal plaque which describes where the building was damaged by German aerial bombs during World War I.

LA FERTÉ-SOUS-JOUARRE

La-Ferté-sous-Jouarre is an attractive town at the junction of the Marne and the Grand and Petit Morin Rivers, those tributaries of the Marne which few English people had heard of before they became sadly familiar names in September 1914. La Ferté is 66 km to the east of Paris.

La Ferté derives its name from a 10th-century fortress, later held by the Bourbons, on a now-vanished island. Louis XVI and Marie Antoinette, after the arrest of their flight at Varennes, were brought here on their way to Paris in 1791.

In 1918 the population of the town was about 5,000 people.

La Ferté is what one might call a border town. Back in the early summer of 1914 it was a flourishing trade center for that section of France. Unfortunately, La Ferté lay in the direct path of the German Army on its march down the Marne to Paris. Because of its position, the town suffered along with the other martyred cities, towns and villages of the front. On the eighth of September, 1914, the weary soldiers of Marshal French's British Army, restored to splendid energy by the prospect of forward fighting once more, struck the advance elements of von Kluck's hosts and forced them northward across this sluggish little vein of water and its more formidable trough of hills to finally reach the Marne bridges of La Ferté and win a passage across them against bitter opposition. All about the hill of Jouarre the British soldiers then swarmed, their coming saving the old town and the larger community at its feet from further molestation by the enemy.

About 14 June 1918, U.S. 4th Division headquarters was located in La Ferté.

The I American Corps (organized in January, 1918) located its headquarters at La Ferté from 18 June to 21 July and from 13 to 18 August, removing to Neufchâteau three days later. The town was a railhead and supply base for the 2nd Division in 1918. The AEF also used La Ferté as a rest and recuperation area for battle-weary soldiers.

The First United States Army was organized at La Ferté on 10 August, 1918 for the St. Mihiel offensive.

An advance airfield for the I Corps Observation Group, AEF, had its location near La Ferté, close to BgGen Mitchell's headquarters. Although the airfield was small and rocky, it had space for six hangars. Messenger and alert planes came and went daily. Often several of the observer teams touched down as darkness fell and the air crews stayed at this field overnight.

Field Hospital No. 23 moved forward from Meaux to La Ferté on 9 June, where it continued to treat the seriously wounded.

Field Hospital No. 103, at La Ferté-sous-Jouarre, received the seriously wounded. This surgical hospital, with 6 operating teams and 35 female nurses, was completely equipped and was established in an old, large convent. Field Hospital No. 103 evidently moved out of La Ferté after mid-July, 1918.

In 1918 there were 344 American soldiers interred in the American Section of the French Communal Cemetery at La-Ferté-sous-Jouarre. These bodies were later moved to larger and more consolidated American military cemeteries.

The following is a short excerpt, from *The Marne, Historic and Picturesque*, written by an AEF officer Joseph M. Hansen just after the war:

> The explanation of the cordiality of the people of La Ferté to Americans is not far to seek. In June and July, 1918, while the United States Divisions were fighting their first battles along the Marne salient and in the valley of the Ourcq, General Pershing spent the greater part of his time at La Ferté, observing the operations of his troops and caring for their welfare, though they were still directly under French army command. Here, on August 10, 1918, the First American Army came officially into being and its staff organization was

"Bridge over the Marne at La Ferté"

The bridge at La Ferté blown up (top). Engineers repairing the bridge across the Marne at La Ferté-sous-Jouarre (middle). Notice how expertly the bridge has been reconstructed and in the original design (bottom).

perfected. Hence, for several months during the very crisis of the war, the city was the rendezvous for large numbers of American soldiers and a great many of their prominent officers, all of whom appear to have produced upon the inhabitants a profoundly favorable impression.

IN THEIR OWN WORDS

Pvt Leo J. Bailey, 9th Infantry, 2nd Division, wrote in his diary:

By midnight May 31–June 1, the infantry was marching somewhere on the road to Château-Thierry. Bailey's squad, burdened under two Chauchats, ammunition clips, Springfield rifles and bandoliers, heavy packs, field rations, and two hundred pistol rounds, stretched upon the cobblestones of a deserted town square. Eighteen hours of marching hip to hip with a seventy-two pound pack, dry throated in a cloud of dust, had wearied them. Most men lay in full equipment on the cobbles and slept, but some scroungers with keener noses smelled brandy. 'If there is a brandy distillery there,' Bailey recalled: 'then the place must have been La Ferté-sous-Jouarre. Some of the fellows for a while forgot their fatigue.' By dawn, remnants of French regiments were streaming through the square as doughboys tightened belts and fell into company lines. "Many of the men told us we would never stop the Boches. Pointing dramatically at the bloody bandage on his head, one of the Frenchmen shouted: *'Voyez ça? J'ai tué trois boches avant de la recevoir.'* [See this? I killed three Germans before I got hit].

Harry E. Townsend, a combat artist of the AEF, wrote in his diary:

The trip there thro Trilport, then on to La Ferté, is a very beautiful trip. We found it a slow one owing to the great numbers of troops and amount of material going up. There seemed to be American troops everywhere and the Marne seemed to be full of them in places. They seemed to relish the chance to not only get a bath, but to have a real swim as well, and every fancy diver in the AEF seemed to be on the job that morning. What a contrast it was...this young, enthusiastic American youth enjoying himself in what seemed his element, to the Marne a little farther down filled with the dead Boche killed along its banks and even on its bosom. La Ferté we found simply packed with Americans. We saw the wreck that the German raiders had made of the R.R. [railroad] station there with their bombs, but troops and supplies were still being unloaded there, for it's a very important and necessary point at this particular moment. La Ferté we found a very beautiful old town with many marks of the Hun still on it from the first battle of the Marne. The ruined bridge, perhaps wisely, has never been rebuilt, a temporary one-way or single crossing span having been thrown across. This we found very congested owing to the traffic in both directions, which meant long waiting.

The transport was unloaded at La Ferté, which was the farthest advanced station with an unloading platform, and went overland to Nanteuil-sur-Marne.

According to *The History of Company A, 102nd Machine Gun Battalion, 26th Division*, by Arthur C. Havlin:

> La Ferté was a bon town in many respects, containing numerous well-stocked stores and cafés. To be specific, one fellow bought there a fountain pen of a well-known American manufacturer. However, many francs were required in order to enjoy the town. Incidently, there were more than sufficient M.P.'s in La Ferté, for it served as headquarters of the First American Army.

COULOMMIERS

Coulommiers is 17 km south of La-Ferté-sous-Jouarre on D-402. Coulommiers was the location of Evacuation Hospital No. 7 and of Mobile Unit One. Evacuation Seven was located in the Château Montanglaust, located just on the northern outskirts of Coulommiers.

IN THEIR OWN WORDS

Frederick Pottle, an aid-man in the AEF, wrote as in his book, *Stretchers: The Story of a Hospital Unit on the Western Front*:

> I shall take the liberty to describe the care of the American wounded in the great Marne battles of the summer of 1918, by means of a letter written by a member of the company who was not at Juilly, but on detached service at Coulommiers. I do this because this letter, which he wrote on his return, is fuller and more graphic than anything which I have describing the work at Evacuation Eight. Much of it is intensely personal, and in no way a history of the experience of the whole company, but in tone and atmosphere it is representative. And it seems to me that this elusive inner core of experience is more important in our record than the bare outward details of chronology.
>
> Since we had set up at Juilly, the American front line had not changed to any extent, but other hospital units had established themselves in localities more directly south of that part of the line which bore the brunt of the offensive.

Railroad station at La Ferté now

Inscription on the wall of the railroad station, La Ferté

American soldiers, Company B, 166th Infantry Regiment entering La Ferté-sous-Jouarre, 23 July 1918. The house number is "13."

American military cemetery at La Ferté

When the German attack was launched, the first great wave of wounded reached these hospitals and threatened to swamp them. Evacuation Seven and Mobile Unit One were at Coulommiers. In response to their appeals for assistance, two surgical teams were detached from Evacuation Eight to help them out.

…I was sent on detached service with a surgical team to a hospital nearer the front. There were two teams of us—four surgeons, four nurses, another enlisted man, and myself. I was ill with a severe attack of tonsillitis at the time, but, as I thought I might get nearer the front, I said nothing about it, but rolled my pack and reported to go. We traveled about thirty kilometers in a Ford ambulance, leaving about supper-time. I wish you could see these French roads. They are broad, hard, and straight, generally provided with a curb, white, always clean, and always lined with evenly spaced rows of symmetrical pollarded trees—sycamore, horse chesnuts, or lindens. We had hardly started when we ran into what seemed like an endless line of trucks filled with soldiers headed for the front, an unbroken procession of huge Army camions stretching back for miles, each one about thirty feet behind the one in front. The sun was going down in one of the most gorgeous sunsets I ever saw. Our road ran through broad fields of wheat, now yellow and ripe, dotted here and there by solitary crosses, which mark the graves of poor French lads who were buried where they fell in 1914. And moving past us endlessly that stream of great brown trucks filled with brown clad men, like the endless belt of some great machine, feeding them into a gigantic hopper. As the glow of the sunset faded and the dusk came on, the dusty brown uniforms blended with the brown of the trucks, and one might not have realized that they were filled with men if he had not seen occasionally the flash of white teeth as they spoke to one another.

We had better than thirty kilometers to go, and our driver wasn't sure of the road. It was ten o'clock and quite dark when we reached our destination. We drove through the unlighted and quiet streets of a town—whether large or small it was impossible to say—climbed a steep ascent, and stopped before a building on the hill top which, from its mass and dark shadow of a grove of trees behind it, seemed to be a mansion of considerable importance. We walked up a graveled driveway with trampled hedges and flower beds on either side, up two or three broad stone steps, and into a dark hallway. There was not a ray of light, and we stumbled over something that moaned with pain. The floor was covered, except for the narrowest of passage-ways, with litters on which were wounded men. We turned to the left, toward a door around which could be seen a narrow chink of bright light, pulled it open, and, shutting it quickly, paused a moment to gaze at one of the strangest sights man ever beheld. Two units were at work here on this hill top, an evacuation hospital, and a mobile unit or 'auto-chir.' This was the operating room of the evacuation. It was evidently the most splendid parlor of the château; a fairly large room, elaborately decorated with a hand-painted landscape frieze, and had, at the side opposite the entrance, a fire-place with an immense rococo mantel and mirror. Now it was jammed full of operating tables, and several teams were hard at work. Bloody gauze and towels were everywhere—on the floor, in the fireplace, simply trodden underfoot. The rush was so terrific that the orderlies had only time to mop off the top of the table as one man was carried out and another brought in. There was no electricity, the light being furnished by portable acetylene generators, bubbling smelly tanks which stood on the floor beside each table, with a bare jet of flame at the height of about five feet. The shutters (which must have been made of solid plank) were all tightly closed for fear of air raids, and the air was terribly close, reeking with ether and acetylene, and shimmering with the heat. To one slightly light-headed with fever like myself, the room was an impossible nightmare of unearthly shapes: silent and prostrate forms cumbering the tables, tense and busy groups of surgeons and nurses with their ghostly white gowns and ghoulish gloved hands, like black claws, wielding the glittering little instruments in a silence broken only by the oppressed breathing of the men under the ether, the click of the instruments, and occasional curt commands.

I had to assist for two tables. We started with a patient. I held his arms as he went under the ether, and as I did so, gazed uncomprehendingly at what was going on at the next table. The surgeons there (a man with an unpleasantly loud and cheerful voice) had amputated one of the patient's legs and was starting to amputate the other. For some reason, he had the patient laid on the table with his feet where the others' heads were. It looked to me as though he were amputating the man's head, which at the time did not seem in the least surprising. It came over me that I was about to faint. But there was no one to pay any attention to an assistant with a silly case of tonsillitis while all these desperately wounded men waited. Besides, the anesthetist just then had her hands full, and all the others were scrubbed up. And if I let go the patient, he might struggle and throw himself off the table. So I stood, holding his arms, hoping that if I fell I should go across his chest. Everything went black. I could see nothing, though I could hear the talking and the vicious gritting of the hemostats. Suddenly the lights came back with a blaze, and I was out of it. The major, seeing me sag, had flopped me down on a stool and pushed my head between my knees. He had just got himself ready to begin the operation, and in touching me broke his asepsis, which quite properly annoyed him. He told

La Ferté-sous-Jouarre — L'Hôtel-de-Ville

German prisoners captured on the night of 1 July 1918 by the 9th and 23rd Infantry Regiments, 2nd Division at Château-Thierry

me to go out doors and stay there until I was steady enough to be of some use. I stumbled out through the hall (tripping over the wounded men again), and collapsed on the grass in front of the château. Then I got up, crawled into the hallway, found my pack and belt, and drank some aromatic spirits of ammonia. It tasted vilely of the rubber stopper of the flask, but seemed to have no effect at all. I thought that if I walked about a bit it might steady me. I skirted the side of the château, and had just got well around into the trees behind, when BANG!! a terrific explosion almost lifted me from the ground. A German plane had dropped a bomb within a hundred yards. In the interval between that bomb and the next, I heard the motor of the plane right overhead. Then a battery of antiaircraft guns opened fire. They were so near that for a moment I thought it was more bombs. I was standing beside a good sized oak tree, and I remember that I embraced it firmly. What good I thought it would do me, I don't know. The German dropped two more bombs, neither so near as the first, and departed. The shock had cleared my head completely. I went back to the operating room and worked without stopping until noon the next day. Just before we went off, a patient died on the table. I helped carry him to the morgue, a small white tent on the lawn. It stood quite in the open, under the direct rays of the scorching sun. Before we got to it, I could hear quite clearly the heavy buzzing, like that of many swarms of bees, made by the hordes of flies that filled it. We went off until seven that evening. I hunted up a stretcher and pulled it into an empty ward tent on the lawn. The tent was one of those fussy English contraptions with three great poles, and peaks like a circus tent. It was made of glaring white canvas, and lined with flaming yellow. It seemed to me that every ray of the blistering sun came through to torture me. Officers and men coming off duty or going on again were continually passing by and talking. I lay in a heavy stupor, unable to sleep, and yet got some rest.

When we went on duty again it was with the mobile unit. All their equipment was in tents, or on wheels. Their kitchen was on wheels, their sterilizer was a truck, and a portable generator furnished electric light. The operating room was a long tent with twelve tables in a row. A person who had not seen it would be unable to believe that so commodious and efficient an operating room could be set up in a tent.

We worked twelve hours this time—until seven the next morning. My knees soon gave out completely, so that to bend them hurt me as though I had rheumatism. I walked stiff-legged. I was the only orderly for two teams of surgeons, but I managed to get through somehow. I remember only one thing that happened. I tried to remove the wet and matted hair from the head of a poor chap with a scalp wound, first using a pair of dull scissors, and then a pair of duller clippers. The clippers (which I hadn't the slightest idea how to use) stuck in the hair so that I had to unscrew the blades to get them out again. I must have almost scalped the patient, but he made no protest, though he looked rather reproachful.

This time we had twelve hours off, but again I had no luck in getting to sleep. The heat was as bad as ever, and as soon as I stretched out my legs, my knees would cramp and force me to sit up. We went on again at seven, but about midnight the supply of wounded ran out. I got a bloody stretcher, covered it with a blanket, and lay down on the operating room floor. I was just dropping sweetly off to sleep when an orderly waked me and made me get up so that he could scrub the floor. But I got to sleep again and rested a lot. We went on again the next noon, and worked until six, when we received orders to report back to Evacuation Eight. So back we came, to find our own hospital as jammed with wounded as those with which we had been working. The ground space of the great cobble-paved courtyard was literally completely covered with wounded men, some lying on stretchers, and some sitting. You found them everywhere—lying in corridors, sitting on stairs, filling the wards, patiently waiting for attention. We had four awful days, but we seem now to be pretty well cleared up.

I have run some of the impressions of that first night at the château together into a few lines of verse. Would you like to see them?

THE MAN ON THE TABLE
CHÂTEAU MONTANGLAUST, COULOMMIERS, JULY 15, 1918

THERE were four of us there by ourselves, the tired-faced nurse and I,
And the man on the table who lay with his teeth tight shut on a cry,
And the surgeon who turned to his task with a weary nod and a sigh.
For the man on the table was young, with a pain-twisted boyish face,
And rounded and smooth were the lines of his long naked body's grace,
Like the slender forms of the youths round the curve of a Grecian vase.
As I held his hands till he breathed through the ether mask deep and slow,
I saw as a dream the walls of the room in that old château,
With the elegant woodland frieze, and the fireplace carved and low.
But now, how the room was filled! White tables, white figures between,
And the thick air shook with the heat of bare flames of acetylene,
And reeked with spent ether fumes, and the stench of the gas gangrene.
My heavy head throbbed and burned; there was not a breath of air,

American soldiers shopping in La Ferté

FRENCH FAMILIES FLEEING FROM THE GERMANS, ON THE ROAD OUT

FRENCH REFUGEES
ON THE MOVE

REFUGEES FROM THE CHATEAU-THIERRY SALIENT

Suicide Battalions, Wendell   G. P. Putnam's Sons

And great black circles wheeled, and met my eyes everywhere,
And I felt myself slipping and falling, but something held me there.
For I saw how the nurse's eyes, in spite of herself, would close,
And the surgeon's face set like a mask, though his busy hands fell and rose,
And I knew they were tired as I, who was weary to death, God knows.
Then I heard my voice, far away: "His pulse is bad, sir," it said,
And the surgeon lifted his eyes, then "Pulse! Great God, man, he's dead!
And gathered up in a heap his instruments, sticky and red.
Then he stripped off his gloves and his gown, and said, "Get him out in the hall;
And the nurse said, "Cover his face up," and I said, "Look out, men, he'll fall;
But the man on the table lay still, and smiled, and said nothing at all.

We received greater numbers of wounded during this drive than at any time previous. But our service was now better organized, and the routine operated more smoothly. An extract from a diary will serve to indicate the mixed spirit of idealistic altruism and matter-of-factness which characterized the greater part of our war work. Caring for wounded men becomes a job like everything else, and to carry on this job efficiently for a long period demands a reasonable attention to one's own physical and mental health. This diary was, of course, never intended for public inspection. But the naiveté of its entries is therefore all the more illuminating.

(Diary A.) "Monday, July 15. Played tennis until 11.00 A.M. [This man was on night duty.] Beaten once, but did not play to finish. Holiday for all the boys. Slept some. Took shower and got ready for dance. Alas! 7.00 P.M. Evac. 8 luck. Dance called off account of big drive. From 8.00 P.M. carried our boys from Battle of Marne to operating room and then to ward.

"Tuesday, July 16. 4.45 A.M. carried the last poor mate to operating room. News said Huns had crossed Marne, but were pushed back. Slept 5.00 to 7.00 A.M., then [I suppose after eating breakfast] slept all day, as I was very tired. Got up for dinner and supper. Reported at 7.30 P.M. Carried a few patients, then slept after supper [at midnight] of pork, bread and butter, lettuce, and cocoa. [This midnight mess was-prepared by the sisters, and served in the refectory of the Collège itself.]

"Wednesday, July 17. Up at 7.00 A.M. Sat around and talked. Germans at Marne had advanced ten miles, but losses were great, and victory conceded to U.S. To bed after dinner and slept until 6.00 P.M. Reported for duty. Nothing to do. Slept until 12.00, then supper. 1.30 A.M. called and helped with man in A Ward. He died, then I slept until 7.00 A.M.

"Thursday, July 18. Played tennis with B. and lost 6–3, 6–2, 6–4. Slept well until 4.00 P.M. Company had dance, but did not go, account of big rush of our boys. Some had legs amputated, and litter bearing in an operating room is surely some job. Took delight in helping to make the boys comfortable. Had supper at midnight, beef, lettuce, and bread. Then back to work.

"Friday, July 19. Reported off at 7.30 A.M. and was surely tired, sick at stomach, etc., and went right to bed. Good news says we drove the Huns back six or eight miles. Up at 6.00 P.M. Worked hard all night carrying. Saw some mean wounds. Had no time for supper at midnight. Court filled with wounded.

"Saturday, July 20. Did not report off duty until 1.00 P.M. after strenuous time all night. [At least eighteen hours of lifting and carrying wounded.] Slept three hours after reading letters from home. Worked hard evacuating until midnight and was about all in. Finished work after a big night. News says our boys are still going ahead. Received six more letters.

Sunday, July 21. Breakfast, oatmeal and bacon. To bed very tired and weak at 8.00 A.M. after short prayer. Up at 6.00 P.M. Went to church in Ward F. Grover [Walters] read text, Mark [John] 14: In my father's house, etc. No patients came in, so talked with nurses until midnight, then had supper, and to bed on litter, very tired.

This strenuous-week completed our busy work for the summer. From then until we left Juilly, our days moved on in the sleepy routine into which they had settled before the Marne battles. The wards were still well filled, but the receiving office and operating rooms might almost as well have been closed, and in fact one of them finally was. Diaries speak of bicycle excursions, attempts at making ice cream without ice, movies, entertainments by infantry bands passing through, and inspections, besides such work as cleaning instruments, rolling bandages, and burying the dead. Whether we admitted wounded or not, we had a few deaths nearly every day. Our living conditions were by no means as comfortable as they had been during the sunny days of June. From July 23 to August 6 it rained almost continuously. The French farmers were then just ready to harvest the glorious fields of grain which had been ripening so auspiciously. With cruel persistence the rain continued to pour, soaking down again and again the soggy and blackening harvest which the peasants—more than half women because most of the men were at the front—strove doggedly to save. Our kitchens were still out of doors, so that we often had to stand in our slickers in the downpour for mess. The flies and wasps were innumerable. The wasps had been rather amusing at first when we shooed them away and marveled at their persistence. By this time they had become an intolerable nuisance. They settled down in swarms over our food, and had actually to be brushed off with

FRENCH REFUGEES ON THE MOVE

THESE FRENCH REFUGEES SAVED WHAT THEY COULD

Foraging

our hands or fished out with our spoons. There were wasps in everything we ate. One could leave nothing uncovered a moment without finding it filled with wasps. Our open latrines probably furnished most of the flies, and the flies furnished various unpleasant infections. We all suffered from painful stomach and intestinal disorders. Inaction began to get on our nerves, and rumors began to circulate to the effect that we were soon to leave.

The death and funeral of a French aviator created a diversion for at least the fatigue gang. "How do you suppose I celebrated my coming of age?" asks a letter from one of those unfortunates. "In blue denim overalls pushing a cart around and collecting rubbish! Operating Room B is closed until another drive, and the surgical assistants are now in the chain gang. Being on fatigue has brought me one rather memorable experience. A French aviator fell last week a few kilometres from here. A wing of his plane broke off, I believe, and dropped him more than a mile. He was terribly smashed up, they say. He was given a fine military funeral in the village church. The officers of his escadrille were here, and a guard of ten infantrymen, with their rifles. As a mark of respect, we Americans were asked to furnish eight bearers. That was the fatigue gang. We carried the coffin—a plain plank box covered with the tricolor on which rested one great bunch of flowers from his family—into the church, and up to the altar. His father and mother were there; the father a short rotund gentleman with a fierce moustache, the mother a handsome woman of middle age. She was in deep mourning and wept bitterly, but the father seemed almost unmoved. The service, a high mass of requiem, was naturally all in Latin, except for a brief but very powerful address in French by the curé. We then bore the coffin to the French cemetery. I wish I could give you some idea of the procession. First, side by side, went the little crucifer and an acolyte carrying the holy water. One wore an American trench cap with an infantry button, the other an horizon-blue French cap with infantry numeral. Each wore a white cotta trimmed with lace. Then came the curé and his deacon in their vestments, chanting a Latin hymn, with pauses between the verses. (I strongly suspect that the curé timed the verses by the regularly spaced trees alongside the road.) Then we followed, carrying the coffin on a bier, with five French infantrymen marching on each side; then the father and mother, and the rest of the funeral cortège.

After a short burial service we lowered the coffin into the grave. The dead man's captain read a panegyric of his military achievements. Then, for the first time, the father showed signs of emotion. One big tear rolled down his cheek and was shaken fiercely off the point of his moustache. The mother gently thanked us for our services.

Sections from a diary (Diary B):

August 9. Went to a nearby town and had a three-egg omelet with *vin blanc* and *citron* . . .

August 10. Very little out of the ordinary happened, and in fact things were so quiet that the air was oppressive with its stillness . . .

August 11. Sunday, and a very peaceful day. It seems anything but the war zone here. I had a very fine bath, and after the evening repast of goldfish, went to the next town. . . . We started for Dammartin, but missed the train, so went to the regular booze joint [a rather cruel name for the café in St. Mard] and played some time on the piano.

August 10. P.S. From now on each day I will put in the various rumors and their sources, so far as possible. Reported by a nurse that we were moving to Toul very soon. It was also rumored that we were about to leave for Oulchy le Château.

August 11, 12, 13, 14. Nothing special doing, except on the IA. I washed clothes [in the town lavoir]. Didn't seem to suit the French woman next to me. She took some of my clothes and did them for me. Pay came about 8.00 P.M., but on account of lack of change we were not paid. Probably will be on Wednesday. The latest rumors say either Italy or Toul. Probably neither."

Our last days at Juilly are well described by the entries in another diary (Diary A):

Thursday, August 15. Up at 6.00 A.M. Worked little all day, which was warm and bright. Took short walk at night. Bought box of chocolates [from the quartermaster at St. Mard] and to bed at 10.30 P.M.

Friday, August 16. Beautiful day. Sat around, had letter from home. Played tennis after supper of eggs and good bread and butter. To bed at 10.00 P.M. after short walk.

Saturday, August 17. Beautiful day. Little to do and no excitement. Rested in P.M. and to bed early, tired of doing nothing.

Sunday, August 18. Beautiful day. Orders to move, and spend day loading an army of French trucks [with all our surgical equipment and company stores]. Took walk after shower . . . until 9.00 P.M., then to bed. . . .

Monday, August 19. [The writing of this entry is extremely uneven, having been written on board a jostling freight car.] Roll call at 6.15. Oatmeal. Packs rolled. Carried patients until 11.00 A.M. Sat around all P.M. Pie from sisters at 5.00 P.M., at 6.00 P.M. lined up and marched to St. Mard. Hun prisoners along the way. Piled aboard singing, and by 7.30 nurses and men were leaving Juilly behind forever.

I have before me as I write a condensed daily summary of our work at Juilly. The totals are perhaps more impressive than one would suspect from a casual

Refugees from the Château-Thierry section

FRENCH REFUGEES ON THE MOVE

French refugees at the railroad station in Montmirail. Also shown are French and British wounded fresh from the battle and American soldiers who are replacing them at the front. It is not a sack of potatoes that is being boosted up onto the railroad flat-car by the American soldier, but a very aged French woman.

French refugees fleeing, 31 May 1918

reading of this narrative. During our ten weeks in the Collège we admitted 3,736 American sick, gassed, and wounded. This does not include the 1,700 admitted between June 4 and June 8, about 500 of whom were in the hospital when we arrived. Up to about June 15, all the transportable seriously wounded from the engagement at Belleau Woods passed through Juilly. Our busiest day, in number of admissions, was July 19, when we took in 608 patients. Our total deaths, June 8 to August 19, were only 71. The percentage of death for the period that we were in charge was only 1.9, which is extremely low; in fact, too low to represent adequately our more characteristic work later in the Argonne. At Petit Maujouy, where we received no gassed (unless also wounded), and only men suffering from serious wounds, our mortality was between 7 and 8 per cent. The smaller figure at Juilly is probably to be accounted for by the large number (about 800) of gas patients we received there, and the fact that many of our admissions in the July offensive were of slightly wounded.

"The best of our war time experience," says a letter I received not long ago from a member of the company, "was at Juilly." Life at Oglethorpe was occasionally more fun. Life at Petit Maujouy was constantly more strenuous, often more exciting, but always sterner and bleaker. But when a member of Evacuation Eight pauses in reverie upon the sweetest moments of his months in France, he will linger, I am sure, upon recollections of the grand old white buildings of the Collège, the broad courtyard drowsing sleepily in the heat, the quiet green of its park, the idyllic beauty of its lake and quiet swans. And mingled inseparably with these memories will come back others, touched with pain and regret but still more to be treasured: thoughts of high idealism as yet unspoiled by cynicism, of ungrudging devotion to the labor of alleviating suffering, of friendships made among the many wounded boys whom we sent away from Juilly, or among that other company who rested in the cemetery in the wheat field.

TOUQUIN

The U. S. 1st Pursuit Group, comprised of the 17th, 27th, 94th, 95th, 103rd, 147th and 183rd Aero Squadrons moved to Toul to Touquin aerodrome (Melon Field) on 27–28 June, 1918.

At this time most of the squadrons had about 17 pilots and 24 planes. One of these squadrons, the 95th Aero Squadron, had Quentin Roosevelt (son of Theodore Roosevelt) as a member.

In four weeks in the new sector, the Touquin group shot down 38 Germans, but lost

36 American pilots. Quentin Roosevelt went down to his death over Chamery on 14 July, 1918.

No. 54 Squadron, Royal Air Force was based at Touquin on 14 July 1918, where it remained until 4 August 1918 at which time it moved on to Fienvillers.

To visit the locale of the airfield, take the D-402 south from La Ferté to Coulommiers and on to Rozay en Brie and to Touquin.

IN THEIR OWN WORDS

In his memoir, "*Fighting the Flying Circus,*" leading American ace Captain Edward V. Rickenbacker says:

> The scene of 94 Squadron's operation now changes from the Toul sector to the Château-Thierry region. On June 27th, 1918, all four of our American Fighting Squadrons were ordered to Château-Thierry.
>
> Our new surroundings were of rather a different character. We settled upon the old French aerodrome at Touquin, a small and miserable village some twenty-five miles south of Château-Thierry and the Marne River. The aerodrome was large and smooth and abundantly equipped with the famous French hangars which consist of steel girders with walls and roofs of canvas. They were very spacious, quite cool in summer and camouflaged admirably with the surrounding scenery.
>
> But no provision had been made at Touquin for the pilots and officers.
>
> All of our aeroplanes flew from Toul to Touquin, while the rest of the aerodrome impediments was carted rapidly away to the new quarters in lorries, trucks and trailers. The pilots of Squadrons 27 and 147 were rather new at that time; and it was thought wise to assign some of the older pilots of 94 and 95 Squadrons to the task of leading them through the air to the new field.

According to the war diary of the 94th Pursuit Squadron, "*The Hat in the Ring Gang*":

> GROUP– All officers walked the airdrome at Touquin to locate holes and spots where work was necessary to put the airdrome in flying condition. Offices of the squadron were billeted in a Chateau near the airdrome and enlisted men were billeted in houses in the town.

DOUGHBOYS AND REFUGEES

When the thousands of American soldiers entering the Marne Salient of 1918 met an almost overwhelming number of pitiful French refugees coming out of the salient and ahead of the advancing German Army, their will to defeat the Germans was reinforced

Touquin is about 15 km SW of La Ferté-sous-Jouarre

French refugees fleeing, 31 May 1918

FRENCH REFUGEES
ON THE MOVE

and steeled. Many a Doughboy either said to himself or aloud, "This country and its people are worth fighting for," or "I hate the Germans for what they are doing to these poor people."

To give you, the reader, a feeling for what took place behind the battle lines in June of 1918, the following quotation from the AEF newspaper, *Stars and Stripes*, 1918, tells it all:

Refugees flocking to the rear

A drama poignant with tragedy, is being enacted in the theater of war behind the lines toward which the two American divisions are advancing. For, upon every road and by-path leading out of the Marne salient, including those you will travel going toward the battlefields, weaving their way through the traffic of transport and soldiers going to the front, are war's victims, the refugees, streaming to the rear,—old men and young, decrepit or crippled; women of all ages, and little children, the flotsam and jetsam of war, forced from their homes by the rising tide of battle.

Nondescript Transport and Loads

In contrast to the spick-and-span business-like aspect of military transport, the means employed by the refugees to aid them in their flight present a bewildering and nondescript variety of vehicles drawn by jaded horses, mules and oxen, with an intermingling of carts, varying in size, pulled by donkeys, goats and dogs. Lacking animal friends to aid them, men and women tug at the traces of wagons or push baby carriages and wheelbarrows along; while others, with no means of transport save their own poor bodies, struggle wearily on afoot, burdened to the limit of their strength. Loaded down with whatever they were able to rescue,—bits of furniture, bundles of clothing and food, bottles and casks of wine, chickens, canary birds in cages, kittens and puppies, etc.,—the burdens carried by the refugees present an equally bewildering and nondescript variety of prized possessions, making a picture that lends a touch of the grotesque and humorous to the tragic drama of people thrust from their homes in flight before the enemy.

They play the game in good part

Lest they interfere with the imperative business of rushing men, guns, ammunition and supplies to the front, the flow of refugees to the rear is frequently halted or diverted into fields to relieve congestion and blockades in traffic on the roads and by-paths, but all of them,—old and young,—play the game of war in good part, obeying orders quickly, with sighs of resignation, with tears or smiles and laughter.

It is an indescribable drama in which these refugees play their parts, one that the imagination, with the aid of these word, must visualize. With minds and hearts already filled with fear and hatred of the enemy and preyed upon by wild rumors of impending disaster at the front, fact and fiction inextricably mingled, without the links of truth and reason to connect the twain, they cry."

Our poor Poilus are falling back! Ah, Messieurs, hundreds, nay thousands, have fallen! And the Boches come on! We cannot stop them! Oui, oui, it is true. Messieurs! You can hear Mademoiselle Bertha even now bombarding Paris! Hundreds of thousands are leaving the city and the Capital will fall! Our country is lost!"

Military policemen, regulating traffic at cross-roads, aid them and seek to reassure them in their flight, but rumor, gathering speed and substance on the wings of fancy, had terrified them beyond reason and understanding. Some among them, too old to care, burdened too long with Life's sorrows, are indifferent to further blows from Fate. For them the end has come or will soon come, please God!

"*C'est la guerre, Messieurs!*—and we are old."

The Indomitable Soul of France is Reflected

In spite of the tragedy that weighs so heavily upon their elders, the younger people, boys and girls and young women, though they have suffered, reflect, by word and deed, the indomitable soul of France and with cheerfulness of spirit and courage of heart, laugh at their troubles.

Ah, la, la! Why so glum and fearful, *Mes Vieux*? Did not Papa Joffre stop the Boches once before? Foch will do likewise, never fear. Oui, oui! Our Poilus may be falling back, but it is only to make a stand and stop the Germans. Soon *les Americains* will come to help them and together they will drive the Boches from France!

And thus does youth, with its hope and confidence, seek to comfort and reassure old age and put to shame hysterical and garrulous middle age.

Refugees Meet Advancing American Columns

Meanwhile, the two American divisions, split up into as many detachments as there are thoroughfares available in order to facilitate their march to the front, are gradually approaching the battle lines, and presently encounter the rearward columns of the refugees on all roads and by-paths. When the khaki-clad, happy-go-lucky soldiers of America, with joking and singing in their ranks, troop suddenly into their midst, the weary wayfarers are for a moment spell-bound. It

FRENCH REFUGEES ON THE MOVE

French Refugees
on the Move

is at first difficult for the homeless wanderers to realize what it all means,—that America, with the first of her manpower, backed by her great resources, is going forward into battle! Going forward to throw her sword onto the Scales of War! Finally the truth dawns upon dulled minds and carries hope to fear-stricken hearts. Yes, yes, it is true! These stalwart young men are the Americans, going forward to help the poor Poilus, to stiffen wavering lines, to stop the Huns! Ah, youth, with its hope and confidence, was right!

'*Les Américains! Les Américains!*'

Hope and Courage Revived

Sudden silence falls upon the hysterical and garrulous lips of middle and old age. Rumor and fiction take flight before truth and fact. Old age plucks up hope and courage. Perhaps even they, the old, will still see victory! Little children cease their weeping and gaze with infantile wonder at the passing troops. With the bubbling impulsiveness of youth, young women and girls assail the soldiers and shower flowers upon them. With gladness and laughter, and in utter disregard of impeding accoutrements of war, some of them shamelessly embrace serious young warriors and plant warm kisses upon startled doughboy faces. Old age grasps swinging soldier hands to carry them to trembling lips in benediction; while middle age, gaining voice once more, takes up the cry—"*Vive l'Amérique! Nos sauveurs sont arrivés!*" [Long live America! Our saviors have arrived!"]

Marking the sudden transition from settled hopelessness to quick hopefulness of which the human soul is capable, this cry gives tongue to long pent-up emotions and soon swells to a chorused salutation that greets and follows the soldiers as hey march on all the roads and by-paths toward the front.

And thus heartened and reassured, with a new and growing faith, before which all their fears have now fled, the refugees look at the khaki-clad columns until distance shuts them out from view; then the wayfarers take up their burdens once more and trudge on to the rear, while the young soldiers of America approach closer to the battle lines—and the enemy-to play their real parts in the forthcoming drama. For what we have thus far witnessed, though an essential part of the drama, is in point of fact a prelude to the more important and stirring action that is to follow.

From George B. Ford's book, *Out of the Ruins*:

The refugees were destitute. In 1918 I saw seventy-five thousand of them pour through Paris in the last days of May and the first days of June, driven back by the German advance at Château-Thierry. They arrived a thousand or fifteen hundred to a train at all hours of the day and night, with the stations pitch black while the air raids were going on: bent old men and women, children in arms, with goats and chickens and baby-carriages and endless bundles—whatever they could manage to save and carry away with them. Most of them had only the clothes they wore. Many of them had ridden a day, or even two days, without food. They wandered about in a daze, quite helpless; most of them peasant farmers who had never in their lives been more than a few miles away from their homes.

IN THEIR OWN WORDS

BgGen William A. Mitchell writes in his book, *Leaves from My War Diary:*

The English are badly smashed up and are trying to replace their losses in men and equipment. In the meantime they are putting up what amounts to almost a last stand, as is shown by the order issued by General Haig, commanding the British Army, which is as follows:

Every position must be held to the last man. There must be no retirement. With our backs to the wall, and believing in the justice of our cause, each one of us must fight to the end. The safety of our homes and the freedom of mankind depend alike upon the conduct of each one of us at this critical moment.

Contained in the same war diary is the following letter written by BgGen Mitchell:

June, 1918

The Germans have attacked the French Army in force. The blow came along the Chemin des Dames, the place where the French thought it might come last autumn, which led to the battle of Malmaison in which the French captured the heights that covered that area.

The Germans used very much the same strategy and tactics against the French in this area as they did against the Fifth British Army in March. The German advance toward the Marne was so fast that the French Army units that stood in their path were entirely destroyed, and even the French airdromes were taken, with the airplanes in them—some 200 planes being lost in this way by the French.

Again there is a tremendous hole in the line and the Germans are advancing rapidly on the Marne. General Foch is being criticized a good deal for not having had more troops where the Germans broke through; but if he put all his troops on the line he would have no mass of maneuver with which to hit a movement by the Germans.

Most of his reserves have been used up in helping the British, though. My friend Major Armengaud, who now is on General Foch's staff, tells me that Foch

" "It looks as if the whole world was on the move to-day, said Leon"

(*Page* 148.)

"It looks as if the whole world was on the move to-day, said Leon."

is trying to get a mass of maneuver together, but at the present time the British are powerless to detach any troops, let alone their own. Their army is in terrible shape since the drubbing it got from the Germans, and it will take a couple of months to get on its feet again.

The French have used up their troops that they brought up from Italy to stop the German attack against the English.

The only real reserves are our new American divisions; and these, I understand, General Foch has ordered to the vicinity of Chateau-Thierry to try to stop the German advances.

Of course, what the Germans are now trying to do is to seize the line of the Marne and occupy the mountain of Reims, which is the key point in that area.

If the Germans are successful in this they will be able to bring up their troops and supplies behind the curtain of the Marne. The mountain of Reims will form a great bridgehead and base of operations for an advance into the heart of France. This point not only has great defensive strength, but it is a splendid point from which to take the offensive, because good roads radiate out from it in all directions.

The Germans are unquestionably attempting to end the war now by one great final campaign. They have taken the punch out of the British by the campaign this spring. We are not yet ready as an army, so that the French must stand the full force of the German blow.

If the Germans do not end the war now, we certainly shall have an army of 1,000,000 men this year and 2,000,000 men next year, and they know it. I doubt if they can get very far, because they are not strong enough in the air, their cavalry is used up, and their automobile transport and armored cars have no rubber tires. They are also very weak in tanks.

Our Second Division is already fighting near Chateau-Thierry and has helped to stop the German crossing of the Marne.

General Liggett is preparing to move the headquarters of the First Army Corps to Chateau-Thierry.

The French are terribly afraid of this great German stroke. It is reported that the Germans have shut down all their munitions factories because they have enough ammunition to last them until the end of the war, no matter if it takes two or three years. They have taken all the available men from the factories and from the interior of Germany and put them in the ranks for this great attack.

German troops have been brought up from Italy, and reserves and second-line troops from the Russian frontier. Now is the time for us to get into it, whether we are ready or not.

I immediately went to Chateau-Thierry to the headquarters of the commander of the Third French Army, General Degoutte.

I have never seen a more stunned group of people than were the officers at the headquarters of the Third French Army, and for that matter, the troops also. The French are not at all excitable in the face of danger; in fact, they are probably the coolest of people under that condition. The French troops of the Third Army were away beyond that. They acted as if they had been hit hard in the head with baseball bats.

They had been under constant attack for nearly a month; they had lost miles of territory, thousands of men, and hundreds of airplanes. There were no reserves to give them. They just had to hold the ground or die. The flower of victorious German Aviation is concentrated over their victorious army. The French Air Division, from its constant duty on the front, is having to recuperate and re-equip.

MajGen James G. Harbord remembers in his book, *Leaves from a War Diary*:

My brigade would go out to the northeast of Meaux and billet in four little villages to the west of the Ourcq River and Canal, outposting toward Mareuil [sic]. The Germans were said to be not far away and we might be expect to be attacked before morning. We left, running out north through the green valley of the Ourcq. Every rod of the road was covered. All kinds of French units, artillery at a trot, straggling groups of infantry, lone engineers, Red Cross, trains, wagons, trucks, which sometimes would congest and block the road for half an hour so that there was no movement possible.

Hundreds of refugees crowded the roads, fleeing before the German advance. Men, women, children hurrying toward the rear; tired, worn, with terror in their faces.

Meanwhile we passed a great many French officers and men, but all going from and none towards the front. All afternoon they passed, that motley array which characterized the rear of a routed army. Along towards nightfall there came one unit with its faces turned towards and not from the enemy; a brigade of French cavalry, neat, natty, horses well kept and equipment turned out, headed for the front.

MajGen Harbord gives a very good general account of the start of the second battle of the Marne in his book, *The American Army in France*:

> After the failure of the German Offensive near Armentiéres in mid-April the opinion of the Allies differed as to where the inevitable next blow would fall. Generally they were inclined to agree that the attack would be renewed in the north. So little were the Aisne heights considered that Foch had replaced active units there with seven tired Divisions of both British and French. It was considered so quiet that it was said that for practically two months the French had discontinued their airplane reconnaissance over the enemy's lines to the north. The gathering of German Divisions, the supply installations and other infallible signs of coming activity were carried on unseen.
>
> The American Intelligence Section at Chaumont, studying the German Order of Battle as it varied from day to day, had concluded that the signs pointed to the Aisne as the coming battleground. Particularly a young Intelligence officer, Captain Samuel T. Hubbard, Jr., who had come to Europe on the old Baltic with the Pershing party, had given very good reasons for the faith that was in him, but he found no converts at French G.H.Q. Like a typhoon of the Oriental seas the storm broke behind the Chemin des Dames with the dawn of May 27th, a complete surprise. The enemy had figured this as the nearest approach to Paris. The Paris-Chalons Railway ran just south of the Marne to supply the whole eastern flank of the Allied lines. The principal munitions factories of the Allies were in the environs of Paris. It was a part of the line least convenient of reinforcement by the Allies. The Germans carried the Chemin des Dames in the first dawn dash, crossed the Aisne on bridges that the French had not stopped to destroy, and by evening were across the Vesle. In seventy-two hours they had advanced thirty miles, captured nearly sixty thousand prisoners, six hundred and fifty guns, two thousand machine guns, immense quantities of supplies and munitions, aerodromes, important depots, and considerable railroad rolling stock. By the

evening of May 30th they had the high hills for ten miles along the north bank of the Marne, with outposts on the southern side. The Allied line had been much lengthened and the enemy were dangerously near Paris. A million people had left Paris within a week, and the French government planned to move to Bordeaux.

MajGen Harbord reported to Gen Degoutte, commander of the XXI French Corps about 6:00 AM, 1 June. Degoutte told Harbord:

> Things have been going badly with us. They have been pressing us since the morning of the 27th and have advanced over 50 kilometers in 72 hours. I know that your men need rest. Let them get something to eat. If it can be avoided I shall not call on you today but it may become necessary. Your troops must be ready to go into the line any time after eleven if called on.

In *The American Army in France*, MajGen Harbord continues his memoirs:

> At about the moment I reached Montreuil after my interview with General Degoutte, the Supreme War Council was coming together in gloom at Versailles for its Sixth Session. The circumstances under which it met could hardly have been more depressing. The Council could hear the German guns at a distance from Paris about equal to that which had been spanned in seventy-two hours by the German swoop from the Aisne to the Marne a week before. Chateau-Thierry had fallen. The German were turning westward towards the French capital. The flotsam and jetsam of a beaten army, with a terrified peasantry, were drifting along the highways to Paris. The Government was packing for evacuation to Bordeaux. The Council met in the consciousness that Foch had made a bad guess on where the third blow would fall; and that the trusted Commander of the Group including the VI Army had neglected aerial reconnaissance and permitted thirty German divisions with all their trains and artillery to assemble unseen and unheard behind the Chemin-des-Dames. They might well speculate as to whether the Council would ever meet again, or if its next meeting, if it had one, might not be near the Spanish frontier. The natural, perhaps the inevitable topic with which Clemenceau opened the meeting was his disappointment with the Americans. The only successful Allied offensive since the previous autumn had been the

local but highly successful operation staged by the First Division at Cantigny three days earlier, but even with 200,000 men arriving during May, Pershing now had but 722,000 Americans in France, less than three quarters of a million. Great Britain and France, with command of the sea and their eighty millions of people to the German seventy, who had also fought Russia, Roumania, Servia, and Italy, were now inclined to blame America for the disaster that seemed almost certain to ruin them. A few days later former Prime Minister Barthou at 4th Brigade Headquarters told me of a secret session of the Chamber of Deputies in which they were told that if Caillaux were made Prime Minister and General Sarrail given command of Paris, the War would end in three weeks.

Such was the psychological background against which at the hour of meeting of the Council that June morning, the Second Division A.E.F. (Regular) was moving along the Paris-Metz highway near Montreuil. There was at that fateful hour no American unit more fitted by efficiency and morale for the tremendous responsibilities that faced it.

Jean de Pierrefeu, a staff officer at French Headquarters, later wrote of the feelings of discouraged officers in Pétain's forward headquarters at Provins, only thirty miles by road from Château-Thierry. From his book, *French Headquarters 1915–1918*:

At this time swarms of Americans began to appear on the roads. At Coulommiers and Meaux they passed in interminable columns, closely packed in lorries, with their feet in the air in extraordinary attitudes, some perched on the tilt, almost all bare-headed and bare-chested, singing American airs at the top of their voices amid the enthusiasm of the inhabitants. The spectacle of these magnificent youths from overseas, these beardless children of twenty, radiating strength and health in their equipment, produced a great effect. They contrasted strikingly with our regiments in their faded uniforms, wasted by so many years of war, whose members, thin, their sunken eyes shining with a dull fire, were no more than bundles of nerves held together by a will to heroism and sacrifice. We all had the impression that we were about to see a wonderful operation of transfusion of blood. Life was coming in floods to reanimate the dying body of France, almost bled to death, since for four years that blood had flowed from countless wounds. Nobody thought that perhaps these soldiers were not trained,

that perhaps they had nothing beyond this courage; these were foolish ideas that never entered our minds. In a sort of exalted vision of the future we looked upon them as an inexhaustible source of strength, carrying everything before it, and so, even in those critical days, although the enemy had once again reached the Marne, and might well believe us to be disheartened, the hearts of Frenchmen were filled with new courage. Our soldiers coming out of the trenches, stern and savage, were suddenly reassured and cheered by the sight of their brothers in arms. They said admiringly, "Fine looking chaps, those," without hesitating to add with the Gallic wit that never left them: "Go to it, my lads. You won't look like that in a week's time."

General Pétain was particularly struck by the sight of the Americans whom he met wherever he went. His mind, naturally inclined to see the significance of facts, showed him clearly the life-giving power they represented. At this time the name of the Americans was always on his lips, and he spoke like a builder of imperishable monuments would speak of an inexhaustible material which would allow him to build without fear of shortage.

He was truly pleased, full of confidence and saying so readily. He even embarked upon prophecy, which he as a rule disliked. He said: "The weld will be made, and then we have nothing further to fear. If we can hold on till the end of June, our situation will be excellent. In July we can resume the offensive, after that, victory is ours." I heard this prophecy with my own ears, and it was fulfilled word for word.

He said also that it was unnecessary to subject these magnificent troops to an over-long course of instruction. I fancy that his idea was this. These men were natural fighters; one had only to see these sport-loving young men to understand that they would enter eagerly into the warfare of the moment. They would enter it in open country, like hunters. They would develop an instinct for it in the course of a few days if they were well led.

When the inherent sadness of this crushing disaster had died away, life at Provins went on as before. As elsewhere, there was a surprising renewal of confidence. An extraordinary energy pervaded the departments. It seemed that the end of the nightmare was at hand, no one knew why. This state of mind had its origin, I think, in the sight of the Americans, of whom everyone had doubted whether they would ever arrive in time, and the excellent impression they produced, although it had been prophesied that they could not be turned into soldiers for six months. Then their coming into action at Belleau Wood, where they showed themselves full of courage and dash, delighted the Third Bureau. Colonel Dufieux frequently said to me: "Do not forget the Americans in the *communiqué*; They are admirable."

Alden Brooks, an American who had enlisted in the French Army, and who had retreated with that army from the Chemin des Dames, watched the first troops of the U.S. 3rd Division come into the lines. Brooks wrote in his book, *As I Saw It:*

> It was a pleasure to stand by the road side and watch the long, double files of them come in, watch them pass by, each man with that tightly-rolled knapsack on his back, many a clean young head bare, all in their khaki legs and arms and shoulders moving in a slow easy rhythm, and the dust ever drifting away from them over the hedges.

In a work of fiction, *The Marne*, by Joseph Hansen, is the following description of the evacuees coming out of the Marne salient:

> The east began to redden through the dust-haze of the cloudless air. As they advanced the road became more and more crowded, and the ambulance was caught in the usual dense traffic of the front; artillery, field-kitchens, motor-trucks, horse-wagons, hay-carts packed with refugees, and popping motor-cycles zig-zagging through the tangle of vehicles. The movement seemed more feverish and uncertain than usual, and now and then the road was jammed, and curses shouts, and the crack of heavy whips sounded against the incessant cannonade that hung its iron curtain above the hills to the north-east. The faces of soldiers and officers were unshaved, sallow, and drawn with fatigue and anxiety. Women sat sobbing on their piled-up baggage, and here and there, by the roadside, a little country cart had broken down, and the occupants sat on the bank watching the confusion like impassive lookers-on.
>
> Down a by-road to his left a stream of haggard country people was pouring from the direction of the Marne. This time only a few were in carts: the greater number were flying on their feet, the women carrying their babies, the old people bent under preposterous bundles, blankets, garden utensils, cages with rabbits, an agricultural prize framed and glazed, a wax wedding-wreath

> under a broken globe. Sick and infirm people were dragged and shoved along by the older children: a goitered idiot sat in a wheelbarrow pushed by a girl and laughed and pulled its tongue.
>
> In among the throng was seen the torn blue uniform of wounded soldiers limping on bandaged legs. Others too, not wounded, elderly haggard territorials, with powder-black faces, bristling beards, and the horror of the shell-roar in their eyes. One of them stopped, and in a thick voice begged for a drink, just a drop of anything, for God's sake. Others followed pleading for food and drink. "Gas, gas," a young artilleryman gasped through distorted lips. The Germans were over the Marne, they were coming. It was hell back there, no one could stand it. "The Germans are coming!"—and in a feeble panic they pressed on.
>
> One old man trembling with fatigue, and dragging a shaking little old woman, had spied the stretcher beds inside the ambulance, and without asking leave, scrambled in and pulled his wife after him. They fell like logs onto the grey blankets, and a livid territorial with a bandaged arm drenched in blood crawled in after them and sank to the floor. The rest of the crowd had surged by.
>
> A new sound was heard coming down the road. It was a deep, continuous rumble, the rhythmic growl of a long train of army trucks. The way must have been cleared to let them by, for their was no break or faltering in the ever deepening roar of their approach.
>
> A cloud of dust rolled ahead, growing in volume with the growing noise; now the first trucks were in sight, huge square olive-brown motor-trucks stacked high with scores and scores of bronzed soldiers. It was the American regiment being rushed to the front!
>
> The refugees and the worn-out blue soldiers fell back before the triumphant advance, and a weak shout went up. The bronzed soldiers shouted back, but their faces were grave and set. It was clear that they knew where they were going, and to what work they had been so hurriedly summoned.
>
> "It's hell back there!" a wounded territorial called out, pointing backward over his bandaged shoulder, and another cried: "*Vive l'Amerique!*"
>
> "*Vive la France!*" shouted the nearest truckful of men. A few miles off the battle of the Marne was being fought again, and there were his own brothers rushing forward to help! He felt that his greatest hour had struck.

Irvin S. Cobb wrote in his book, *The Glory of the Coming: What Mine Eyes Have Seen of Americans in Action:*

Civilians were fleeing southwards from Soissons or from evacuated villages within the zone of active hostilities. We seemingly were the only civilians going in; all those we met on that three mile hike were coming out. To me the spectacle was strikingly and pathetically reminiscent of Belgium in mid-August of 1914—old men trudging stolidly ahead with loads upon their bent backs; women, young and old, dragging carts or pushing shabby baby carriages that were piled high with their meagre belongings; grave-faced children trotting along at their elders' skirts; wearied soldiers falling out of line to add to their already heavy burdens as they relieved some half-exhausted member of the exodus of an unwieldy pack. Over the lamentable procession hung a fog of gritty chalk particles that had been winnowed up by the plodding feet. Viewed through the choking dust the figures drifted past us like the unreal shapes of a dream. I saw one middle-aged sergeant, his whiskers powdered white and his face above his whiskers masked in a sweaty white paste like a circus clown's, who, for all that he was in heavy marching order, had a grimed mite of a baby snuggled up to the breast of his stained tunic, with its little feet dangling in the crisscross of his leather gear and its bobbing head on his shoulder. He carried the baby with one hand and with the other he dragged his rifle; and he looked down smiling at the bedraggled little mother who traveled alongside him shoving before her a barrrow in which another child sat on a pillion of bed clothes.

I saw two infantrymen slide down a steep embankment to give aid to an old woman who struggled with a bundle almost as large as herself, and then, having accomplished the job, running with their accoutrements slapping against their legs to catch up with their company. I saw scores of sights such as this, and I did not hear one word of complaint uttered, nor did I look into one face that cxprcsscd aught save courage and patience. And seeing these things, multiplied over and over again, I said to myself then, as I say to myself now, that I do not believe Almighty God in His infinite mercy designed that such people as these should ever be conquered.

Only one person spoke to us. A captain, grinning as he plodded by at the head of his company, said with a rearward flirt of his thumb over his shoulders: "No good, no good! Much boom-boom!"

MajGen Harbord made the following remarks before the Detroit Bond Club, 22 February, 1928:

About the middle of May, 1918, the Second Division had been relieved from the Verdun sector where it had for several months been holding trenches south of that place. After a week of rest and instruction it had been sent to the neighborhood of Gisors, a town about sixty miles northwest of Paris in the ancient province of Picardy. The 1st Division was already engaged near Montdidier and the 2nd was intended to relieve it. Memorial Day was a holiday with us but the Division had orders to march at dawn on May 31st toward Montdidier. Our holiday was interrupted late in the afternoon by notice that our destination was changed, and my midnight we received orders to have the division, except the artillery, machine guns and animal-drawn transport ready to embark in buses at 5 the next morning, with destination unstated. General officers were directed to proceed by motor car to Meaux where orders would be given them. We all knew of the great attack toward Chateau-Thierry, and at times the rumble of the guns could be heard. With that much information and orders for our generals to proceed to Meaux, it took no great prophet to guess that the Second Division was headed for action in front of the German advance toward Paris.

The [2nd] Division was 28,500 strong, only about six thousand men less than the Army we took six weeks in getting to Santiago in 1898. There are many details involved in a change of orders for a body of men that size, when received at night about six hours before the buses are to be in line for embarkation. Some hurry, some confusion, not much sleep,—but the buses moved out next morning from the various villages where the troops had been billeted, making, when finally strung out along the highway, a column about fourteen miles long filled with thousands of somewhat conversational, articulate and audible young Americans.

The route led through country where many people, worn and wearied by four years of war, had heard that the Americans had come but had not seen them, and not seeing had not believed. All say long and until late that night the column rolled through the little French villages of old Picardy, touching the ancient Ile France, skirting the edge of Paris itself, and finally into Champagne and the Valley of the Marne. The moral effect of this movement on the doubting and despairing French who saw it can hardly be overstated. It has its place in song and story both in English and French.

Edward Hungerford wrote in his book, *With the Doughboys in France:*

> The impressions which the great German drive made upon the minds of our workers who fell back before it will remain with them as long as thought and memory cling—the vast conglomeration of men, tired, dirty, unshaven; men and animals and inanimate things, moving quickly, slowly, intermittently, moving not at all, but choking and halting all progress—with the deadly perversity of inanimate things; men not merely tired, dirty and unshaven, but sick and wounded almost unto death, moaning and sobbing under the fearful onslaughts of pain unbearable, sometimes death itself, a blessed relief, and marked by a stop by the roadside, a hurriedly dug grave, prayers, the closing earth, one other soul gone from the millions in order that hundreds of millions of other souls may live in peace and safety. Such traffic, such turmoil, such variety, such blinding, choking dust. Army supply trains, motor trucks, guns, soldiers, civilians, on foot and mounted, of vehicles of every variety conceivable and many inconceivable; motor cars upon which the genius of Renault or Ford had been expended; wheelbarrows, baby carriages, sledges, more motor cars, ranging in age from two weeks to fourteen years, dog carts, wagons creaking and groaning behind scared mules and worse scared negroes who wondered why they had ever left the corn brake—for this. Such traffic, such life. And then—again and again death, more graves, more prayers, more men's souls poured into the vague unknown.

> And here in the midst of death, life. Here in this wagon is a haggard-looking woman. The babe which she clasps to her breast is but four hours old; but the woman is a hundred—seemingly. She stretches her long, bare arms out from the flapping curtains at the rear of the Red Cross camionette. A group of *poilus*, in extremely dirty uniforms, catches her eyes. She shrieks to them in her native French.

> "My *poilus*," she cries, "you shall return. God wills it. You shall return—you and my little son," and falls, sobbing incoherently, into the bottom of the bumping ambulance.

> An old woman with her one precious possession saved—a bewhiskered goat—hears her, and crosses herself. A three-ton motor truck falls into a deep ditch and is abandoned, with all of its contents. This is no hour for salvage. The dust from the traffic grows thicker and thicker. Yet it is naught with the blinding white dust which arises from this shell—which almost struck into the heart of one of the main lines of traffic. The racket is terrific; yet above it one catches the shrieking cry of the young mother in the camionette. Her reason hangs in the balance. And as the noise subsides a detachment of *poilus* falls out beside the roadside and begins opening more graves. The boches aim was quite as good as he might have hoped."

According to marine officer John W. Thomason, Jr., in his unpublished manuscript *The Second Division Northwest of Château-Thierry:*

> During the night camion trains began to roll into the area, driven by yellow Tonquinese and Anamites, and men from Madagascar, small weary heathen in Khaki and crested helmets. The infantry and engineer battalions formed at dawn, gulped breakfast by their rolling kitchens—it was the last hot meal many of them were to have in this world—and got aboard as ordered. the artillery regiments loaded their guns and horses as they received their trains, the first of which left at 5:30 AM: the 4th (divisional) Machine Gun Battalion was also entrained, while the 5th and 6th Machine Gun Battalions, with their guns, were embussed. The motor transportation of the division set out under its own power. By sun-up the leading elements were in motion towards the east. The animal-drawn transport would have to march overland, and it included the regimental and battalion trains, and the field kitchens of the troops. During the afternoon these details were formed in three columns and took up the march. With their departure, the last elements of the 2nd Division, 27000 officers and men, were in motion for the front.

> The camion trains, one to each battalion, had come down from the Chaumont-en-Vexin area through Marines, Pontoise, and St. Denis, that suburb of Paris where the kings of France and the children of the Blood Royal are buried. They swept eastward on the Paris-Metz highway, along the road by which, in September, 1914, Gallieni passed his 7th Division in taxicabs to the battle at La Ferte on the Marne. As the battalions went eastward, beyond Paris, they

began to meet a drift of refugees from the lost country between Soissons and Rheims and Chateau Thierry, and the men who saw the fleeing host remember it as the most pitiful sight of the war.

The weather was clear, and the sun hot and merciless on this last day of May. The hard Rue Nationale and the lesser roads bore a top dressing of dust, as fine and white as talcum powder. The dust rose and hung thick in the still air, so that each motor column went up the right of the road; on the other side, coming down, was the melancholy flow of refugees. There were old men and old women, and children of all ages. They rode in farm wagons and carts, in old barouches and pony-traps, in quaint high-shouldered vehicles of another generation, drawn by oxen and cows and old raw-boned horses rejected by the army, or they went on foot, treading heavily through the dust. Some of them trundled wheel-barrows: an old bent woman pushed one, in which, atop a pile of household odds and ends, rode an ancient of days, clad in a blue smock, sucking with toothless gums at a cold pipe. Every conveyance was loaded with gear, things strangely assorted and precious to householders, not to be left behind; and things as absurd as people snatch up when they run from burning houses. There were featherbeds and quilts and tall clocks, and ducks and chickens tied by the legs, and rabbits in crates, and chairs and bird cages and strings of garlic. The Mayor of a village passed: he limped in tight shoes and wore the high hat, the frock-coat, and the tricolor sash of ceremony. In the throng there were sheep and goats, herded anxiously: men remember a flock of sheep, which, at a cross-roads, went inescapably under the wheels of a battery of French artillery turning into the highway there, and the lamentable cries of the shepherds.

It was a countryside in flight. After 1914, the population of the rich farming lands of the Marne Valley had returned to their homes, and for three years the war had kept away from them. Now the Boche had broken through again, as suddenly as thunder, and they fled. They went with a dazed look, compounded of weariness and terror. Mixed with them came the debris of the French 6th Army, walking wounded, and unwounded men whose organizations had disappeared; malingerers and brave men who had fought to exhaustion. There were artillerymen without guns, and infantry without rifles, and demoralized machine gunners, riding on the gun-

cart mules. The 2nd Division had not looked before upon this side of war; it was apparent to every man there that they proceeded to a serious front, as fast as the lumbering camions could take them."

Henry Berry, who served as a marine in 1918, relates in his book, *Make the Kaiser Dance*:

> The scuttlebutt is flying all around. Hell, they had us going everywhere. I felt it would be exactly where we ended up. I'd read a paper a few days before that explained how the Germans had broken through the Chemin des Dames and were moving toward Paris. We were about to find out what war was all about.
>
> By mid-afternoon we were all ready, full packs, ammunition, everything, so we stacked arms and stood by our gear. You know, those damn camions didn't arrive until seven the next morning. We ended up sleeping right there on our packs. When they did arrive, wham, we were hustled right aboard—and they took off as fast as possible.
>
> My God, what a ride, crammed into those little trucks, bumping over those roads, and most of us with our overcoats on. Hell, this was the first of June, it was hot. And the dust—we could hardly breathe.
>
> Finally, around four o'clock that afternoon, they stopped and let us off. Then the marching started, if you want to call it that. Here we are trying to move up to the front, while all the French refugees are going the other way. It was pathetic as hell: families with baby carriages, bundles on their heads, children in their arms, old men driving carts pulled by nags; old women trying to walk with canes. It was truly the flotsam of war.
>
> Then there were the stragglers, the beaten Poilu in groups of twos and threes. They couldn't believe it when they saw fresh troops moving up.
>
> "*Retournez, retournez!*" they yelled. "*La guerre est fini! Retournez, retournez—La Boche est victorieux.*"
>
> There was one heartening sight—a division of French cavalry moving toward the front. They truly looked magnificent with their horses prancing and their guidons and lances waving. They showed us that France was still very much in the war.
>
> I don't know how many of us who made that march are still around, but I'll bet they all agree with me—it was one hell of a dramatic experience.

Well, they halted us about midnight in this open field. We were so darn tired that no one even bothered to take off his bedroll; we all just collapsed in our packs.

Lt H. R. Long, 6th Machine Gun Battalion, USMC, wrote in one of his letters to his family:

I wish you could have been along the first few days of the battle in this particular section. Of course, you have read of how, after the Boche bursted through at Soissons and came galloping south and West for 35 kilometers, the Marines stopped 'em at Bouresches and Bois de Belleau. It had trench warfare beaten to a stand-still. We were 'way up northeast of Paris, getting organized and screwed up again after two months in the line at Verdun, when the news came that the Germans had broken through west of Rheims and were coming on double for Paris.

With only a few hours of preparations we were hustled on trucks (It took about 200,000,000,000 of them, it seemed like) early in the morning, and tore across country for a whole day. All afternoon our long line of camions passed refugees and refugees (hundreds of them—it was pathetic beyond all words). Farm wagons, baby carriages, wheel barrows, crying kiddies in tired womens' arms, old men, resigned and fatalistic sort of looking, laughing girls riding on hay wagons, holding on to cows and horses, women, bird cages and bundles in their arms, bravely trudging along westward—the women of France are the bravest people in the world,—and the French troops going and coming.

Lt Elliot D. Cooke, an army officer who served with the marines in the 2nd Division, relates in his article, *We Can Take It*:

You can't fool the American lads who lugged their heavy packs over the highways of France as to who won the First World War. American troops fought and won many a decisive battle and I was in one of them. If you will bear with the none too modest observations of a young lieutenant, whose main ambition was to live long enough to spend his next month's pay in Paris, I would like to tell about that battle.

The German shock troops bogged down in the Flanders mud about the middle of May and our division was moved northwest of Paris to a place called Gisors. The French civilians in that part of the country were a discouraged lot—pretty well convinced that Germany had won the war. That gave us a pain. The Boches could not win the war until they licked our 2d Division and they couldn't bring up enough Germans in ten years to do that.

The division was busy drilling and practicing open warfare maneuvers when topside put out the news that we were soon to move up to Cantigny where the 1st Division was fighting. That suited us, because next to our own division we rated the 1st Division the best in the AEF.

Then on Monday, May 27th, the Germans caught the Allies completely by surprise. They smacked the Frenchmen right between Rheims and Soissons and came busting through on their way to Paris.

The French civilians hollered, "Fini la guerre," and about a million of them started pulling out for the Mediterranean. The 2d Division, ready and rarin' to go, got orders to stand by for a move in trucks.

We sat around half the night and nothing happened, so Captain Wass told us we could lie down and get some sleep if we kept our clothes on.

Lieutenant Becker woke me up at four in the morning because I was mess officer and he was always hungry.

"They're blowing reveille," he said. "Let's eat before those trucks come along."

I got up and had the galley crew cook all the chow on hand. We packed what was left after breakfast to take with us in case we actually moved. Lucky we did because the trucks arrived at eight o'clock.

We got aboard with lots of enthusiasm, twelve officers or twenty men to a bus and the whole divided into company and battalion sections. The last man had hardly cleared the tail-board when the slant-eyed little Annamese drivers impatiently ground in their gears and the column began to roll.

"A new way of seeing France," piped Lieutenant Jackson, who had snitched a seat at the rear end of our bus, "and it's a whole lot better than walking."

Everybody agreed at the moment, but in a couple of hours we had different ideas. The board seats were hard and narrow. The wheels of the truck had solid rubber tires and our vertebrae were constantly jerked and jarred like a string of box cars behind a switch engine. But the dust was worst of all.

It billowed in long funnels from the tail of each section. Clouds of grit swirled in through both ends of our truck, and with each jounce of the springs small geysers of dirt squirted up at us from between the floor boards. Some of the men tried wearing their gas masks, but decided that air with dirt was better than no air at all so all took them off again.

On parallel roads other battalions could be spotted by the blankets of dust rising above the distant trees and small hills. The Annamese drivers of two columns, converging on a main highway, would race to get there first and avoid the other's dust.

"Lucky if we don't get killed before reaching the front," yelled Lieutenant Frazier, as we won a race and at the same time missed a tree by six inches.

Twice the columns were halted while staff cars and motorcycles rushed about furiously, like collies herding sheep. About noon the driving became even more difficult when we ran into a continuous stream of refugees moving south—old men, women and children, and an occasional French soldier, all bound for the rear. Peasants mostly, people of the soil. Driven from the land, they carried their remaining possessions with them. Cows and horses pulled small, wobbly wagons top-heavy with household goods. The poorer ones pushed carts or trundled wheelbarrows. Some even carried goods on their backs.

No words passed between these people. Like the beasts hooked to their carts, they plodded on, ignorant of where they were going of what they would do when they got there."

Martin Gulberg, a marine with the U.S 2nd Division, wrote in his diary:

And to plug this weak spot Foch picked the 2nd division.

Our call came a few minutes before taps when most of us were already in bed. I heard first call blow and I thought it mighty funny that first call should blow at this time. Next we heard the sweet voice of our top Sergeant. "Pack up and be ready to shove off in ten minutes."

About twenty minutes later we were on our way. We slept on the streets in the next town until morning and then got into he camions bound for nobody knew where, not even the officers. We always travelled under sealed orders. It was a hell of a ride. No sleep and very little to eat for forty-eight hours.

William Scanlon, a marine in the U.S. 2nd Division, wrote the following fictional account in his book, *God Have Mercy on Us:*

"Fini la guerre!...Fini la guerre...."

The French soldiers came straggling along the road. They were coming south—toward Paris. We were hiking in the opposite direction—north. We hollered at them and beckoned for them to come on with us, but they shook their heads and waved their arms and shouted, pointing back the way they had come:

"Fini la guerre. Boches! Boches! Fini la guerre!"

"They're yelling that the Germans are just up ahead and that the war's over." This from Benvenuto, a 'music,' also known as 'The Wop.' But we knew what the French soldiers were saying just as well as he did, even if he was one of our interpreters.

Then our outfit started yelping—Calahan, Shiel, Conroy, Young, and the rest.

"For Christ's sake, don't tell me the war is over after all I've done to get here."

"Jesus! when I think of all the drilling I put in at Quantico."

"Quantico!...Hell—drilling was a pipe compared to what we did at Parris Island! Say, I made most of that damned island myself."

"The hell you did! I guess I was in that 'Join the Marines and move the world' bunch , too."

"Aw, pipe down on that bootcamp stuff! What gives me a pain in the neck is all the time we wasted up at Verdun in the old trenches when we might have been killing Krautheads...."

We were all sore. When they loaded us into camions at Chaumont-en-Vexin, we thought that at last we were going to see some real action. We were nuts about the camions. They looked like patrol wagons. They had two long seats inside, just like patrol wagons. The drivers were French-Indo-Chinamen. They never knew where they were going. They simply followed the camion ahead. The leading car had an officer in it who knew where the convoy was headed for.

Pvt Walter Scott Hiller wrote this letter home on 16 June 1918. Scott states, in part:

> Somewhere in France June 16, 1918
> Dearest Mother, Dad, Brothers and Sisters:
> When going up to the front some weeks ago, we saw people moving everything they owned out of the towns because the Huns were advancing. It made tears come to my eyes and of several other boys that I have since talked to regarding that scene. My thoughts went home to you folks, and I pictured some things in my mind if the Germans were victorious the world over. I just set my jaw and determined to do everything I possibly could to eliminate that curse from the face of the earth.
> Your loving son and brother
> Walt

Thomas Boyd, who served in the AEF as a marine, wrote the following fictional account of moving toward the front in his book, *Through the Wheat*:

> The platoon assembled and joined the rest of the company along the road. They marched off in the darkness, melting in with the immeasurable stream of olive drab that grew at every cross-road.
> Up and down the hills they marched, evenly wearing away the distance that lay between themselves and their destination. In the night there were no directions, no cool and mysterious little cafés to draw their attention from placing one foot after the other. But after fifteen or twenty kilometers, marching even at night was oppressive.
> At the bottom of the millionth valley they passed through, lay the town. Along the road, leading up the hill on the other side, horizon-blue motor-trucks stood and waited.
> The platoon came to a halt in one of the streets, the butts of their rifles clattering on the cobblestones. It had been quite dark a moment ago, but dawn had come hurriedly, and now Hicks could see the great number of troops that were preparing to embark.
> No one seemed to have the least notion of the direction in which the camions were moving. Though some of the men who had been reading a recent copy of the Paris edition of the *Chicago Tribune*, believed them to be headed for the Somme, where, it was said, there was heavy fighting; others believed that they were on

their way to relieve the First American Division, which a few days earlier had attacked at Cantigny. Apparently the trip was to last for two or more days, for each squad had been apportioned two days' extra rations before entraining. The drivers of the camions were Japanese, which, as purveyors of information, made them as useful as do many "professional" silent men of the President's cabinet. With twenty men in each camion the train bumped and thundered along the road all day. At night they stopped only a few minutes to allow the soldiers to prepare themselves for a still longer journey.

Cpl Fred W. Hill, Headquarters Company, 6th Marines, wrote in a letter home dated 8 June 1918:

> My Dear Mother:
> The war came home to me more this time than it ever has before. One reason being that I saw my first line of refugees coming up here, and it was an impressive sight. As the German advance continued, these people were forced to leave their villages and most of their belongings and flee. Many of them on foot, but the majority had two-wheeled French wagon drawn by one horse. On this they piled all of their needed and desired articles and left. There was an unbroken line of them for several miles, and in some cases they were driving herds of cows and flocks of sheep ahead of them rather than to allow these to fall into German hands. This line of march is one that I will never forget, but the people themselves seemed to bear up bravely under it. The other reason is that there are new faces in the ranks where many of our best friends used to be.

In Marine Maj Frank E. Evans' book, *Daddy Pat of the Marines: Being His Letters from France to His Young Son Townie*, is this letter to his young son:

> France, June 1, 1918
> Dear Townie:
> This is all about the trip we made in big trucks across a lot of France to stop the wicked old Germans from coming to Paris. You never could have dreamed there were so many trucks in the world, and there must have been easy more than a thousand. They came to our four pretty little towns at four o'clock in the morning. It was a beautiful day, and yet it sounded like thunder when they rolled

in; so we lined up all the Marines along the road, and, as soon as the first truck rolled in, it turned right around and started back till it came to the end of the line; and then the first twenty-two Marines hopped in, and then the next, till a whole battalion of a thousand had hopped in, and away they went. They were great big, heavy trucks with a long wooden seat on each side, but most of the Marines sat backward, with their feet hanging outside, so they could see things, and the old trucks looked like big, gray spiders with forty-four brown legs. And they all had funny marks and pictures painted outside in gay colors, about as big as a watermelon, near where the driver sat. The one we had first had big grasshoppers, blue and red, and there were camels, soldier heads, a big cannon on a snail's back, and a donkey's head, a clock face, flowers, a funny old darky with great big, white teeth, and a rooster, and all sorts of funny things. And Daddy rode in a little automobile with a French officer who had been wounded in Belgium and couldn't fight, but who could boss the trucks; and he was just like a man running a big circus, because sometimes a truck would break down, and then we'd fly down the line and bring up a little truck with tools; and when it was all fixed he'd blow his horn, and we'd fly back and he'd yell "En Route! En Route!"—and that's just the way the old horn would sound, "En Route!"— and away we'd go! And pretty soon we came to the prettiest towns, with gardens full of roses and all sorts of pretty flowers; and the French ladies and girls would run out and throw flowers into the trucks and bring milk and red wine and cheese, and loaves of bread as long and round as the biggest hat that Ty Cobb has; and the dear little old ladies would smile and wave their hankerchiefs, and the little bare-legged boys would come flying out to the road and hop up and down and yell, "Les Americains! Voila les bons soldats!" So everybody was happy and smiling, because they knew the Marines were going to kill and capture all the Germans they could and stop them from coming to Paris. And as far back as you could see on all the roads were trucks and such dust that pretty soon all the Marines and the infantry and signal corps and artillery were just gray, like mummies. But they were all happy and having a fine time. And we came to some big towns with rivers, and pretty soon to the nicest little towns we'd seen in France; and we were only 15 miles from Paris, and you could almost see the Eiffel Tower. And the nearer we got to Paris, the gayer the people were; and of course the Marines were smiling at all the pretty French girls and having a time, and the old trucks rolled along, and pretty soon we saw some bad sights. The Germans were driving back the French soldiers, and all the French people had to leave their homes, where they'd lived all their lives, or the Germans would have whipped all the little children, and made their mothers work for them, and burned their little towns; so they were coming into Paris. Some of them were walking, and they had little donkeys hitches up to little carts, and great big horses with wooden collars painted in red and blue, and big white oxen—all pulling big loads, with beds and chairs and mattresses and things piled away up. And the dogs were walking along, and under the wagons were chickens and ducks and geese in crates covered with chicken-yard wire. And nearly all of them had goats, because it's easy to feed goats on old tin cans and paper and get good goat's milk. And there were little tow-headed boys and fat little girls with curls and blue eyes and such short little legs that every time their mothers took a step they had to take four. And they were going away to find a new home, and at night their wagons would stop and they'd camp alongside the road. And Daddy never saw one of them cry, although they were very unhappy. And it made the Marines terribly mad to see them so sad, and they just wished they could find those Germans and drive them away. And there was one big wagon piled up so high that it looked like the big ladder that Jack the Giant-killer climbed (or maybe it was the bean-stalk), and right on top was a beautiful old lady all dressed in her nicest black dress with a little white lace cap on; and her hair was white as snow and just like silver, and she must have been just one of the kindest and prettiest grandmothers in the world.

Here is MajGen Robert L. Bullard's description of the French retreat from the Chemin des Dames as from his book, *American Soldiers Also Fought*:

Picture it. Six days of staggering, exhausting, whimpering retreat. Shells bursting overhead. Machine guns ripping through. Rifle-fire ever at their backs.

In the beginning, some attempt to bring out guns, trucks, carts, kitchens, ambulances. But not for long. Roads and valleys were strewn with the material of war.

Beaten soldiers straggled down across the plateaus into the river valleys, with gaunt, set faces. They fled an enemy believed irresistible. The wounded sank down—to any fate that came, for there are no cleanly, efficient, smoothly functioning hospital trains in a mad retreat. The weak fell, and did not rise.

Emulating the boche, the poilu looted the countryside—his own countryside. General Harbord has attacked them for this. But it is well to remember that what the poilu did not take, Fritz would get. Many threw away rifles, coats, equipment, in order to load up with booty. But in the end Fritz got most of it. Except that which could not be eaten. Even loot is only a burden to be cast by the roadside when men are driven by panic.

Terror swept the countryside—so "safe" but yesterday behind the ridges of fortified hills. Out of the homes and villages of a thousand square miles poured the pitiful souls who were being dispossessed by war.

A tangled mass. Carts, baby-carriages, barrows; goats, cows, chickens. The sick, the old and the very young lagging, resting. The strong push forward, but loaded down like beasts of burden.

Our approaching troops saw them. Thousands of civilians, with fear in their eyes, moving always to the rear. Soldiers and officers too, dogged, purposeful, not turning, struggling along to the rear.

Up front somewhere—on an elastic, elusive "front"—steadier and braver men maintained at least some semblance of contact with each other in a wavering "line."

But through the tidal wave of retreating humanity, our Second Division (Regulars and Marines) moved forward, stiffened by the knowledge that only they stood between Germany and a Paris from which one million persons fled in hopeless consternation.

A tactical distraction had become a great strategic victory.

A wedge, fifty miles across the base and thirty-five miles in depth, had a point driving toward the very heart of France, the capital which was also the dominant rail center and the home of war industries.

Daniel E. Morgan, a marine in 1918, writes in his book, *When the World Went Mad:*

As we neared the battle area we witnessed the most horrible sights that up to that time had ever greeted our eyes. We saw hundreds of old men, old women and little children carrying in their hands loaves of bread, chickens, rabbits and pieces of bed clothing, or pushing barrows with all of their life's possessions in them. Some were leading cows: others were pushing baby carriages full of their earthly goods. With tears in their eyes they cried out to us as we passed, "Long live the Americans."

On toward the front we went. The villages were now vacated, with all their possessions, exactly as one would leave home on a Saturday afternoon, to go shopping. The chickens were in the yard, the cattle in the field, the horses in the barn, and everything else that goes to make up life in a country village was in its usual place.

Private E. A. Wahl, a marine, wrote in a letter home:

Decoration Day, just after I had written you my last letter we received sudden orders to pack and move from the quiet little country place just outside of Paris where we were resting. At midnight we started off. Motor trucks were to have transported us, but they didn't seem to have enough to carry us all even though there were hundreds continually passing. So it was a case of hike again for the Seventy-third (for which, by the way, we're quite noted) and several other Marine companies. That hike is pretty much a blur. I hope I will never have to do one like it again. We had one rest from twelve noon until nine in the evening of the first day. The rest of the time it was just tramp, tramp along until dusk of June 3ᵈ, when a string of motor trucks hove in sight to take us the rest of the way. (We were then in the region where the refugees were trundling past in their many pathetic states.) Did those trucks look good to us! Tired out beyond description, we didn't care where we were or where we were going, just so we could ride. We learned from the weary, dust-covered drivers (many of whom hadn't slept for several days) that the situation was serious and that we were badly needed. We bumped along all night at tremendous speed, passing the long lines of dim-shaped wagon trains, truck trains, cannon, troops, and the poor refugees, who, of course, were bound in the opposite direction.

From the diary of 1ˢᵗLt Elmer Hess, 15ᵗʰ Field Artillery, 2ⁿᵈ Division, about the march to May-en-Multien on 31 May, 1918:

Finally we arrived at the town of Nanteuil-le-Haudouin where we were told to detrain. The village station was certainly a sight for the gods. One might have thought the Germans were coming down the road by the enormous clouds of dust which could be seen. The station was filled with women, children and very old men, sitting upon piles of household goods, waiting for the next train to Paris, which the station-master told them would never come; and too thoroughly exhausted to go any farther, they sat there in silent grief.

When our animals, guns and other belongings were unloaded, the train pulled back to the rear. Over our heads airships with little black crosses, indicating they were Germans, hovered, and once in a while dropped small bombs upon us at this village and at other villages along the railroad, trying to stop the detraining of troops.

Down the road out of these clouds of dust came no Germans nor retreating French soldiers but thousands of women, children, old men, mules and cattle, with carts piled high with household goods, fleeing from the invader.

The road was lined with refugees. Old women pushing wheelbarrows, with a few personal rags and a pen of chickens or rabbits on it. Two-wheeled carts, the type used almost entirely by the French farmer, — great cumbersome things, loaded with hay, a few personal belongings, one to ten children. A couple of old women drawn by three horses, one behind the other. Tied to the rear are usually a donkey or some cows, occasionally a flock of sheep or some dogs. I saw not one such party but literally thousands of them. The women and children do not cry—they are beyond the crying stage, but the agony at leaving their homes is written all over their faces. Even the dumb animals plodding along with them have the same look.

From the memoirs of Cpl Frank W. Anderson, Company M, 23rd Infantry:

At three o'clock in the morning of May 31st, we were called out of our bunks by the bugler blowing his old bugle! Orders were that we were to move at once, so we make up our full packs, had a hurried breakfast, policed up the town, fell in line, and marched to the next town about two miles away.

A line of trucks awaited us here. We waited about a half an hour before embusing and were on the road all day. When we

were within fifty kilometers of the front line, we began to see signs of why we had been called to the front line of battle so quickly. Refugees lined the left side of the road from this point up to within two kilometers of the front. The Germans were driving down from the northeast towards Paris. These people were the peasants who had been peacefully tilling the soil and attending their livestock. Naturally, they were all old men, women, and young children; the others were fighting at the front and nursing the soldiers in the hospitals. They were going miles from their homes to start anew in some strange locality until a time when they confidently believed the Boche would be driven back and they could return to their old homes. Everything they owned except their buildings and crops they took with them. An old hay wagon with oxen drawing it, loaded down with furniture and farm tools, and on top were the mattresses and bedding; and here the family slept. A little boy or girl of ten leading the oxen along the road in bare feet. A cow, a few pigs, hens, ducks and sheep herded by little children or old women. This was the make-up of the average family, and we passed dozens just the same. There were hundreds of these families travelling the different roads away from the front, and in spite of all this, these people still had the courage to smile upon us as we passed by.

We rode through the town of Meaux. A French cavalry regiment was at rest in a field a few miles beyond Meaux; their long spears stacked in uniform rows making a veritable field of spear points. This sight denoted open warfare.

From *Combat and Construction: U.S. Army Engineers in World War I*, by Charles Hendricks:

The March to Battle. It was Decoration Day, May 30, 1918, and a more beautiful day was never seen in the 2nd Division area, 30 kilometers northwest of Paris. A holiday was declared, and the 2nd Division stopped its intensive training and spent the day at racing, running, jumping and swimming.

Several days previous, the Division had received maps of the British front, the 1st Division expected to relieve the 1st Division. At 8:00 P.M. that day the 2nd Engineers got orders to be ready to move in three hours, but to go in another direction. Heavy packs were made, the wagons loaded, and the billets and stables cleaned. The companies fell in, stacked arms and unslung equipment; then they fell out again to get as much rest as possible.

About 1:30 A.M., May 31ˢᵗ, 1918, orders came for the regiment to march about four kilometers to a highway where it would embus in camions. Arriving there, the whole regiment found itself together for the first time since arrival in France. Word came that the trucks could not be expected before 8:00 or 9:00 A.M. and a hurry-up call was sent for the rolling kitchens, which had been left behind to follow with the wagon train. They arrived about 7:00 A.M. and the regiment received a meal that was the last real cooked meal for many days.

About 10:00 A.M. the trucks arrived. They were little light French ones, driven by French and Chinese drivers. The regiment climbed on and started for [original town name censored out of letter in 1918] they knew not where.

The men were packed rather tight and the sun kept getting hotter and hotter. The dust arose in great clouds and the men were soon covered with a thick greyish powder. The truck train headed towards Paris, which fact gave rise to all sorts of speculations. Civilians along the route waved and shouted, and at every halt gave the men water, etc.

From John W. Thomason's unpublished manuscript, *The Second Division Northwest of Château-Thierry*:

Early in the morning of 1 June, between May-en-Multien and Montreuil and the Ourcq towns, the troops had picked their way forward through the last of the tide of refugees, but the country where in the afternoon they left the roads and went into position, was drained of life. Around the farmhouses, they found cows, and rabbits and fowls; left behind, unfed. At Cocherel, Colonel Chamberlain related, they read a scrawled message on the door of the house in which Artillery Headquarters was established: "*Papa, nous sommes parties á Rue___, Lizy-sur-Ourcq*"; The women and children had been obliged to take the road while their man was in his fields. In the area where they deployed, they found a few groups of French artillery and scattered details of infantry. "Which way," said a young man in the Marine Machine Gun Battalion, as they left their trucks and went across the fields from the highway, "is this here line?"

"Line, Hell!" a sergeant told him. "We're going to make one—"

The situation on June 2ᵈ was critical. Corps orders defining and organizing the new line said: "No retirement will be thought of on any pretext whatsoever."

The following selection, from a work of fiction *Jimmie Higgins* by Sinclair Upton, is included here because it gives a spirited description of the American soldier:

But most of the time now the spirit of the herd mastered Jimmie; he wanted what all the men about him wanted—to hold back the Beast from these fair French fields and quaint old villages, and these American hospitals and rest-camps and Y.M.C.A. huts—to say nothing of the motor-cycle repair-sheds with Jimmie Higgins in them! And the trouble was that the Beast was not being held back; he was coming nearer and nearer—one bull rush after another! Jimmie's village was near the valley of the Marne, and that was the road to Paris; the Beast wanted to get to Paris, he really expected to get to Paris!

The sound of guns grew louder and louder, and the rumor flew wild-eyed and wild-tongued about the country. The traffic on the roads grew denser, but moving more slowly now, for the Germans were shelling the road ahead, and blockades were frequent.

There were long trains of refugees streaming back from the battle-fields; pitiful peasant people with horse-carts and dog carts and even wheel-barrows, toothless old men and women trudging alongside, children and babies stuck in amidst bedding and furniture and sauce-pans and bird-cages. This was war, as common people saw it.

"And these Frenchies?" The doughboy looked at the others. "You savvy their lingo?" When Jimmie shook his head, he turned to the battle-worn hairy ones. "You fellows go back," he said. "We don't need you now." When they stared uncomprehendingly, he asked: 'Polly voo Francy?"

"We, we!" cried they, in one voice.

"Well, then," said the doughboy, "go back! Go home! Toot sweet! Have sleep! Rest! We lick'em Heinies!" As the poilus did not show much grasp of this kind of "Francy," the doughboy boosted them to their feet, pointed to the rear, patted them on the back, and grinned with his wide mouth. "Good boy! Go home! American! American!"—as if that was enough to make clear that the work of France in this war was done! The poilus looked over the top of the shell-hole, and saw a swarm of those new fashion-plate soldiers, darting forward through the woods, throwing themselves down and shooting at the sockray Bosh. They looked at the rosy cheeked boy with the grateful faces of dogs, and shouldered their packs and rifles and set out for the rear.

These doughboys had a song that Jimmie had heard all the time: "The Yanks are coming!" And now the song needed to be rewritten: "The Yanks are here!" All these woods through which Jimmie had blundered with his motor-cycle were now swarming with nice, new, clean-shaven, freshly-tailored soldier-boys, turned loose to get their first chance at the Hun. Four years they had been reading about him and hating him, a year and a half they had been getting ready to hit him—and now at last they were turned loose and told to go to it! Back on the roads was an endless procession of motor-trucks, with doughboys, and also marines, or "leather-necks," as they were called. They had started at four o'clock that morning, and ridden all day packed in like sardines; and here, a mile or two back in the woods, the trucks had come to a halt, and the sardines had jumped out and gone into this war!

Jimmie did not realize till long afterwards what a world-drama he had been witnessing. For four months the Beast had been driving at Paris; irresistibly, incessantly, eating his way like a forest fire, spreading ever wider and more fearful desolation—this Beast with the Brains of an Engineer! The world had shuddered and held its breath, knowing that if he got to Paris it would mean the end of the war, and of all things that free men value. And how here he made his last supreme rush, and the French lines wavered and cracked and gave way, and so in this desperate crisis they had brought up the truck loads of doughboys for their first real test against the Beast.

The orders had been to hold at all hazards; but that had not been enough for the doughboys, they and the leather-necks had seized the offensive and sent the Germans reeling back. The very pride of the Prussian army had been worsted by these new troops from overseas, at whom they had mocked, whose very existence they had doubted.

It was a blow from which "Fritz" never recovered; he never gained another foot, and it was the beginning of a retreat that did not stop until it reached the Rhine. And the Yanks had done it.

Another fictional work which graphically portrays the French refugees is from *With Pershing at the Front* by Kay Ross:

A short time later the Ninety-eighty was swinging down the road, bound for the front again. The faces of the men were set and stern. They knew what lay ahead of them. They knew the Germans were surging forward wave after wave in overwhelming numbers, and they realized what it meant to stop their rush.

The thunder of the guns sounded louder and louder in their ears. The road they traveled was crowded with soldiers, with trucks, and with refugees, poor homeless people of France driven from their homes by the invaders. Some were pushing wheelbarrows, others had curious little carts drawn by sturdy dogs, while now and again an ox team lumbered past. For the most part, however, the people were on foot, carrying a few precious belongings on their heads or in bundles, or pulling them in tiny wagons. Little children and old men and women were everywhere to be seen in the throng, a sad but quiet and patient procession. Sometimes a truck, returning from the front, came along, and in every case the driver had loaded his vehicle to capacity with those who were least able to stand the journey on foot.

As the Ninety-eighth passed along on the other side of the road, its members could not help but catch, even though unconsciously, the splendid spirit of France. Here were people who had lost not only their homes, and most of their earthly possessions as well, but in most cases sons, husbands, or brothers. But they had no thought of not continuing the war to a victorious conclusion. They knew Germany and German methods from first-hand experience; they realized what it would mean to France if Germany should win the war. Rather than have such a thing happen they were ready and determined to pay any price asked of them. The American soldiers in the regiment with Leon and Earl could see all this from the expression on the faces of the refugees and it gave them new spirit and determination. Every man resolved that in so far as it lay in his power, and even though his life was the price, this German menace should once and for all be removed from the world.

Ambulances hurried by with their freight of wounded humanity. Soldiers limping, or with heads or arms bandaged, passed by. All the wreckage of a great battle was on one side of the road. On the other side were the fresh troops, new batteries, and supplies of those who were to take the place of what had been used up or destroyed.

"It looks as if the whole world was on the move to-day," said Leon to his brother during a short halt. "I never saw a road so choked up."

"Nor I," Earl agreed. "It's terrible."

They sat down by the roadside and watched the procession file past. They sat in silence, thinking busily.

A few minutes later the long column of khaki-clad men were on the march once more. As they neared the front the refugees became less and less numerous, the noise of the guns sounded louder and louder, and the faces of the men became more and more set and determined.

MajGen Melvin L. Krulewitch, USMC, who fought as a marine sergeant in Belleau Wood, gives the following account of his journey to the battle in his *Marine Corps Gazette* article, "Belleau Wood":

We bounced and rattled in the boxcars, detrucked near Fountainebleau, and piled into the waiting camions lined up along the Paris-Metz road. The front was less than 40 miles from Paris and we could hear the guns. Heading for our regimental headquarters, 6th Marines, we were replacements for the wounded and the dead, casualties of the last week's fighting. We were 20 in the truck including Red McGrath of Massachusetts, Buddy O'Neil of Alabama, Lou Diamond of Chicago, Friedman and Fitzpatrick.

We rolled through the villages and towns East of Paris for the Second Battle of the Marne. Along this road, Gallieni's taxicab army had turned the German flank, four years before, when Joffre had outwitted Von Kluck. The convoy passed through village streets, lined with all who remained, tearful and cheering their American defenders. Many a skirt hem was lifted to dry eye, a revealing sight.

For the first time, we bumped along a road pitted by old and new shell holes. Long distance shelling dropped on the fields along the road as we passed the still visible scars of the four-year-old trenches of the First Battle of the Marne. We laughed like hell at Lou Diamond, who mindful of boot camp instruction to protect the front sight of your Springfield at all costs shouted, "Fellows, take off your front sight covers." We were five miles from the front. On we rolled. We lay over for chow, at regimental headquarters.

Pvt Leo J. Bailey, 9th Infantry, 2nd Division, wrote:

The Chauchat gunner and his squad were soon marching northward again in the summer heat through the disheartened and retreating Frenchmen. The gas saturation in the inactive sectors began to tell on men returned from hospitals. By noon the column saw no more of the defeated French. The furious pace slackened when the doughboys began to pass forlorn poilus at siege guns firing by map into fields and woods beyond them. The column then halted for a brunch of corned-beef hash eaten from the cans. It aggravated thirst, but [the lieutenant] drove Bailey's platoon from a small stream which he believed polluted.

Lacey Gibbs, a marine in the 2nd Division, wrote in his diary:

Finally we were pulled out of the line and replaced by French soldiers who seemed to be all old men. We were tired and ragged and lousy and we hiked back to the railroad almost all night long and were loaded on an old freight train. When we stopped, it was at a large camp where they had lots of supplies with only one guard, and we began stealing canned tomatoes and potatoes and onions, filling our pockets.

We drilled and rested for several days and got onto a freight again and the rumor was we were to be part of a large offensive. We passed the outskirts of Paris and soon unloaded. There were about 4,000 men there. We were told to rest, but I and some other boys set out scouting for food. Before long we started out on a 65 mile hike. By 10 o'clock it was awful hot. We hiked all day and one boy died from the heat. We hiked until 11 that night without dinner or supper. The last 4½ miles was on hard cobblestone. We slept in the rain in a cloverfield that night and began again at 6 a.m. We hiked until 8 that night before we got chow. We were so tired that we could hardly stand.

We lay around for two days waiting then on May 30th at 11 p.m. we heard the call to arms blow and orders came to pack up and be ready to leave in 30 minutes. We were being called to the Battle of the Marne at Chateau Thierry 26 miles from Paris.

We hiked three miles then loaded up in French trucks, 18 to a truck. We rode all day and night without food or water. About 6 in the morning we went through a village and one of the boys jumped out and bought 3 bottles of rum. The next stop was 11 at night. I bought some moldy bread from a Chinese cook. It was so bad that we just ate the crust off it then threw it on the ground. Some other Marine would stumble over it and pick it up and chew on it for a while then he would throw it down and some one else would pick it up. I saw at least 10 Marines try to eat off the loaf.

The rest of the run was all night long. We unloaded the next morning 8 miles from the Front near a large aviation field and started to hike. The roads were lined with families that lived in the small villages nearby. We hiked until 8 that night before we had a ten minute rest. As we hiked on toward the front, trucks and ambulances of all kinds were hauling back wounded French soldiers. We asked them how it was, and they said worse than hell."

LtGen Merwin H. Silverthorn, USMC (Ret), wrote of his experiences as a young lieutenant during the fighting in early 1918 in the *Marine Corps Gazette*, "A Brigade of Marines":

The war had come suddenly upon the civilian population. They were flooding the roads, carrying or pushing in carts what prized possessions they could transport—the balance remaining behind—lost forever to the vicissitudes of war. Around the farmhouses one could still see cows, rabbits and fowl left behind, unfed. Here the soldier came face to face with the hardships and heartaches of war—old men, women and children trudging down the dusty highway with a look of wonderment in their faces— "Which way, which way?"—they seemed to say. To the soldier, the sight was not one taught in the books, in the distance could be heard the sound of artillery.

Frederick Palmer, a staff officer in the AEF, wrote in his book, *Our Gallant Madness:*

So They Called Us Heroes

They were fresh; they were ready; they were made soldiers, and in the pink. I had seen too many soldiers marching to the front not to realize this. The picture of the men of that battalion on the Paris-Chateau-Thierry road remains clear in more vivid significance than it did twenty years ago, while much detail which seemed important then has been fused into the atmosphere of the crisis.

The year's training was graven in their faces. It had become a second sense. To say that they were "in the army now" did not apply. They had been a long time in the army; they were regulars.

Lafayette, we are not just here, but we are on the way to battle. What the hell do we care? Take the word to Mademoissele from Armentiéres. The men broke into "Hail! Hail! The Gang's All Here!" It had a metallic definite ring beating time with tempered steel.

This carried more weight than Clemenceau's, "I will fight in front of Paris, I will fight in Paris, I will fight behind Paris," which lives with his name as "the father of victory." But he was just a valiant old man speaking to the helpless members of the Chamber of Deputies when the French government had started moving its papers out of Paris, which the people were beginning to evacuate.

At Versailles the members of the Supreme War Council could hear the sound of the guns. What could the elders of the council do in the darkest hour of the war since Von Kluck threatened Paris? They could only hope and wait and ask America to send more soldiers such as those on the Paris–Chateau-Thierry road.

I rode on toward the Front and to learn where the Front was. We had known where it was yesterday. But where would it be today? I saw one of the contrasts of war, as old as war, that had been pictured again and again, but in which we had a part for the first time in this war. There was no new scene in the movement of women big with child, they and other women carrying children, carts piled with family belongings with chickens tied to chairs, and horses and led milch cows. Young and old exclaimed, *"les Américains!"* in wonder, and then with hope in their faces, which carried more feeling than that of the women who always stuck flowers in our rifle barrels on the grand propagandic day of "Layfayette, we are here" in Paris.

But mixed with the refugees were straggling French soldiers, now just human beings in flight. Their exclamations of *"les Américains!"* was that of men too weary and too satiated for any enthusiasms. It said to me:

"So you are here, too. Go on, and then tell us how you like it after you have more than three years of it. Have your turn, but we know this show is over."

So far as these French soldiers were concerned, Clemenceau, Foch and Pétain, President "Veelson" and General "Pershaing" might have this war. All they asked was a night's sleep, and then, tomorrow, they would look after themselves and throw out the latest of the governments that had betrayed them.

If the French army as a whole had been in such mood it would have been a routed, broken army; attrition would have done its work. But these were not the whole French army; their attitude was only significant of how fatalism may spread in an army that has fought very long and finds the enemy's latest blow too much.

Against this tide marches the Americans in their heartening precision. If you are going to war they are the kind of soldiers you need; and if you are going to make a crusade of force in foreign lands they are the kind of crusaders you need.

They did not know where they were going. This was not their business. They would be told where to go and what to do as they always would be while they were in the army. They did not know why they were going except that apparently the frogs had suffered a hard wallop. But they did know what was expected of them in trench and in battle, these regulars.

The Germans were over the Aisne, over the Vesle, beyond all the old trench lines, their left close to sacred Rheims. They took Soissons. They were making days' marches of their swift progress. They took Château-Thierry there on the banks of the Marne, sacred river of national defense to the French. Then they scaled the heights beyond Château-Thierry moving on along the Paris–Château-Thierry road straight toward Paris, hampered less by resistance than by their own fatigue.

They were nearer Paris than they had been since Von Kluck threatened it in 1914. They had gone faster than Ludendorff had anticipated, run away from their transport in their eagerness to make an end to this war.

The battle maps showed where the German line was that night of June 3rd. How much nearer would it be to Paris tomorrow. Would Ludendorff have fresh reserves up to press his advantage?

The American soldiers I had seen marching past the refugees and stragglers now knew their destination. It was to take over on a line across the Paris road than held by tired French reserves just beyond the village of Lucy le Bocage. The fields had known no excitement except grazing and growing crops, they had been free of shell craters since the Germans had been thrown back from the Marne in 1914. Now the war with its destruction had returned here to say that all the nearly four years of fighting and agony had been waste, and the million French dead might have died in vain.

The American soldiers knew, too, just what they had to do. It was to hold that line where it was. And when it remained in the same place the next day and the next, the French government stopped packing up its papers to move then out of Paris; the elders of the Supreme War Council ceased worrying for the moment; and all the peoples of the Allied world breathed a prayer of thanks whether they believed in God or not.

From the book, *The German Offensive of July 15, 1918*, U.S. Army Service Schools:

Reputation Of American Soldiers Among German Divisions

Officers of the 84th Division, captured by the French on July 9 in their attack in the vicinity of Antheuil, state that fear of and respect for American soldiers has spread generally through the German divisions. The 84th Division has not been engaged against Americans and has not been nearer than 20 kilometers to any part of the front held by any American troops. The French Third Army Bulletin of July 11, reporting an examination of these officers states: "They expressed the fear of American soldiers: All of them are strapping and determined young fellows (gaillards). The French have great confidence in the Americans and unfortunately they are not wrong.

From Dale van Every's book, *The A.E.F. in Battle:*

During that time the Third Division, less its artillery and engineers, travelling by train and truck to Provins, some 35 miles south of the Marne, and by forced march from there, passing on their way a stream of refugees who had only half believed in the existence of American soldiers, reached the river on June 1 and joined the French Thirty-eighth Corps in defending the crossings of the Marne from Château-Thierry to Damery, a stretch of 25 miles.

Ahead of the Germans came a pitiful horde of refugees bound, like the enemy, for Paris. Some had time to organize their retreat and they marched beside farm wagons laden with their effects. Others had no draft stock, and the women tugged between the shafts of carts or pushed barrows and baby carriages top-heavy with their cargo. Goats, dogs, kittens, burros, pigs, milch cows and crates of chickens were in the ragged columns. And as in the panic of fire we are prone to salvage the least essential of our goods, every last umbrella and bird cage in the department appeared to have been saved, whatever else was left behind.

The war-evicted peasantry plodded with dogged patience and resignation past and through the hurrying-up American and French reinforcements and transport columns, but once they reached Paris they began to mill like frightened cattle. For the most part they had neither money nor food and no destination, beyond escaping the enemy. More than 1,000,000 of the inhabitants of Paris, or about one in three, had fled the city as the German advance reached the Marne. The city's food supply was low and the municipal government was disorganized. The national government was straining every ligament to stop the breach at Château-Thierry and could not concern itself with civilian woes.

The possibilities of riot and looting, with a further breakdown of the national morale, were ominous, and here the American Red Cross performed one of the greatest of its many great services to the Allied cause. With an admirable absence of red tape, it waited neither for requests nor for orders, but took over the task of feeding, sheltering and clothing this pitiful horde to the limits of its resources. I do not think it is an exaggeration to say that the Red Cross saved Paris from having pillage and riot added to panic in those early days of June.

Paris had been the capital, metropolis and the railroad center of France in 1914 when the Germans first reached the Marne. In the intervening four years it had become the great munitions center of the nation, its military heart in all senses of the word, and its

capture now might well be decisive. On June 4, with the refugee columns pouring out the south gates, Clemenceau had faced the Chamber of Deputies and said, "*Je me bats devant Paris; je me bats a Paris; je me bats derriére Paris.*" ["I will fight before Paris; I will fight in Paris; I will fight behind Paris."]

At a historic meeting of the Supreme War Council at Versailles on June 1 and 2, Clemenceau, Lloyd George and Orlando had cabled a dramatic appeal to President Wilson.

"We desire to express our warmest thanks for the remarkable promptness with which American aid in excess of what at one time seemed practicable has been rendered to the Allies during the past month to meet a great emergency," the message read.

"The crisis, however, still continues. General Foch has presented to us a statement of the utmost gravity. One hundred and sixty-one Allied divisions now oppose 200 German divisions.

"There is no possibility of the British and French increasing their forces; on the contrary they are put to extreme straits to keep them up. There is a great danger of the war being lost unless the numerical inferiority of the Allies can be remedied as rapidly as possible by the advent of American troops. He therefore urges with the utmost insistence that the maximum possible number of infantry and machine gunners, in which respect the shortage on the Allied side is most marked, should continue to be shipped from America to avert the immediate danger of an Allied defeat in the present campaign owing to the Allied reserves being exhausted before those of the enemy. He represents that it is impossible to foresee ultimate victory in the war unless America is able to provide such an army as will establish numerical superiority. He places the total American forces required for this at not less than 100 divisions"—equal to 200 European divisions.

Ruth Gaines, a Red Cross worker in France, wrote in her book, *Helping France: The Red Cross in the Devastated Areas:*

One of the girls has just returned from Paris. She says the rumors there are dreadful—hints of treachery in the air raid and people are leaving by the hundreds. We are awfully overworked here and some are getting peevish. We never have enough people to go around for we have a huge place here and this last week we have fed thousands, all going back to the Front with new trappings. Everybody is being called in to resist the attack. We can tell so much from the appearance and attitude of the men and just now France is banking on the Americans. How I hope it isn't too late!

What a week it has been! The dreaded prophesies have come true and the Line has not been held. Day after day for three weeks the refugees have been pouring through the country and every day long trains of *blessés* going down to the South. I had given word to feed all *repatriés* and today I went down at seven in the morning as one girl was ill. When I went in I was greeted with shouts from the girls on the night shift who were still working and was rushed hastily to look in the Refectory. There was a sight never to be forgotten, crammed, packed in were 300 refugees who had been there most of the night waiting for trains to take them on. From Amiens and Noyon they had fled, carrying what they could and leaving their homes in ruins. Old men, crippled and lame—some had fallen from fatigue. Women and babies, babies everywhere—tiny ones in blankets, little toddlers, each clutching a treasure. There they were and they even laughed with me when a rooster crowed from a covered basket.

There were several baskets with tiny chickens, here and there a hen and last of all, a poor tired goat, huddled by the stove. The women told how they had brought him and cared for him because of the milk he (or rather, she) gave the children. She, poor, dear, seemed quite wan, so we fed her a huge basket of potato peelings and she was quite her own goatish self before she left. We managed to feed everyone in the crowd and sent them further down the line to new adventures.

Paris is in a state—everyone leaving who can and the destruction of the church has had the effect of spreading terror everywhere. It seems to have done more to break down the morale of the French people than anything else that has happened. The American Red Cross has set up temporary *Cantines* at every station and fed everyone coming from the North. Two large *Cantines* in the war zone have been under fire but the people have stayed on to help with the refugees, and so it goes. We are each doing a small part and I suppose it helps to hold the whole thing together; although I sometimes wonder what it is all about.

It is quite a problem to keep the food going and ready for emergencies of 800 to 1000 extra every day. The refugees pour through here on their way to the South, carrying bundles and babies. Old, old men, women and children, each with a few treasures, with a desolate and despairing look, having left everything behind them as they fled from the enemy. The trains of wounded hurt me just as much every time I see them. The soldiers go through with their guns and *musettes* to the Front, and every day long trains come back with broken wrecks, and such horrible wrecks, dying or made helpless for their few remaining years. At times it seems as if we couldn't go on, and then it is a joy to walk through the trains with hot chocolate, and when you give each one a tiny American flag, everything changes. They are like children, they smile and salute and if they have a hand, they go off waving happily from a window. They all just worship the Americans, can't do enough for them and look to them for the end of the War. I often wonder if our boys will have the courage to meet life and death like that. And even that isn't the worst, for most of them have not only offered their lives but have lost their families as well. I was putting a dressing on a little old man yesterday and the tears streamed down his face as he told me how he went home on *permission* to find the family had fled without leaving a trace, the village was in ruins, and there was nothing for him to do but to go back and fight again.

MajGen John A. Lejeune, USMC, in his book *The Reminiscences of a Marine*, remembers that:

French camions appeared at early dawn on May 31st, and at once there began the great parade of 28,000 fighting Americans through the outskirts of Paris and the streets of Meaux and over the country roads to the stretch of country lying just west of Château-Thierry and north of the Marne. The roads were jammed with French refugees. Mothers with babes in their arms, little children, old men and women carrying their most precious belongings or driving loaded ox-carts, were wearily plodding along. Their numbers seemed unending; their woe seemed undescribable. The hearts of the men of the Second Division were touched as never before, and their will to conquer and their determination to drive the invaders from the soil of France became immutable.

From *The War Diary of a Combat Artist*, by Harry E. Townsend:

At last we neared the front, or the immediate zone back of it, passing long trains of refugees for many miles, grey in the dust, patient-faced, leaving their homes for the second time to who knows what fate, and going back to the more-or-less unknown rear to await the final day. Many of them were smiling as they waved their hands at us as we passed, and always were the children gay. Little did they seem to comprehend the meaning of it all. Lucky they!

Two of these groups of evacuees I shall never forget. One was led by the father, a more-or-less ordinary looking man, kind-faced, not over-strong, who struggled up the slight hill pushing a barrow loaded to the skies with things that he had felt he must not leave behind. Behind him was a lovely girl of eleven or twelve years with big, wide-brimmed, beribboned straw hat and in white dress who was carrying, with great difficulty, a roll of rugs on her shoulder. And behind her was her mother, a wonderfully refined and handsome woman, bareheaded, who pushed a baby carriage loaded to overflowing with bundles and clothes and parcels hanging from the handles, and down in the midst of the carriage was a wee, smiling baby. I couldn't help wondering about this family or where they were from—what sort of home—or where did they think to go? How full of this sort of sad flight, tho, France has been.

Later, we met or passed, as she rested by the roadside and gazed at us with strange, distant look, a tall, rather gaunt, woman, along with all the belongings she was apparently able to bring with her. She stood at the head of a large, black horse hitched to a cart loaded with furniture and bedding and hay, and with a coop on top filled to overflowing, almost with chickens and ducks. She was hatless and shaded her eyes with her left hand from the glaring sun. With the other hand she held the leash on three fine cows who struggled and tugged to reach the grass at the roadside. Beneath the cart a faithful dog panted in the heat. She seemed along in the world. Her *marié* at the front, living or dead, and she left behind to manage their apparently prosperous little farm. The great threat had come again to them and she had to pack and flee, as she had once before done, till the menace was passed. Alone but not alone, for "*enceinte*" as she was, she carried with her that great hope, to give joy soon to that soldier husband of hers when he heard the news

that he was father to a son, another soldier someday for his beloved France. And failing his return, or even her return ever to their old home, she stood there looking, as it were, into a future that bore for her a son, consecrated to her and to that other mother, France. One glance at her and one sensed all this.

Further on we pass a small boy in an old, dilapidated "peram" who, hitched on behind a large cart, was having the time of his young life, innocent of the crisis at hand. When one thinks of the countless children that have been born and raised their few young years within sound of the guns, and even under or within gun fire, and know nothing of a world beautiful and at peace.

James B. Wharton wrote in his fictional novel, *The Squad*:

Noon of a July day. The sun dazzles out of a cloudless sky and heats to a touch the stones that protrude through the hard macadam of the road, yellows the grass of the unfenced fields and dulls the green of the orchards and woods.

Along a white road that runs away from Paris toward the northeast, a column of infantry is on the march. From under the shuffling feet rises a white cloud of dust. It envelopes and follows the slow moving column, so that it seems to carry the cloud along with it, as part of itself. The dust whitens the heavy, iron-shod shoes and tightly wrapped leggins. It settles thickly over steel helmets, packs, rifles and shoulders of heavy woolen blouses. It penetrates painfully through nostrils and mouths, grits against teeth, burns throats and chokes lungs.

"Way to the ri-ght!"

Up and down the column, carried along from man to man, comes the command. And the infantry, in column of twos, thickens toward the right of the way. Traffic passes constantly up and down the clear half of the road.

The lieutenants and sergeants weave up and down on the outside of the column. Hoarsely, they shout through the dust:

"Close up—close up—close up—don't straggle!"

And the soldiers bunch closer for a few minutes, until the natural inequity of gaits again irregularizes the column.

"Yuh-all reckon we're jus' doin' this fo' trainin'?" asks Anderson, "Or, yuh reckon we're goin' somewheah?"

"Hell, yes, we're goin' somewhere," says O'Connors. "Lookit them

Frogs. Whadda you think—they're just goin' on vacation er what?"

A huge-wheeled cart, its two horses in tandem, driven by an ancient peasant baanced sideways on the shafts, creaks by. On top of the mountainous load of beds, mattresses, wardrobe, chairs, tables and kitchen wear, sprawls a wrinkled woman. Barefoot children follow alongside. The refugees take no notice of the troops. Their minds' eyes are filled with visions of the homes and country they've just quit.

"Les Boches viennent, allez-y!"

A wagon creaks by, laden heavily with bottles of beer from a village bistro somewhere up ahead, cleared out under the threat of war. Here, too, the driver takes no notice of the troops until O'Connors veers out from the column to snatch at a bottle. Then the Frenchman shouts terrifyingly and cracks his long whip. O'Connors ducks back into the column, while laughs and jibes pass through the Squad.

"Scared you off, huh?"

"Aw, hell, I wuz just kiddin' th' old man. Who wants to steal a bottle o' beer from a pore old Frog like that? Yet, I won't say I couldn't use a drink right now. I'm so dry I can't spit.

Come ambulances and trucks. Over the tailboards hang filthy soldiers, in torn, muddy clothing, with red-soaked bandages on heads, shoulders and arms. They appear stupid, these wounded, with the stupidity of the mind which has met with something too colossal to comprehend.

"What's it like up dere?" Marzulak shouts out.

"Hell!"

From the rear, overtaking the infantry, dusty French camions, driven by yellow-faced Annamites in crude, goatskin coats, pound and flap by. Rolling kitchens and batteries of 75's go by with a snap of leather harness. The horses are unkempt and emaciated. Occasionally, the infantry passes a horse dying in the ditch beside the road. The war is through with the animal, cast off as it reached the end of its tether.

Ahead, low in the sky, appear great, sausage like balloons, turning lazily in the wind and showing on each side huge eyes of concentric red, white and blue circles. Overhead, high up, is a

constant whir of avions. Tiny puffs of the white smoke of shell-bursts appear about them, as they dip and fall, and climb and glide, with the rattle of their machine-guns coming faintly to earth.

At intervals along the roadside are camouflaged guns—155 mm. G.P.F.'s—manned by Frenchmen in soiled, blue uniforms mingled with the dun of civilian clothes. A sharp command. The long snout shoots back in recoil. Flame and black smoke belch forth. An unseen projectile reverberates through the air—to burst miles away, beyond sight or sound of here, somewhere among the enemy lines.

"Close up—close up—close up—don't straggle!" the Lieutenants and the Sergeants shout as they ply up and down on the outside of the column of twos.

And again the stragglers bunch forward with an eccentric movement and hold the proper distance for a few minutes.

"Say, Mike," says Waglith. "Know what it is today?"

"A hell of a hike. That's easy."

"It's the Fourth of July."

"No! It ain't!"

"Dam' right it is."

"Christ, th' Army don't take no 'count o' day er night, Sundays er holidays—Some one oughta give th' Colonel a calendar."

"What'd they take awaiy arh B.V.D.'s fo? Ah'm sweatin' like a hoss an' this lousy woolen underweah chafes like hell," says Anderson.

"My pack feels like a ball and chain—the doughboy's sentence for life," adds Allen.

"It gives me an awful kink in the back and the straps cut hell outa my shoulders," says Whittaker.

"I'd like to have th' guy that invented it here now. I'd pile th' eight packs on his goddam back an' then whip him forward along th' road wit' bullets," O'Connors growls.

The Squad grumbles along through the hot dust. Helmets, hung over slung rifles, jangle against the barrels. Sweat pours down faces from under the O.S. caps.

Suddenly, through the dust, the Lieutenant's voice breaks out angrily:

"Pick 'em up, God dam' it. If those bandoliers're missin' at th' end of th' march, you'll stand court-martial!"

Gray looks around. Whittaker has chucked his bandoliers, heavy with clips of rifle cartridges, into the ditch. Frightened, he now picks up the canvas pouches and reshoulders them. With the Lieutenant out of earshot, he mutters:

"He can talk, but what's he carrying but a pack without even a blanket roll in it."

In *Circuits of Victory*, Capt William C. Elmore, 55th Regular Signal Battalion, remembers:

I saw some of the horrors of war when unloading refugees. I witnesses one old man caring for six little tots, now knowing who any of them were. An old couple carried their all tied up in a bandanna handkerchief: family clock, marriage certificate and some money. These people came in on flat cars, and had no place to go. The 410th Telegraph Battalion (Chicago and Wisconsin Bell) took care of them.

Daniel Strickland wrote in his book, *Connecticut Fights, the Story of the 102nd Regiment, 26th Division:*

July fourth saw the battalions of the regiment either in or near Paris. As each troop train drew nearer and nearer to the city, rumors continued to spread that the regiment and perhaps the division was to parade there in recognition of the fine service performed on the Chemin des Dames and in the Toul sector. Poor deluded doughboys began polishing their hob-nailed trench shoes, putting clothes into shape, and so on. And one train after another did draw into Paris, but as the engine was uncoupled from one end, another backed down on the opposite end, and the regiment was dragged up toward Chateau-Thierry! Some of the units it is true, did detrain later at towns close enough to permit a hasty trip to the great city for a few hours, but those boys who did manage the trip found Paris very different from the city they had expected to see. The place was dark and the streets more or less deserted because of the proximity of the enemy. The most important business on every one's mind, was that of keeping the Germans out of Paris.

By evening of July fourth the regiment had detrained at Lizy sur Ourcq and Trilport, and went into billets as follows:

Headquarters. Poincy

Headquarters Company. Poincy

First Battalion. Isles les Meldeuses

Second Battalion. St. Fiaere and Villemareuil. Third Battalion. Tanerou, Jaignes, Changis sur Marne. Machine Gun Company. Changis sur Marne

Supply Company. Woods west of Poincy

This area was from four to fifteen kilometers east of Meaux along the Marne, between Meaux and Chateau-Thierry. The German offensive against Chateau-Thierry (and Paris) had just been checked; the Marine Brigade had made its memorable attack in Bois de Belleau, and had stopped, at least for the time, that seemingly irresistible wave sweeping into that heart of France. These were tense times; no one knew what to expect. Enemy avions in squadrons flew at will over the country; it was necessary to conceal everything resembling troop movements or concentrations; night bombings were frequent all over the area; anti-aircraft guns were always firing; at night searchlights attempted to locate the source of the ever-present hum of the Boche motor. The fourth of July was celebrated in this area with games, band concerts, and whatever festivities were feasible.

George Pattullo, a newspaper correspondent with the AEF, wrote a fictional book, *Horrors of Moonlight.* His book vividly portrays the times of 1918. This excerpt is from the book chapter, "Hellwood, 1918":

A wonderful thing has come to pass. A small force of Americans has put new life into the Allied armies and raised the drooping spirits of two nations.

Bouresches and the Bois de Belleau of themselves would not stand out in war's chronicle as military feats because both were small affairs in these days of human tidal waves and, desperate as was the fighting, there have been others as desperate and will doubtless be many more. But the stout blows that the Second Division delivered in the month of June cannot be measured by the toll of enemy dead and prisoners, by the capture of ground or guns and material; they must be gauged by their moral effect and that has been tremendous.

I have never seen anything like it. The German offensives had been sweeping forward like a flood, lapping up territory here, then swerving to lap up there, but always coming on, so that their whole battle line drew inexorably nearer to Paris. The British had suffered cruel losses; the French were fighting with their backs to the wall. And American aid—where was it? On that they had banked for a year, on that they had built all their hopes.

For months and months the poilu had been fed abundantly with promises of American support and what the glorious allies from overseas would do when they got in—and all he had seen of them was in the training camps or in quiet sectors where the only activity was intermittent shelling, an infrequent raid, or minor operations carried out under French tutelage. Meanwhile the Germans drove against the Allied front again and again and the poilu had to do the fighting.

Where WAS this American aid? Was it to prove as illusory as the Russian? Small wonder that Jacques grew skeptical and angrily contemptuous of the newspaper propaganda which endeavored to stiffen the nation's morale by still more roseate pictures of what the United States would do in the future. It was always and always the future! When would they come in force and help bear the brunt?

Hope deferred maketh the heart sick. They had almost despaired of us. It is my firm conviction that our army did not enter seriously into their calculations for this emergency; certain it is that the average French and British soldier had given over expecting substantial aid in the 1918 crisis. We saw their spirits go down, down, down.

The German hordes pressed on toward Paris. They veered and swirled; held at one point, they surged forward at another. Word came that they were in Chateau-Thierry. Men looked at each other in dumb foreboding. Where would they be stopped?

And then suddenly the boche flood-tide recoiled. The broad gap they had opened in the line was closed and the magic news flashed throughout the army and nation that the French were counter-attacking, that they were hurling the enemy back at critical points and that the road to Paris was barred.

How had it been done? An American force was mentioned in the first announcement, but Americans had shared in undertakings before and the French remained unimpressed and apathetic until the full story of the part the Third and Second Divisions had played came out several days later.

They went wild. From the Channel ports to the remotest villages the news ran like a prairie fire. The Americans had stopped the boche—they had beaten him. In the darkest hour—just when it seemed that Hindenburg had opened a road to Paris and picked German divisions were developing the success—the Americans had smashed into them and, fighting in their own way in the open, they had thrown back superior numbers, wresting from them positions that were essential to farther advance. And they were holding these positions! Beating off all counter-attacks, they had reestablished the broken line.

Vive l'Amerique! The French let out a yell, gave a hitch to their braces, and went into the fray with fresh ardor. After all their disappointment their ally could fight! Not only could he fight, he was a bearcat at fighting. This was the great outstanding fact to the poilu. And suddenly, too, this ally began pouring men into France by the hundreds of thousands, until all the villages and valleys and roads were choked with stalwarts in khaki and every passing train showed them grinning cheerfully through the windows.

Instantly the whole French nation rose to a frenzy of enthusiasm. Six months ago American popularity had fallen to a new ebb; to the soldiery the overseas force were "Boy Scoots"; the French had grown to feel that America in the war threatened to prolong it without lifting any of the burden.

Today, the population pours pell-mell into the streets to cheer when American soldiers march past; the poilu cries "C'est bien, ca!" and borrows some tobacco. Last winter he might not have bothered to rise from his seat at the roadside when an American major-general drove by; today he will jump nimbly to his feet and give a smart salute to a shave-tail lieutenant.

The Second were in a rest area back of the First, which was holding a portion of the Montdidier Front. It was certainly a he-sector; I was up there with them and I know. What the communiqués describe as fairly active artillery fire took its toll of dead and wounded by day and by night. Now, holding the line under constant shelling is the toughest work that soldiers have to do. The sum total of losses over a period of a month will usually exceed those suffered in a heavy attack and the strain on the nerves is greater because prolonged.

The staunch old First naturally expected to be relieved. They had taken Cantigny by assault and had stubbornly held it against bombardment and counter-attacks. Therefore it cheered them mightily when it was whispered that the Second Division was behind and would shortly take over. Officers from the Second came up to make a reconnaissance, a step preliminary to a relief.

Then the situation to the southeast became critical. The boche offensive was sweeping forward. His original intention had been to advance his front only as far as Fismes on the Rheims-Soissons line, but success in the center so greatly exceeded expectations that the German command decided to develop it into a push for Paris and swiftly threw an enormous mass of men into the breach. Already they were in Chateau-Thierry. Unless the enemy was speedily stopped the capital would be brought under his guns. And then what?

In this emergency it became a question of what reserves to employ. The French generalissimo decided to send American.

It was four o'clock on the morning of May thirtieth when the Second climbed into their trucks and headed for the great battle. The men were jubilant. They had enjoyed a fine rest, in a fat land of green trees and fields of yellowing grain and burnt-almond colored clover—a fair, quiet land of beautiful chateaux and well-ordered villages, of rich-pastures grazed by sleek cattle. A considerable number of the men had been evacuated with the grippe, but the Division was in first-class shape and up on its toes for a whack at the Heinie. Hadn't most of them been doing police work and construction jobs and other such things along lines of communication most of the time since arrival in France?

The long caravan of trucks took a route that brought them very close to Paris. In every town and village they threaded, the people ran out to huzza and shower them with flowers. The population of this region had never seen American soldiers in any numbers and here were camions pouring through the streets hour after hour, all loaded to the guards with big, husky, rollicking men in khaki, who laughed and joked with them and stuck flowers in their buttonholes, and behaved for all the world as though bound for a picnic. And with them went guns and horses and mules and machine-gun carts, beyond count.

The inhabitants guessed what all this activity meant: The Americans were going into battle. So they came running from their houses to run beside the trucks. Old grandfathers saluted and waved their hats; women threw roses or kept pace beside the wheels to talk and wish them *bonne chance*; the children scrambled wildly everywhere, shrilling "*Vive l'Amerique!*" half frantic with joy.

It was a long, hard trip. Just before reaching Meaux they encountered the first of the refugees. Beyond that, from Meaux northward, the roads were crawling with them—an unbroken stream of heaped carts and plodding peasants, of bleating sheep and swaying, rumbling cattle, weary unto death.

They saw toothless, doddering octogenarians in that line, and also babes at the breast. They saw there bedraggled, tear-stained mothers and strapping, broad-backed girls, sullen from fatigue and hate. Men long past the prime of life urged the tired horses forward. Their women and children either perched amid the mass of mattresses and bedding with chairs and mirrors, of bird cages and rabbit hutches, of crucifixes and plaster figures of Our Lady, or trudged along in the dust with the family dog or cow.

Some of the children wailed; some took it as an adventure. The very old just rocked in their carts, silently rumpling and rumpling their aprons.

Up the road came the men of the Second Division, camion after camion, mile on mile. They passed this saddest of all processions under a pall of dust. The refugees stared at them apathetically, without enthusiasm, apparently without interest. They were sunk in the lethargy of despair. What did it mean to them now that soldiers from beyond the seas were going into the maelstrom up there? All was lost—homes property—everything made precious by a life-time's association.

So they gazed at the Second Division and the big guns and the little guns trundling northward to battle and gave no sign. But the men of the Second grew stern. Showers of flowers and the glad shouts of admiring allies were heartening incidents, but here before their eyes was the tragic business of war. Those hordes of exhausted, stained, hurrying refugees, pressing southward, every southward, steeled them for the job. All their hilarity ceased. How long now before they would go against the boches?

The bulk of the division were in the trucks fully thirty hours.

Some battalions lost their means of transportation while still far from the Front and had to hike it, but the American soldier has grown hardened to that.

They reached some little towns behind the battle front at long last and bivouacked. For bedding they had ponchos and one blanket to a man. The nights were cold, but that was nothing new to them. The men could hear the artillery booming in the distance like a heavy surf, and in the darkest hours of the night boche avions came droning overhead to drop bombs on adjacent villages. Yet the noise of battle was less than they had anticipated.

Up to this time the resistance offered to the German thrust had not been sufficiently determined to stop them. The plan of the French was to delay the enemy as long as possible by rear-guard actions until the arrival of reserves in sufficient strength to stabilize the situation. Therefore the Americans were to take up support positions on which the French would fall back, and then these positions would become the front line. Such was the plan.

"Why not stop them where they are?" inquired the American commander.

Which was all very well, but how was it to be done? The French were plainly dubious about intrusting an enterprise of such importance to what they regarded as untried troops. To be sure, a regiment of Americans had captured Cantigny; they had showed dash and courage and tenacity; and other divisions had some fine performances to their credit. But the Battle of Cantigny belonged to the established order of trench warfare. It had been elaborately prepared and French staff work had contributed to its preparation. It was rehearsed under the eyes of a French general and French tanks and flame projectors and much French artillery had contributed to the success of the attack.

This was different. Here was open warfare, whose aspect changed from hour to hour—a style of warfare demanding the highest form of military skill and initiative. They never doubted the pluck of our men, which had been proved on numberless occasions since last November, but they did entertain serious doubts of the ability of the American staff and unit commanders to swing it, solely because no American staff had so far been permitted to undertake an operation on its own.

Consequently they demurred. Their proposal was to brigade the Americans among seasoned French troops. Then the Allies could exact what toll they might while falling back.

"Let us fight this in our own way and we'll stop 'em," declared the American commander.

The situation was growing hazardous; a few more gains and the boche could train his heavy guns on Paris. The French general consented. The Division could go in as a division, fight it out in their own way—and heaven have them in its keeping.

Howard O'Brien, an officer in the AEF, wrote in his book, *Wine, Women and War: a Diary of Disillusionment:*

Friday, 12 April. To station. Saw number of refugees from war zone. Piteous. All aged and infirm, many scarce able to walk. Very poor. One old woman, in rags, tottering along on home-made crutches, assisted, almost carried by a young poilu. Tenderness of helpers for these unhappy derelicts most striking. Sight of these feeble old creatures after lifetime of toil, reduced to this, filled me with a great loathing for war. Sudden gust of hate for swine who had loosed such a dreadful thing on the world.

The same sorrowful picture again on station platforms en route to Paris. Many young women—and little children. One pair, little boy about four, leading little sister by the hand through crowd, guarding her from the jostle of the unthinking, comforting her when she wept…

May, 1918. Curious murmur outside, like rustle of branches in wind. Clatter of many feet on cobbles. Street black with sorry picture. Refugees, pattering wearily along toward their barracks. Small children, leading still smaller ones. The very old, trying awkwardly to help each other. Pitiful vestiges of homes—dingy little bags, an extra hat, a pair of shoes, a bird cage, one old woman leading three small dogs. And then…clump, clump, clump—company of soldiers, 60 lbs. apiece on their backs, steps dragging. So, on this street, all day long, and all night too. Dirty war. Never a band. No flags. Just hanging on. Dreaming that tomorrow *la guerre va finir.*

In *Fighting the Flying Circus* (Stokes, 1919), Captain Edward V. Rickenbacker, the leading American aerial ace of World War I, wrote about the flood of refugees from the Marne salient:

Paris in wartime is well enough known to millions of my fellow countrymen, but the scene that presented itself to my eyes as I alighted at the Gare de l'Est on the morning of June 6, 1918, merits a description. That date, it will be remembered, marked probably the lowest ebb in the spirits of the Parisian populace.

The Germans were along the Marne and but thirty miles from the capital. Château-Thierry was in their hands. The villagers in that vicinity who had braved four years of adjacent warfare were now swept away from their homes. Thousands of these poor refugees were arriving in Paris on the morning I entered it.

Used as I was to the various horrors of war, there was a terror in the countenances of these homeless people that made a lasting impression on me. Old women, young women, all clothed in wretched garments and disheveled headgear wandered blindly through the streets adjoining the stations, with swarms of crying children clinging to their skirts. Pathetic as this scene was, it had its comic features in the extraordinary articles that these fleeing peasants had chosen to carry with them.

Umbrellas seemed to be the most precious thing that they had tried to save. A little bundle, probably containing a loaf of bread and a few articles of clothing was carried by each woman. The children were loaded down with such strange treasures as axes, parrot cages, wooden buckets, and farm implements. The few old men who accompanied them hobbled along empty-handed, with the utmost patience and abandon. Evidently the whole care of the migration was left to the energetic women of France.

They had been walking for many miles; this was very evident. Their clothing was dusty, worn and crumpled. Their faces were pinched and wretched and an indescribable look of misery and suffering filled every countenance. The pathos of this scene will never leave my memory.

And here I desire to express my appreciation of the magnificent work of the American Red Cross and American YMCA organizations. In that one case of the Château-Thierry refugees these American societies repaid their American subscribers for the

sacrifices they made to support them. Indeed, without the help of this American agency I can easily imagine that the French capital, overwhelmed and crushed under the burden and horror of these calamities would long since have abandoned all hope, and riots and disorders would have prostrated the authorities in control of the nation.

Thousands of refugees swarmed throughout a more or less demoralized Paris. They had no money, no food, no idea of where they wanted to go. The spirit was gone from their bodies. Only the call of hunger served to remind them that they still must live.

Preparations were immediately made to care for this new demand upon the American charitable organizations. It was a very critical period of the war. Every available soldier was at the front and these must have the undivided attention of the supply officers, the commissary department and government authorities. Refugees were of no consequence toward winning the war. They deserved pity but could not be permitted to divert the attention of the defenders of the nation.

How dangerous this subtle menace might have been will never be known, for the American Red Cross threw itself into the situation and cared for this increasing army of unfed in Paris. Had they been neglected a day or two longer such riots might have been started in Paris as would have demoralized the whole system of the French organization.

The secret of their success was undoubtedly due to the elasticity and absence of red tape in their organization. But whatever it may have been, the fact that the American Red Cross did successfully feed and clothe these bedraggled thousands was in itself a marvel and made me appreciate how valuable an asset our Red Cross Society was and is in war time.

It was easy to read in the faces of the people one met the deadly fear that gripped them. Thousands had already fled from Paris. The authorities were even that morning considering again moving the seat of the government to more distant Bordeaux. The capture of Paris before the American aid could arrive was a possibility that worried every Parisian.

I tried to fancy the exulting German officers walking down these same beautiful avenues, driving their motorcars through these splendid woods and occupying such of these magnificent palaces as happened to tempt their cupidity. Then I thought of the "Spirit of the Marne" which had so strengthened the French people in those cruel days of 1914. Studying the set faces of these passers-by I could discover that the same indomitable spirit still held them. Their faces held something of the same expression that was pictured on that famous French Liberty Loan poster—a poilu standing with fixed bayonet defending his native land. Underneath the poster was written the immortal phrase, *Ils ne Passeront Pas!*

LUZANCY

In 1914 Luzancy was on the right flank of the advance of the British 4th Division.

5.5 km NNE of La Ferté on D-402 there is a bridge which crosses the Marne river. The BEF had destroyed this bridge during its retreat southward in 1914. On its northward offensive in the same year, the infantry of the BEF had to cross the river on a weir (dam) which is just north of this bridge.

A large detachment from AEF Evacuation Hospital No. 8 in Juilly was sent in early June to Luzancy.

AEF Field Hospital No. 15 moved from the Château la Rue on the La Ferté-sous-Jouarre–Château-Thierry Road to Luzancy on 16 June, 1918. It remained in Luzancy until 6 July where it operated a hospital for sick and gassed patients.

An American military hospital used the château of Luzancy. AEF Field Hospitals Nos. 15 and 16 (animal-drawn) were located in an old school building in Luzancy where they used this location to treat gassed and wounded soldiers. Gas casualties were washed in the nearby Marne river. Field Hospital No.16 had moved to from Meaux to Luzancy on 11 June 1918. Here a building, formerly used by the French for hospital purposes, was supplemented by tentage, and shelter was thus provided for 800 beds.

During their stay in Luzancy, the two field hospitals operated as a division hospital for gassed and sick and treated 3317 soldiers. They started with accommodations for only 250, but on June 14, their second day, they had 756 cases from the region of Bouresches [see editor's note below].

On 9 July 1918 the 101st Sanitary Train, 26th Division took over the hospital in Luzancy.

Field Hospitals Nos. 101 and 104 together cared for the slightly wounded, gassed, and sick in a large school building at Luzancy. Field Hospital No. 165 started at Luzancy on 23 July and moved on to Villiers-sur-Marne on 27 July.

An all-woman medical unit of the American Women's Hospital (AWH) operated a hospital at Luzancy. From their arrival in August, 1918 through March, 1919, its first overseas hospital, AWH No. 1 treated military and civilian wounded. They also ran an ambulance service and created mobile clinics, dispensaries and the only dental service available to both military and civilian personnel.

Luzancy was well to the rear of the front lines, but not beyond extreme artillery range.

Editor's note: On 9 June 1918, LtCol Derby succeeded in obtaining permission from the French authorities to move two hospitals, one for non-transportable wounded and the other for gas cases, closer to the front lines. This was none too soon, for, as it happened, the Germans launched a major mustard gas attack five days later against the Marines, resulting in the evacuation of almost 800 members of the 2nd Battalion, 6th Marines to the newly relocated Field Hospital 16 at Luzancy.

IN THEIR OWN WORDS

LtCol Richard Derby, Chief Surgeon, U.S. 2nd Division, AEF, wrote in his book, *Wade in Sanitary! The Story of the Division Surgeon in France*:

> I stopped off at Bézu on the way back to headquarters. Ambulances just in from the front were unloading wounded at the door of the church.
>
> At Bézu everyone was stripped and as many bathed as facilities permitted. Those that could not be bathed here were put into pyjamas or suits of underclothing and sent at once to Luzancy where good facilities existed. Later that afternoon, I saw a large number of the very slightly gassed being bathed in the Marne, beneath the suspension bridge crossing to Luzancy.

Frederick A. Pottle, an enlisted member of Evacuation Hospital No. 8 in Juilly, wrote a series of articles which provide a graphic description of hospital work at the front during a major engagement. Here, from the October, 1929 edition of the periodical *Outlook and Independent*, is a part of Pottle's article, "The Backwash of Battle, A Hospital Unit on the Western Front":

> Not all of our men were in Juilly during those first days. Immediately on our arrival several groups were detached for service

Before Endeavours Fade, Rose Coombs

with other units. I have no complete list of those details. Some of our men went to the Red Cross hospital at Neuilly, twin to Juilly, and a larger detachment was sent to Luzancy. A noncomissioned officer who went in charge of this last detail has preserved a record which I shall quote practically entire.

June 12. Moved up front about 15 kil. To town of Luzancy. Evac. 8 men had no gas masks but had to risk it just the same. Luzancy is right on the Marne, about 5 or 6 kil. behind Belleau Woods. Quiet all day.

June 13. During day all was quiet, and I slept, being on night duty. At night few patients, but an awful barrage. The hospital was set between the heavy artillery and the front lines, so that the shells went overhead all night. No sleeping.

June 14. Day about as usual, with a few gas cases coming in. At night an air raid, and the anti-aircraft guns on the Marne sure did raise some noise. Terrific barrage all night. Germans hammering Americans hard.

June 15. Hard fighting all day, and Belleau Woods captured by Americans at night. Germans put over a box barrage entirely around the wood, hemming our boys in. Then they shot gas over, and it sure was a success for them. The night was muggy and rainy, which helped the gas to do its awful work.

June 16. Early this forenoon soldiers came in great numbers, and by noon the courtyard was full of blinded men, crying, moaning, and begging for help. The worst sight I ever saw. All day they kept coming in, and all night we tried to evacuate. I was on duty all night the 15th, all day the 16th, and am evacuating all night as well. Carried litters, gave dope, baths and everything all day.

June 17. 500 cases evacuated during the night, and everyone almost all in. A few were evacuated on the trucks this a.m. Hellish barrage all day and night, but Americans holding everywhere, and gaining in some places. Almost all Marines coming in, 5th and 6th Regiments. Had my first sleep this a.m., but was called to evacuate at noon. Seven hours sleep since the 15th. Had all night to sleep on the 17th, and the morning of the 18th was sent back with the rest of the boys to Evac. 8.

Frederick A. Pottle, the author of *Stretchers: The Story of a Hospital Unit on The Western Front,* relates this anecdote:

The men brought back from Luzancy a yarn that became one of the most popular in the company's repertoire. I cannot vouch for the truth of any part of it, but I can cite it as typical of the cycles of legends which all companies accumulated. The hospital at Luzancy was using the buildings of a large estate with a porter's lodge. This lodge was serving as the morgue, but the officer in charge of billets either forgot it, or was a humorist, for he assigned sleeping quarters there to two Evacuation Eight men. They went to the place after dark and made their beds on the floor, without striking a light because of the danger of air raids, naturally supposing that the other men over whom they stumbled were asleep. The night was cold, and they had only one blanket apiece. Being chilly and uncomfortable on the hard floor, they began telling each other stories, expecting, if not applause, at least a protest, but the other occupants of the room maintained an obstinate silence. One of the men finally rose, cautiously struck a light, and discovered that they were all corpses. He considered the situation a moment, then said: "Well, that being the case, you don't need the blanket"; divesting a dead man of his covering, and put it over himself.

MÉRY-SUR-MARNE

Méry-sur-Marne, 5.5 km NNE of La Ferté, on D-402, was 26th Division headquarters during the period 15–20 July 1918.

IN THEIR OWN WORDS

Clarence Richmond, a young marine in 1918, remembers arriving in the village of Méry-sur-Marne:

> About 4 o'clock in the afternoon our truck ride ended. There was some delay in assigning us to the different units. Some here, some there, and soon we were all apportioned out. I found myself assigned to a unit stationed in the small village of Merry [sic]. It was several days before I knew my company, battalion, etc. As soon as we were assigned, we were taken to the galley for supper. The food was the best I had had for many a day. The Red Cross had provided an abundance of canned peaches and I went for seconds, thirds, fourths, and I was ashamed to ask for any more. I wanted to get one square meal before I was killed.
>
> The company to which I was assigned had as a mascot, an ant bear, which had been secured in Vera Cruz. This same animal was later to receive quite a lot of newspaper publicity in the states. He was known as "Jimmie the Ant Bear."

American Doughboy

NANTEUIL-SUR-MARNE

Nanteuil-sur-Marne is 8 km NE of La Ferté, on D-402. The U.S. 26th Division established in its headquarters in Nantieul on 2 July 1918.

American Doughboy at rest

IN THEIR OWN WORDS

Dean L. Robertson, 79th Company, 6th Marines, wrote in his memoirs:

We spent the next few days in two or three different woods and not doing much but rest. We drew some new clothes too, and it's lucky for me that we did because mine were just about torn off me. This fighting business sure is hard on clothes. The 13th of July we moved into a town and slept in a house the first time in six weeks. That night like once before I determined to have a good night's rest and took off most of my clothes. And sure enough about midnight the Germans dropped a few shells on the town and we got up and beat it for the cellar. They were trying to destroy the railroad bridge across the Marne River. It was the main road to Paris. This town was Nanteuil-Sur-Marne, and was built so close to the high ridge along the Marne River that it was almost safe from shell fire. The view from the top of this ridge was wonderful. The river with its level valley land and growing crops, and the little villages scattered here and there, I guess there were about ten in sight, all made a picture that I never tired of looking at. Sunday, the 14th, France's national holiday, was a busy day for me. I went swimming and washed clothes in the morning, then went to church. After dinner a couple of us took a hike along the river, then came back in time to go to a show in the next village, given by men of the 26th Div. The guns were pretty loud that day and we heard there had been more fighting at Chateau Thierry, which was 20 km east of us.

William Scanlon, a marine who served in the Fourth Marine Brigade in 1918, wrote in his fictional novel, *God Have Mercy on Us:*

Early in the morning of July 3 we left our positions near the Paris road and hiked down to a point between Sainte-Aude and Nanteuil-sur-Marne, on the Marne River.

Orders were to take a bath and wash clothes. We did not have a change of underwear or socks, so first we scrubbed clothes and while they were drying we took our bath and went in swimming. It was the first bath we had in months.

I washed my dog-tag ribbon and hung it on a tree, tags and all. After our clothes were dry, we got out and dressed. Orders came to fall in, and we marched away toward Sainte-Aude. I left my dog-tags hanging on the tree.

Gus M. Gulberg, a member of the Marine Brigade in 1918, had this to say about Nanteuil after he was relieved in Belleau Wood by the 7th Infantry Regiment:

We got into Nanteul [sic] at five AM, and as soon as we were billeted we unslung our equipment and threw ourselves in the hay to sleep. I think I slept about twelve hours without a break. In the evening we had a swim in the icy "Marne," and then shaved off the six days growth of whiskers. The next day a Y.M.C.A. truck rolled into the town with a load of goodies. Behind them came the Red Cross and supplied our mess Sergeant with jam, cakes and other sweets. It was good to be alive, just then; and for a time we forgot our nightmare of a few days ago. We lived high for a few days, but we also drilled the usual eight hours per day. We received replacements and were re-equipped at this town before starting for the front again.

MONTREUIL-AUX-LIONS

According to historical legend, the town of Montreuil-aux-Lions got its name from a very old château that had sculpted stone lions guarding its entranceway.

On your right and in the center of the village is the city hall (Hotel de Ville). This old building contained the headquarters of the 2nd Division from 31 May to 10 June 1918, during the early part of its fighting in the vicinity of Belleau Wood and Château-Thierry. After several 210 mm shells fell nearby on 7 June, Division headquarters was moved from Montreuil to Genevrois Farm.

The 101st Field Artillery, 26th Division set up its regimental aid station at Montreuil. Battalion aid stations of the 102nd Artillery, 26th Division were located in Domptin and one-half kilometer (0.9 miles) east of Montreuil. On 9 June the headquarters of the 3rd Brigade, 2nd Division was established in the *Mairie* (Town Hall) at Domptin.

Outside of Montreuil is where the infantry of the 2nd Division, hot and exhausted, but high spirited despite their forced march of twenty-four hours, took up their positions during the afternoon of 1 June 1918. The Marine Brigade went to the north side of the main road and the Brigade of Regulars on the south side.

They reported this road crowded, and in some places, blocked with French civilians and troops endeavoring to get out of the way of the German advance.

Montreuil billeted many thousands of American reserve troops who were going into the Marne salient during the 1918 fighting.

IN THEIR OWN WORDS

The following report was written during the occupation of Germany in 1919, and by W. A. Mitchell, Colonel, Engineers. The report, from *Records of the Second Division (Regular)* states, in part:

36. That it may be of record, it is desired to state the conditions that prevailed in the village of MONTREUIL-aux-LIONS at the time of its occupancy by the 2d Engineers.

The *Mairie*, Montreuil-aux-Lions. Headquarters 2d Div., June 1, 1918. During morning of same day headquarters of Fourth Brigade of Marines was established in this town also for half an hour in an automobile.

The town hall today

ANTI AIRCRAFT BATTERY IN ACTION
Men of the Second Division, near Montreuil aux Lions

A gun of Battery B, 1st Anti-Aircraft Bn, 2nd Division, in action at Montreuil-aux-Lions, June 15, 1918.

This regiment arrived in the town of MONTREUIL-aux-LIONS on June 1, just at the time when the last civilian population was making a hasty departure, thinking that the enemy might continue his advance and capture the town.

All homes were left unguarded and very little furniture or other private property was carried away by the owners. In one building in particular, a great quantity of wine was stored.

The officer assigned to the headquarters of the 2d Engineers and a small detail of enlisted men were billeted in this town, and were among the first American troops to be stationed there.

An inspection was made of the various houses that had been abandoned, with a view to occupying them as billets. In numerous cases, the houses had been entered by troops other than Americans, and literally wrecked. Furniture was broken; glassware smashed; trunks and bureaus ransacked and their contents scattered all over the house; small articles of value were presumably stolen; chickens, cows, sheep, rabbits, etc., were confiscated and other stores, such as wines and edibles, were carried away; conditions in general were deplorable and shameful.

The American troops were not responsible for the above conditions.

Dean L. Robertson, 79th Company, 6th Marines relates in his diary how he continued his journey from Meaux:

This was Sat. the 8th of June, and about noon trucks came and took us towards the front, to the town of Montrilielaux-Lions[sic], where we stopped and rested for a short while. We were also given ammunition until every man had two hundred and twenty rounds. Towards evening we pushed on towards the front. We were in two single files, one on either side of the road, with a wide interval between men, this being the way troops always moved when close to the front. This lessens the chance for observation and keeps down casualties.

Lt Elliot D. Cooke, continues his narrative of marching toward the front lines in early June, 1918. In his article, *"We Can Take It,"* Cooke says:

A halt was called and we fell to the ground like dead men. Trucks rolled up and some iron rations were issued—canned meat and French war bread. A stream ran beside the road and medical personnel put up signs saying the water was not potable. The men used the signs to kneel on while filling their canteens. Beck and I sent our orderlies down to do the same for us. We had to eat, and war bread and corned beef wouldn't go down without water.

The respite was short and again we started marching, but no longer on a course parallel to the main German drive. This time we were moving east—

going straight to meet the Boche. Not to encounter the shadowy beings of trench raids and night patrols, but the German storm troops, real fighters. And we would come together in the open, in the light of day, where Americans liked to fight. Heads went up and the swing of cadence returned to the marching.

A month later we were to come back over that same road-hard, hollow-eyed veterans, leaving hundreds of our buddies behind us, scattered through the wheat fields of Lucy, in the cellars of Bouresches, and beneath the underbrush of Belleau Wood. But that Saturday evening we eagerly marched up the hill to Montreuil-aux-Lions, anxious to show the world that we were the equals of the best German-shock troops ever born.

We passed French soldiers going to the rear, on the roads and in the fields, the backwash of an army in retreat. Some turned their heads away, others saluted us disparagingly, while a few even shouted "Fini la guerre," and waved for us to go back. They had small faith in our ability to stop the Germans. Well, we had plenty of doubts about theirs, too.

In Montreuil more men in blue uniforms were, from all appearances, looting and pillaging the homes of their countrymen. We looked askance, for the rules of war specify that looters shall be shot. But the conduct of the poilus was no affair of ours, even if they did make it look like a bad day for France.

In George G. Strott's book, *The Medical Department of the U.S. Navy with the Army and Marine Corps in France,* comes the following excerpt from, "Journal of an Unidentified Battalion Surgeon":

1 June (0330): Started toward Montreul au Lyons [sic]—all men eager. Hiked until 1300, moving 55 minutes and resting 5, covering 26 kilometers. Little rations—excessive heat. Detachments of French Chasseurs met along the road, tired and worn. Poured their red wine (pinard) and gave it to the grateful marines as they passed. Altogether the command went along in good condition. The few who fell out caught up with the main body as it reached the heights east of this town. Rations issued with 2 days reserve. Each man kept his issue intact.

Pvt Leo J. Bailey, 9th Infantry, 2nd Division, wrote in his diary:

The regiment halted in the abandoned town of Montreuil-aux-Lions in the early afternoon of June 1, and word was passed to forage liberally—for the first time since Sherman gave the word to his Georgia bummers. Cider, wine, and brandy were in many abandoned shops, and the 9th Infantry had a brief carouse before resuming the march, inebriated comics in some squads now caparisoned in corsets, lace-trimmed drawers, and large organdy hats. Bailey carried a live chicken

American Doughboy

Anti-aircraft defense at Montreal-aux-Lyons, 2nd Division headquarters during assault on Belleau Wood. July 8, 1918

with trussed legs, and a buddy had a large iron cookpot. Bailey had been unable to raid a kitchen garden for a chicken stew, being barred by a poilu sentry who was saving it for his general. 'Tell the general,' said the doughboy, congenial after so much hard cider, 'that I'll take the house next door.' The battalion turned again and soon was single file in a patch of woods. The German was ahead and coming on. It was June second before the regiment found itself on the fighting line.

Martin Gulberg, a marine in the Marine Brigade, wrote in his war diary:

> At Montreal-aux-Lions we unloaded. Refugees were pouring down the road going west. It was a most pitiful sight. There were old women, old men and babies, all wandering like lost souls in a chaos of confusion. Everything and everybody seemed to be in a hurry to get away from the battle line, except a few marines. It was about six A.M. when we arrived in Montreal-aux-Lyons. We stayed here until 1:00 P.M., and had the time of our lives feasting. The inhabitants had left a few hours before we came and we fell heir to everything they could not carry with them. The French officers told us to help ourselves to anything we wanted, because the Germans would get everything eventually. I heard one of the boys remarked, 'Gee, that Frog officer ain't got much confidence in us, had he?' We visited the wine cellars and helped ourselves to the choicest wines; raided rabbit and chicken coops and feasted royally. We didn't leave much for Fritz in case he should get through. I was sitting near the road devouring my fried rabbit, when I heard a commotion down the way. It was a marine coming down the road yelling, 'Pork Chops,' with a squealing pig under his arm. In the line of march that day one could see dressed rabbits and chickens slung over many knapsacks. But it was excess baggage, for a lot of them never got a chance to eat their prizes.

William Scanlon, a marine in the 2nd Division, wrote the following fictional account in his novel *God Have Mercy on Us*:

> When we got to Montreuil-aux-Lions, we unloaded from the camions and watched them drive off. We were assigned to billets in barns and told that we had better turn in and get some rest. But we were too excited and curious to go to sleep. From the looks of the town the people must have left it in a hurry. We had a fine time rooting around. We rummaged the houses over from cellar to garret. We found wine and cider and were warned not to eat or drink anything we found for fear of poison. We took a chance. Nobody got poisoned.
>
> It was after twelve o'clock noon before we began to turn in. Some of the fellows went to sleep in the beds in the houses instead of the straw in the barns. I had just about got to sleep when the whistles began to blow and orders were

shouted around to dress and fall in at once. We had been told that we were to rest until evening and it was now one-thirty. But we didn't belly-ache very much. Something must be doing at last. We fell in and marched out of town, toward the northeast.

It was at the edge of this town, Montreuil-aux-Lions, that we began to meet French soldiers. And they said the war was over. Most of them carried packs, but few of them had rifles, and those that did have rifles were throwing them away.

After passing the first bunch of French soldiers, we were shoved over to the side of the road to let a string of camions go through us. They were loaded with soldiers dressed like us in regular army uniforms without any distinguishing marks, and as they went by we yelled at them, "What outfit?"

And they said, "First Battalion, Sixth Marines."

The camions with the First Battalion had passed on and we were running into more French. Some were on horses and we tried to wise crack them, but they did not pay any attention to us. Another French soldier came along on foot, slowly. His coat sleeve was cut off and his arm was bandaged. The bandage was red. "Wonder what happened to that guy."

"He must have been cleaning his rifle and didn't know it was loaded."

AEF combat artist Harry E. Townsend wrote in his war diary:

We are only a few kilometers here from the action that is taking place on the road that leads out past Ferme de Paris to Chateau-Thierry. The division headquarters are at Montreuil-aux-Lions where we are going to report. The roads here are alive with all sorts of activity. The country on either side of the roads is filled with French reserve troops, infantry and cavalry. Ammunition trucks come and go, and one hears at all times the roar of the artillery on ahead.

We soon come to the evacuation hospital which is unloading ambulances as fast as they arrive. We meet them coming. There is a large well-guarded ammunition dump farther on. Trucks here are busy loading and officers and clerks are busy pegging typewriters here and there.

As we arrive at HQ, a lone German prisoner is being brought in looking as tho he really believed he was to be killed soon, as they are taught by their officers. This one was quite a young boy, and seemed so scared. We were told that many had been brought in earlier in the morning.

We reported, and were soon on our way up the road to where the batteries were.

Editor's note: The older French farms, built during the Middle Ages, served not only as working farms, but as veritable fortresses to which local residents would retreat in times of invasion or of other dangers. Being square or rectangular in shape, they have

Infantry of the 4th Division with their German prisoners near Montreuil, 22 July 1918

Men of the 2d Division, including the 4th Brigade of Marines, wounded in the operations northwest of Château-Thierry, arriving at 15th Field Hospital near Montreuil-aux-Lions, June 7, 1918.

Photos of BEF cemetery, Montreuil-aux-Lions

very thick and strong walls of stone. The living quarters are on one side of the four sides of a square court, and the barns and cattle sheds on the other three. These farms make admirable forts because of their heavy stone construction. They also have deep wine cellars and underground storage areas. Most of the farms had a big pile of manure in the center of the courtyard, and a well in the center of the pile.

The French farm thus became a self-contained entity, with everything the peasants needed: a well for water, ample food and numerous farm animals. The people living inside the farm could withstand a siege, if it became necessary for them to do so.

Looking at one of these farms today, one can well understand why they saw extensive use in military capacities. They were utilized as headquarters, command-posts, first-aid stations, hospitals, and as fortifications by both the Germans and the Franco-American forces. Although usually few and spaced far apart, the farms were easily recognizable from afar on the level land of the Marne salient. If a wounded soldier was told to walk "down the road to the big, white farm building," he and his buddies would easily find the site of an aid station or field hospital.

Aid stations were established preferably in cellars of farm buildings, but if these were not available they were opened at suitable locations under stone culverts, in dry watercourses, or in small, shallow excavations.

Even if the above-ground structures suffered destruction, or severe damage, the underground vaults, wine cellars and basements would survive to be used for military purposes. If there were enough of these sturdily-built farms in a battle area, they could be used as retreats for an entire garrison during a bombardment.

It is unfortunate today that many of the old farms are derelict and badly in need or repair. Most of the farms and their associated dwellings were already several hundred years old when used by the soldiers of World War I. Some of the farm houses are now so decayed that French authorities will no longer allow them to be used as dwellings and they have been simply abandoned and left for time to take its eventual toll. Others become victims of development in the form of high-speed transit lines and widening of highways. It appears as if it will not be very long at all before many of these once magnificent farms will no longer exist.

MONTREUIL-AUX-LIONS BRITISH CEMETERY

Just after leaving Montreuil, and on the right, is a British Commonwealth military cemetery containing the graves of 139 men of the original BEF who died near here in September 1914 during the retreat from Mons and through this area. The large cross erected therein is that of St. George. An inscription behind this cross of sacrifice records eight men of the 1st Battalion Dorsetshire Regiment who were killed on 9 September and who are known to be buried in this cemetery.

The cemetery was made after the Armistice by the concentration of graves from the battlefields of the Aisne. There are now over 150 soldiers from 1914–1918 and a small number of 1939–45 war casualties commemorated in this site. Of these, over half from the 1914–18 War are unidentified and the names of 16 soldiers known or believed to be buried among them, are recorded on special memorials (in the case of eight men of the 1st Dorset the special memorial is a panel behind the cross of sacrifice.) The cemetery covers an area of 154 square metres and is enclosed by a low rubble wall.

Stop and visit this cemetery. Please feel free to read the comments written in the cemetery visitors book and to enter therein your own remarks.

VENTELET FARM

Ventelet Farm is 1 km south on D-84, and on the left side of the road.

The 3rd Brigade, U.S. 2nd Division established its headquarters at Ventelet Farm on 1 June 1918. Ambulance Company No. 16 established a brigade dressing station here, just off the Paris–Metz Road. This location enabled the walking wounded to obtain first-aid on the same road which they had taken when they had gone into action. The wounded would naturally follow the same route out of the fighting. Military police, stationed at the intersection of D-3 and D-84 directed the walking wounded southward to the dressing station and to the field hospital.

In serving the walking cases the Ventelet Farm station much relieved the congestion in the overcrowded battalion aid-stations. It also reduced considerably the number of wounded requiring treatment at Field Hospital No. 1 at Bézu-le-Guery, farther to the south along this same road.

BÉZU-LE-GUERY

Bézu-le-Guery is about 2 km ESE of Montreuil-aux-Lions. To visit this village, turn south on N-3 at its intersection with D-84, the Marigny to Bèzu-le-Guery Road.

During the 1918 fighting, Bézu was anywhere from one to eight kilometers behind the battalion aid stations, and at all times beyond the enemy artillery zone.

The church, the village school, and tentage at Bézu were part of a triage and field hospital for the non-transportable wounded established there by Field Hospital No. 1. Patients were removed by regimental and ambulance company litter bearers from battalion and regimental aid stations to ambulance posts, and thence to the triage at Bézu-le-Guery, where gassed cases were bathed and re-clothed before being sent to Field Hospitals Nos.15 and 16, at Luzancy, whither also the seriously wounded were sent. In

At the first crossroad beyond the British monument, turn left on the RUE DE COND 600 meters farther on, turn left again, crossing the MARNE RIVER.

Continue on N-3 in the direction of MONTREUIL-AUX-LIONS.

Ventelet Farm — Three different views

The barn where the German prisoners were questioned

caring for the gassed cases, Field Hospital No.1 bathed, treated, and dressed them at the rate of 100 an hour. On July 18, the first day of the Allied offensive, 1648 wounded passed through the triage at Bézu-le-Guéry.

Ambulance Company No. 1 had moved to Bézu-le-Guéry on June 1 and established liaison with the front but on June 2 it moved to Vendrest, where it established a dressing station at a place then occupied by a battalion aid station on the 23rd Infantry. On June 4 it returned to Bézu-le-Guery, and there remained during the rest of its stay in this sector.

Ambulance Company No. 23 began operating an ambulance post at Meaux on June 1, but the next day, leaving four ambulances to serve the 23rd Field Hospital, it moved to Bézu-le-Guery, where it remained until the U.S. 2nd Division was relieved. At this point it operated in conjunction with Ambulance Company No. 1.

At Bézu-le-Guery, Ambulance Companies Nos.101 and 102 were stationed. Bézu Wood also concealed the kitchens and wagon trains of the 26th Division.

The ambulance head was established at Bézu-le-Guery on June 3 and all ambulances were pooled for service directly under the orders of the director of ambulance companies.

Location of the triage here also facilitated coordination and conservation of the ambulance service, both to forward points and to the rear. During attacks in which ambulances were insufficient for rapid evacuation of all wounded, all trucks of the sanitary train were utilized, and if these did not suffice trucks from the supply train were called for.

United States Army Ambulance Section No. 502, with 20 Ford ambulances, arrived June 4, and working from the ambulance park at Bézu-le-Guery, evacuated from battalion and regimental aid stations, thus relieving the larger General Motors Company ambulances from the longer run to the rear.

The little building in Bézu which held all of the amputated arms and legs as described next, and in the fictional setting of William Scanlon's *God Have Mercy on Us!* is located at the southwest end of town, along the road to Nanteuil-sur-Marne. It is the last little building as you leave Bézu, on the left side of the road.

IN THEIR OWN WORDS

William Scanlon, a marine who was there, wrote as follows in his fictional novel, *God Have Mercy on Us:*

The next morning we fell in and hiked to the town of Bézu-le-Guéry. Up on a hill outside this town we took up reserve positions in rear of an American division. We dug a complete system of trenches, north, along a road leading up to Ventelet Farm.

We had regular positions assigned to us which we were to occupy in case the Germans broke through the line up ahead. Every time a barrage was turned loose, we would drop whatever we were doing, grab our rifles and belts, and rush to our positions.

There was a large hospital in the town of Bézu-le-Guéry and they had a small canteen just for the accommodation of convalescent soldiers. They wouldn't sell to outside outfits such as ours.

It opened at certain hours to sell stuff—cigarettes, chewing, candles, cookies. We tried to buy things at this canteen several times and couldn't, so then we doped out a system. The men that had been wounded would go limping around on canes or with bandaged arms and heads. We borrowed canes or used our first-aid kits to bandage up our arms or heads and then we limped over to the canteen window and bought whatever we wanted.

Three or four of us were walking along the road just outside of town—the main road leading in from the southwest. We noticed a stone building at the left and one of the fellows ran down and looked in a window. He hollered for us to come down. We went down and looked in. It was more than half full of arms and legs. They covered the whole area up to the windows. Some had leggings on and some were bare. There were arms from the wrist up to the shoulders. Some legs had blue leggings on, but more had khaki. They were dumped there from the hospital.

In Alexander Woolcott's book, *A Friendly Guide for American Pilgrims to the Shrines Between the Marne and the Vesle:*

> Then go on to Bézu-le-Guéry, and, as you peek into the church and the village school, remember that they once constituted the buildings of an overflowing field hospital, carpeted, all through June with the undiscouraged, grinning wounded, brought back by the ambulances from the fight just up the road.

LtCol Richard Derby, Division Surgeon, U.S. 2nd Division, AEF describes his visit to Field Hospital One, Bézu-le-Guéry on 1 June 1918:

> My first duty on reaching Montreuil was to visit Field Hospital One at Bézu-le-Guéry.
>
> Bézu was situated in almost the exact center of the sector which we were holding, and was easily accessible by good roads from almost any point of the front. It was an ideal location for the triage, or sorting station, and for the general supervision of the medical activities of the front area.
>
> Bézu was a village of not more than fifty buildings, placed on the heights to the north of the Marne, built about one winding street. At the extreme northern end was a small church with a two-story school house adjoining. These two buildings were taken over by the hospital and served a most useful purpose during the five weeks that the Division fought on this front.

"The little house that was full up to the level of the second story window with arms and legs that had been amputated in the nearby field hospital at Bézu-le-Guery."

The school and church at Bézu-le-Guery

The schoolroom was high-ceilinged, with one wall a black-board. It was a room of ghosts. Under date of May twenty-ninth, still stood the composition lesson of that day. *Un jour de grand vent.* It must have been more than a day of great wind to the children attending that last class; truly a day of much alarm, borne on the wings of a great Hun advance. Under the caption, *La Pensée* the lesson went on: *L'homme libre obeit a sa conscience et aux lois de son pays.* Almost in the presence of the enemy, the children of France were being taught the righteousness of their fathers' cause. Then came a column of words, the last word unfinished. The lesson had been interrupted.

As I gazed upon the room I saw again the figures of the little children leaning over their desks and writing industriously in their copy-books. I saw the teacher pouring her soul into the sentences on the board. I heard the approach of a horse. He was reined up at the door. The loud knock, followed by the appearance of a French soldier, who told of the oncoming enemy hordes, counseling immediate flight. Something else told me that flight was dignified, not precipitate; that the children were reminded that it was ennobling to suffer *pour la France*, and that the interrupted lesson would be continued *apres la victoire.*

Field Hospital One had installed itself in the church and schoolroom. The pews and desks had been removed and given place to litter racks, each with its blanket draped litter. A portion of the schoolroom had been partitioned off by means of blankets in to a resuscitation ward where the heat from several primus stoves was conserved to the maximum. The remainder of the schoolroom was arranged as a dressing room for the seriously wounded. In the courtyard a tent had been erected in which men exposed to mustard gas could be undressed preparatory to their bath in a small concrete chamber adjoining. Here one of the portable shower baths always carried by this hospital, had been set up, and was supplied with water by pump from an adjacent well. Another small tent adjoining afforded a dressing room, and was kept well supplied with pyjamas, underclothing, socks, and towels. Under a shed in the corner was piled the men's discarded equipment, which was removed daily by a salvage truck. The church was used as a temporary refuge for the slightly gassed and wounded while awaiting evacuation farther to the rear.

The interior presented a weird and somber picture. The whole floor space, except for three aisles running the length of the church, was filled with blanketed figures lying upon stretchers. The church was lit by candles upon the altar and pulpit railing. The chancel was occupied entirely by prisoner wounded, placed there for the ostensible purpose of guarding against their escape. This refinement in their security was hardly necessary judging from the serious nature of their wounds.

Seated on a bench against one of the side walls was a long row of slightly wounded men, along which passed a medical officer followed by an assistant with a tray of syringes. Each man received an injection of antitetanic serum, and as a witness of the fact a broad T was marked by means of an iodine swab upon his forehead. Captain Evans, the C.O. of the field hospital, was passing up and down the aisles, designating the men to be loaded on the waiting ambulances.

From the book *Iodine and Gasoline, a History of the 117th Sanitary Train* by Josiah C. Chatfield, et al:

July 25th was moving day for all the hospitals. Oregon's [the origin state of the medical unit] destination was Bézu-le-Guéry, Aisne. It was only a few hours' ride from Luzancy, but the road they planned to follow had been mined and they were forced to travel several times the original distance on a detour, arriving in the small hours of the night. Upon their arrival, however, they assumed charge of a hospital operated by a 26th Division unit in the village church, and stretching their tentage to use as a gas hospital, and went to bed after daybreak to await developments. They were thus the first hospital to function on the Chateau-Thierry front.

Floyd Gibbons, a correspondent for *The Chicago Tribune*, was gravely wounded at Belleau Wood, 6 June 1918. Here is an excerpt from his book, *And They Thought We Wouldn't Fight*, in which he writes a vivid description of the 1st Field Hospital at Bézu-le-Guéry.

Floyd Gibbons was an intrepid young newspaperman who, in the days of the Mexican Revolution, in the face of Pancho Villa's decree that any gringos found in Mexico would be killed on sight, not only rode straight into Mexico alone, but accompanied Villa through three major battles and became the first correspondent to bring authoritative news of the revolution out of Mexico. It was this same intrepidity which, in February 1917, helped Gibbons to survive the sinking of the *Laconia* by German torpedoes two hundred miles off the Irish coast and which, on the 6th of June, in the following year, caused him to be present in the first-wave assault on Belleau Wood, immediately at the side of Major John Berry who was leading the attack. Both Berry and Gibbons were hit, but whereas Berry was able to regain his feet and continue into the wood, Gibbons was more severely hurt. The first two bullets tore into his shoulder and arm, but it was the third which nearly finished him. He was on the ground when it hit, and glanced off a rock, penetrated his left eye from below, and ripped out through his forehead.

Astonishingly, Gibbons never lost consciousness and was later able to record his experience in detail, as well as to relate the little he was able to see and hear of the battle around him. For three hours he lay in the wheatfield in front of Belleau Wood, pinned

Bézu-le-Guery—the church today

Interior of school room showing the blackboard

Modern view of the interior of the Church at Bézu-le-Guery, France, used as a ward for the wounded by Field Hospital No. 1, 2nd Division, June 16, 1918. Compare this photo with the one on page 125 opposite.

down by intense machine gun fire until, under cover of darkness, and assisted by fellow correspondent Lt. Oscar Hartzell, he first crawled for some twenty minutes into a small wood, and then walked and stumbled for about a mile to a small relief dugout where he received his first medical attention. Unfortunately, due to a total absence of water, the corpsman was unable to clean Gibbon's wounds, and he had no choice but to continue on, still helped by Hartzell, for another half mile or so until they came to the edge of another wooded area where they found a number of wounded men lying about with a few corpsmen working among them. There were shells flying overhead, some exploding nearby, but the work continued as though it were quiet. Gibbons lay flat out on the ground and rested until a corpsman came by to look him over. He lifted the dressing from Gibbon's eye and simply put it back again, they cleaned and dressed his other two wounds.

There was a severe scarcity of ambulances, so rather than simply lie untreated on the ground, Gibbons decided it would be better to keep walking. Lt. Hartzell walked slightly in front of him and to the side, providing a kind of platform for Gibbon's wounded arm with his shoulder. In this manner they continued on, with the German shells still occasionally dropping around them, until a small American ambulance, brimming with wounded and steaming and sputtering from its radiator cap, came up slowly behind them, picking its way over the rough and pitch-black road.

When apprised of Gibbon's condition, in spite of being already badly overloaded, they managed to squeeze him into the front seat. Ten miles later, after an interminable, jolting, and excruciating ride, the destination was reached: the little church in Bézu-le-Guéry which served as a clearing station. It is at this point in the story that we take up the narrative in Gibbons own words:

…The clearing station was located in an old church on the outskirts of a little village. Four times during this war the flow and ebb of battle had passed about this old edifice. Hartzell half carried me off the ambulance seat and into the church. As I felt my feet scrape on the flag-stoned flooring underneath the Gothic entrance arch, I opened my right eye for a painful survey of the interior.

The walls, gray with age, appeared yellow in the light of the candles and lanterns that were used for illumination. Blankets, and bits of canvas and carpet had been tacked over the apertures where once stained glass windows and huge oaken doors had been. These precautions were necessary to prevent the lights from shining outside the building and betraying our location to the hospital-loving eyes of German bombing planes whose motors we could hear even at that minute, humming in the black sky above us.

Our American wounded were lying on stretchers all over the floor. Near the door, where I entered, a number of pews had been pushed to one side and on these our walking wounded were seated. They were smoking cigarettes and talking and passing observations on every fresh case that came through the door. They all seemed to be looking at me. My appearance must have been sufficient to have shocked them. I was hatless and my hair was matted with blood. The red-stained bandage around my forehead and extending down over my left cheek did not hide the rest of my face, which was unwashed, and consequently red with fresh blood.

On my left side I was completely bare from the shoulder to the waist with the exception of the strips of white-cloth about my arm and shoulder. My chest was splashed with red from the two body wounds. Such was my entrance. I must have looked somewhat gruesome because I happened to catch and involuntary shudder as it passed over the face of one of my observers among the walking wounded and I heard him remark to the man next to him: 'My God, look what they're bringing in.'

Hartzell placed me on a stretcher on the floor and went for water, which I sorely needed. I heard someone stop beside my stretcher and bend over me, while a kindly voice said: "Would you like a cigarette old man?" "Yes," I replied. He lighted me one in his own lips and placed it in my mouth. I wanted to know my benefactor. I asked him for his name and organization. "I am not a soldier," he said; "I am a non-combatant, the same as you. My name is Slater and I'm from the Y.M.C.A." The cigarette tasted mighty good. If you who read this are one of those whose contributions to the Y.M.C.A. made that distribution possible, I wish to herewith express to you my gratefulness and the gratefulness of the other men who enjoyed your generosity that night.

In front of what had been the altar of the church, there had been erected a rudely constructed operation table. The table was surrounded with a tall candelabrum of brass and gilded wood. These ornate accessories had been removed from the altar for the purpose of providing better light for the surgeons who busied themselves about the table in their long gowns of white, stained with red.

I was placed on that table for an examination and I heard a peculiar conversation going on about me. One doctor said, "We haven't any more of it." Then the other doctor said, "But I thought we had plenty." The first voice replied, "Yes, but we didn't expect so many wounded. We have used up all we had." Then the second voice said, "Well, we certainly need it now. I don't know what we are going to do without it."

From their further conversation I learned that the subject under discussion was anti-tetanus serum—the all important inoculation that prevents lockjaw

Floyd Gibbons, a correspondent for *The Chicago Tribune*

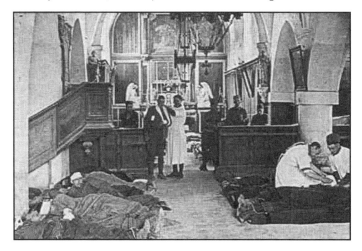

Church at Bézu-le-Guery, France, used as a ward for the wounded by Field Hospital No. 1, 2nd Division, June 16, 1918

GENEVROIS FARM

15925

Premier Clemenceau congratulates the Americans
On June 30, 1918, Clemenceau visited the front in order to congratulate the American leaders. MajGen Omar Bundy, commanding the Second Division, stands next to Clemenceau (with cane), and Gen Degoutte of the French Army. Col. Edward L. King, later commander of the 65th Brigade, 33rd Division is third from the left end.

Château-Thierry, June 30, 1918

Genevrois Farm—the modern view

and is also an antidote for the germs of gas gangrene. You may be sure I became more than mildly interested in the absence of this valuable boon, but there was nothing I could say that would help the case, so I remained quiet. In several minutes my composure was rewarded. I heard hurried footsteps across the flagstone flooring and a minute later felt a steel needle penetrating my abdomen. Then a cheery voice said: "It's all right now, we've got plenty of it. We've just got piles of it. The Red Cross just shot it out from Paris in limousines."

After the injection Hartzell informed me that the doctors could do nothing for me at that place and that I was to be moved farther to the rear. He said ambulances were scarce but he had found a place for me in a returning ammunition truck. I was carried out of the church and somewhere in the outer darkness was lifted up into the body of the truck and laid down on some straw in the bottom. There were some fifteen or twenty other men lying there beside me.

A long and severely jolting ride through the night was to be Gibbon's lot until, shortly after dawn, he would arrive at the U. S. Military Base Hospital at Neuilly-sur-Seine on the outskirts of Paris where the surgeon's knife and the anesthesiologist's mask were awaiting him.

GENEVROIS FARM

Genevrois Farm is near Bézu-le-Guéry (3 km SE of Montreuil-aux-Lions). The farm was 2nd Division Headquarters, 10 June to 10 July 1918; 26th Division Headquarters, 10–15 July and on 20 July 1918.

IN THEIR OWN WORDS

From Alexander Woolcott's book, *A Friendly Guide For American Pilgrims to the Shrines Between the Marne and the Vesle*:

Before you turn back to Chateau-Thierry, walk down the byway from Bézu-le-Guéry to the fine old rambling house of the Genevrois Farm, so peaceful and prosperous that it seems impossible that war ever reached its gates. But remember that its well-stocked tool-shed was a pen for German prisoners, that its long stable, where the cows now munch contentedly, was once a thing of telephones and maps and colonels. Pause contemplate the aromatic manure pile in the court-yard, for it was present during all our occupation, left there heroically lest the winged cameras of the German air fleets should note its removal and suspect the whereabouts of the precious staff.

Here is an excerpt from Alexander Woolcott's book, *The Command is Forward—Tales of the A.E.F. Battlefields* as they appeared in the *Stars and Stripes:*

The tourist was almost sure to miss the sleepy old farmhouse just outside of Bézu-le-Guéry, where the headquarters of the Second Division was established during the period of the Belleau Wood fighting. Time was when no car could approach the spot, and the vast, aromatic manure pile was heroically left undisturbed lest its sudden disappearance should hint something to the photographers of the enemy air-fleet. At the end of summer the pile was miraculously still undisturbed. The tool-shed, which once served as a witness-box for the long procession of German prisoners, reopened for business as a tool shed, and the old army telephone exchange was packed with newly garnered grain. The long stable, once crowded with maps and fire-eating colonels and the like, is now again crowded with bovine pacifists—a long row of them, placidly chewing their cuds.

Mme Bellanger, mistress of the farm has nothing left to recall the American invasion except her uplifting memory of having had four generals at once in her spare room, and her rueful recollection that, although the Americans had sworn to her the enemy would never reach her farm, she lost heart in the nervous first fortnight of July and sold all her livestock to some Parisian robbers of her acquaintance.

From *Circuits of Victory*, by A. Lincoln Lavine:

Lieutenant Price, who had been dispatched on a motor-cycle on the night of the alert to locate and stay with the Signal Officer of the 26th Division, was having his troubles.

"You may find the Major," he had been told, "in a little town called Mery, but if he is not there, try Genevrois Farm." Driving Price was a young daredevil named Magill. Two others, Giles and Halgren, also of the 406th, accompanied them on another motor-cycle with bedding and rations for the group. It was essential to the American advance that the Signal Officer of the 26th Division be located, in order that no hitch should occur in maintaining communications with his ever-moving telephone headquarters.

Squirming, turning, twisting and shooting in and out through congested and almost impossible roads—sometimes, indeed, leaving the road to make it—these men finally located Mery and Genevrois, only to find that they were scarcely more than mere names, had been shelled almost out of existence, and were totally uninhabited.

LA LOGE FARM

Photo credit: Where the Marines fought in France, Antrim, 1919

La Loge Farm—On June 4, 1918 the Fourth Brigade of Marines changed its headquarters to La Loge Farm.

La Loge Farm—Now. Notice how the barn roof evidently has not been repaired since the war.

Modern view of the interior courtyard

BrigGen Harbord (right) and Col Marius McCloskey (left) questioning a German prisoner at La Loge Farm, June 12, 1918. By this time, Gen Harbord had been adopted by the Marines. Note the Marine collar device that had been conferred by Col Neville.

"It seemed to me the seal of approval by my comrades in the Marine Corps," wrote Gen Harbord later, "knowing the circumstances it meant everything to me."

LA LOGE FARM

About 2 km farther on N-3 and off on a track to the left, is La Loge Farm. This farm still holds the old house from which MajGen Harbord directed the operations of the Fourth Brigade, 2nd Division, June, 1918. MajGen Harbord moved his headquarters here from Issonges Farm, as Issonges was in too exposed a position.

The 3rd Battalion, 5th Marines, less two companies, was stationed at La Loge Farm as Corps Reserve on 1 June. Gen Michel, commander of the 43rd French Division had his headquarters at La Loge Farm about 1 June 1918.

About 8 July 1918, the 52nd Brigade, 26th Division established its headquarters at La Loge Farm.

In August 1918 Battery B, 305th Field Artillery Brigade, U. S. 77th Division was briefly billeted at La Loge Farm.

IN THEIR OWN WORDS

In Alexander Woolcott's, *A Friendly Guide For American Pilgrims to the Shrines Between the Marne and the Vesle*:

> La Loge Farm holds the old house whence General Harbord directed the operations of the Marine Brigade. There, too, by the way, the Twelfth Field Artillery had its home—one of the regiments of guns which raced across country for that battle and, when it reached it, strung out any old way in the open fields where, without waiting for shelter or nice adjustment, the gunners went to it and fired for seventy hours without pause for food, drink or sleep.

In an address before the Detroit Bond Club in February, 1928, MajGen Harbord said, in part:

> My headquarters were established at Yssonge [sic] a house with a red roof, on a little hill, which proved so attractive to shells that three days later I took over La Loge Farm, vacated by the French General when his troops withdrew on June 4th. We were then responsible for what happened on that front, though served under French Corps and Army Command for our entire stay in the neighborhood.

According to MajGen James G. Harbord, in his book, *The American Army in France:*

> To me personally the first effect of the withdrawal of our Allies from our front was the vacating by the French Division Commander of La Loge Farm, which he had occupied as Headquarters. I left Yssonge [sic] and promptly moved to La Loge. It was a small farmhouse about three hundred yards north

of the Paris-Metz highway, much less conspicuous than Yssonge and equally convenient. It was to be my house and office until the 5th of July, when I turned it over to General Charles H. Cole of the 26th Division.

We were very chary about evening lights at La Loge, for they attracted shell fire. There was no embargo on noise, however. Colonel McCloskey's 12th Field Artillery was the artillery support of the Marine Brigade as long as I was commanding it. His headquarters were at La Loge with mine, and nearly every evening a group of us sat around in the half-light and listened to each other, and to the rumble of the guns.

When prisoners were sent back they were usually lined up in he stable-yard which dominated the scene at La Loge, and were questioned and looked over before being sent to the rear. When our first hundred prisoners were brought in, I went out to inspect them. They were rather down-in-the-mouth, and more or less mussed up. I stopped in front of an undersized Prussian officer who wore the Iron Cross. It was the first one I had seen at close range, and I examined it with some curiosity while he glared at me. Prisoners of war, of course, are entitled to retain their decorations and articles of a personal nature. I completed my inspection, returned to my office and the prisoners were marched away.

A few minutes later there was a knock at my door, and in came a smiling Marine Sergeant. He saluted with great formality, and held out an Iron Cross to me. I looked him in the eye and his smile broadened. I recall that he wore a long bayonet at his belt. What he said was: "Sir, that officer who was wearin' this cross hopes the General will accept it."

What could I do? The prisoners were gone. The cross was still there on the table. The Sergeant looked honest. I have always had some doubts as to the spontaneity of the gift.

During my stay at La Loge I had for office a small, very narrow room, behind a room used by us for telephones. A small table served as a desk, and a set of bookshelves of worn volumes stood against the wall within easy reach. Sometimes when there was mail I shoved the letters in between the nearest books, until able to dispose of them. In 1922, four years later, I visited La Loge with my wife. The peasant farmer's wife who knew it had been my Headquarters brought out a letter which she had found between the books, forgotten there when the Brigade left. It was a letter from my wife, written from Washington on June 6th, saying among other things: "The morning papers say the Marines are doing fine work." The farmer's wife had no idea from whom the letter had come, and not knowing the lady with me that morning rather surreptitiously handed the letter to me, remarking that in four years she had never shown it to anyone. The lady was moved to say that it was fortunate it happened to be from my wife.

LA LOGE FARM

Dugout at the La Loge Farm, used as a shelter from artillery fire.

Col. McCloskey supervises the construction of a dugout at La Loge farm to be used as Marine and Artillery headquarters during the operations at Belleau Wood.

Dugout at the La Loge Farm at the time. The caption reads: Col McCloskey supervises the construction of a dugout at La Loge Farm to be used as Marine and Artillery headquarters during the operations at Belleau Wood.

ISSONGES FARM

Issonges Farm–then, with benches in front (top)

courtyard view

Issonges Farm–now

ISSONGES FARM

About 0.5 km after La Loge Farm, and 1 km to the left on D-84, is Issonges Farm. The Fourth Marine Brigade set up at Issonges Farm at 4:45 P.M., 1 June, having held forth from the Brigadier's automobile during the day. BgGen Harbord, Commander of the Marine Brigade, did not stay long at Issonges Farm. Two days after he established his headquarters there, a large-caliber shell landed in the courtyard, killing several horses and wounding two men. That same day he packed up and moved south to a more isolated farmhouse called La Loge.

The battalion aid station of the 101st Artillery, 26th Division was set up at Issonges Farm.

IN THEIR OWN WORDS

In an address before the Detroit Bond Club in 1928, MajGen Harbord said:

> My headquarters were established at Yssonge Farm, a house with a red roof, on a little hill, which proved so attractive to shells that three days later I took over La Loge Farm, vacated by the French General when his troops withdrew on June 4th.

PARIS FARM

About 4.5 km after leaving Montreuil-aux-Lions, at the intersection of D-11 with N-3, look to your left just before crossing the D-11. The large group of farm buildings seen there is the very old farm Paris Farm, at the crossroad leading to Marigny. Once a post for horses, it was already existing in 1750.

The farm was several miles in the rear of the battle line during June and July, and it suffered frequent bombardments by German heavy artillery. Paris Farm was an exposed crossing, subjected to observation by German "sausage" balloons (so called because of their shape) and airplanes. Despite this hazard, the farm had to be necessarily passed day and night by ammunition trains and troops. The lines had to be supplied while the fighting was in progress and the National Road (N-3) passing beside the farm was a critical supply route. The direction of travel by the Americans was on N-3 seen to your front, and from your rear (west) to front (east) on the road.

Immediately after the Allied offensive of 18 July, Paris Farm became an aid station for the care of gassed and wounded men. Like La Maison Blanche (the White House), a short distance down the road, Paris Farm was an easily recognizable feature on the landscape. The wounded would be told to "look for the large farm at the crossroads," or "the large white house beside the road."

In 1997, portions of Paris Farm were being torn down. The reason for the demolition is unknown at this date of writing, but it is very probable that Paris Farm is suffering from the same ailment as do many of the farms, old age and decrepitude. There is also the distinct possibility of the N-3 being widened, in which case Paris Farm could completely disappear.

IN THEIR OWN WORDS

Raymond Wunderlich, 101st Engineer Regiment, 26th Division, wrote in his book, *From Trench and Dugout:*

> One night the call came for us to go up to Paris Farms, I think it was, to dig support trenches. Companies D,E and F were details to do the job. We went up in motor trucks, about thirty men to each truck. F Company had hard luck that night. On the way up a shell struck their tool wagon, demolishing it. They arrived without picks and shovels and could not do any work. Over across the rolling hills about a thousand yards away, were the enemy trenches. We couldn't see them for the low hills intervened, but the flares lit up the sky-line. I know it couldn't have been more than a thousand yards because that is the range limit for one pounders, and they were dropping around us pretty regular. Company E, our company, began digging across the top of a hill. F Company was placed down the hillside in ravine. The Germans began dropping shells into that ravine and the boys had a miserable time of it. Being without tools, they had to dig themselves in with their bayonets and mess kit covers. They lost several men. Frits also hurled mustard gas at them, and many of the boys were frightfully burned.

> After we had finished our work on the hill, F Company came up and took the shelter which we had just dug, and we went out into the open again. Towards morning we expected the Germans to come over and make an attack as they had been shelling us continuously, but they didn't come. Just before daybreak we started back. Our way lay across an open field, and there we had to run the gauntlet. The Germans started shelling the field, and we had to dash across in little groups.

From *Circuits of Victory,* by A. Lincoln Lavine:

> One line of twisted pair wire was run from Montreuil-aux-Lions (Headquarters 2nd Division) to Ferme de Paris. Here a telephone exchange was opened to serve as forward information point, lines being extended therefrom to the Brigade Headquarters on either flank, (the 3rd Brigade, including the 9th and 23rd Infantry, and the 4th Brigade, including the 5th and 6th Marines). The next day a telephone operator at this board, Pvt. First Class Andrew Casey, asked permission to move the switchboard outside the building, which had been hit twice by shells. The board was taken into the open field 100 yards away.

THE PARIS FARM

From the West

From the East

If you so desire, *carefully* pull over from N-3 and park on the road shoulder in the vicinity of the farm and read the vivid descriptions of Paris Farm as it was during the hot summer of 1918. If you do not feel like stopping at this time, we will be returning to Paris Farm a little later on in this tour.

A note of caution—The intersection of N-3 with D-11 is the scene of frequent accidents. N-3 is a very high speed road and automobiles seen at a distance will come up on you very rapidly because of the speed at which they are travelling, usually much faster than the maximum allowed by law. Allow more than ample time when pulling onto or off the N-3 roadway.

The Paris Farm

The Courtyard (top and middle)–It is unknown if the state of physical deterioration is due to the effects of wartime shelling, natural aging, or perhaps even deliberate demolition.

The main farmhouse

LA MAISON BLANCHE (THE WHITE HOUSE)

One kilometer past Paris Farm on N-3 the roadway begins to bend to the right. On the left side of the road is La Maison Blanche (The White House). La Maison Blanche was the Command Post of 3/6, June, 1918. After the start of the Allied offensive of 18 July, La Maison Blanche became an aid station for the care of gassed and wounded men. It is said that some marines were buried in the garden of the house. In 1997 La Maison Blanche was derelict and abandoned. The old house faces extinction because it lies between N-3 and A-4 highways and there is talk of expanding both roads.

Directly to the right of and beside La Maison Blanche is the small patch of woods in which the men of 3/6 sheltered themselves while the officers lived in the house. These woods still contain the old foxholes of the marines and, even today, many of the household implements which they 'liberated' from the big, white house can still be found in this wooded area. Please respect this area which is still private property and do not rummage around in the wood beside the house.

At La Maison Blanche there was a very old and very beautiful cedar tree which was there for at least 250 years. The tree was marked on a map dated 1750, a time when La Maison Blanche did not exist. The name of the old tree was Arbre Gobart, like the name of the small stream which flows down from this area, near Lucy-le-Bocage and on to Belleau Wood. The tree no longer exists.

La Maison Blanche was also called "White Farm," and "Blanche Farm."

IN THEIR OWN WORDS

Col Albertus Catlin, commander of the Sixth Marines, wrote the following selection in his book, *With the Help of God and a Few Marines*:

> I established by first Post of Command [P.C.] in a corner of the woods near Lucy-le-Bocage, but this soon proved to be too exposed a position as German shells began to burst in the neighborhood, and on June 2nd I moved by P.C. over to La Voie du Chatel, a little village west of Lucy and south of Champillon. Later on, however, when the line was shortened, I moved again still farther south to the wooded cover of Mont Blanche, and Colonel Neville of the Fifth moved to my old P.C.
>
> It was on the 5th that, owing to the likelihood of early action, I moved my P.C. again, leaving Mont Blanche and returning to the neighborhood of Lucy. By this move to an apparently more dangerous location it is probable that my life was saved, for a German shell reduced to a heap of ruins the room I had occupied at Blanche Farm very soon after I vacated it.

Pvt William A. Carter, a marine, remembers that the troops were just falling asleep at Montreuil-aux-Lions where they were bivouacked on the hill side along the road. From his book, *The Tale of a Devildog*:

> We were ordered to re-roll our packs and march further on, about five kilometers, to a place called White Farm. Some of us slept here in barn lofts and others in the woods nearby.

If you pull off N-3 and onto the road shoulder to look at La Maison Blanche, do so very carefully while driving eastward.

LA MAISON BLANCHE

La Maison Blanche, 6th Regimental P.C., June 1918

Photo: Where the Marines Fought in France, Antrim, 1919

Plaque on the entrance gate to Maison Blanche

La Maison Blanche–Now

Continue on N-3, entering CHÂTEAU-THIERRY on the AVENUE DE PARIS.

Pass through the traffic circle at "PLACE A. BRIAND" and on to the AVENUE JULES LEFEBVRE.

Keep straight on and pass the traffic light intersection at the AVENUE DE SOISSONS.

Just after passing the AVENUE DE SOISSONS you will see a large parking lot on your left.

Go into this lot from AVENUE JULES LEFEBVRE and park your automobile.

If you have gone to or past the main bridge over the Marne River, or as far as Brasles, then you have gone too far. Turn around and return in the opposite direction on Avenue Jules Lefebvre. From the parking lot you can ascertain the location of your hotel.

A PAUSE IN YOUR TOUR

You have so far looked at several monuments, one national military cemetery, and observed a few other sites of interest on your way to Château-Thierry. At this point you are advised to continue to Château-Thierry, obtain your lodgings, rest for the night and take the walking tour of Château-Thierry the next day.

Having read in this book about the AEF and Allied sites behind the battle-lines from the airport to Château-Thierry, in the next and last section you will read about the Franco-American defense of, and take a detailed tour, of Château-Thierry, a town well-known to several hundred thousand American soldiers of World War I. You will also see and visit the sites where the men of the U.S. 3rd Division fought to defend Château-Thierry.

The interior of Regimental Headquarters, J. Andre Smith

VIEW OF CHATEAU THIERRY AND THE FAMOUS BRIDGE WHERE THE MARINE (DEVIL DOGS) STOPPED THE HUN HORDES ON THEIR MARCH ON PARIS.

NO. 102-F

THE BRIDGE AT CHATEAU-THIERRY

CROQUIS DE GUERRE par FRANÇOIS FLAMENG.

SECTION THREE

CHÂTEAU-THIERRY

Thru the night winds wet and dreary,
Word goes on to Château-Thierry,
Ghostly Phantoms hear the call—
Gather those who gave their all

From Phantoms,
Pvt L. C. McCollum, American Expeditionary Forces, 1918

THERE'S A GIRL IN CHATEAU THIERRY

Words by E. Ray Goetz. Music by Melville Gideon. Published 1919: Leo Feist Inc., New York, NY.

One September I'll remember,
Never to forget. Battle weary Chateau Thierry,
That was where we met,
'Mong the ruins I still can see,
Suzette smiling out on me,
Somehow it just had to be,
This love that bids me tell you:

Chorus 1: [repeat after each verse]

There's a girl in Chateau-Thierry,
A girl who waits for me.
There's a weary heart made cheery,
By love and victory.
And her buddy boy's devotion,
Burns a trail across the ocean,
To Chateau-Thierry, where she waits for me.

There's a girl in Chateau-Thierry,
A girl who waits for me.
There's a weary heart made cheery,
By love and victory.
And her buddy boy's devotion,
Burns a trail across the ocean,
To Chateau-Thierry, where she waits for me across the sea.

Cherie, Cherie, I'm so very
Sad here over the sea,
Battle weary Chateau-Thierry,
Seems much brighter to me,
Loved ones ask on ev'ry hand,
Why I'm sad in Yankee land,
Maybe they would understand
If I could only tell them:

CHÂTEAU-THIERRY AND THE U.S. 3RD DIVISION

CHÂTEAU-THIERRY

Château-Thierry, once only a small village on the Marne River, 55 miles from Paris, will stay forever a name for Americans to conjure. Suddenly, in the late spring of 1918, the name blazed up in the world press as a beacon for everyone to see. Château-Thierry, where American soldier footsteps turned in 1918, is indelibly written into the pages of American World War I military history. To Château-Thierry American footsteps will always turn. The town is remembered for the struggle of May–July, 1918, when the splendid defense of the French and American armies barred the road to Paris. Château-Thierry saw many a young soldier fall, French, British, German and American.

Château-Thierry is a little town so picturesque that its smiling aspect has tempted many a traveler to break his journey on the way from Paris to Epernay. Dominated on the north by the ruined towers of its ancient castle, the town lies closely nestled in a valley, between the wooded sides of which winds the River Marne. Approaching from the east the Marne bends sharply upon passing the town, as if to avoid a bare knoll known as Hill 204, which bars its direct course to the west. At no point more than 70 meters wide, the river is too deep to be forded. The Marne meanders through a lovely valley walled in by two parallel ranges of hills. East of the town the crests of these lie about two kilometers apart, a narrow plain stretching along the base of the hills on the southern bank. South of the town the valley expands to a greater breadth. The valley slopes ascend from the northern banks of the Marne to a plateau about 500 feet above the river.

Château-Thierry, with a normal pre-war population of about 8,000 inhabitants in 1914, is still an attractive town of stone buildings whose principal streets, each rising terrace-like above the other, parallel the stream. Below the edge of the plateau, the ancient Château, with crenellated and bastioned walls, rears itself above the trees and gardens which surround it. From the old castle, a wonderful panorama of hills, ridges, valleys, rivers, towns, villages and hamlets is seen. Along the main boulevard at the level of the river there are many lovely houses with walled gardens. Château-Thierry was once the home of the poet and writer of fables, Jean de la Fontaine.

This ancient city, scarred with the memories of a hundred wars, had its origin in a Gallo-Roman village known as Otmus. The name of the town comes from the castle on a hill on the northern side of the Marne River. Legend says that Charles Martel built

3RD DIVISION INSIGNIA

View of Château-Thierry from Hill 204 by E. Piexotto

Aerial view of Château-Thierry in August 1918. In this sector the American 3rd Division immortalized themselves in the defense of the Marne. The wrecked stone bridge was repaired by American engineers. The two new pontoon bridges under construction are clearly shown.

the castle in 720 AD as a prison for King Thierry II. Martel's victory over the Saracens had given him control of the region. Château-Thierry was afterwards held by the counts of Champagne.

The King of the Franks, Thierry IV (d.1737) used the castle as a residence. Captured by English archers, Spanish troops and earlier Prussian hordes in the sundry sieges of which the city has been the target, the castle of today lies in ruins.

There are four roads that go out from Château-Thierry: one up the north bank of the Marne, one to Soissons, one to Fere-en-Tardenois, and one to La Ferté and Paris. The position of the city, however, explains its long history, for it has ever stood as a citadel in the path of the endless succession of invasions aimed at Paris.

Leaving the Marne at La Ferté-sous-Jouarre, 16 miles southwest of Château-Thierry, an important national highway forms a chord to the bend which the river makes between those points. The road passes to the north of Hill 204, then crosses the Marne River at Château-Thierry. Thence it follows the southern bank of the Marne to Épernay and Chalons. A main line of railway also follows the southern bank of the river, connecting Meaux, la Ferté-sous-Jouarre, Château-Thierry, and Épernay. Branch lines connect Château-Thierry with Soissons, about 30 miles to the north, and with Montmirail, about half that distance to the south.

War had come to Château-Thierry many times over the centuries. Normans, Danes, the English, and pillaging bands all took their turn at spreading destruction and terror in the vicinity. Destroyed by the Huns in the 5th century, captured by the English in 1421, by Charles V in 1544, and by the Leaguers in 1591 and again pillaged in 1652 during the War of the Fronde, Château-Thierry's sufferings were not yet at an end. In 1814 Napoleon bombarded the city when he defeated the Russians and Prussians under Blücher in this neighborhood. The city would again suffer during the two World Wars of the 20th Century.

The Germans held Château-Thierry for a few days in early September, 1914, during the first battle of the Marne. On 9 September 1914, when the Allies began to advance, the I Corps of the British Expeditionary Forces (BEF) crossed the Marne here and moved north to Fere-en-Tardenois.

After the first battle of the Marne, Château-Thierry remained far behind the lines and in Allied hands until the German advance in May of 1918. Breaking through Allied lines on the Chemin des Dames in their offensive of 27 May 1918, the Germans drove the French rapidly southward. On 30 May the French rear-guard reached Château-Thierry. On the following day, German Gen Max von Boehn's vanguard entered the town. The Germans thoroughly sacked the town in the following weeks.

For the second time in its history, this little town on the banks of the Marne occupied the attention of the civilized world. The second battle of the Marne was in progress, the Germans were making their last and most desperate thrust at Paris. Château-Thierry became the apex battle-point of a very large salient that the Germans had driven into the French lines. From this apex, thrust into the town of Château-Thierry itself, the battle lines drew sharply back, north west for 21 miles to Soissons and north east for 30 miles to Reims, forming the western and eastern faces of the gigantic triangle known as the Marne salient.

Château-Thierry is a railway junction of considerable importance in the Marne system of communications. It was very important to prevent the enemy from occupying the town.

Divided into two sections by the river Marne passing through it, with three bridges spanning the stream, Château-Thierry constituted the key-point of the Marne barrier against the German advance toward Paris. It was extremely vital to hold the bridgeheads from the enemy. If Château-Thierry held, it would present a front on which to shatter the German spearhead.

At Château-Thierry, and in the surrounding area, the fresh young fighting men from America halted the most successful offensive that the Germans launched during the war. The Americans saved Paris and received credit for it from a world in arms.

Eight U.S. Divisions of the American Expeditionary Forces (AEF) got their baptism of fire in this region during June and July of 1918. And, all proved that the American soldier was second to none.

Rushed up from their training area in half-ton Ford motor trucks the 7th Motorized Machine Gun Battalion of the U.S. 3rd Division met the retiring French in the town and took up positions on the northern riverbank. Here they fought off the Germans for two days and then were withdrawn to the south bank by the French who then blew up the town's bridges. From that time on the Marne became the dividing line between the opposing forces. Neither side attempted to cross the river in Château-Thierry until the Germans evacuated the town on July 19–20 as a result of the Allied attacks to the east and west of it.

Château-Thierry became the tip of a large battlefield when American machine gunners met the Germans in its streets on the last day of May, 1918. From its streets, on the night that May turned into June, the word went forth that American soldiers had jumped into the fight to block the German drive. Here, in June of 1918, in front of this provincial city nestled in the bend of the Marne, the raw American Army stopped Ludendorff's lunge for Paris.

Château-Thierry itself saw only a few days of active fighting, but a few miles east and west of it and to the north occurred some of the most bitter struggles of the war. The 2nd U.S. Division fought bitter actions just outside of Château-Thierry in the area of Belleau Wood, Bouresches and Vaux in June, 1918. Particularly ferocious was the 20-day long struggle between the Marine Brigade and the Germans for control of Belleau Wood. The 3rd U.S. Division fought tenaciously in the area of the Jaulgonne Bend of the Marne, to the east of the city. Despite many attacks the allied line held. The morale

Officer's Mess in the cellar of a house in Château-Thierry, 7 June 1918

A frying pan used by the Germans as a gas alarm in Château-Thierry.

Smithsonian Institution

A Battery of French 75's shelling the Germans on the Ridge to the left of Château-Thierry. W. J. Duncan, June, 1918.

of the Allies went up to a point where they could again take up the offensive, never to relinquish it. Thus, Château-Thierry is sometimes alluded to as the "Gettysburg of Europe." On 21 July 1918, U.S. Divisions pushed forward into the wooded hills north of the Château-Thierry.

Original orders had it that the Americans would take Château-Thierry, but the French had requested that the honor of taking the city be given them. The French took Château-Thierry on 21 July 1918, the Americans advancing with them on both sides of the city.

Either when entering the battle area or when leaving it, most of the 310,000 U.S. soldiers engaged in this great battle passed through Château-Thierry. Most of the 67,000 American casualties during their battles within the Marne salient left from the railroad station in Château-Thierry to be transported to hospitals in the rear areas.

To the American soldiers, therefore, their battles in the Marne salient of 1918 would forever bear the name of "The Battle of Château-Thierry." The doughboys got into the habit of calling the entire campaign that of "Château-Thierry." Thus the city would forever bear the name of the great offensive through which they had just passed. Although officially known as "The Aisne-Marne Offensive," in the American soldiers vernacular it was most likely to be "The Battle of Chatto Teary," "Chatoo Terry," "Chatty Terry," or some other variant name.

Those American soldiers who were in Château-Thierry during the stormy days of June, July and August recalled many scenes of needless, wanton destruction. The Germans forced open and ransacked almost every house. They even scarred many beautiful pieces of ancient furniture with their battle cry: "Gott mit uns!" The Germans missed sacking the rock-cellars, which were old, when Napoleon visited them. The cellars, with their millions of bottles, lie beneath the Faubourg de la Folie where stand the sumptuous houses of the rich vine growers whose names such as Chandon and Périer, are of worldwide solace.

Oddly enough, this center of a genial commerce just escaped the worst of the war. During the German occupation of Château-Thierry, the Americans and the French preferred to spare the town. Evidently the Germans had the same idea after they evacuated Château-Thierry, as German aerial bombing caused most of the damage in town. Château-Thierry, although hit by a number of randomly thrown artillery shells from both sides, was spared the prolonged bombardments which could have easily destroyed the town.

Château-Thierry is remembered by the doughboys of the American 1st, 2nd, 3rd, 4th, 26th, 28th, 32nd, 42nd and 77th Divisions that fought to clear the Germans from the Marne salient of 1918. Frequent mention of the town is made in American military unit histories and in other literature that describes the fighting in the Marne salient.

The soldiers remember the town as being the central point of operations from which they either entered or departed from the Marne salient. They remember it as being the town to which they returned for whatever brief rest periods it was possible to give the troops. Thousands of doughboys were never too tired to walk around the city whenever presented with even a brief opportunity to do so.

Most of the American soldiers who passed through Château-Thierry were full of fun. Many of them would get hold of high hats, derbies, colored parasols, and a lot of other foolish things in the town. The next morning they would march or drive along wearing silk hats and carrying parasols and wearing ladies underwear, as their own had long ago worn out!

The name of Château-Thierry, more than any other French town, will always stands out in American World War I history. Château-Thierry will always be an American shrine in France—not the old Marne City alone or chiefly, but rather the American battlefields which surround the city. Château-Thierry still occupies a major position large in our national military traditions for it was there that our military forces first participated in a great battle and first figured in a large offensive.

IN THEIR OWN WORDS

Col Robert H. C. Kelton, General Staff, U.S.A., wrote "The Miracle of Château-Thierry," *Century Magazine*, May, 1919:

> Château-Thierry was an emergency; it had no part whatsoever in the plans prepared by the general staff of the American Expeditionary Forces or in the original French scheme for the entry of the American forces upon the Western Front.
>
> The result of the German attack on the morning of May 27th was a rude and startling surprise to the Allied headquarters. In four days, or on the evening of May 30th, the leading elements of the German troops were at Château-Thierry, and on the following day the Boche stated in his communique, "We Stand on the Marne." No greater measure of self-satisfaction was ever reflected in his pompous announcements than this.
>
> But on the same fourth day at Château-Thierry the German troops found a small American fighting unit, the 7th Machine Gun Battalion of the 3rd U.S. Division, which had come a distance of 110 miles in 30 hours by motor transport, and the Boche failed to cross the Marne.
>
> For 72 hours the 7th Machine Gun Battalion successfully contested the crossing, and by the second day of June the 3rd U.S. Division was in position along the river from Château-Thierry to the east for a distance of 12 miles....it signified the fact that the tide of military fortune had turned at that point, and that we had taken the measure of the Boche, and were no longer anxious as to the final result.

American soldiers in Château-Thierry.
After the battle, the remains of the German barricade on Bridge Street (Rue du Pont).

Smithsonian Institute

A Franco-American conference in a wine cellar of Château-Thierry. May, 1918.

George Harding, AEF

German bombardment of Château-Thierry, 7 June 1918.
The Germans are shelling the town, where several buildings are
burning. The main part of the fighting is in the ridge to the left.

Claggett Wilson

Stragglers. French wounded in the retreat from Château-Thierry.

From the *New York Times Current History Magazine*, October, 1916 by Gabriel Alphaud,
"The Desecrated Birthplace of La Fontaine":

La Fontaine, the famous French writer of fables, was born at Château-Thierry, and his birthplace is still reverently preserved by the State as a shrine.

In the Elysian Fields, whither it has gone to join the souls of other vanished sages, the shade of La Fontaine must feel some inquietude. He did not love children, not even his own, whom he saluted one day in a crowd without recognizing them. "Youth is without pity," he wrote of them. Now the school children of the Aisne have been driven by the German invasion as far as Château-Thierry, where they are living today in the house where the philosopher prolonged the reveries he had begun in the highways and meadows of the neighborhood.

Against the façade of the house, with its softened tones of age, the crime of treason against beauty had been committed before the war: back of the grille of forged ironwork, and in the inner court, a horrible whitewash, insolent in its whiteness, covered the panels of the walls. It is in the apartments themselves that a new upheaval—has just taken place. The picture of Desbrosses, of L'hermite, of Teniers, of Vithoos, the drawings of Daubigny, relics of La Fontaine's birthplace, which had been transformed into a municipal museum, have been removed. School mottoes and geography maps have replaced them: in the halls and rooms now are found classes of boys and girls. The shade of La Fontaine is compelled to desert the precipitous streets, paved with loose cobblestones, and to descend to the banks where the Marne, peaceful and beautiful, flows between two paths of fine sand.

Never, indeed, has the Marne seemed more graceful, or flowed in an atmosphere more simple. Its recent immortality, the noise made in the world by the victory that has rendered it famous, has not altered its habits: in its new glory it seems to have acquired a new indifference, an indifference to battle, to cannon.

Not far from it, however, the great guns of the warring nations still mingle their wild voices day and night. These voices were heard by Château-Thierry and the Marne for the first time on Aug. 31, 1914. It was the retreat. On the 2d of September, in the afternoon, the enemy entered the town by the Soissons road. With their rifles on their shoulders, in columns by eights, and keeping parade step, the regiments of Von Kluck filed in and stacked their arms in Champ de Mars square [now the Place des Etats Unis, the municipal parking lot] on the right bank of the river. Their patrols were stationed on the crossings and streets in every direction on both sides of the bridges. After a lively combat the soldiers who formed our rearguard had cut their way out with rifle and bayonet, and had disappeared.

An order was given by Prussian authority to occupy and barricade the principal houses. On the public square the Court Houses was immediately invaded. In the hall where President Magnaud had once decreed as a "good Judge" the acquittal of the poor woman who had stolen bread, the Prussians put everything to pillage. The clerk's records, torn, shredded, honeycombed, served to build improvised loopholes at the windows and doors.

On the other side of the river, facing the Court House, lies a beautiful estate. The buildings of the north wing are used as a factory. Those of the south wing have been transformed into a château of sumptuous appearance. Between the two a park spreads the foliage of its magnificent forest trees, hiding the factory from the château. The Prussian command chose the château as the headquarters of its General Staff, and from the first hour announced—already!—its intention of seizing the important stocks of copper in the factory.

The estate had been left in charge of two old servants, Hector and his wife Fanny, who has a blue-ribbon reputation as a cook. Hector received the German officers who first appeared. They spoke French without the slightest accent. They knew the inhabitants and contents of the house, the names of the two domestics, even the fact that Fanny cooked certain dishes divinely, especially rabbit a la royale. The news that she had remained, with the affirmation that she would prepare appetizing meals on condition that the estate be not molested, put the German officers into a good humor.

A last quick inquiry, made in a tone of apparent indifference, sought to discover whether the stocks of copper were still there. This was enough to cause the wily Hector to invent diplomatic stratagems each day, with a view to making von Kluck's officers forget the supplies which they coveted. The fare was exquisite, the best wines came from the cellars for every meal, old liqueurs and choice cigars were lavished upon the guests. Chance also favored Hector. Through the edges of the battle of the Marne the German offices went and came and went again, giving the place to others and taking it back by turns. On the 9th of September, after seven whole days of occupation, General von Kluck suddenly gave the order for his army to retreat toward the north. The copper was saved.

A piquant detail: When von Kluck's order reached Château-Thierry it was about noon. A fat Prussian General quartered in the château was preparing to sit down at the table and enjoy a juicy beefsteak which Fanny had declared to be unusually good. Though he sprang to the saddle on receiving the order, he demanded that Hector serve the steak to him as he sat on horseback; and as events moved swiftly, the General, in order not to lose a mouthful, seized the enormous slice of meat, all hot and sticky with sauce, carried it in his right hand, and with

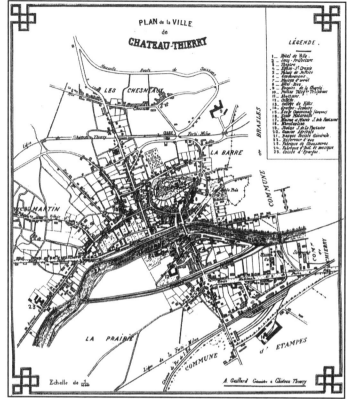

Château-Thierry in 1913 — Plan de Ville.

A dead German soldier near Château-Thierry, 21 July 1918.

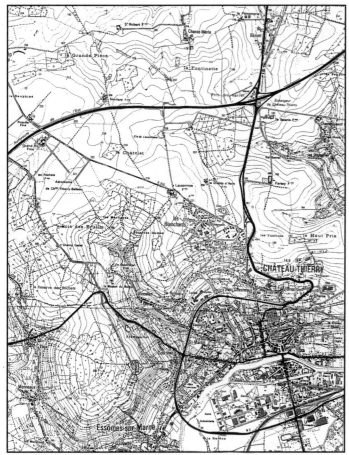
Map of the Château-Thierry vicinity.

his left gave the reins to his beast for flight. He was wise in his Teutonic gluttony, too, for six other German officers who were at a table a few paces away in the Swan Hotel, and who refused to believe in the victorious return of the French, were made prisoner in the turn of a hand by two little "glaziers." One of them fired on the group from the rear court, which opens on the street. The bullet went through the wall and carved a beautiful spider's web in the dining room mirror, at the center of which it still remains in full sight. "Surrender!" cried the chasseur, as he leapt over the threshold; and the six German officers, seeing a second French military cap appear behind the first, surrendered.

The city of la Fontaine was freed, but not all the Department of the Aisne. Out of 37 cantons, barely 11 were to regain their liberties and the joys of their native land. Today out of 841 communities only 265 have escaped German occupation. Of the 550,000 inhabitants who lived in this department before the war, 125,000 now occupy the soil on which they were born and welcomed. Many have taken refuge in other provinces, notably in those of Yonne, Loiret, Orne, and Aude. There are 12,000 in Paris. About 15,000, civil and military, are prisoners in Germany, where their number is diminishing daily, thanks to the work of repatriation. Few remained on this side of the German lines: the frontier populations particularly detest the invader.

Château-Thierry, a sub-prefecture of 7,000 inhabitants, might have kept this number; but after the victory of the Marne the report spread of a second victory on the Aisne. Those who had fled before the enemy believed their whole department liberated, and flowed back, impelled by love of the earth, by devotion to their buried dead, by the passion of their grief's and hopes. The firing line stopped them. They refused to depart again, intoxicated again by the odor of their native soil, plunging their gaze beyond the horizon to the belfry or village, to the cherished field or house where they had known the happiness of home. Thus, Château-Thierry and the liberated cantons saw their population doubled.

In the town itself, where most of the houses had been left uninjured, it was relatively easy to reorganize a normal life. It was less easy, however, in the hamlets and farming communities, where the peasants, despoiled of everything by the soldiers of von Kluck, no longer had linen, furniture, or food. From all over France came help for these. Prefects and Sub-Prefects might be seen in their silver-embroidered uniforms and gold-laced caps, transporting, now in rude wagons, now in luxurious automobiles, great sacks of supplies for the ruined villages. Everybody was shouting at once in more than 200 communes: Food, more food, still more food! It seemed as if it would never be possible to satisfy them. Salt, which caused so many insurrections in the ancient days of the salt tax, was lacking everywhere: it had never before seemed so indispensable. Then it was clothes and bedding. In each community there were episodes of rare beauty. At Epieds three women who were still sucking their infants took refuge. Under their weight of misery and hunger they had crept into a muddy shed and were sleeping on a pile of dirty straw. A poor old woman of 80, wrinkled and broken, found them there and called the attention of the officials to their plight. By way of example, she returned a quarter of an hour later carrying in her trembling hands a woolen comforter which she had brought, with the slow steps of an old woman, from her home.

"The Germans have robbed me of everything," she said, "but I still have this. I already have one foot in the grave, and am perhaps more accustomed to suffering. Give it to them, monsieur, for the babies."

Two years have passed over these miseries. In the freed territory life has returned, and acts of devotion have multiplied. Soissons is under shell fire. Of 14,000 inhabitants, scarcely 400 have remained, among whom are a baker who fills his ovens daily, two grocers, a butcher who sells fish, wine, preserves, and one photographer.

The capital of the Aisne today is Château-Thierry. In its Town Hall are assembled all the administrative services of the department. Nor do all the provisions come from Paris. The fields sown by the peasants of the Aisne furnish anew their tribute, in which is found once more the savory perfume of the soil of the Ile-de-France. From the Marne to the Aisne there is not a corner left fallow.

The families scattered by the war are gradually reuniting. In the evening, "between dog and wolf," at the hour when light vapors rise from the river and spread along the lanes like a protecting and favoring veil, it is not rare to see the girls and young men of the neighborhood going arm in arm to gay betrothal parties. Some of the men, decorated with the War Cross, have undergone glorious amputations; their love is all the livelier on that account; in their arms the girls seem more beautiful, and all are laughter. The couples flee under the foliage of the fine trees, far from the populous section where stands the statue of the fabulist. Yet he would not be the one to say unkind things to them if he were living. La Fontaine described himself as "a light thing," lovable and loving, lively and delicate, whom a pretty face, a prepossessing manner, a fresh laugh, a floating lock of hair, a white hand carelessly arranging the fold of a gown, have always rendered glamorous and dreamy. His frivolity, his skepticism, his indulgence would bestow upon the romantic couples only the happiest of smiles.

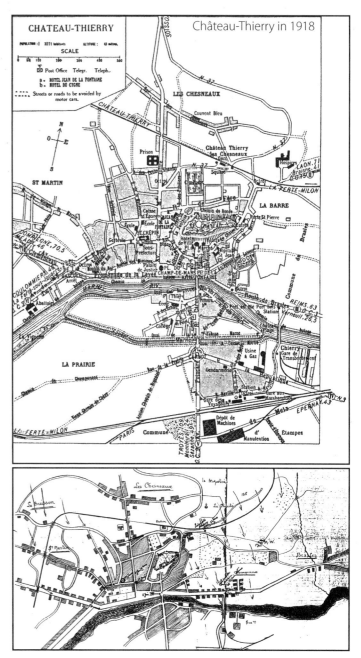

French map showing direction (arrows) of German attack on Château-Thierry.

Halt For A Rest
Men of the 111th Infantry on their way through Château-Thierry
on the afternoon of 21 July 1918.

Hotel de la Giraffe — then, above and now, below

H. A. Gibbons wrote an article, "An Ancient Village on the Marne" in *Harper's Magazine*, April 16, 1916. Shortly after this article was written Château-Thierry saw for the third time in a hundred years the German helmets. It was occupied for several days by the German Army and suffered from the cannon of both armies in the battle of the Marne.

We went through Essomes with hardly a look at its abbey church. For night, we thought, was not as far distant as Château-Thierry, and we had set our hearts upon entering the gateway to Champagne before sunset.

The towns were nearer together than we anticipated. Just beyond Essomes the Marne makes one of its every-kilometer bends. As we hurried along the tow-path, Château-Thierry, hidden by a railway bridge until we had passes beneath its span, stood suddenly before us. Quaint houses in rows at cow-path angles crowded down to the water's edge on both sides of the river. They were joined by a stone bridge of three arches. The towers of Saint Crépin and Balhan rose above the jumble of roofs awry. Dominating the city, the crumbling ramparts of the castle made a frame of striking severity for graceful clusters of trees, whose summer foliage showed dark against the Mont de Chesneaux in the background. We were in Champagne.

The hotels of Château-Thierry are fittingly named after animals. For Château-Thierry is the birthplace of La Fontaine. The prices at the "Giraffe" were so alluring to us that we gave no thought to the more pretentious "Elephant" and "Swan" and "Deer." We had no misgivings. In cheap hotels one sometimes runs a risk in the matter of beds; but good cooking is generally easier to find in France at five francs a day than at twenty-five. *Vive la cuisine bourgoise!*

What matters it, then, if you have hot water in your room by the gill and beer on your table by the quart, if you are afraid to put out your russet shoes for a shine because you are morally certain that the establishment possesses only one brush, and that a black one, if sunrise brings through your window the usual barn-yard chorus reinforced by teamsters' oaths and the stamping of horses.

The "Giraffe" is between the tow-path and the Paris road, just outside the octroi [tollhouse], the road from Paris becomes an avenue of stately elms, in four rows. At the end of the avenue, a statue stands out in sharp relief against a background of closely interlaced lime-trees. This is Château-Thierry's memorial to La Fontaine. The first thing you see in Château-Thierry is this statue, and in your rambles through the town you are never one moment allowed to forget the fact that La Fontaine was born here. The principal café, the principal quai, the principal street bear his name.

"Aux grands hommes la patrie reconnaissante." The inscription over the Panthéon is indicative of the attitude of French cities toward their famous

children. We Americans lack the perspective of those who count history by centuries where we have difficulty in mentally spanning decades. It is not that the French live in the past, but that they are able to recognize the category of imperishable achievement. If Pittsburgh were in France, one would hear less of the forty-odd "steel kings" and more of Stephen Foster and Ethelbert Nevin. Château-Thierry, for its size, shows unmistakable evidences of wealth and prosperity. On the other side of the river is a large factory, kindly sheltered by luxurious hedges and rows of tall poplars, in which the larger part of the population of the town is employed. But we did not hear the manufacturer's name, nor did we see it on the town library or hospital.

The Artist was up early in the morning. I know it must have been early, for he was fully dressed and rummaging in his sack when I opened my eyes at eight o'clock. All day on the tow-path gives long sleep to a city man.

After coffee, we started for Saint Crépin, intending to go from there directly to the citadel. But two gamins, with light hair and blue eyes and freckles, reminiscent of unmixed Frankish ancestors, hailed us. They knew better what we wanted than we did. No excuses were allowed. We were evidently strangers. We were evidently out to see the sights. Ergo, we must first be led to the house where La Fontaine was born. In vain we explained that we had no birthplace. Their eyes opened wide with incredulity. They saw only a stratagem to shake them and save a pourboire [tip]. The evident remonstrance in their "Mais, Messieurs" put us in the wrong. We were forced to justify ourselves. We pointed to the fleeting sun and spoke of the glorious view that could be seen now from the hill, and might be lacking later. No use! To La Fontaine's birthplace we had to go.

In the courtyard of the Hôtel Swan the upper rooms from whose casements one looks out over the lovely landscape to Champagne, from some remote cell came the lines:

La cigale, ayant chantée
Tout l'été,
Se trouvait fort dépourvue
Quand la bise fut venue.
Pas un morceau
Dublé ou de vermisseau…

Rare is the skill of writing for childhood, and the choice spirits who have possessed it hold high rank among the immortals. Their fame is as universal as it is imperishable. The audience is the same the world over. It does not change in taste and sympathies as do succeeding generations of "grown-ups." I have

An impromptu concert by members of the Pennsylvania National Guard amongst the ruins of Château-Thierry, France. 24 July 1918.

Trench and barricade used as Machine Gun Position by Germans in Street of Château-Thierry. Château-Thierry, France, 24 July 1918.

A dining room at 26 rue St. Martin

Refugees returning home to Château-Thierry, 10 August 1918.

found the Thousand and One Nights as successful for a rainy day in Idaho as in Constantinople. Mother Goose, Cinderella, Little Red Riding Hood, The Tortoise and the Hare, Br'er Rabbit, Alladin, Ali Baba, Alice in Wonderland, and Sleeping Beauty—are they not written on the tablets of early Mesopotamia? They must be! For the themes of stories for children are world-old.

Translators are damned by the criticism that their work, however fine, is not creative. It is really Chapman's Homer or a certain sonnet that makes us know who Chapman was? But, La Fontaine is esteemed none the less because there was an Aesop before him. In fairy-tales, folklore, and fables the gift is not in the subject matter, but in the telling. He strikes a chord of understanding in the child heart who peoples the world with imaginary folk and makes the animals talk. Yet, one could easier deceive a master financier or the shrewdest buyer among the merchant princes than an ordinary child. To children miracles need no explanation, for the supernatural is not super. The world of make-believe is real. It exists. How ridiculous, and at the same time how much to be pitied, are the people who gravely discuss the ethical side of the Santa Claus legend every time Christmas comes around. "For shame!" We cry the moment they begin to argue. And we are very sorry for their children. Imagination is the salt of life. Without it the world has no savor.

La Fontaine's naivéte, his irresponsibility, his effervescence, his quickly varying moods made possible the fables. That he could write the Contes, tales of shameless licentiousness, that he could lead a life of idleness excess, and yet be neither a worthless nor a vicious man, is explainable only by the hypothesis that he never grew up. He thought as a child and saw as a child. How else could he have been able to place before millions of children the picture of Mr. Crow seated on a branch of a tree, holding in his claws a bit of cheese, while Mr. Fox, watering at the mouth, looked up slyly from below? I saw that tree—also the curve of Mr. Fox's tongue, the flash in his eye, the smiling beak of Mr. Crow, and the coy droop of his left shoulder.

We were in a room that might have been the nursery of La Fontaine's childhood. I was wondering to myself whether I could test my theories on our guides. They were still young enough. The Artist was gazing with half-closed eyes out of the window. "There is no other country like this," he said. "The light is never two minutes the same. The clouds are continually chasing one another over the sun, who is playing peek-a-boo with the earth." I looked at him curiously. The fact upon which he was commenting was striking enough to arouse one's interest, but it was the way he put it which delighted me. *Bien entenndu,* it was not his usual method of expressing his thoughts. "The sun, who is playing peek-a-boo." Was he under the spell of the house?

A fascinating landscape lay before us. The Marne was flowing in as leisurely a fashion as the canal-boat whose horses were a reincarnation of tortoises. On the hillsides were the first of the vineyards which, nestled on every bit of sloping ground for fifty miles to the east and northeast, yield the most highly prized (and priced!) grape-juice in the world. In the valley, wheat and oat fields were ablaze with red poppies, yellow mustard, and blue bachelor's buttons, the useful hidden by the beautiful. The foliage of the trees, still dripping from the morning mist, sparkled under the sun.

When we left La Fontaine's house, the boys felt that they had done their duty, and that we had done ours. In fact, as they pocketed their pourboire and pointed out the road to the castle, they explained that we could get through up there in an hour, and that there was a train for Paris at 2:46! We were amused, until it occurred to us that this idea of values had been imposed upon these youngsters by their dealings with our fellow-countrymen.

Turning to the left, we continued to climb the street that bears the poet's name. In a few minutes, we had on our right tiers of ancient walls which formed the outer defenses of one of the historic castles of France. Nearly up to the level of the castle site was an old city gate, the Porte St. Pierre. Passing through it, we found ourselves in front of the Porte St. Jean as it appears when you are leaving the castle's enclosure.

I did not go immediately. Perhaps it was the attractive footpath in the moat, flanked by lime-trees, perhaps it was two massive polygonal towers peeking out at an angle a few hundred feet away, that drew me. A sign read, "Chemin de Ronde." I followed it. Past the Tour Rouge, the Tour Bouillon, the Tour du Roi, the Tour du Guet, a ruined postern and the bastions that protected it I walked, and had gone almost down into the town and up again before I completed the circuit of the castle as it stands to-day.

The enciente of the castle is in ruins. With the exception of the towers mentioned above, the walls have fallen, and their line of stone, peeping out from ivy and bushes, is distinguishable only by the terraced sub-structure. The plan of the fortifications is manifest, but one has to use imagination to conceive the picture that must have been present to the eyes of the past centuries. The acropolis on which the castle was built seems to have fallen from the mountain behind, and to have stopped in some mysterious way on its downward course a few hundred feet from the Marne. On the lower side, toward the city, one looks up the sheer mass of stone which the hands of man has placed upon, or rather against, the precipitate slope of the acropolis. On the upper side, when the tour of the enciente is completed, one does not observe a very deep depression

The Old City Gate of St. Pierre, on the road to Soissons.

Port St. Jean gate to Château-Thierry. Above as it is now, below with a group of American soldiers. This entrance was built in the 11th and 12th centuries.

to mark the separation of the castle site from the Mont des Chesneaux. That this must have always been a pregnable side would be a natural inference, even if remains of many lines of outer walls did not tell the story of chatelains endeavoring to raise an artificial barrier where nature had failed.

This time I entered the Porte St. Jean. The Artist was still camped in the roadway, puffing at a long pipe to keep the mosquitoes from tasting his watercolors. "Do you know," I asked, "that on this spot" (I dug my cane into the grassy mound beside where he sat) "Louis XIII had a house—it must have been a large one from the extent of these lines—built in six weeks for Cardinal Richelieu? When Louis brought the court to Château-Thierry, Richelieu made a big kick because there was no place within the castle enclosure where he could be properly housed. It is a pretty keen indication of how thoroughly Richelieu was on the job that he had the house put where he could keep his eye on every one that went in or out. In those days it was a case of see the cardinal first, and the king only if Richelieu so decided."

"I haven't read the guide-book yet," answered the Artist. "But isn't it great the way the road dips under that arch, and how those bushes crowd down there on the left? Now, you see, in this light—" But I had turned away to pace out the size of Richelieu's dwelling. The Artist was not interested in the fruits of historical research.

From time immemorial there has been a fortress on this spot. When Attila destroyed the Roman city of Ottmus on the Mont de Chesneaux, shortly before his defeat at near-by Châlons, men were just beginning to build in the valleys rather than on the hilltops. So the inhabitants of the country used Ottmus as a quarry for the new city which grew up on the Marne under the shadow of the advantageous acropolis. Charles Martel, after the battle of Soissons, chose this site for the prison—although it was ostensibly a gala residence—of Theodoric IV. Château-Thierry first saw the shadow of the Merovingians. Within a few years the house of Clovis was supplanted by the house of Pepin. By an odd coincidence—a retribution, might one call it?—Château-Thierry just two centuries later became the prison of the last really independent descendant of Pepin, Charles the Simple.

Owing to its strategic position in the valley of the Marne and at the gateway to Champagne, Château-Thierry has seen more of the vicissitudes of war than any other fortress of France. Visited by the Huns when they threatened Paris; won and lost in the civil wars of Franks and Burgundians; pawn in the resistance of the great French vassals to the growing power of the monarchy; stormed by the English in the Hundred Years' War, and retaken by Jeanne d'Arc on the triumphal coronation march to Reims; captured by Charles V. and the Spaniards, by the Duke of Mayenne and the Leaguers, by Charles of Lorraine and the Frondeurs, by the Bavarians after the retreat from Leipzig, by the Russians after Waterloo, and by the Germans after Sedan; scene, under the name of Egalité-sur-le-Marne, of the wildest excesses and orgies of the Revolution—is there any humiliation in the history of France in which Château-Thierry has not had its part?

Napoleon I, regarding the castle as no longer valuable for military purposes, gave it to the municipal authorities, who in the course of the 19th century turned the whole castle area into a park. If they had kept it as it was until the time of Napoleon III, the reconstruction of the medieval castle might have been entrusted to Viollet-le-Duc, and the confines of Champagne might have boasted of another Pierrefonds. No, not another Pierrefonds would France have had today, but a different and earlier type of castle. For Château-Thierry, as one can see from the plans preserved at the national archives, was laid out in an age before the convenience and comfort of the chatelain came to be considered as an important factor by architect and builder. It is difficult to trace in wandering through the modern park—at least I found it so—the scheme of buildings, but one readily sees that the home of the chatelain was an insignificant factor in comparison with the claims of the defense. The enclosure is divided in half by a deep, wide ditch, the inner moat. The outer court contained buildings for mercenaries, who were not trusted when it came to a question of final defense. Here were the stores and windmills, and here the people of the city took refuge in time of danger. Passing to the castle proper, a rustic bridge has replaced the portcullis. The walls of the donjon just beyond are still partly standing. When you have successfully resisted the importunities of a guardian who wants to show you subterranean galleries, which, from his description, would make the miners of Butte or the builders of a New York subway envious, you find that everything else within the castle enclosure has disappeared.

Beautiful as the park is, my first thought was to regret it and to curse the imbecility and lack of appreciation of the city fathers, who had so little respect for the treasure entrusted to their care by Napoleon. As I walked around, my second thought was not so harsh. A park like this is well worth the climb, even if one is not a pilgrim bent on historical memories. And there is historical continuity in this park, for it signifies that the spot is still adapted to the uses of the age, as it has always been. The impatient protests of travelers over the desecration of historic places must seem ludicrous to the natives who hear them. In our own land we should do what we condemn here. Each generation lives for itself and for the future, never for the past. It is not the park, with

Port St. Jean today

A View of Château-Thierry by J. Andre Smith.

"In connection with this 'World War', the name of Château-Thierry will forever stand in our memories as the proving ground of American valor. The long months of watchfulness in our trenches in the Vosges, the sharp and bitter struggle at Seicheprey, the show of splendid courage and fighting at Cantigny which marked our first encounter with the Germans on their way to Paris, all these were overshadowed by the triumph of our faith in our arms when we put our untried strength to the fullest test against the Château-Thierry salient, and found it not unworthy of our highest hopes. In our minds thereafter, we saw Château-Thierry as the gate which, held by our unfailing strength, barred the Germans from their hopes of victory and peace. And although they made one more effort to break this barrier, it failed; and when this gate was opened again it swung wide to give way to the charge of our triumphant forces in pursuit of a beaten enemy. Château-Thierry was the flood-gate that marked the turning point of the war. The drawing gives one an idea of the location of the city in its setting of hills. The River Marne is not visible, but is marked by the line of taller buildings above the row of trees in the center of this picture."

its trees and grass, its rhododendrons and wild flowers, its winding paths and occasional welcome bench, far better than the dust of distant ruins, or than the endowments of a hospital sunk into the reconstruction—only a guesswork, after all—of an obsolete and useless institution?

It is a warm day, my bench is comfortable, and the view of the city below and the winding valley of the Marne is far more pleasing than if I were standing in the glaring sun, precariously perched on a crumbling wall, fearful of the union of blue serge and lime dust, and of arousing bats, and annoyed by the unpastoral tinkle of thoughtless visitors' sardine cans from the persistent efforts of goats to eat off attractive paper labels. Ought not historical memories to come as easily at Baux as at Carcassonne, at Château-Thierry as at Pierrefonds? We travelers have sensibilities, we have imagination, and can build as we dream. Why let Viollet-le-Duc and his ilk do it all for us? Why do we feel that we ought to be grateful for restorations? For example, those flying buttresses at— The Artist is calling me, and I am going, because my pipe is cold and I have no more tobacco.

Friday is market-day at Château-Thierry. The square of the Hôtel de Ville, with its background of houses rising in terraces and a street of steps leading up to the castle, is given over to the immemorial occupation of the human race. It is morning, and the country is selling to the city. Peasants have left their wagons and carts on the quay, and are squatting here wherever they find room to display their wares. Only a few have improvised booths. For the most part, their fruits and vegetables, their chickens and rabbits, their cheese and butter and eggs, their meat and fish are sold directly from the producer's hamper to the townswoman's basket.

Everything good to eat produced in Champagne one finds here in artless confusion. You pick up a rabbit by his ears to judge his weight, and his angry protest comes not from rough handling or from presentiment of his fate, but because you have removed him from delightful proximity from a bunch of carrots which he had been nibbling. Your butter is given to you in grape-leaves, your eggs are dished out of a basket of spinach or lettuce, you bargain for blackberries with the same merry-eyed grandmother who assures you that her bones are not entirely meatless and make the best sort of soup.

On the market-place there is no distinction of sex, no limit of age, no privilege of large producer. Men and women, seventy and seven, the rich farmer with the huge panniers of vegetables and fruits, tubs of butter and pyramids of cheeses, and coops crowded with fowls, rub shoulders and share the pavement with the old woman who has brought two chickens and the little boy with a kerchief full of eggs. Each has equal opportunity to sell.

The trading instinct is alert when once you stop to inspect; it becomes keen when you want to buy. But there is no importunity, no undue solicitation, as you wander along through the rows; no unpleasantness if you ask a price and then move on. Everything is fresh, everything is useful. The peasants are serene in the knowledge that what they have to sell man must have. If a local purchase does not come, there is always the Paris buyer waiting to take at market prices what is left.

After selling comes buying. What is life but an exchange of things? Market-day is not over when the last of the peasants tie together their empty baskets, rub the legs that have gone to sleep, and lift skirts to shake off dust and to stow away the purse in some mysterious hiding-place. For in Château-Thierry, as elsewhere, there is at work the inexorable law which forbids purses to stay hidden and baskets empty till the farm is reached. There is a second market. Now is the townsman's turn. He wants his money back.

While the Hôtel de Ville has been looking down benevolently upon its weekly guests, while housewives have been replenishing their larders, the shopkeepers of the city have been hurrying their goods out into the alleys or elms along the quay. Booths are erected in the twinkling of an eye. When the peasants are ready to leave the marketplace, they are confronted by the bewildering display of all that Château-Thierry has to sell. Here it is, clothing, finery, household goods, knick-knacks, the things needful cleverly mixed with the things ornamental and useless. This is ever the story of the city. It cannot buy if it does not sell, but what it sells represents neither the work nor the worth of the country's offerings.

Not all, however, that the morning brought is turned back in the afternoon. These peasants of Champagne are ants, not grasshoppers, even if they do sing as well as, and while, they work. In France, every city of the size of Château-Thierry, every city large enough to boast of such a market, has three buildings bearing the signs of Crédit Lyonnais, Société Générale, and Caisse de Épargne. These are visited before the townsmen's market. Here is the secret of the happiness and prosperity of France. Each week something is laid aside for the rainy day, for the daughter's dot, for the son's marriage portion.

The atmosphere of a Champagne market-day is more than that of good nature. It is an atmosphere of good cheer, of gaiety. For to the Champenois work is a pleasure. Out of the everyday round of life they get their joy of being content.

It is the last evening of our stay. The proprietor-chef of the "Giraffe" has done his duty well, and Madame-waitress generously urges us to second helps. So we are quite content with ourselves and the world when we leave the dining room. Some of the long day's light lingers. Down the avenue of elms the statue

Members of 112th Ambulance Company, 28th Division getting water from the Fountain in Château-Thierry, France, July 24, 1918

Château-Thierry water fountain — Now

306th Infantry, 77th Division passing through Château-Thierry on their way to the Front. On the right, French artillery is seen passing into town.

Mr. & Mrs. Rutherford, Y Entertainers, with piano on wagon, Château-Thierry, 13 August 1918.

of Bon Jean can still be distinguished. We go to the Café de la Fontaine for our coffee, and sit out on the pavement nearly opposite the end of the bridge.

A crowd has gathered on the quay in front of us in a three-quarters circle around four chairs which the garçon has placed in the street not many yards from the terrace of the café. Tied to two of them are torches, the like of which I have not seen since I had the joy as a little shaver of carrying one in a procession to celebrate a Cleveland presidential victory or defeat—I forget which. In the midst of loud applause and good-natured witticisms, four men in civilian clothes come into the ring and occupy importantly the chairs. It is a concert, a band concert! As soon as they start to play we realize that their instruments, of local origin, are not a good advertisement for the factory across the river.

Our delight, however, is not to be in music. The leader and soloist introduces his *collaborateurs* in turn with pointed flourishes of his flute as *ancien soldat de la musique* of such and such a regiment of the line. Before each selection he impresses upon the audience with an impassioned speech the difficulty of the heralded rendition, and how much better they can play if encouraged by a generous pourboire. The musicians, while he speaks, pass through the crowd, holding forth the yawning ends of cornet, trombone, and bass-horn as receptacles for the quete.

The proprietor of the café does his share. He sends the *garçon* out with a table, and orders him to keep full the demi-litre glasses. French musicians are averse to the strains of "Die Wacht am Rhein," but they imbibe the same inspiration—even at the gateway to Champagne! Night has now mercifully hidden from view the reproached vineyards.

As we look around us we see that almost everyone is drinking beer. But the atmosphere is far from optimum. The Champenois are children—perhaps "half-tiger and half-monkey," like other Frenchmen, but always children. It is no fete that we are witnessing. And yet the people are having the best of a time. The world is without cares. But we know that if, at the moment, a vine-grower on the Paris side should try under stealth of night to introduce a load of grapes across that bridge, every man in the merry group would join instantly in dumping the cart into the Marne. No outside grapes can enter Champagne.

Effervescent like their wine, quick to tears and as quick to laughter like their climate, hiding their well-rewarded industry and the suffering of toil under a gay mien like their wild-flower-dominated grain-fields, the people of Champagne are a product of the land that nurtures them.

One of the most descriptive articles written in 1918 about the American soldiers and Château-Thierry comes from American writer Dorothy Canfield in her article "Khaki Confidences at Château-Thierry," which appeared in *Harper's Monthly Magazine*:

They were detraining in dense brown crowds at what had been the station before German guns had knocked it into a shapeless heap of tumbled bricks; they were pouring in on foot along the road from the west; and when I made my way along the main street to the river I found other khaki-clad lines leaving the little town, marching heavily, unrhythmically, and strongly out across the narrow, temporary wooden bridge, laid heavily across the massive stone pillars which were all that remained of the old bridge.

An old, white-capped woman, who had been one of my neighbors in the days before the little town had known German guns or American soldiers, called out to me:

"Oh, Madame! See them! Isn't it wonderful? Just look at them! All day like that, all night like that. Are there any people left in America? And are all you people so big, so fine?"

"Where are they going?" I asked her, taking refuge for a moment in her doorway..

"To the front directly, the poor boys. They'll be fighting in two hours.… Do you hear the big guns off there banging away? And they so good, like nice big boys! Their poor mothers!"

I addressed myself in English to a soldier loitering near, watching the troops pass, "So they are going to the front, these boys?"

After a stare of intense surprise, a broad smile came over his face. He came closer. "No, ma'am," he said, looking at me hard. No, these are the Alabama boys just coming back from the front. They've been fighting steadily for five days." He added: "My! It seems good to talk to an American woman. I haven't seen one for four months!"

"Where are you from?" I asked him.

"Just from the Champagne front, with the Third Division. Two of our regiments out there were…." He began pouring out exact, detailed military information which I would not have dreamed of asking him. The simple-hearted open confidence of the American soldier was startling and alarming to one who had for long breathed the thick air of universal suspicion. I stopped his fluent statement of which was his regiment, where they had been, what their losses were, where they were going.

"No, no. I mean where are you from in the States?"

I raised my voice to make myself heard above the sudden thunder of a

A street in Château-Thierry showing barricades and the result of the bombardment. 1 June 1918.

Château-Thierry, the Town Hall (l'Hôtel de Ville) in the background (above), and now (below)

convoy of munitions-camions passing by and filling the narrow street front from side to side.

"Oh! From Kansas City, Missouri. It's just eight months and seven days since I last saw the old town."

"And how do you like France?"

"Oh, it's all right, I guess! The climate's not so bad. And the towns wouldn't be much off if they'd clean up their manure-piles better."

"And the people, how do you get on with them?"

The camions had passed, and the street was again filled with American infantry, trudging forward with an air of resolute endurance.

"Well enough. They don't cheat you. I forgot and left a fifty-franc bill lying on the table of a house where I'd bought some eggs, and the next morning the woman sent her little girl over to camp to give it back. Real poor-appearing folks they were, too. But I've had enough. I want to get home. Uncle Sam's good enough for me. I want to hurry up and win the war and beat it back to God's country."

He fell away before the sudden assault upon me of an old, old man and his old wife, with the dirt, the hunted look, the crumpled clothes, the desperate eyes of refugees.

"Madame, Madame, help us! We cannot make them understand, the Americans! We want to go back to Villers-le-Petit. We want to see what is left of our home and garden. We want to start to repair the house…and our potatoes must be dug."

I had passed that morning through what was left of their village. For a moment I saw their old, tired, anxious faces dimly, as though across the long stretch of shattered heaps of masonry. I answered evasively:

"But you know they are not allowing the civilian populace to go back as yet. All this region is still being shelled. It's far too dangerous."

They gave together an exclamation of impatience as though at the futilities of children's talk. "But, Madame, if we do not care about the danger? We never cared! We should not have left, ever, if the soldiers had not taken us away in camions…our garden and vineyard just at the time when they needed attention every hour. Well, we will not wait for permission. We will go back, anyhow. The American soldiers are not bad, are they, Madame? They will surely would not fire on an old man and his wife going back to their homes? If Madame would only write on a piece of paper that we only want to go back to take care of it…."

Their quivering old voices came to me indistinctly through the steady thudding advance of all those feet, come from so far, on so great, so high, so perilous a mission; come so far, many of them to meet death more than halfway…the poor, old, cramped people before me, blind and deaf to the immensity of the earthquake, seeing nothing but that the comfort of their own lives was in danger. I had a nervous revulsion of feeling and broke the news to them more abruptly than I should have thought possible a moment before:

"There is nothing left of Villers-le-Petit. There is nothing left to go back to."

Well, they were not so cramped, so blind, so small, my poor old people. They took the news standing, and after the first clutch of their wrinkled hands, after the first paling of their already ashen faces, they did not flinch.

"But the crops, Madame. The vineyards. Are they all gone, too?"

"No, very little damage done there. Everything was kept, of course, intact for camouflage, and the retreat was so rapid there was not enough time for destruction."

"Then we will still go back, Madame. We have brought the things for spraying the vineyards as far as here; surely we can get them to Villers-le-Petit, it is so near now. We can sleep on the ground, anywhere. In another week, you see, Madame, it will be too late to spray. We have enough for ours, and our neighbors' too. We can save them if we go now. If Madame would only write on a piece of paper in their language that…"

So I did it. I tore a fly-leaf out of a book lying in the heap of rubbish before the ruins of a bombarded house (it was a treatise on Bach's chorales by the French organist, Widor!) and wrote: "These are two brave old people, inhabitants of Villers-le-Petit, who wish to go back there to work under shell-fire to save what they can of their own and their neighbors' crops. Theirs is the spirit that is keeping France alive."

"It probably won't do you a bit of good," I said, "but here it is for what it is worth."

"Oh, once the American soldiers know what we want, they will let us pass, we know." They went off trustfully, holding my foolish "pass" in their hands.

I turned from them to find another young American soldier standing near me. "How do you do?" I said, smiling at him.

He gave a great start of amazement at the sound of my American accent.

"Well, how do you like being in France?" I asked him.

"Gee! Are you really an American woman?" he said, incredulously, his young face lighting up as though he saw a member of his own family. "I haven't talked to one in so long! Why, yes, I like France fine. It's the loveliest country to look at, isn't it? I didn't know any country could be kept us so, like a garden. How they do it without any men left? They must be awfully fine people. I wish I could talk to them some."

Château-Thierry — Place de l'Hôtel-de-Ville and Rue du Pont.

Above in July 1918

Below as it is now

Port St. Pierre outside and inside

"Who are these soldiers going through today?" I asked. "Are they going out to the front-line trenches or coming back? I've been told both things."

He answered with perfect certainty and precision. "Neither. They are Second Division troops, from Ohio, mostly, just out of their French training camp, going up to hold the reserve line. They have never been in action yet."

Our attention was distracted to the inside of a fruit-shop across the street: a group of American soldiers struggling with the sign-language, a flushed, tired, distracted woman shopkeeper, volubly unable to conceive that men with all their senses could not understand her native tongue. I went across to interpret. One of the soldiers in a strong Southern accent said:

"Oh, golly, yes! If you would do the talkin' fo' us. We cyan't make out whetheh we've paid heh or not, and we wondeh if she'd 'low us to sit heah and eat ouh fruit."

From the Frenchwoman: "Oh, Madame, please, what is it they want now? I have shown them everything in sight. How strange that they can't understand the simplest language!"

The little misunderstanding was soon cleared away. I lingered by the counter. "How do you like our American troops, Madame?" I asked.

"Very much indeed, if only they could talk. They don't do any harm. They are good to the children. They are certainly as brave as men can be. But there is one thing about them I don't understand. They overpay you, often, more than you ask…won't take change…and yet if you leave things open, as we always do, in front of the shop, they just put their hands in and help themselves as they go by. I have lost a great deal that way. If they have so much money, why do they steal?"

I contemplated making a short disquisition on the peculiarities of the American orchard-robbing tradition, with its ramifications, but gave it up as too difficult, and instead sat down at the table with the Americans, who gave me the greeting they always repeated: "Great Scott! It's good to talk to an American woman!"

A fresh-faced, splendidly built lad looked up from the first bite of his melon, crying: "Yes, suh, a cantaloup, a' honest-to-the-Lawd cantaloup! I neveh thought they'd hcahd of such a thing in France."

They explained to me, all talking at once, pounding out unasked for military information till my hair rose up scandalized, that this was their first experience with semi-normal civilian life in France, because they belonged to the troops from Georgia—volunteers; that they had been in the first-line trenches at exactly such a place for precisely so many weeks, where such and such things happened, and before that at such another place, where they were so many strong, etc., etc. "So we neveh saw real sto's to buy things till we struck this town. And when I saw a cantaloup I mighty nigh dropped daid! I don't reckon I'm likely to run into a watermelon, am I? I suahly would have to be ca'ied back to camp on a stretcheh if I did!" He laughed out, a boy's cloudless laughter. "But, say, what do you-all think? I paid fo'ty-five cents for this slice—yes, ma'am, fo'ty five cents for a slice, and back home in Geo'gia you pay a nickel for the biggest one in the sto'!" He buried his face in the yellow fruit.

The house began to shake to the ponderous passage of artillery. The boys in khaki turned their staglike heads toward the street, glanced at the long, motley-colored, mule-drawn guns, and pronounced expertly: "The Forty-third heavy artillery going out to Nolepieds; the fellows from Illinois. They've just been up in the Verdun sector and are coming down to reinforce the One hundred and second."

For the first time the idea crossed my head that possibly their mania for pouring out military information to the first comer might not be as fatal to necessary secrecy as it seemed. I rather pitied the spy who might attempt to make coherent profit out of their candor.

"How do you like being in France?" I asked the boy who was devouring the melon.

He looked up, his eyes kindling. "Well, I was plumb crazy to get heah, and, now I'm heah, I like it mo' even than I 'lowed I would."

I looked at his fresh, unlined boy's cheeks, his clear, bright boy's eyes, and felt a great wave of pity. "You haven't been in active service yet?" I surmised.

Unconsciously, gaily, he flung my pity back in my face: "You bet yo' life I have. We've just come from the Champagne front, and the service we saw theah was suah active. How about it, boys?"

They all burst out again in rapid, high-keyed, excited voices, longing above everything else for a listener, leaning forward over the table toward me, their healthy faces flushed with their ardor, talking hurriedly because there was so much to say, their tense young voices a staccato clatter of words which brought to me, in jerks, horribly familiar war pictures, barrage-fires meeting, advancing over dead comrades, hideous hand-to-hand combats…all chanted in those eager young voices….

In a pause, I asked, perhaps rather faintly: "And you like it? You are not ever home-sick?"

The boy with the melon spoke for them all. He stretched out his long arms, his hands clenched to knotty masses of muscles; he set his jaw, his blue eyes were like steel, his beautiful young face was all aflame. "Oh, you just got to love it!" he cried, shaking with the intensity of his feeling. "You just love it! Why, I neveh want to go home! I want to stay over heah and go right on killin' boches all my life!"

The Americans at Château-Thierry. Infantry at rest in the advance on Soisson 1918.

The River Marne at Château-Thierry in 1918

The Home Coming. The French soldier returns to what the retreating Germans have left of his home.

At this I felt stricken with the collective remorse over the war which belongs to the older generation. I said good-by to them and left them to their child-like ecstasy over their peaches and melons.

The artillery had passed. The street was again solidly filled with dusty, heavily laden young men in khaki, tramping silently and resolutely forward, their brown steel helmets, shaped like ancient Greek shepherds hats, giving to their rounded young faces a curious air of classic rusticity.

An older man, with a stern, rough, plain face stood near me.

"How do you do?" I asked. "Can you tell me which troops these are and where they are going?" I wondered what confident and uninformed answer I should receive this time.

Showing no surprise at my speech, he answered: "I don't know who they be. You don't ever know anything about any but your own regiment. The kids always think they do. They'll tell you this and they'll tell you that, but the truth is we don't know no more than Ann…not even where we are ourselves, not where we're going, most of the time."

His accent made me say. "I wonder if you are not from my part of the country. I live in Vermont, when I'm at home."

"I'm from Maine," he said, soberly, "a farmer, over draft age, of course. But it looked to me like a kind o' mean trick to make the boys do it all for us, so I come along, too." He added, as in partial explanation, "One of my uncles was with John Brown at Harper's Ferry."

How do you like it, now you're here?" I asked.

He looked at me heavily. "Like it? It's hell!" he said.

"Have you been in active service?" I used my usual cowardly evasive phrase.

"Yes, ma'am. I've killed some of 'em," he answered me, with brutal courageous directness. He looked down at his hands as he spoke—big, calloused farmer's hands, crooked by holding the plow handles. As plainly as he saw it there, I saw the blood on them, too. His stern, dark, middle-aged face glowered down solemnly on those strong farmer's hands. "It's dirty work, but it's got to be done," he said, gravely, "and I ain't a-going to dodge my share of it."

A very dark-eyed, gracefully-built young soldier came loitering by, and stopped near us, ostensibly to look at the passing troops, but evidently in order to share in the phenomenon of a talk in English with an American woman. I took him into the conversation with the usual query.

"How do you do, and how do you like being in France?"

He answered with a strong Italian accent, and I dived into a dusty mental corner to bring out my half-forgotten Italian. In a moment we were talking like old friends. He had been born in Italy, yes, but brought up in Waterbury,

Connecticut. His grandfather had been one of Garibaldi's Thousand, so of course he had joined the American army and come to France among the first.

"Well, there are more than a thousand of you, this time," I said, looking at the endless procession defiling before us.

Si, signora, but it is a part of the same war. We are here to go on with what the Thousand began."

Yes, that was true; John Brown's soul, and Garibaldi's, and those of how many other fierce old fighting lovers of freedom, were marching there before my eyes, carried like invisible banners by all those young strong arms.

An elderly woman in well-brushed, dowdy black came down the street toward us, an expression of care on her face. When she saw me she said: "Well, I've found you. They said you were in town today. Won't you come back to the house with me? Something important. I'm terribly troubled with some American officers….Oh, the war!"

I went, apprehensive of trouble, and found her house, save for a total absence of window-glass, in its customary speck-less and shining order. She took me up-stairs to what had been a bedroom and was now an office in the Quartermaster's Department. It was filled with packing-cases, improvised desks, and with serious-faced, youngish American officers who, in their astonishment at seeing me, forgot to take their long black cigars out of their mouths.

"There!" said the woman-with-a-grievance, pointing to the floor, "just look at that! Just look! I tell them and I tell them, not to put their horrid boxes on the floor, but to keep them on the linoleum, but they are so stupid they can't understand language that any child can take in! And they drag those boxes just full of nails, all over the floor. I'm sick of them and their scratches!"

A big gun boomed solemnly off on the horizon as accompaniment to this speech.

I explained in a neutral tone to the officers, looking expectantly at me, what was at issue. I made no comments. None was needed, evidently, for they said, with a gravity which I found lovable, that they would endeavor to be more careful of the floor, that indeed they had not understood what their landlady had been trying to tell them. I gave her their assurance and she went away satisfied.

As the door closed on her they broke into broad grins and pungent exclamations: "Well, how about that! Wouldn't that get you? With the town bombarded every night, to think the old lady was working herself up to a froth about her floor-varnish!"

One of them said: "I never thought of it before, but I bet you my Aunt Selina would do just that! I just bet that if her town was bombarded she'd go

Dead German soldier near Château-Thierry

"Boudoir of Madame" by Claggett Wilson. This drawing purportedly shows a German suicide in a lady's boudoir in Château-Thierry

VIEWS FROM THE CASTLE OF CHÂTEAU-THIERRY IN 1918

right on shooing the flies out of her kitchen and mopping up her pantry floor with skim-milk! Why, the French are just like anybody, aren't they? Just like our own folks!"

"They are," I assured him, "so exactly like our own folks, like everybody's folks, that it's impossible to tell the difference."

When I went away the owner of the house was sweeping the garden path clear of broken glass. "This bombardment is such a nuisance!" she said, disapprovingly. "I'd like to know what the place would be like if I didn't stay to look after it.

I looked at her enviously, securely shut away as she was by the rigid littleness of her outlook from any blighting comprehension of what is going on is not blighting. No, on the whole, I did not envy her.

Outside the gate I fell in at once with a group of American soldiers. It was impossible to take a step in any direction in town without doing this. After the invariable expressions of surprise and pleasure over seeing an American woman, came the invariable burst of eager narration of where they had been and what had been happening to them. They seemed to me touchingly like children who have had an absorbing, exciting adventure and must tumble it all out to the first person who will listen. Their haste, their speaking all at once, gave me only an incoherent idea of what they wished to say. I caught odd phrases, disconnected sentences, glimpses through pin-holes.

"One of the fellows, a conscript, that came to fill a vacant place in our lines, he was only over in France two weeks, and it was his first time in a trench. He landed there at six o'clock in the evening, and just like I'm telling you, at a quarter past six a shell up and exploded and buried him right where he stood. Yes, ma'am, you certainly do see some very peculiar things in this war."

From another, "We took the whole lot of 'em prisoners, and passed 'em back to the rear, but out of the fifteen we took, eight died of sudden heart-failure before they got back to the prisoner's camp."

I tried not to believe this, but the fact that it was told with a laugh, and received with a laugh reminded me gruesomely that we are the nation that tolerates the lynching of helpless men by the mob.

From another: "Some of the fellows say they think about the Lusitania when they go after the boche. I don't have to come down as far as that. Belgium's plenty good enough a whetstone for my bayonet."

This reminded me with a thrill that we are a nation that has always ultimately risen in defense of the defenseless.

From another: "Oh, I can't stand the French! They make me tired! And their jabber! I seen some of 'em talk it so fast they couldn't even understand each other! Honest, I did."

From another: There's something that sort of takes me about the life over here. I'm not going to be in any hurry to go back to the States and hustle my head off after the war's over."

From another: "Not for mine. Me for Chicago the day after the boches are licked."

I listened to their home voices, running up and down the scale of all the American accents, and reflected on the universality of human nature. Just such entirely varying and contradictory sentiments, just such a mixture of idealism, materialism, narrowness, generosity, invariably came clattering out from any group of French soldiers speaking their minds freely. There was a good deal of nonsense about this talk of racial differences, I thought to myself.

They were swept away by a counter-current somewhere in the khaki ebb and flow about us, and I found myself with a start next to a poilu, yes, a real poilu, with a faded, horizon-blue uniform and a domed, battered French helmet.

"Well!" I said to him, "things have changed here since the One-hundred-and-forty-second used to come back from the trenches. The town's khaki, and not blue.

He looked at me out of light brown eyes, smiled, and entered into conversation; and at once I was acutely aware of a strong, unmistakable racial difference. As we talked, I tried desperately with the back of my brain to analyze what it was that made him so different from all the American soldiers I had been seeing. He was a very ordinary little poilu, indeed, such as you see by thousands—a rather short, strongly built, well-knit man, with a rather ugly face, not at all distinguished in line, not at all remarkably clean as to bluish, unshaven chin, not even as to dingy neck…but there was about his every accent, gesture, expression, an amenity, a finish, an ease that not one of the Americans had had, in spite of their perfect self-possession and fluency. Fresh from talking to so many of them, I had a vivid impression of difference.

What was the difference? I racked my brains wildly to put my finger on it, knowing that in a moment my perception of the phenomenon would pass, my familiarity with the type would reassert itself, and my interlocutor would slip back into the great mass of all other dingy, shabby, polite little poilus with whom I have chatted.

We talked, of course, of the American soldiers, one of whom came up and stood at my elbow, listening with amused astonishment to what seemed to him the insane volubility of our talk.

"Gee!" he said, when I stopped to talk to him, "I wish I could rip it off

VIEWS FROM THE CASTLE OF CHÂTEAU-THIERRY IN 1918

VIEWS FROM THE CASTLE OF CHÂTEAU-THIERRY IN 1918

like that! I have got combien and oui down fine, but I don't get on any beyond that. Say what does the Frenchman say about us? Now since that little affair at the Bois de Belleau they think we know a thing or two about the war ourselves, what? They're all right, of course, mighty fine soldiers, but, Lord! you'd know by the way any one of them does business, as if he had all the day for it, that they couldn't run a war fast, like the way it ought to be run, now we're here."

I did not think it necessary to translate all of this to the bright-eyed little Frenchman on my other side, who began to talk as the American stopped.

"You asked my opinion of the American troops, Madame. I will give it to you frankly. The first who came over made a very bad impression indeed. All who have come since have made the best of impressions. They are remarkably courageous, they really fight like lions, and there could be no better comrades in the world, but, oh, Madame! as far as really knowing how to make modern war, they are children, just children. They make all the mistakes we made four years ago. They have so much to learn of the technique of war and they will lose so many men in learning it!"

I did not think it necessary to translate all this to the American, who now shook hands with the both of us and turned away. The Frenchman, too, after a quick look at the clock in the church tower, made his compliments, saluted, and disappeared.

I watched his back retreating fixedly, feeling that in an instant more I should have had my hand on that slippery, ineffable, racial difference. There! It swam up, full and round under my fingers. I closed on it, held it triumphantly to look at it hard…and, lo! it was not a racial difference at all, but an infinite difference of age, of maturity. Not that the poilu was so much older than our boys, but between them lay the unfathomable abyss of four years of war experience. I realized that he alone, of all the soldiers to whom I had talked, had been able to look outside of himself and see another person there, that he alone had been in a normal frame of mind, had been conscious of what he had been saying, had really looked at the person to whom he was talking. This conscious recognition of social contact had given his manner that appearance of social ease which all the familiarity of the Americans had failed to have. They were not conversing, in spite of the fact that they were all talking incessantly; they were simply so full of the exciting, rending, up-heaving experience of their lives that they must needs express their excitement, somehow, anyhow, to anyone, or choke. The poilu, alas! had lived so long in the rending, exciting, up-heaving experience that it was second nature to him, that he moved with ease among portents and could turn a phrase and make a gesture among horrors.

Pondering the meaning of this, I walked forward, and, coming to the church door, stepped inside.

It was as though I had stepped into another world. I had found the only place in town where there were no soldiers. The great, grey, dim vaulted interior was empty. After the beat of the marching feet outside, after the shuffling to and fro of the innumerable men quartered in town, after the noisy shops crowded with khaki uniforms, after the incessant thunderous passage of the artillery and ammunition-trucks, the long hushed quiet of the empty church rang loud in my ears. I wondered for just an instant if there could be any military regulation forbidding our soldiers to enter the church; and even as I wondered the door opened and a boy in khaki stepped in…one out of all those hordes. He crossed himself, took a rosary out of his pocket, knelt, and began his prayers.

Thirty thousand soldiers were in town that day.

Whatever else we are, I reflected, we are not a people of mystics. But then I remembered the American soldier who had said that Belgium was a good enough whetstone for his bayonet. I remembered the rough, gloomy farmer who did not want to shirk his share of the world's dirty work. Perhaps there are various kinds of mystics.

Once outside the church, I turned to look up at Madame Larçonneur, the valiant market-gardener who had been one of my neighbors, a tired young widow with two young children, whom I had watched toiling early and late, day and night, to keep intact the little property left her by her dead soldier husband. I had watched her drawing from the soil of her big garden, wet quite literally by her sweat, the livelihood for her fatherless little girls. I wondered what the bombardment of the town had done to her and her small, priceless home. I found the street, I found the other houses there, but where her little, painfully well-kept home had stood was a heap of stones and rubble, and in place of her long, carefully tended rows of beans and cabbages and potatoes were shell-holes where the chalky barren subsoil streaked the surface and where the fertile black earth, fruits of years of labor, was irrevocably buried out of sight. Before all of this, in her poor, neat black, stood the widow with her children.

I sprang forward, horrified, the tears on my cheeks. "Oh, Madame Larçonneur, how awful! How awful!" I cried, putting out both hands to her.

She turned a white, quiet face on me and smiled, a smile that made me feel infinitely humble. "My little girls are not hurt," she said, drawing them to her, "and as for all this…why, if it is a part of getting other people's homes restored to them…" Her gesture said that the price was not too high.

The look in her sunken eyes took me for an instant up into a very high place

VIEWS FROM THE CASTLE OF CHÂTEAU-THIERRY IN 1918

Château-Thierry from the Terrace of the Old Château
This drawing was made a few days after the Germans had
evacuated the city

of courage and steadfastness. For the first time that day the knot in my throat stopped aching. I was proud to have her put her work-deformed hands in mine and to feel on my cheek her sister's kiss.

It steadied me somewhat during the difficult next hour, when in the falling twilight I walked up and down between the long rows of raw earth, with the innumerable crosses, each with its new, bright American flag fluttering in the sweet country air. I needed to recall that selfless courage, for my heart was breaking with sorrow, with guilt-consciousness, with protest, as I stood there, thinking of my own little son, of the mothers of the boys who lay there. A squad of soldiers were preparing graves for the next day. As they dug in the old, old soil of the cemetery to make a place for the new flesh come from so far to lie there forever, I looked away toward the little town lying below us, in its lovely green setting, still shaking rhythmically to the ponderous passage of the guns, of the troops, of the trucks.

At one side were a few recent German graves, marked with black crosses, and others, marked with stones, dating from the war of 1870, that other nightmare when all this smiling countryside was blood-soaked. Above me, dominating the cemetery, stood a great monument of white marble, holding up to all those graves the ironic inscription, "Love ye one another."

The twilight fell more and more deeply, and became darkness. The dull, steady surge of advancing troops grew louder. Night had come, night no longer used for rest after labor in the sunlight, night which must be used to hurry troops and more troops forward over roads shelled by day.

They passed by hundreds, by thousands, an endless, endless procession— horses, mules, trucks, artillery, infantry, cavalry; obscure, shadowy forms no longer in uniform, no longer from Illinois or Georgia or Vermont, no longer even American; only human young men crowned with the splendor of their strength, going out gloriously through the darkness to victory through sacrifice.

From "Château-Thierry Now Has a Place in American History" in the *Literary Digest*, August, 1918:

Rudely roused by the clangor of war, old French towns and villages have awakened from the peaceful slumber of centuries to play their parts once again in the strife of the world, and to receive fresh wounds where time had softened the scars of long-forgotten battles.

Ancient towns that loomed large in the wars of long ago, and with the passing years had withdrawn behind a curtain of peaceful obscurity, have sprung into the light of the world again to take their place in the events of to-day that are binding France and America still closer in the pages of history.

Château-Thierry, where the German armies in their drive for Paris first met the resistance of American troops, stands out prominently among those old French towns that have been engulfed in the maelstrom of the world-war. Of its stirring history, dimmed by the passing years, a writer in *The Stars and Stripes* [the newspaper of the AEF] says:

"Château-Thierry is a little town on a hill. Past its foot flow the slow, untroubled waters of the Marne. From the grey-stone, red-tiled outskirts on the other side of the river you cross a three-arched bridge of stone to mount by winding paths to where the ancient church lifts its sixteenth-century belfry to the heavens. House by house and street by street, the town has grown up through the centuries around a squat, deep-dungeoned château. Of this château only two vine-hung gates and the fragments of a thick-set wall are left to tell the story of many a bitter siege.

The château was built in 720 by Charles Martel, the great "hammer" of the Franks and grandfather of the still greater Charlemagne—the same Charles Martel who saved Europe for Christendom when, twelve years later, he met and vanquished the turbaned hosts of the all-conquering Saracens in the battle of Poitiers. Little remains of the castle itself, but you can still see the base of the tower where one of his feeble successors, Charles the Simple, was held prisoner.

When in the early days of June, 1918, men once more fought hand to hand in the narrow streets of Château-Thierry and the thunder of the guns stirred ancient echoes in the crumbling ruins of the castle, history was but repeating itself. The river valleys, converging upon the plain of Paris and finding there a barrier of hills, have ever turned that basin into the final battlefield of an invasion with the capital as the goal. That is why around Château-Thierry, reared like a stubborn bastion on the rim of that basin, the soldiers of many a forgotten cause have fought and died. It has always blocked the path to Paris.

Not held as a watchtower by the dukes of France, now as an outpost by the courts of Champagne, the castle changed hands again and again through the early centuries.

English archers took and held it in 1421, toward the close of the weary Hundred Years' War between England and France, the interminable war which finally brought Joan of Arc up out of the fields of Lorraine to lead the armies of the king, and which, at the end, lost to the English crown all its rich French jewels save only Calais.

In the first half of the 16th century, while adventurers on the other side of the Atlantic were exploring with fear and wonder the mysteries of the wilderness

Copyright by Underwood & Underwood.

"Château-Thierry Forever Will be Linked With Most Sacred Memories in America. The Deeds of the 8,000 Heroic Marines here in July, 1918, Will Never be Forgotten."

Scenes of the main wagon bridge and its destruction along the Marne

Le pont détruit de Château-Thierry.

CROQUIS DE GUERRE par FRANÇOIS FLAMENG.

known as America, the Old World shook with the trampling armies of Francis I., King of France, and his enemy, the mighty Charles V., Emperor of Germany, who had made a pact with England for his undoing.

Then—and not for the last time—the dwellers along the Marne saw an army of Germans march upon Paris. For, leading his troops through Champagne, Charles pressed his invasion to within twenty-four leagues of the capital, and in that invasion the Germans took Château-Thierry.

A half-century later, the Spaniards sacked it in the course of that terrible war of religion, when Catholics and Huguenots fought such bitter battles for the control of France that, in the course of thirty years, a million Frenchmen perished. Spanish troops entered France as allies of the Catholics. Those were the days when a Spanish garrison held Paris, not for all his sieges, could the Protestant chieftain, Henry of Navarre, enter its gates till he had marched through crowds of joyous people to the church of Saint-Denis, and there, in the presence of the prelate, asked to be received "into the pale of the Catholic Apostolic and Roman Church."

At Château-Thierry Napoleon, with an army of 20,000 young conscripts, smashed an army of 50,000, representing the alliance of England, Prussia, the German states, Spain, Portugal, Russia, Sweden and Austria. It was in February that the little Emperor made his final stand against onrushing odds. In March his enemies entered Paris, and in a few weeks Napoleon was on his way to Elba. This was in 1814. One hundred years later the scarred walls of Château-Thierry saw the German Triple Alliance in retreat before the armies of the Entente Allies. Says the writer in *The Stars and Stripes*:

Visiting Château-Thierry in the spring of this year, you would have found a town set in a fair and peaceful countryside, proud of its sheep-crowded pasturage and rich in its vines and cherry-trees—a little town of 7,000 people, no larger than Rochester, Minn., or Red Bank, N.J.

And this town is a shrine for French pilgrims, not because of the battles fought in its streets, but because it was the home of the master of fables, La Fontaine.

The French of all ranks and ages love their poet of Château-Thierry. When in the early stages of the Revolution the infuriated mob in Paris gave themselves over to the September massacres of bloody memory, and thousands of prisoners were butchered, one woman was spared for no other reason than because she was the granddaughter of La Fontaine. French children hear his fables in the nursery and know them by heart. Their fathers and mothers find summed up in them all their philosophy of life.

It was in Château-Thierry that La Fontaine was Master of the Waters and the Forests. It was there he made friends with the wandering dog, the toiling ant, the mounting lark—all the animals of the countryside who move in his fables. It was there he wrote, "The Wolves and the Ewe," of which the moral is the motto of his people in this year of trial.

"We can conclude from this that one must war continually with the wicked. Peace is all very well in itself, I admit, but of what use is it with enemies who are faithless."

The following article, "The American Château-Thierry," appeared in the September 14, 1918 edition of *The Literary Digest:*

Château-Thierry was in a sense put upon the American map "when Marshal Foch picked the American new Army for the spear-head thrust of the great drive," on July 18. In the secret recesses of more than one American family is the feeling that some corner of this Marne region is forever American. But Château-Thierry was in still another sense long ago put upon the American map by Elizur Wright, a citizen of Medford, Mass., who, says "The Listener" in the *Boston Transcript*, was the translator of the accepted English version, now a classic, of La Fontaine's fables. The birthplace of the great fabulist was Château-Thierry, and his statue stands, or stood, in the public square. Perhaps it stands there no more, since the blight of German occupation makes way with such tributes to civilization. A cartoon in the Écho de Paris by Abel Faivre shows the wise Frenchman re-uttering his own words from "The Wolves and the Ewe"—the "very moth for the hour," says "The Listener": "Peace is all very well in itself, I admit, but of what use is it with enemies who are faithless?" The Massachusetts translator, we are told, prefixes a long essay to his La Fontaine (over thirty pages) to the first edition.

It shows the facility and the patient industry at once with which the young Wright performed this labor of love for his idol that he speaks of this preface as no worthy and adequate critique, but just an introduction hastily thrown off by the translator to round out his work. There is in this time-stained and dog-eared copy of the fifth edition a notice preceding the preface, signed, 'The Translator,' and dated Dorchester, March 3, 1842, in which he says:

"'The fables of La Fontaine were the delight of Fénelon and have been in high favor with the best and wisest teachers of youth ever since. In translating them, it was my endeavor to follow the original as closely as I could and produce readable English. The testimonies of my success in respect are extremely gratifying. But, having reason to suppose, from criticisms both friendly and unfriendly, that the work might be rendered more acceptable to parents and

SCENES OF THE MAIN WAGON BRIDGE AND ITS DESTRUCTION ALONG THE MARNE

"Where we crossed the Marne at Château-Thierry."

American machine-gunners defending the wagon bridge

teachers in other respects, I have with some care, revised it for that purpose, changing many expressions, altering some fables, and entirely omitting a few.

…After all, I am not so foolish to expect that these time-honored fables will entirely escape censure. In this age, distinguished for almost everything more than sincerity, there are some people who seem too delicate and refined to read their Bibles. They are themselves so far removed from reality that the very word fable seems to disturb them, as the word hemp does a person whose relative has been hanged. But the unsophisticated lovers of nature who have not had the opportunity to acquaint themselves with the French language, I have no doubt will thank me for interpreting to them these honest and truthful fictions of the frank old Jean, and will beg me to proceed no farther in the work of expurgation.

A taste of the translator's work is given in these lines from his version of "The Animals Sick of the Plague": He places it at the top of La Fontaine's achievements, as did Voltaire, Madam de Sévigné, and other good judges, and it may well be imagined our Boston translator put his very best effort into its translation. To the animals assembled the Lion says:

> Let us our guiltiest beast resign,
> A sacrifice to wrath divine.

Then begins the soul-searching of the respective representative beasts; the Lion, continuing, remarks:

> For me, my appetite has played the glutton
> Too much and too often upon mutton.
> What harm had o'er my victims done?
> I answer, truly, None.
> Perhaps, sometimes, by hunger prest,
> I've ate the shepherd with the rest.
> I yield myself, if need there be:
> And yet, I think in equity,
> Each should confess his sins with me.
> "The next speaker is Reynard, the lawyer fox. He protests with animation
> against calling eating stupid sheep a crime:
> It rather was an act of grace,
> A mark of honor to their race.

> Loud applause followed Reynard, and neither Tiger, Boar, nor Bear was
> asked to confess their crimes:
> The fighter, biters, scratchers all
> From every mortal sin were free

The very dogs, both great and small
Were saints as far as dogs could be.

But the Ass, confessing in his turn, admitted in tones of deep concern
that he had 'browsed the bigness of my tongue,' on tender grass, while the
monks, its owners, were at mass.

On this a hue and cry arose
As if the beasts were all his foes:
A wolf, haranguing, lawyer-wise,
Denounced the ass for sacrifice—
The bald-pate, scabby, ragged lout,
By whom the plague had come, no doubt.
His face was judged a hanging crime.
What? Eat another's grass? Oh shame!
The noose of rope and death sublime.
For that offense, were all too tame!
And soon poor Grizzle felt the same.
Thus human courts acquit the strong.
And doom the weak as therefore wrong.

Something in the way of "currents set up in the spiritual atmosphere" between Medford and Château-Thierry, speculates "The Listener," may have "moved the countrymen of La Fontaine, Moliere, and Voltaire, through their 20th century genius, Marshal Foch, to send the Americans in at that point." Of the place itself we read:

It was Charles Martel, A. D. 720, who built the château, and his glory was to have saved Europe from the Saracens. English archers took it in the Hundred Years' War, which Joan of Arc, in whose Lorraine fields other Americans are waiting the word on the German flank, entered in triumph. Charles V., Emperor of Germany, in the first half of the 16th century, got as far as Château-Thierry in a march upon Paris, and half a century later the Spaniards sacked it in the wars between Catholics and Huguenots. Again in 1814, it was at Château-Thierry that Napoleon made a stand with 20,000 young conscripts against 50,000 troops of the allied rest of Europe. This was in February, but in March his enemies entered Paris, and in a few weeks Napoleon was on his way to Elba. One who saw Château-Thierry early in the spring of this year describes it as a sweet, old, fortified town of 7,000 people, no larger than Wellesley or Ipswich, set in a fair and peaceful countryside. In the French Revolution, the story runs, one woman was spared by the mob simply and expressly because she was the granddaughter of La Fontaine.

American Machine Gunners Defending Château-Thierry
H.T. Dunn, AEF August 1918

THE WASH BOATS OF THE MARNE

Between 1860 and about 1950, there were groupings of large, wooden boat wash-houses established on the Marne River at La-Ferté-sous-Jouarre and at Château-Thierry. During the fighting of 1914 at La Ferté and in 1918 at Château-Thierry, a number of these wash-boats were destroyed or badly damaged when the adjacent river bridges were blown up by French army engineers. A number of these barges were requisitioned to provide a bridge of boats. Several wartime photographs show what appears to be very large railroad freight cars sunk in the Marne River. These are not wooden freight cars—they are the remains of sunken wash-boats.

These boats were anchored on the left and right banks of the Marne, upstream and downstream and very close to the bridge crossings so as to provide easy access to their customers. They were moored not more than five feet from the river bank so as to not obstruct the navigable river channel. None of the boats was communual, they were all private properties.

The wash-boats often had cold and hot baths personal baths and a drier as well as laundry facilities. Some of the larger boats even had living facilities on the second level. The boats employed washerwomen and professional ironers. At both La Ferté and Château-Thierry some 150 to 200 women were employed on these large barges.

Here is an excerpt from "Emptying the Bag, Part III" of "On the German Heels," by James Hopper, as it appeared in *Collier's*, 30 November 1918:

A French Noncom's Cap

One of our excursions took us one morning into Château-Thierry just after it had been evacuated. Our troops and some of the French had pressed on beyond; their artillery was pounding near by to the north, but the city itself was empty—empty both of the conqueror and the conquered. The streets leading to the quay were still barred by heavy barricades; on the quay itself lay a lone cow, which must have strayed innocently there in the zone of fire weeks ago, and which since had flattened and dissolved till it looked like a mere dun-colored rug, there in the center of the place. Above it the statue of La Fontaine poised minus a leg; on the parapet of what was left of the bridge, which had been blown up, lay a machine gun with several belts of cartridges gleaming like jeweled festoons in the sun. But down on the river bank were the small mementos of a tragedy—a French noncom's cap, by it a shattered rifle, next to that a clean towel, a piece of soap, a toothbrush. The man must have been surprised weeks before by the Germans as he knelt there, stealing a moment to clean up after the hard retreat.

The Hun's Hurry

I went into a small store on the river-bank which had been No Man's Land ever since the German had entered the town. It was a small "bistro"—a wine and tobacco shop. Half-drained glasses lay on the zinc counter, tied together by fine cobwebs; in a rack were the newspapers of several weeks ago, which had come in that day from Paris, all bearing the date of the German invasion of May 29. But what puzzled me more was the fact that this small wine shop was full of clocks. They lay all over the floor, some shattered, some intact; one was on its beam-ends on the counter. I went through a great hole in the partition into the next shop, and understood.

The next shop was a jeweler's; the clocks had come from there. But the jeweler's shop, in turn, was full of hats! Most of them straw hats—the spring stock; they lay all over, scattered as small bits of paper are scattered by the breath of a child. Again I went through a big hole into the next shop, and understood; I was now in the hat store. A shell had gone through the hat store, jeweler's, and the "bistro." It had forced the hats of the hat store into the jeweler's shop and the clocks of the jeweler into the wine shop.

We went up to the old castle on a hill rising in the center of the city, the old Château-Thierry, from which the city has gained its name and which is believed to be a relic of the Merovingian times. There, in the vast vaults and galleries of the ruins, we found—all warm and still—the evidence of a very late boche occupation. There was, of course, the usual litter of arms and ammunition, of clothes, equipment, and rags, and, besides the strange heaping of loot—chosen by minds, one feels, not quite developed—which one finds where German troops have lived. But, also, there was a table upon which cards lay spread as they lie spread when one throws down one's hand in disgust, except that here all four hands lay thus spread, expressive more of haste than disgust. In and about the cards were glasses of wine, one full, the other half drained, a third with just a little at the bottom, while under the table were three uncorked bottles and another still corked. In another dug-out the colonel had just been about to wash his hands before dinner. Here was the basin, all ready, full of nice clean water, and by its side the soap, and by its side the clean towel, carefully laid within easy reach of one rising from ablution with eyes tight shut against the danger of suds. But the soap had not been used, the towel was still folded, the water pellucid and unsoiled. The colonel had gone away without washing his hands.

Mail for Germany

Here and there, everywhere, were great baskets in which all sorts of objects made of copper had been collected; there were scales and weights, clock-works, trombones, bells, and kettles. The baskets were already ticketed for departure for Germany; all this brass was the official and governmental loot, what might be called the suzerain's first rights in pillage. But we found something still more interesting. In one of the galleries we came upon a pyramid of packages. They were neat packages, all the same size, wrapped in the same stout brown paper, tied securely with the best quality of twine and with no careless knots or loose ends. At first we thought this was the German mail come in, parcels sent from German homes to their fighters. But a short study proved the contrary; they were all addressed to good German Frauen; they had been on the point of departing for Germany in the mail when our advance had thrown all plans, even the best, into disorder. We opened one of them. Our curiosity then whetted, we kept on—tearing open package after package—and found spread before our eyes all that which was missing in Château-Thierry shops and homes. Those excellent, naïve, thrifty, and family-loving German soldiers were, at this distance, stocking their chests and linen closets. All the sturdy domestic virtues of their race were displayed in their choice: what we found most in the parcels were those garments at which a young man blushed when, as he walks with his girl, she stops to view with tenderness and entire window full of them. He stands by then, pretending to be absorbed by the passing streetcars. The first thought of those good Germans had been for their good wives: there were filmy waists, and

The remains of a wash boat on the right

Boat wash-houses served a definite need and purpose in their day. There were no commercial laundry facilities in town, and the French homes of the day had no washing machines or bathing facilities.

It was very hard work for these washerwomen—their day was made up primarily of washing, heavy work made even more tiring by the climatic conditions during the season of winter when the frozen water of the river turned fingers numb, making the linens more difficult to rinse. The women's knees were rubbed raw, despite the pads that were kneeled upon. The wages were also quite thin at the end of each working day.

Although the working conditions aboard the wash-boats were difficult and the hours long, the washerwomen were of good mood and often cheerfulness. The "salted" remarks of the washerwomen were well known. Their time was passed in exchanging local news with each other, as long as this distraction did not block their work. Their language would become animated at the rate/rhythm of the beater, the grass brush and the movement of the water of the river rinsing the large pieces of linen.

With the increasing availability of modern land-based commercial laundry companies and indoor plumbing and bathtubs in French homes, the era of the wooden wash-boats slowly disappeared, until about 1950 when they were all gone from the Marne River.

American machine-gunner by Dunn

good stout woolen stockings, and sheets and tablecloths and napkins—and many other things. I remember, as if I had seen it in a nightmare, a monstrous pantalet made seemingly for a giantess. But paternal love had also a place beside conjugal affection; the small Hanses and the small Gretchens had not been forgotten. There were little shoes and stockings, blouses and pinafores, dolls and tops and marbles and balls. In the heart center of a package, I found six little French soldiers—a brilliant Zouave, a horse chasseur with sky-blue tunic, a red-képiet pioupiou, a natty alpin, a black artilleur, and an armored cuirassier—small ghosts of the brilliant, gay, and naïve army of France before the Great War. I took those, I recaptured them. And now they are on my table, all in a row, looking on as I write, and seemingly quite well pleased to be here rather than in Germany.

We lunched on the provisions we had taken with us in the court of a big building which had been a convent before the war and a hospital since. A burst water main made a pretty gurgling sound and gave the illusion of an old fountain. Nearby was a half-wild garden; when we looked amid the flowers though, we found graves—simple French graves with the inscription: "Here rest three French soldiers," and more pretentious German graves each with a headstone proclaiming that a "Deutsche Held"—a German Hero—lay there, who had "died in defense of his Fatherland." Extraordinary how far one has to go to defend the Fatherland. The place was quiet, though our cannon thundered not a thousand yards away, and the city seemed not only deserted, but never to have been peopled.

AEF officer Joseph Hansen, in his book *The Marne, Historic and Picturesque*, states:

Here Dwelt The Sluggard Kings

At Château-Thierry, which, from Blesmes and Chierry, the traveler comes at by the Paris road passing through the southern suburbs and across two bridges into the main part of the city, the flavor of romance in pre-war days must have been mainly supplied by legends of Jean de la Fontaine and Charles Martel, two widely diverse characters, truly. To these legends, in future generations, will be added another group, those of les Américains. The three facts are obvious, immediately one enters the city. At the northern end of the last bridge, facing west along the broad boulevard which borders the right bank of the Marne, stands a statue, by Laitié, of the great fabulist; chipped by German and American machine-gun bullets and with its left leg broken by a shell splinter, but still intact in the main. Set in the pavement almost at La Fontaine's feet is a square stone tablet on which are chiseled the words: "Dedicated to the 3rd Division, U.S.A., Aug. 9, 1919." This tablet, placed on the date mentioned by representatives of the "Marne Division," indicates the first step in the construction of the monumental bridge across the Marne which that divisions intends eventually to erect as its own memorial in France and, at the same time, as a gift to the City of Château-Thierry to replace the bridge, built in 1768, which was blown up by the Americans on the night of June 1, 1918, to prevent the Germans from crossing the river. Finally, if one stand beside the tablet and look up the street formerly called the Rue du Pont but now the Rue du Maréschal Pétain, which, narrow and walled by high buildings, leads northward from the bridge into the Place du Marché, he sees, towering up beyond the Hôtel de Ville, a steep slope crowned by decayed but massive walls. These are the remains of the once mighty château of the "Sluggard King," Thierry IV of Neustria, built for him in 720 A.D. by his all-powerful Mayor of the Palace, Charles Martel, who saved Europe to Christianity by his defeat of the Saracens at Tours in 732 and who united France and left it to become the greatest nation of earth under the genius of his grandson, Charlemagne.

Thus, standing on one spot in this quaint city whose very center is traversed by the lucid current of the Marne, one may reflect upon a panorama of events covering twelve centuries and profoundly affecting the whole course of civilization; the rise of France to greatness and power, the eminence of its intellectual estate, and its recent salvation from submergence by a spurious kultur.

But the physical aspects of the city, with which we are chiefly concerned, are most agreeably revealed from the elevated ramparts of the ancient château, beneath which roll away to the west, south and east the closely built streets and the wide stretches of countryside, rich in associations, whose every vista is enlivened by the ample bends of the Marne. At mid-height of the hillside a road, leading round through a quarter of the city which is very quiet and very medieval in aspect, comes curving presently to the château gateway. Its low, deep arch, pierced between the ponderous octagonal towers of the barbican, gives access to the long, narrow interior court which was formerly occupied by the crowded structures of the citadel, but is now given over to a park whose drives and pathways wind between large, dense trees.

The château was a place of almost impregnable strength before the introduction of artillery, but it was besieged and captured by the English in 1421 and again in 1544 by the Germans of Charles V. Standing at the southeastern side of its razed and moss-grown battlements one looks across the wheat fields to the white walls of Brasles, nestled at the foot of the towering Bois de Barbillon Hill, and across the Marne by Chierry and Blesmes to the fair

"American soldiers halted by the roadside in a small picturesque French village."

150th Field Artillery, Rainbow (42nd) Division marching through Château-Thierry

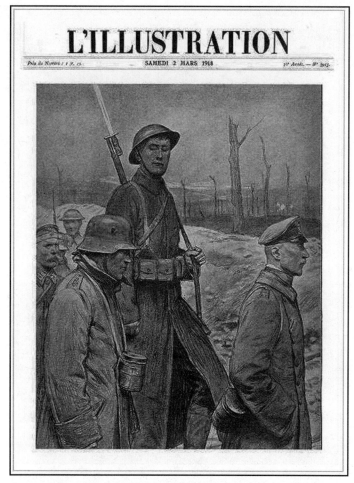

L'ILLUSTRATION

SAMEDI 2 MARS 1918

Georges Scott's cover depicting an American soldier alongside
German prisoners

downs and woodlands beloved of Fontaine. One may fancy the writer, as a boy, wandering over the precincts of the deserted château, in his day still covered with a maze of ruined halls and passageways, and from the decaying battlements peopling the distant countryside with the odd creatures, half brute and half human, of his awakening imagination.

Walking on to the southern side of the height, at the head of a long flight of steps which ascends from the Place de la Hôtel de Ville, one contemplates a scene which rouses thoughts more stirring than pensive. Far across the Marne, where the hills rise beyond Nesles, there runs between checkerboard fragments of woodland the straight road to Fontenelle and Montmirail. Over that road, in the chill dusk of the evening of February 11, 1814, a watcher on the château would have seen a terrified mass of fugitives, the Russians of Sacken and the Prussians of d'York, encumbered with wagons and artillery, pouring northward from the battlefield of Montmirail toward the bridges of Château-Thierry, pursued and belabored by the exultant cuirassiers of Napoleon. As the darkness deepened, he would have seen the demoralized fugitives, or such of them as had not been slain or captured by the French, spreading through the streets of the unfortunate city and, stung by defeat and the lust for vengeance, giving themselves over to pillage and every species of outrage upon the citizens. Then, as the dawn of the twelfth broke after the fearful night, he would have seen the 24 squadrons of Prussian horse under General Horn, as yet unscathed in battle, maneuver into position on the open grounds south of the city for the purpose of stopping the French pursuit; he would have seen the dark columns of Ney's cavalry corps swing into position on the slopes beyond and then, charging in clouds of dust and with thunder of hoofs, under the eye of the emperor himself sweep the hapless foe from their path and gallop on into Château-Thierry, greeted before they could gain its streets by throngs of men and women and children pouring forth to welcome their deliverers. He would have seen these civilians working furiously to repair the Marne bridge for the pursuing French cavalry and also, alas! He would have seen many of them, goaded to a frenzy by the horrors of the preceding night, slaying without mercy the scattered wounded and prisoners of the enemy as the latter fled northward into the hills of Orxois.

From the same battlements on September 2, 1914, the observer would have looked down upon other German hosts swarming over the surrounding hills, but now advancing and encircling the town. At about 5:00 o'clock in the afternoon the field-gray uniforms would have been noted filtering into the streets from the west, along the Paris and the Essomes roads, while the French rear guards, firing sullenly, fell back southward. Next day Château-Thierry would again have been disclosed, writhing under the hands of pillagers no less brutal than their ancestors of a century before. Then would have been seen, in the words of the acting mayor as quoted by Mr. Toynbee:

> Château-Thierry completely pillaged. The work was done under the officers' eyes and the loot was carried away in wagons. German prisoners have been found in possession of jewels, stolen here, and articles of clothing, obtained from the plunder of the shops, have likewise been found among the effects of German doctors who remained behind at Château-Thierry when their army left—and this at the moment when these doctors were being exchanged."

These conditions obtained until the ninth of September, when the invaders again, as always, recoiled from their implacable foe, the Marne, pursued by the French and the British.

But Château-Thierry and the castle which watches the centuries flow by like leaves upon the bosom of the guardian river, still had to look once more—and may it have been the last time forever!—upon the faces of the enemies from beyond the Rhine. It was on the last day of May in 1918 that the hated field-gray uniforms again came creeping down the hillsides and into the streets. But now, beside their French antagonists of immemorial years, there stood to welcome them among the houses and along the shores of the Marne, a new foe; one which neither Charles Martel nor Charles V nor even Napoleon would have dreamed to see battling on the soil of Europe. And when, beneath the shells of Allied and German artillery which crossed above the roofs and crashed with shattering detonations into the narrow streets, there vibrated the rat-tat-tat of the guns of the American Seventh Machine Gun Battalion, the Germans knew that behind the moat of the Marne the New World, too, was at bay in the name of civilization. For five long days they fought there, French poilus and Yankee doughboys behind mined walls and splintered trees and in hastily dug pits along the waterside, doggedly clinging to the positions they had been ordered to hold against the withering fire and oft-repeated attacks of men who hesitated at no effort or sacrifice to win their way across the narrow river which alone barred them from victory. By that time the Allied artillery and infantry were firmly established on the hills to the southward, from which they were to never move until they moved forward in pursuit of the finally beaten foe.

It is from the western summit of the château hill, looking between the tree branches and past the rough-hewn tower of St. Crépin's Church, rising like a huge Druid's stone above the jumble of roofs almost at the foot of the hill, that the panorama reaches out and over heaving crest and valley and knots of woodland blasted here and there by shell fire, to other fields which are now immortalized for Americans. Hill 204, its slopes mounting up from the Marne

Here are some of the American boys who advanced across a wheat field in the face of a line of machine guns and heavy field pieces. They cleaned up the machine-gun nests and captured the field pieces. It was near the Marne. The Germans insisted it was impossible even after they had done it

"Here are some of the American boys who advanced across a wheat field in the fact of a line of machine guns and heavy field pieces. They cleaned up the machine-gun nests and captured the field pieces. It was near the Marne. The Germans insisted it was impossible even after they had done it."

Rue Petain as the citizens returned

Rue du Pont — Directly after the battle [sic] in the bridge street.

at the southwestern edge of the city, is conspicuous in the nearer distance, with the shapeless ruins of Vaux just beyond it. These were places for which the Germans fought furiously throughout the June and early July of the war, to finally lose the village to the Ninth United States Infantry, Second Division, and the hill to the Tenth French Colonial and Third American Divisions.

Northwest and farther away, just beyond the depression of the Gobert Creek, is the curving, dark outline of the famous Bois de Belleau, called now by the French the Bois de la Brigade de Marine, from which, in stubborn fighting throughout the month of June, 1918, the gallant marines and infantrymen of the Second American Division forced the Germans foot by foot down into the creek valley. Within the latter, just hidden from view by intervening hills, are the villages of Bouresches and Belleau and Torcy and those poppied wheat fields over which the men of the "Yankee Division" charged to victory on the misty morning of July 18. And there, also, a bright flash of color against the verdure of the renowned woods, are visible on a clear day the folds of Old Glory, floating above the white rows of crosses of the Belleau Wood cemetery, where rest the remains of 3600 Americans killed in the fighting in that region of battles.

Northward of Château-Thierry, but hidden from the castle by the mounting hills and forests, are the open fields before Trugny and Épieds and the tangles of the Bois de Trugny battle fields of the New Englanders. Beyond them lie the aisles of the Forest of Fére, and La Ferme Le Croix Rouge, set in the midst of it, where the Rainbow Division came into line, and still farther away, the deadly slopes along the Ourcq where not only the Forty-second, but the Thirty-second and the Twenty-eighth Divisions wrote glory upon their standards. In fact, on every side of Château-Thierry is country which will be visited by patriotic pilgrims from the New World of generations yet unborn, for it was in this land that the sons of America gave their first virile aid to the cause of the Allies in the campaign which turned the tide of the war.

In the streets of the city itself the effects of the battle were distressingly evident after the armistice. The Rue du Maréschal Pétain and many other of the narrow streets were piled feet deep with the dèbris of ruined buildings and blocked by the Germans with barricades made of stones and the furniture from adjacent houses. In front of 27 Rue du Maréschal Pètain, just north of the bridge was the barricade of their first line of resistance, facing upon the wide esplanade of the Champ de Mars. The handsome Hôtel de Ville lost one of its towers in the bombardments, though a little farther down the street the sixteenth-century belfry of the old Belhan Mansion escaped material injury, as did St. Crépin's Church on the Rue St. Crépin. The massive fifteenth-century tower of St. Crépin's has already been mentioned. The church is nobly conceived, with carved buttresses and a roof line of deep, saw-toothed gables, and its low groined interior and sixteenth-century organ loft, carved with figures of the prophetesses, are impressive.

When the French and Americans advanced into the city after he enemy's evacuation, they found in many places heaps of packing cases and sorted booty, systematically collected by the Germans from the stores and houses and much of it already marked for shipment to Germany. What they had not already carried away or prepared for transportation, they had wantonly destroyed or mutilated. This was attested by the condition of the interiors of scores of houses wherein mirrors hung broken and pictures slit on the walls, and upholstered furniture stood ripped open with bayonets, and polished tables hacked to pieces.

Gentler memories are stirred as one ascends the steep Rue de la Fontaine, at the western base of the château hill, and pauses at Number 13, where the light of day was first seen by the erratic son of Charles de la Fontaine, "master of waters and forests" of the Duchy of Château-Thierry, and his wife, François Pidoux. Here one is reminded, too, of the fabulist's suzeraine and generous patroness of later years, who generally resided in Château-Thierry; Anne Mancini, Duchess of Bouillon and youngest of Mazerin's nieces; a young woman who was, according to Mignard's still-existing portrait of her, as lovely as she was gracious. Garbed to represent "the Muse of the Marne," in that portrait she is revivified down the years; "dressed to charm, her hair falling upon one white shoulder in Italian curls—a young woman, beautiful, darkly piquant, and vivacious." Is it any wonder that by such a creature her talented liegeman should have been inspired to write his collections of famous Tales and a large number of his imperishable Fables?

Going out of the principal, or northern part of the city across the Marne bridge repaired with steel on the piers of the structure destroyed by the Americans, one comes to the row of shattered houses along the southern river bank wherein fought the Seventh Machine-Gun Battalion, and then, passing across the "false Marne," or canal, which shortens the natural bend before the city, he enters the circular Place Carnot, where the American battalion commander, Major Taylor, made his post of command on the evening of May 31, 1918, in touch with his two companies, A, under Captain Houghton, and B, under Captain Mendenhall, which were fighting along the river bank.

From the *American Legion Weekly*, June 3, 1921:

Company B was assigned to the defense of the railroad bridge and the portion of the river bank lying in and immediately beyond the eastern sector of

Georges Scott's *Soldiers of the Foch*

Destruction in Château-Thierry on the rue General de Gaulle

Rue General de Gaulle today

the town. Company A took over the defense of the western portion, including the wagon bridge in the center of the city. The squads were conducted to their places by French officers or soldiers and the Americans spent the night in preparing their positions, receiving some German shell fire from the hills north of the Marne and an occasional burst of machine-gun fire from the lowlands near the river. For these detachments the serious work had not yet begun. But a handful of 14 men of Company A, under First Lieutenant John T. Bissell, had a wild night and following day on the north side of the river, where, with a few French Colonial troops who were holding on there, they engaged in continuous hot street fighting with the German advance guards.

So, with a last impression of it as a city all-French, yet with an aroma of America now hovering about it perpetually, we must leave Château-Thierry, though with only a fragment of all its traditions and its romances told.

CHÂTEAU-THIERRY AFTER THE WAR

From Alexander Woolcott's book, *The Command is Forward*:

Immediately after the war Château-Thierry became a mecca for battlefield tourism, with soldiers, nurses and civilians coming into the old town by the thousands to stay in the hotels and to hire taxis to take them to such memorable places as Belleau Wood, Torcy and Bouresches. They all wanted to see where it was that "America had won the war." In the 1920s and 30s many ex-soldiers returned to see their old battlefields and the newly established American military cemeteries. Château-Thierry became then and still is a name synonymous with American participation in the war.

Not all the American visitors in the Château-Thierry area are sightseers. There are the ambulance men and the photographic squads on duty there. There are the occasional line officers back on the old terrain to point out the best subjects for the cameras to record. There are the men of the Graves Registration Service who are gathering the scattered dead into little, neatly-fenced, roadside cemeteries. Five hundred here, one hundred and fifty there, thousands of bare, sod-less mounds, each with its wooden cross and metal tag, with here and there a stupefying funeral wreath laid there by some French friend, or perhaps a cluster of pansies, planted by French hands on the grave of "An unknown American, buried beside the Paris highway he died defending."

From a little AEF pamphlet, *American Battlefields in France*, published in 1919 by First Section, General Staff (Visitor's Bureau), Headquarters American Forces in France:

Itinerary 1ST Day

The town of Château-Thierry is divided into two parts by the Marne River. The entire city was occupied by the Germans in early September 1917, but they were driven out of it that month in the 1st Battle of the Marne. The north half was again occupied by the Germans on May 31, 1918, but they were unable to get into the south half. This northern half did not suffer much from hostile bombardment as the Germans occupied it in 1918 without much opposition, and while the enemy held it the Allies did not shell it. At the time that the French re-occupied the north half on July 21, 1918, there was very little fighting as the Germans were then evacuating the whole of the Château-Thierry salient on account of the French-American successes near Soissons. The original stone bridge near the center of the city was destroyed by the French at about 11 o'clock PM, June 2, 1918, in anticipation of a German attempt at crossing. When the bridge was blown up there were a few French and American troops on the north bank. They either swam the river or crossed by the railroad bridge to the east of the town. This latter bridge was blown up June 7.

The 7th Machine Gun Battalion of the 3rd Division which figured so prominently in stopping the German advance across the Marne on May 31 in the vicinity of Château-Thierry had its guns located on the south side of the river. That part of the city was divided into two parts, the western part being assigned for defense to Company "A," 7th Machine Gun Battalion, and the eastern half to Company "B." This division placed the bridge near the center of the city under the protection of Company "A" and the railroad bridge under that of Company "B." On June 5 this Machine Gun Battalion was replaced by a French unit. It then went back to a reserve position. Between June 4 and July 15 this sector was quiet. On the north side of the city is located the Hotel de Ville, in the tower of which is a clock. At the center of the clock can be noticed a hole through which the Germans fired a machine gun on anything moving on the main road running through the south side of the city. Behind the Hotel de Ville on the high hill may be noticed the remnants of the old fortifications surrounding the Chateau of Charlemagne. If the party arrives at Château-Thierry the day before starting the trip, the members should go up to those fortifications to get a view of the surrounding country.

Cleaning up Rue Carnot

Rue Carnot

From "The Festive Rubberneck Wagon in France's Battle-Fields," printed in *Literary Digest*, November, 1920:

> Nowhere is the stamp of "Touristia" more apparent than at Château-Thierry. The town has settled quite naturally into being what it is destined to be for the rest of its days—a shrine for Americans. You see the Stars and Stripes frequently among its ruins. Signs in English are commonplaces. The pretty little waitress at the place where you lunch speaks charming English.

From Somerville Story's 1920 book, *Present Day Paris and the Battlefields*:

> Château-Thierry is a little town on the Marne (about eight thousand inhabitants in 1914), which has always been a kind of citadel on the road to Paris, protecting it. There is a ruined château, which is supposed to have been originally built for Charles Martel. The town is especially famous as the birthplace of La Fontaine, the famous writer of fables. His house, which still stands and was a library and museum, was used as a dugout by the German officers. The chief square at Château-Thierry is now known as the Place des Etats-Unis, in honor of the great stand made by the Americans.
>
> It was at the end of May and in the first days of June, 1918, that the American machine-gunners made their great stand in the streets of Château-Thierry, which was the center of a great battle. The German offensive had begun a few days before the end of May, had easily smashed through the thinly held line, and was pushing forward (for the second time) for the Marne. Then the Americans made their dramatic entry into the war, the Second and Third Divisions being sent forward to help, ill-trained and ill-equipped though they were. The two bridges of Château-Thierry were for four days and nights raked by fire from seventeen machine guns in the doors and windows of a row of houses on the river bank. One of the bridges was completely demolished, being blown up as a party of Germans, who had pushed forward, had reached the middle of it. The American gunners made a methodical retreat and installed themselves on the other side of the Marne in positions which enabled them to support French Colonial troops as they fell back.

From *Literary Digest*, April, 1921, "They Used to Call It the Front":

> Château-Thierry has patched its roofs, plastered its chimneys, painted its shutters, and decided to forget the war. At first every villager dreamed of making his fortune as a tourist guide. They are all back now at their old trades. It is only the good housewife who still pays attention to tourists, and then only to think black thoughts of the dust raised by the rubberneck automobiles that plunge without a stop through the village streets.
>
> Over the bridge, our famous bridge, that crosses the Marne come the jolting market-carts filled with beets and cabbages grown in the farmlands at the foot of Belleau Wood. There is a great deal of grumbling about the temporary wood structure that now spans the Marne, and the peasants tell you that they can not imagine why the soldiers did not build it wide enough to let two carts pass each other. In the Café des Mariniers they talk no more of the war. Instead one hears only the idle gossip that the river-men have picked up. Château-Thierry is no place for the sentimentalist who has imagined that this town of towns would live forever in awe of its memories.
>
> A walk through the streets reveals few marks of either the German or the American occupations. In a field on the outskirts stands the skeleton of a "tin lizzie" that once did ambulance service. On the door-jambs of several houses one can still read the billeting officer's stencils telling how many soldiers each house would accommodate. In one instance the owner had purposely left unpainted a square around these sacred numbers as a delicate tribute to his departed guests.
>
> But if Château-Thierry itself has tried to erase all signs of the occupation, the Marne still reveals its tale of a ghastly yesterday. It was once a sparkling stream flowing through a charming valley that was particularly noted for its wooded scenery. Nowadays the Marne writhes through a valley of tree corpses. Its waters are discolored and foul. Its surface is covered with a thick, oily scum. The stream flows with great weariness, and as though in great pain.
>
> Even then, you must look beneath the murky waters to appreciate the full horror of the Marne. The story of what this river has mirrored in its troubled waters of yesterday is best told by the accumulation of rubbish that clutters the riverbed. There one sees rusted shells and broken artillery pieces, sometimes old shoes, broken rifles, helmets, for the Marne, as those who fought there will testify, is a continuous sepulcher to the unknown dead.

CHÂTEAU-THIERRY TODAY

Château-Thierry has changed very little from its appearance during 1918. Today, the town is dominated by the gigantic American memorial on nearby Hill 204. The site of the castle is now a public park where the ruined walls are still visible. On many occasions through the passing centuries the castle was damaged and rebuilt.

CHÂTEAU-THIERRY DURING THE WAR

From *The Americans in the Great War*, published in 1920 by the Michelin Tire Company of France:

> Château-Thierry—The name comes from a hill on the northern side of the Marne which, legend says, was built by Charles Martel for the King of the Franks, Thierry IV. The site of the castle is now a public park where the ruined walls are still visible.
>
> On September 9, 1914, a most important date in the First Battle of the Marne (when the Allies began to advance), the British First Corps (Haig) crossed the Marne here and moved forward to Fere-en-Tardenois. Château-Thierry remained far behind the line until the German advance in May, 1918. As it had been with the British in 1914, Château-Thierry was to be the scene of the first American offensive. Despite many attacks the allied line held and the town, which had fallen to the Germans on May 31, was retaken on July 21, the American divisions pushing forward into the wooded hills north of the town. Dominating the town from the summit of Hill 204 is the huge American Memorial.

Château-Thierry During The War

September, 1914

On September 2, 1914, the town was almost encircled by the Germans. While the German batteries posted above Courteau were firing on the railway station and the Place-du-Champ-de-Mars, their troops debouched by the Essomes and Paris roads about five in the afternoon. The French fell back at 11 PM On September 3, German troops pillaged the town. On the 9th, the Franco-British troops relieved the town.

June–July, 1918

On June 1, 1918, the town was retaken by the German Conta Corps [the German Army Corps of General Richard von Conta] after fierce street fighting, in which the French Colonial Infantry, gallantly supported by American troops,

The ruins of Château-Thierry after the Germans had retreated. This photograph was taken in the suburb of Courteau

American soldiers working on the road through Courteau, a suburb of Château-Thierry

German machine gun crew

German soldiers advancing over a hill

inflicted severe losses on the enemy. The defense of Château-Thierry is one of the episodes of which the Americans are justly proud.

On May 31, sections of the American Machine-Gun Corps were placed at the disposal of the French Commander, who was defending the town, which was in danger of being outflanked. They were hardly out of the trucks, when they were rushed into battle in support of the French Colonials. Throughout the long street fighting their fine marksmanship, cool courage and clever maneuvering excited the admiration of their French comrades. When night fell, thanks to their aid, the enemy had been forced back to the outskirts of town.

At 9 PM on June 1, the Germans, under cover of night, and protected by a dense smoke screen, counter-attacked, creeping along the river-side towards the great bridge, the defense of which had been entrusted to the Americans, with orders to hold it until the Colonials, who were fighting on the far side of the river, should fall back. This they did until the last of the French troops had passed over, when they withdrew. When the Germans debouched in front of the bridge, the latter blew up, and the few who had succeeded in crossing before the explosion were taken prisoner by the Americans, who had calmly posted their guns on the south bank of the river.

From July onwards, the Allies, by a series of local operations, approached the town. The Allies successful counter-offensive of July 18 completely cleared Château-Thierry.

On July 21, with their front pierced on the north and east, the enemy was forced to abandon the town, which was then entered by General Degoutte's Army.

Château-Thierry Plundered By The Germans

When the Franco-American troops entered Château-Thierry, the town had been methodically sacked. The enemy emptied the houses of everything portable, including mattresses, metallic articles, etc. The churches were likewise despoiled. In the case of St. Crépin's Church the Germans had not had time to carry off the whole of the plunder. The photographs show what was hurriedly left behind, part being packed in cases, the rest, including a fireman's brass helmet stolen from the fire station, lying scattered about.

That portion of the population which had remained in the town was locked up in this church on the night before the deliverance.

The houses had literally been turned upside down, as the Americans, who entered the town with the French, can testify. Packing cases full of clothing, linen, and all kinds of objects had been got ready to send to Germany, as the labels on the cases prove.

What the Germans could not carry away they broke, mutilated, or spoilt. Here was another example of their practice of spreading systematic ruin and desolation wherever they went. To use the Kaiser's own expression, the entire region was left 'a barren waste.' Special detachments of troops had orders to collect and remove all machinery, tools, raw materials, furniture, food, etc., in the districts occupied."

That the Germans regarded the towns and cities they captured as being providers of booty for the German war economy is shown in their official documents. One German report, relating to the town of Château-Thierry, states, in part:

The idea of establishing a bridge-head on the south bank of the Marne had to be abandoned in consideration of the heavy casualties which had to be expected in connection with an operation of that sort, so the next few days were utilized to prepare the captured positions for the defense and to salvage the rich supplies of provisions, clothing and military equipment of all kinds, above all, the medical supplies in the city.

George B. Ford tells us in his 1919 book, *Out of the Ruins*:

The greatest destruction of all occurred as the Germans were driven back in the summer of 1918. They evidently felt that all was lost and that the time had come to harm France economically as much as they could. It was then that they carried out feverishly their long-prepared plans of systematic pillage and destruction; every piece of furniture and clothing, every trinket and work of art, all copper and brass, every machine or part of a machine, all cattle and farming implements, anything that could be of any use in Germany, they carried off. Everything that was not carried off, if it could be of economic use to France, they destroyed. It was then that they burned and blew up the factories and flooded the mines. It was then that they scientifically destroyed the industrial towns.

The Germans everywhere carried off any furniture, furnishings, or household utensils they thought they could use, and they broke or burned the rest. The insurance companies estimate the damage at about ten billion francs.

In *The Outlook*, Wednesday, June, 26, 1918, is the following article by Eliza R. Scidmore, which is included here as a 'tone of the times' piece:

In The War Swept Marne Country
American history is fast being made across the water, and Château-Thierry and Cantigny are now as much household words as Santiago or Vera Cruz.

Château-Thierry, fifty miles east of Paris by railway or motor road, is the

German soldiers

Bottom photos courtesy Great War Association–George Gaadt

The Boche Looter, by Dunn

first large town on the Marne after Meaux. Motorists must remember the aisles of lofty trees along the avenues of the new part of town south of the Marne and the imposing modern Mairie. A certain homely but delectable inn at the fork of the main shopping street near the stone bridge very likely lives in the grateful memory of those who have had the luck to lunch or dine there. Even in war time the rich brownish-yellow war bread was the best in France, the omelets and salads beyond compare, and the cheery proprietress could regale one with tales of the Boches of 1914 and the Prussians of 1870. Bismarck has his headquarters at the Rothchild villa outside the town, and the first peace negotiations went on there before the Chancellor moved to Versailles—and left the Rothchild cellars absolutely empty.

And just now, in 1918, came the lapping edges of the returning waves of Boches, and the American Marines came to meet them and help hold the four bridges across the Marne until the French engineers could blow them up.

Gone is the old stone bridge, built in 1621, and the quay with its statue of La Fontaine, and even that philosopher's house in one of the old stony streets.

Gone, too, are the picturesque ruins of Charles Martel's old castle, from which one had such beautiful views of the town, the river, and the encircling hills to the westward. The castle was built in 730. It was captured by the English in 1411, sacked by the Spaniards in 1501, captured by Charles V in 1544, and riddled with cannon shot in 1814, when Napoleon with only 24,000 men soundly thrashed some 50,000 Prussians! All the old town across the Marne has now been ground to rubble and powder by high explosives, a desolate No Man's Land probably never to be rebuilt; and St. Crépin's square tower and its precious sixteenth-century stained glass no longer exist.

At the time of the first battle of the Marne, in September, 1914, Château-Thierry was not greatly damaged by the Germans. Their stay was short, their exit hurried, and they had the intention to hold it and Epernay and Châlons for their own use as way stations to Berlin, as they did in 1870. They contented themselves with immediate plunder—jewelry, silverware, securities and money, food, wine, and supplies. Their retreat was so hurried that they had no time to burn or blow up. Racing southward along the valley of the Petit Morin a few miles, they reached the Route de Paris or Route de Châlons, the broad, direct highway that cuts from Meaux to La Ferté, Montmirail and Epernay. At Viels Maisons Château they spent a night and wrecked the pretty villa with their occupancy, and wreaked a speedy vengeance on the charming old Château de Villers-les-Maillets. They defiled the little Château de Rieux near Montmirail, where Lamartine lived, and General von Einem, commanding the Seventh

Army occupied as his headquarters the great château of the Duc de la Rochefoucauld at Montmirail. Some Imperial prince was with him there during the four days of the German occupation. The staff put up at the hotel, where they incidentally packed up the linen and silver as methodically as the All-Highest one was doing at the château, and all the plunder was promptly despatched toward Germany on the second day. Cellars were emptied, of course. They laid the paved streets thick with straw while their artillery rumbled through, and installed a battery in the park behind the château, exchanging shots with a French battery across the Petit Morin until the German gun and crew were struck by neat French shots. Two crosses in the roads near the ramparts mark the spot where they fell—one the grave of a von der Goltz, nephew of the re-creator of the Turkish army.

As the French came on the Germans prepared to burn Montmirail in the pleasing way by which they had made sure the destruction of so many Belgian towns. Sacks full of tiny black pastillon were thrown in all the open doors and windows; but before the men with flaming pinwheels could follow, the French came swarming through the woods to the château gates, and the last of the Boches went pell-mell in the darkness. Sixty German wounded were left behind with one German surgeon, knowing quite well that they would be treated humanely and with the consideration that international conventions provide.

The German artillery headed straight on down the valley road in the afternoon, and at dusk they floundered in the byways of the great swamp of St. Gond, where they were finished off completely the next day. The rear-guard fought all across the beautiful stretches of farming country and the forest lands, villages and country houses towards Epernay, the battle fiercest at the very gates of the Rochefoucauld's other château, that of Montmort. There the tide decisively turned, the last resistance ended, and the German retreat was then a rout, a frantic flight, with Foch biting at their heels clear to the height beyond Rheims and the edge of the Châlons plain. They had only time to fine the town of Epernay eighty thousand bottles of champagne, when there were millions of bottles in the great cellars, and no time for great destruction before retiring. They could only fill their pockets and knapsacks at the last moment. They have

vented their wrath ever since by bombing Epernay and all the railway towns every moonlight season.

Château-Thierry's big hospitals have received the wounded from nearby Rheims and from Verdun all these years, but they were hastily evacuated when the Boches broke through last month and came down to the Marne from the Rheims sector. Little Montmirail had three military hospitals, because of its fortunate position and wonderful air, and cable messages have recently told how the wounded sent down from the recent fighting at Château-Thierry swamped the medical staffs; and how two American women, Mrs. Herbert Squiers and Miss Olga Wiborg, with two nuns, working twenty-four hours at one stretch, cleaning and dressing the wounds of six hundred men. Mrs. Squiers, who knew perilous times during the siege of Peking, has been the only American or foreigner in Montmirail for three years, in charge of the operating-room at the French military hospital of St. Vincent de Paul. The wounded American marines were amazed to find themselves in American hands in the heart of France, and, like all the patients in Mrs. Squiers's wards, will probably protest if moved.

Another 'tone of the times' piece comes from *The Outlook*, September 11, 1918. From "The Battle of Château-Thierry and Beyond," by Joseph H. Odell, special correspondent of the *Outlook* in France:

CHÂTEAU-THIERRY! The name has been hanging over the consciousness of Paris for many weeks and about it has clustered all the hopes and fears of the Allied cause. The battle was on a conflict which many believe to be the turning-point of the war. It was also the first time in which division after division of American fighting men were thrown into the fray. It seemed to us like either the first or last syllable of Armageddon. The old town is only about forty miles from Paris, and the Huns held it in the middle of July. Château-Thierry! What would it prove to be? Some thought only the starting point on the last lap of the Boches' journey, and then the sack of the richest and fairest city in the world! But Château-Thierry is on the Marne, and the Marne has proved to be the River of Death to Kaiserism. On the south side of the river lay more than one division of American troops—pure blooded, high-spirited United States men, who strained upon the leash which wise

Artillery on the March

Really Homesick, from *Stars & Stripes,* 1918

generalship imposed upon them. They were told to hold the line, but they did not. The American idea of holding the line against the enemy is to advance and drive the fox from his positions. That is exactly what happened—one of those splendid plus-duty affairs which history will write about stupidly for many a generation to come unless some poet appears who loosens an epic and startles the world.

Good fortune placed me near enough to this Gettysburg of the world war to get into it. Clarence Buddington Kelland, of the *Saturday Evening Post,* and now of the Y.M.C.A. Publicity Department accompanied me. We had a French automobile, which we loaded to capacity with cigarettes, gum, chocolate and tobacco. The driver was a wounded American soldier wearing the Croix de Guerre who had never manipulated a French car before. We started out of the city on a zigzag, ricocheting from almost everything we met. The time was three o'clock in the afternoon, and our progress for the next ten hours was thick with thrills, alarms, perils, and labors. We stuck in the mud and needed a platoon of infantry to push us out. We ran out of gasoline and it costs a liberal libation of American cigarettes to bribe a supply from a French convoy commandant. Our radiator dried up and the engine threatened to incinerate itself; but an artillery outfit furnished water from a swamp a full half-mile off the road. We got mixed up with a division going to the front, and had to take our place in a thousand slow moving camions. We threaded our light-less way through heaps of ruins which once were respectable, the only illumination being the lurid horizon, on which the artillery belched a dull-red fire. At 1:30 AM we pulled into the desolation which had once been Château-Thierry and found the headquarters of the Military Police. The M.P.'s were Philadelphia policemen at home, and there amid the Boche devastations we discussed the most baffling of all municipal themes—how not to govern Philadelphia on civilized lines; and the Vares and McNichols and Penroses and the Wanamakers and the Rittenhouse Square accessories would have been amazed and somewhat pained to have heard what we said about them in the early morning drizzle with the German rear-guard guns punctuating our conversation.

Why do Americans persist in differentiating between the German military caste and the German people? They were ordinary Boche regiments which held Château-Thierry, and they set about to destroy and pollute everything within reach. Remember, this is not hearsay; I went into Château-Thierry on the heels of the American advance and saw things with my own eyes. Every vandalistic, Hunnish, fiendish, filthy thing that men could do these Huns did in Château-Thierry just before they left. The streets were littered with the private possessions of the citizens thrown through the windows; every bureau and chiffonier drawer was rifled and its contents destroyed; in the better-class houses the paintings were ripped and the china and porcelain smashed; furniture was broken or hacked; mirrors were slivered into a thousand fragments; mattresses and upholstery were slashed; richly bound books were ripped; in fact, there was hardly a thing in the city left intact. The houses of the poor, in which the German privates had been billeted, were just as badly pillaged and devastated as the houses of the well-to-do. The church, grand enough for a cathedral, had not been spared. Its paintings and altars and crucifixes and stations of the cross had been ruthlessly battered and defiled. Yet even this does not tell the story—a story which cannot be told to people who respect decency—for the Germans left tokens of physical and mental obscenity in every house I visited, and I entered scores. If hell had been let loose in a choice suburban town for a half a day, in could not have put its obscene and diabolical mark on a place more unmistakably than the Germans put theirs on Château-Thierry. I stood amazed that there could be so much unrelieved vileness, such organized beastliness, in the world….

Of course there were casualties in Château-Thierry and to the north. The Allies could not wipe out that impertinent and audacious salient between Soissons and Rheims without paying toll. Château-Thierry had several field hospitals, at least one for each division engaged. Francis Sayre and I worked in one of them, and particularly with the men who were being carried in from the ambulances. They came in a sickening stream; doctors, orderlies and stretcher-bearers were tired out and were working on their nerve; the patients ranged all the way from shattered and perishing hulks of humanity to slightly gassed cases and mere flesh wounds. Every one was too busy to answer questions, so we read the dressing station tags tied to the patients and avoided giving cigarettes to the gas cases. How wonderful those men were! As we lit a cigarette in our own lips and put it between the lips of the wounded man he looked his gratitude far more eloquently than words could have fashioned. Only once, and that in the surgical ward, did we hear a cry from those broken men, and then it was a dying boy who sighed with his last breath, "Mother, oh, mother."

Far spent and on the verge of nervous collapse, Sayre and I turned away and walked silently back to the Y.M.C.A. The canteen was in a stately mansion, or what had once been a stately mansion before the dastardly Hun had blasted its beauty. In the courtyard and far out into the street there stretched an apparently endless line of men awaiting their turn to get to the counter. After the foodless days and bedless nights and bloody battles all they asked was a package of cigarettes, a square of chewing tobacco, a bar of chocolate, or a quarter of a

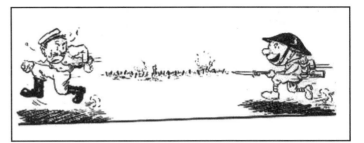
Americans chasing Germans in the cartoons of the era

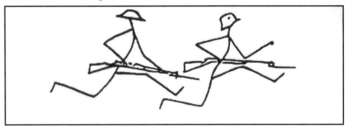

Left to right —
Lt. Turner, Capt.
Hammond, Corp Ripp̈e,
Lt. D.S. Hose, Sgt. Dell,
Lt. Dickerhoff
Co. 'B.' 7ᵗʰ M.G.Bn.,
in Germany

pound of crackers; they were willing to stand in line for one or two hours for the privilege of making that simple purchase; they were as quiet and orderly as if they had been entering church. Then, darkness fell. In one sense it was a mercy, for the Y.M.C.A. canteen men were ready to drop from sheer weariness; in another sense it was a tragedy, because several hundred war-weary and nerve-spent men could not buy what they wanted most. Then it was that the spirit and the mission of the Y.M.C.A. were revealed; in order to give no guidance to the Boche airplanes lights were not allowed in Château-Thierry and the secretaries could not see to sell or make change. So they solved the problem by walking down the long waiting line with baskets, and giving, absolutely free, to each man what he wanted most—cigarettes, tobacco, sweet biscuits, or chocolate. Then the line melted away….

THE 7ᵀᴴ MOTORIZED MACHINE GUN BATTALION AT CHÂTEAU-THIERRY

British Major-General Sir Frederick Maurice, Chief of Operations of the British Army, wrote for the McClure Newspaper Syndicate, July, 1919:

The Campaign of 1918—How Victory Was Won—Foch on the Defensive
The weak and weary allied divisions were overwhelmed, and the German Crown Prince drove through to the Marne, where his further progress was just checked in time by the arrival at Château-Thierry of a machine gun battalion (the 7ᵗʰ) of the 3ʳᵈ American division, followed almost immediately by the remainder of the division. This German drive brought the enemy within forty miles of Paris, and was a rude shock both to Foch and the French people.

From *Harper's Pictorial Record of the World War*, 1920, comes the following statement:

The French-American defense of Château-Thierry gave General Foch time to plan for the Allied defense northwest of and east of Château-Thierry along the Marne River.

From *The Medical Department of the United States in the World War*:

On May 27 the Germans began their offensive between the Aisne and the Marne, and within the next few days elements of the 3ᵈ Division, which had been placed at the disposal of the French, began their move toward Château-Thierry. The 7ᵗʰ Machine Gun Battalion was the first organization of the division to enter the lines, reaching the defenses of the bridgehead at Château-

Thierry late in the afternoon of May 31, there reinforcing a battalion of the 10th Moroccan Division at a very critical moment. The main body of advancing German troops reached the Marne the next day, but were prevented from crossing at Château-Thierry. The prompt arrival and stubborn defense of this important point by untried troops (May 31 to June 1) are well worthy of special mention. Continuing operations through the following days, the 7th Machine Gun Battalion was relieved by the 9th Machine Gun Battalion on June 4. The first battle casualties of the 3d Division occurred here. When relieved on 4 June, the 7th Machine Gun Battalion had suffered 32 casualties.

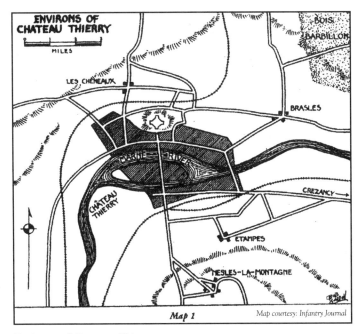

Environs of Chateau-Thierry

IN THEIR OWN WORDS

STORY OF THE 7TH MACHINE BATTALION

By 1st Lieut. Luther W. Cobbey

The 7th Machine Gun Battalion was in training at La Ferte-sur-Aube, Haute Marne, until May 30, 1918. We had spent the days on a range which had been built by Lieutenant Paul T. Funkhouser. We went out to the range in the mornings in Fords and returned in the evenings.

At that time Major Edward G. Taylor was the commanding officer of the battalion.

The officers of Company "B" were:

Captains John O. Mendenhall and Lloyd H. Cook; 1st Lieutenants Thomas W. Goddard, John H. Ransdell and Charles Montgomery; and 2nd Lieutenants Paul Taylor Funkhouser, DeWitte S. Hose, Luther W. Cobbey and Joseph G. Hanus.

We Move to Château-Thierry

On May 30th, at three o'clock in the afternoon we started for a destination unknown, loaded in Ford vans. We had twenty four vans for the company. Paul rode a motorcycle all of the way, keeping liaison between the different cars and leading or showing the route. We traveled the rest of that day, all that night and all the following day without a voluntary stop. We had several stops caused by lack of gasoline or losing the route. We loaded machine gun clips en route.

We reached Montmirail, thirty kilometers south of Château-Thierry, about nine o'clock in the morning of May 31st, having passed through Bar-sur-Aube, Jaucourt, Vendeuvre, Lusigny, Troyes, Rimilly, Anglure, Sezanne, Moeurs and Le Gault. A considerable part of our route followed the rivers Aube and the Seine. From Montmirail on into Nailles we passed refugees coming away from the front. It was a wonderful, a pitiful sight; the French women and old men leading

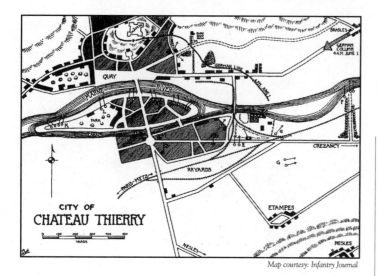

City of Chateau Thierry

Map courtesy: Infantry Journal

cows and sheep; some with a few belongings loaded on one-horse wagons, or on wagons drawn by ox-teams; some pushing hand carts, and moving in every conceivable way. Some carried bundles on their backs and drove herds of cows or sheep. These refugees took up most of the road. It was very hard for us to get our Company post. We finally reached Nailles that evening about seven o'clock, at which place we received orders from a French Commander to go into Château-Thierry to hold the bridgeheads at that place. (Still the officers and men, outside of the Battalion Commander, knew nothing of where we were, not knowing the name of the towns). We were tired and worn out, having traveled 110 miles without rest or sleep.

Lieut. Goddard, who had sprained his ankle before we started, stayed with the vans in order to handle rations and ammunition which he was to bring into town for us. Lieut. Montgomery was given two guns with the personnel. Paul was given two guns with men, and I was given two guns. The reason there were only two guns apiece was that we lost so many vans en route, and that was all of the guns we had left in the Company, we having made such a quick trip. At six o'clock that evening we rushed into the town in vans, going under shell fire for the first time.

Our Battalion was the first of the American forces to reach the Château-Thierry territory and is the unit referred to by General Pershing in his official report (See Annual Report of the Secretary of War, 1918, p. 73) as "the motorized machine gun battalion" of the Third Division which "preceded the other units (of the American Army) and successfully held the bridgehead at the Marne, opposite Château-Thierry."

From this time I will try to give only what happened to Paul and myself, not knowing personally about the rest of the Battalion, or what they did. Paul was taken by a Frenchman to the east end of the town and went into position at the edge of the town in a little wood on the bank of the Marne River. His guns were right on the south bank of the Marne. The position I was given was about 200 meters to his left at the bridgehead, which bridge was the east bridge across the Marne. The other guns of the Battalion, I understood, were placed or were to be placed at the lower bridge and west of us along the south side of the Marne in South Château-Thierry. Nothing particular happened that evening. At five o'clock the next morning it became light. However, during the night a few shells were thrown around by the Germans, and also a few shots from machine guns. By this time we actually realized that we were at the line, still not knowing just where we were.

At eight o'clock this morning, June 1st, we saw the dutchmen coming

Americans worked their way through the streets.

forward, coming across the open flat space across the river, which space at that time was green wheat about waist high. Paul and myself were the only ones out of the whole Battalion that had guns in position that could reach this attack, the attack coming from the northeast. The dutchmen made nine attempts to effect a crossing. They would come up and be driven back by the machine gun fire from the four guns that Paul and I had. We accounted for a good many dutchmen during this attack. Paul was driven out of his position by German machine guns. He lost, as I remember, three men. He took up a position a little farther back, in a more protected place, and stuck the day out in this position. He had an opportunity in about the middle of the afternoon to prevent the Germans from throwing across a pontoon bridge. By machine gun fire he chased some of the dutchmen away who were half dressed and who had stripped in order to get into the river to place this bridge. The attempt to cross the river stopped about seven o'clock that evening.

During the day Paul and myself placed men in buildings and along the banks, scattered out, and armed with their pistols, and any detachment seen crawling in the wheat towards the river were met by our men with pistols. The river at this point was about 60 to 75 feet wide. Paul came to me after the battle was over, crowing about having two notches in his pistol, which he showed me. I told him he had nothing on me for I had gotten two that same day. Ever since that time his only desire was to add another notch to his pistol in order to outstrip me.

At eight o'clock that night, at which time it was dark, some men were seen crossing the bridge that I was guarding. We commenced firing and stopped them from crossing. We could hear a great amount of talking across the river. The Germans, as well as my guns, were machine gunning the bridge. Through the noise could be heard the cry "Cease fire." Fearing that it was a German trick I would not allow the men to cease but went to the bridge and called across to find out who it was, finding that it was Lieut. Bissel of "A" Company. The bridge in the center of the town had been blown up, cutting Bissel and his platoon off from retreat. Knowing his only way to cross to the south side would be to cross the bridge I was guarding, he attempted to cross at that bridge. When I found it was Bissel I ran back to my men, taking my men across the bridge and carrying the wounded and killed back to our side. Going back to the guns we were able to open up fire in time to stop a crossing by the Germans who had been pressing Lieut. Bissel from the north side. Their attempt lasted about an hour.

The False Alarm

About 9:30 PM a runner came to me with an order to retreat with all possible speed; that the Germans had crossed the river and were in our side of

Here was the crisis.

Guns were kept well back from the window to prevent their discovery

Warn the Americans not to fire.

Ford Model T Touring Car
This type of Ford Model T touring car was used by the U.S. 7th Motorized Machine Gun Battalion to transport staff and other officers.

View from the Mill to Crezancy

Château-Thierry. Supposing that the Germans had made a crossing without my knowing it and fearing that we would all be captured, I followed instructions given, which instructions were nothing less than to "beat it." Going through an enemy barrage, which consisted of three lines of barrage on a road, railroad and canal, we went to the rear about four kilometers up a hill overlooking the river, where the French had previously retreated to and prepared as a line of resistance. On arriving I found Paul and his platoon already there, Paul having received the same order as I. We waited on this hill, after putting our guns into position, expecting the Germans at any moment to make further attack.

At about one o'clock in the morning Paul said to me: "What do you think we had better do?" I asked him what he meant, and he said: "Don't you think we had better go back into Chateau Thierry? (having found out the name of the town) and find out whether or not the Germans were actually in the town?" This to me was one of the bravest things that any man has ever done. I had thought about the thing myself, but hesitated in saying anything, Paul ranking me in command, but Paul says: "We had better do it," and we, Paul and I, took one runner and started back for Château-Thierry to find out, if possible, why the dutchmen were not on our trail. We each took a pistol in one hand and a trench knife in the other. We worked our way back through the same barrage that the Germans were still firing and crept into Château-Thierry. I wish it were only possible to give an idea of what doing this meant, every moment expecting to run into dutchmen and every moment expecting to be bumped off by a shell. We finally reached the place where we started from, and to our surprise we found that there were no dutchmen on our side of the river. We immediately went to Battalion Headquarters for information as to why we had been ordered to retreat. The Major denied any knowledge of our retreat, and showed no interest in the matter, and didn't seem to give a darn what we had done or might do. It seems that on account of his condition the order had been given by another officer at Headquarters. Paul and I felt that under the circumstances as we found things at Headquarters an effort might be made to hold us responsible for the retreat, and that the only thing for us to do was to go back and get our men and guns and get into action again in our old positions, which we were finally able to do about daylight that morning. We both decided at that time that if another order came for retreat we would never obey it. We learned afterward that it had been reported at Headquarters that the dutchmen had made a crossing at the bridge which we had been guarding, which, of course, was not true.

It was this same morning that Paul had a chance to annihilate a German platoon which was seen coming down the hill on the opposite side of the river.

He afterwards made the remark that it was to "square up for the retreat that he had gone through. Nothing in particular happened until the night of June 5th, except a continuous bombardment by the enemy artillery. On the night of June 5th a rumor had been started that the Germans were going to make another attempt to cross the east bridge. (Both bridges were stone; the west bridge had a stone railing and the east bridge a steel hand rail). In order to strengthen the defense of the bridge Paul brought his two guns and placed them so as to fire on the bridge with the four guns that I now had, which made six guns on the bridge. We stayed in a small dug-out which had about a foot of dirt for a roof.

How the Bridge Was Destroyed

About nine o'clock that night we received a message from Company Headquarters that we were to be relieved, which news, of course, was received with great rejoicing, but our troubles were not yet over. About ten o'clock in the evening a French officer came to our Post of Command (P. C.) and commenced to talk. Neither Paul nor I being able to understand him, we secured an interpreter. Through the interpreter we learned that this Frenchman was to bring in a company of French, on account of the expected crossing by the Germans. This Frenchman wished to make a reconnaissance on the bridge in order to get the lay of the ground. Mind you, it was dark. Paul and I, neither one knowing just whose guns were firing on the bridge, except our own, did not care to take a chance in taking this Frenchman out, so we sent him to Battalion Headquarters. While he was gone another Frenchman came, and we found that he wanted to blow up the bridge. Going to the Battalion Headquarters with this Frenchman we joined the Major with this other Frenchman to receive instructions. We found the Major in the same unfortunate condition, and he turned the proposition over to Paul and I, telling us to handle it in the best way that we could.

The Frenchmen asked him what assurance he could give that they would not be shot while they were on the bridge doing their work. I asked the Major if there were any other guns firing on the bridge except the guns Paul and I had, and the Major said "No," so Paul and I told the Frenchmen that we would take them out personally to guarantee to them that they would not be fired upon by our guns. Leaving Battalion Headquarters we returned to our gun positions. Paul sent orders to his guns to this effect, I sending the same to mine: "Cease firing on bridge because we are going out on the bridge personally." We went out on the bridge, taking these Frenchmen with us in order for them to do the work they were sent out to do, but while on the bridge we were fired upon, and the fire came from our side of the river, which we afterward learned was from the guns of Company A. Naturally, we did not stick on the bridge very long. Out

The field of fire of Lt. Bissell's machine gun located on the top of the medieval stone tower.

G Company had its guns positioned to the left and right of where the railroad spur line meets the main line. The mill property is to the left.

F Company, top of the road

E Company, the sunken area

of the party the Frenchmen were the first ones to get back to where we started from. Paul and I were not far behind, however. Knowing that we could receive no satisfaction from the Major, we went and found these other three guns which were firing on the bridge and gave them orders not to fire any more that night. About four o'clock in the morning of June 6th, the bridge was finally blown up and we were relieved about five o'clock and started back to the back area.

We had been sent into Château-Thierry with the hope that we could delay the enemy with a rear guard action in order to give the French time to prepare a line of resistance on the hill to which Paul and I had retreated June 1st, and which was about 4 kilometers south of the Marne. Instead of merely conducting a rear guard action, as was intended, our Battalion stopped the dutch and held them and they got no further on their wild drive for Paris. For this our Battalion was decorated by the French government.

Wilbur Forrest, an accredited correspondent with the AEF in 1918, later (1924) wrote *Behind the Front Page*. In his book, Forrest presents an explanation of how the Marines garnered the larger share of the credit for having fought at or in Château-Thierry:

I shall never forget many stories on which the war censor fell with a resounding clash as he bayoneted them with keen shears and obliterated them with smudges of heavy blue.

One particular incident stands out in my mind. It was at dawn on May 27, 1918 that the army of the German Crown Prince came forward after a short gas bombardment against British troops holding the tableland of Vauclerc, scattered them, then routed the French Tenth Army to the west. By late afternoon the enemy forces had put the famous Chemin des Dames behind them, had taken and held the three bridge-heads of the Meuse, Oeuilly, and Pont-d'Arch, then by night had forged southward to the Vesle at Fismes with its ammunition dumps, ambulance units, and army parks. The following day the Germans took Soissons, and on May 29th, advance guards reached the Marne at Jaulgonne.

The Germans had reached the Marne a second time. There were no Americans within a hundred miles of that river at this time. There were American troops in training here and there in France, and the war spirit at home had been livened for the first time with the capture of Cantigny.

A story of the Americans on the Marne was a great story as far as American newspapers were concerned, one designed to stir the war spirit at home to fever pitch. There was talk about the Germans reaching Paris. The eyes of the world, as well as of the United States, were upon this battle. We had sent thousands of troops to France. Where were they? Cantigny had been taken. That fact located some of them without telling who or what these troops were. But what of the rest? Where were they, and what were they doing?

Late in the afternoon of May 31ˢᵗ, two correspondents were sitting in a camouflaged position with French artillery men on the south bank of the Marne near Dormans watching the Germans maneuver down this historic stream towards Château-Thierry. Advance German elements had already filtered through the town from the north and held the houses on that side of the stream. Two bridges over the Marne linked Château-Thierry, north and south, and it was imperative to prevent the Germans from crossing.

Paul Scott Mowrer of the *Chicago Daily News* and I were the newspaper observers. Our minds were not on Americans at all. We were gathering local color, which we intended to cable that night, supplementing information contained in the official communiqué. Two routes led into Dormans, one paralleling the river along the main street, and another descending sharply from the rolling, wood-covered hills above. The latter route passed directly across the main street to the bridge, an ancient fifty-yard long, suspension affair. Beyond lay the north bank of the Marne.

Leaving headquarters that morning we had intended to go as far as possible and near enough to observe events, but not at the risk of capture. Our chauffeur, a French *poilu*, was so advised, and acted accordingly. Our car was a staff Renault, painted battleship gray and bearing the usual military numerals. It was headed down the steep hill, and it came to a crunching halt on the bridge before we discovered anything wrong.

There were Germans with machine-guns at the far end of that bridge. We expected a well-directed stream of hot lead at any moment. Our chauffeur, with the quick wit of his race, shifted his gears to reverse. The car moved backward with a roar. Yet no fire. It gathered speed and still the enemy machine-gunners hesitated. Like a frightened crab our Renault scuttled backwards up the hill and took cover behind the friendly fringe of trees. We scrambled out, taking personal cover in the ditches at the roadside. Still the expected sputter of machine-guns did not come. The element of surprise may explain this. It all happened quickly and the Germans were as much astonished as we were. Undoubtedly we had neatly escaped capture, for once across the bridge into the enemy's line, he could have dealt with us at his leisure. Under international laws of war, a correspondent does not go armed. Resistance would have been worse than useless.

When it was evident that we were well concealed after our successful reverse maneuver, we got aboard the Renault again and proceeded to parts less hostile. Our new field of action was the road along the crest of hills which flank the south bank of the river. Here we found our friends, the French. They were the giant blacks of Senegal, strongly ensconced among the trees, ready adversaries for the

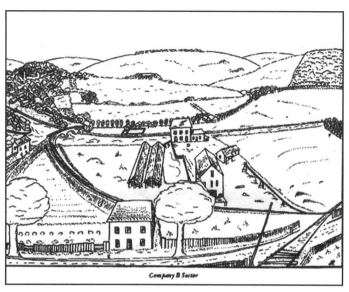

Company B Sector

F Company's view to the NE

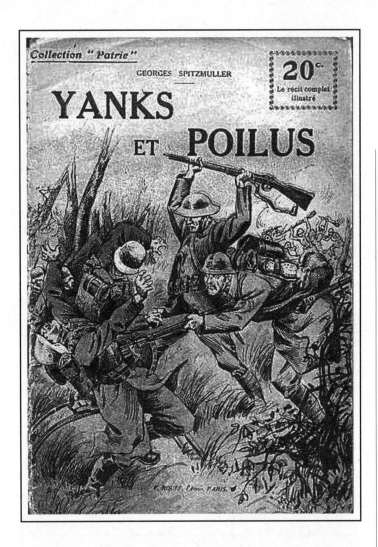

Collection "Patrie"

GEORGES SPITZMULLER

20ᶜ
Le récit complet
illustré

YANKS ET POILUS

Germans if there should be a move to cross the river. Batteries of snappy little 75's were mounted in position to blow the Dormans bridge off of the map once the enemy set foot upon it. Likewise, any considerable grouping of enemy troops could have been similarly dealt with by direct fire. As a last resort there were the Senegalese, expert hand-to-hand battlers. They were of the hard-fighting colonial forces of General Mangin, ordered to the Marne to prevent a German crossing. What we did not know was that American troops also had been ordered up.

The German design, however, was not to cross the river at that time. Theirs was obviously a concentration of effort near Château-Thierry.

When Mowrer and I had gathered sufficient material for a color story, we started back to headquarters itching to get our fingers on the typewriter. Our Renault had carried us only a short distance when we met the wholly unexpected. It was a dusty flivver containing four men who had either much reason or none at all to be in that locality. They wore the brimmed felt had of the United States Army, an article of equipment which Americans usually put aside in favor of the cloth forage cap soon after arrival in France.

"Americans!" I shouted. "Americans!" shouted back Mowrer. They had passed and were disappearing down the road in a cloud of dust. Under excited command our chauffeur wheeled the Renault around sharply and took after them. They were the first Americans to reach the Marne and we were intensely interested in them. Once we halted the flivver, there began a series of rapid-fire questioning without preliminaries. Our compatriots were all second lieutenants.

"You're American?" we queried. They admitted as much.

"Are you up here on a pleasure and sight-seeing tour, or for fighting?" we demanded.

They were reticent, obviously nervous and somewhat suspicious. Our own status was not quite clear to them. We wore the English uniform which was de rigeur for correspondents with the French armies. We explained this before one replied:

"We're hardly up here for pleasure. We're here for business. Where's Château-Thierry?"

We explained that Château-Thierry was up the road "a piece," but in the opposite direction, and that it might be dangerous to tear into the town in a dust-kicking flivver. In fact, we advised, in might be expedient to proceed with some caution as, at the moment, beyond the screen of trees and across the Marne, about three hundred yards away, there were many Germans also en route to Château-Thierry. We indicated French troops in the brush not far off, which they had not observed. This confirmed our suspicions that these compatriots of ours were so green at the war game that they needed chaperoning.

The four second lieutenants were not only the first American combatants to reach the Marne in those stirring days but they were the vanguard of the Seventh Machine Gun Battalion of the Third Division—General Dickman's force, which had arrived in France a few weeks before.

Eventually we picked up the Seventh Battalion, a motorized unit which had been on the road more than eighteen hours, dusty and tired but fired with the desire to "mix it" with the enemy.

Mowrer and I chaperoned this battalion into Château-Thierry on that evening of May 31, 1918. We pointed out heavy black shell-bursts of enemy fire, and explained that these were nothing more than the welcome of an ill-intentioned army which objected to their presence. These shell-bursts were the first that members of the Seventh Battalion had ever seen. The true significance of their situation was only realized when a section of the battalion had received the full force of a German 155 with dead and wounded. This occurred in a village on the outskirts of Château-Thierry. Shortly after we left the battalion that night, it had planted its guns in the houses along the south bank of the river to command the two big bridges. Here it fought with great bravery for many days.

Naturally, my companion and I lost little time in returning to French headquarters. We had a story that would thrill America. It had a kick in it for every American heart, that tale of these superbly green youngsters and their baptism of fire on that famous river, the Marne. It was a picture story as well, the trickling of Feldgrauen towards Château-Thierry on one side, the olive green of America and the coal black giants of France on the other. How would it all end? It was a brand-new kind of war, the campaign of maneuver.

We arrived at French headquarters and went beyond to the château in which the Anglo-American correspondents lived. This story was under our hats. There had not been another American or even British correspondent within twenty miles of the Marne. The story was ours exclusively. We settled down to our typewriters and wrote throughout the night.

Early the next morning we appeared at headquarters, with carefully worded copy. It was necessary to get the O.K. of the field censor before the copy could proceed by wire to the Paris Bourse, and then from Paris to the cable head at Brest. But our prize story only got to headquarters. Here it was killed by the censor. An American major assisted in the execution. He was attached to French headquarters as press liaison officer. I have forgotten his name, but I hope he reads this and repents before it is too late.

Three days after the Seventh Machine Gun Battalion entered Château-Thierry, the United States Marines took up their positions in Belleau Wood, barring the road to Paris. Most of the American correspondents were concentrating on this

American machine gunner and his French Hotchkiss machine gun, 1918

event. When censorial authorities sought to delete all mention of the Marines, there was a concerted protest which raised the roof and shook the morale of the censor.

Demands were made by the American correspondents in the name of the American people to set aside a rule of censorship which forbade identity of troops which the enemy had every reason to know were opposite him. The Germans had no illusions about the Marines. Those doughty fighters had begun to do what their Regular Army brothers of the Third Division had been doing in Château-Thierry for three days, unknown to everybody but the Germans, the censor (especially the censor at French headquarters), Mowrer and me.

Suddenly under heavy persuasion the American censor department, after consultation with our own and the other staffs, agreed that the magic word "Marines" might be used. Consequently the exploits of this brave brigade swept across the cables in such force that within 24 hours all America was thrilled to the marrow.

Belleau Wood is near Château-Thierry. In the confusion which resulted from that fact, the latter became a magic name associated with the Marine Brigade, yet not a single Marine fought in the battle of Château-Thierry.

It was our Seventh Machine Gun Battalion which was at the moment fighting the desperate battle of Château-Thierry. The battle went on, unheralded, piling up the enemy forces who attempted to take the bridges. Fighting became so hot that French engineers sent first one, then the other of the bridges into the air with TNT. The first bridge that was destroyed cut off an American squad on reconnaissance duty in German territory.

Because of censorship rules the whole story of the Seventh Machine Gun Battalion at Château-Thierry was smothered, or rather, overshadowed by the equally thrilling story of the Marine Brigade. Thus was the news of the arrival of the first Americans on the Marne virtually killed.

When Mowrer and I were permitted many days later to cable the tale of the heroic machine-gunners, the censor ruthlessly blue-penciled any mention of their unit which might have identified them with the Third American Division, Regular Army. They were just "machine-gunners."

American newspaper readers already had the story of the Marines, hence the deleted dispatches gave the impression that our "machine-gunners" were Soldiers of the Sea. In fact, so strong was this belief that a headline writer in New York carefully labeled my lengthy cable: "Marines at Château-Thierry."

Without in the least minimizing the great valor of the Marine Brigade at Belleau Wood, I believe, even after years of reflection, that this was one of the greatest crimes of the war censor. His sin was that of commission and omission. He (I speak in the collective sense) weakened under clamor to permit mention of the Marines, an order which he rescinded within forty-eight hours.

Thus were the Marines permitted to take credit for one of the greatest single exploits of the untrained, untried soldiers of the nation. He also ruined one of the best stories that individual war correspondents might hope to write through personal initiative. And it required many weeks to convince the General commanding the Third Division that Mowrer and I were not responsible for this theft of glory from his gallant men.

In the July, 1918 issue of *New York Times Current History Magazine* appeared the following article, "American's Defense of Château-Thierry":

UNITED STATES troops, mostly inexperienced in actual warfare, on June 1 played a brilliant part in the defense of Château-Thierry. By their prompt and resolute support to the French they assisted in driving the Germans from the south bank of the Marne at that vital point, and were largely responsible for blocking the enemy's determined advance across the river toward Paris, thus preventing the development of a most serious situation for the Allies. The French official report of the incident was as follows:

"American troops checked German advanced forces which were seeking to penetrate Neuilly Wood, and by a magnificent counterattack hurled back the Germans north of this wood.

Further south the Germans were not able to make any gains. On the Marne front an enemy battalion which had crept across to the left bank of the river above Jaulgonne was counterattacked by French and American troops and hurled back to the other bank, after having suffered heavy losses. A footbridge which the enemy used was destroyed and 100 prisoners remained in our hands.

A BRITISH ACCOUNT

The Reuters correspondent under date of June 5 described the feat of the Americans at Château-Thierry in these words:

On May 31, when the Germans were already in the outskirts of Château-Thierry, an American machine-gun unit was hurried thither in motor lorries. Château-Thierry lies on both banks of the Marne, which is spanned by a big bridge. A little to the northward a canal runs parallel to the river and is crossed by a smaller bridge

The Americans had scarcely reached their quarters when news was received that the Germans had broken into the northern part of Château-Thierry, having made their way through the gap they had driven in our lines to the left of the town and then pouring along the streets to the bridge, intending to establish themselves firmly on the south bank and capture the town.

The American machine gunners and French colonials were thrown into Château-Thierry together. The Americans immediately took over the defense of the river bank, especially the approaches to the bridge. Fighting with their habitual courage and using their guns with an accuracy which won the highest encomiums from the French, they brought the enemy to a standstill.

Already wavering under the American fire, the Germans were counterattacked by the French colonials and driven from the town. They returned to the attack the next night and under cover of darkness crept into the town along the river bank and began to work their way through the streets toward the main bridge. At the same moment a tremendous artillery bombardment was opened up upon the southern half of the town.

Blowing Up The Bridge

When within range of the machine guns the Germans advanced under the cover of clouds of thick white smoke from smoke bombs, in order to baffle the aim of the American gunners. A surprise, however, was in store for them. They were already crossing the bridge, evidently believing themselves masters of both banks, when a thunderous explosion blew the center of the bridge and a number of Germans with it into the river. Those who reached the southern bank were immediately captured.

In this battle in the streets, and again at night, the young American soldiers showed a courage and determination which aroused the admiration of their French colonial comrades. With their machine guns they covered the withdrawal of troops across the bridge before its destruction, and although under severe fire themselves, kept all the approaches to the bank under a rain of bullets which nullified all the subsequent efforts of the enemy to cross the river. Every attempt of the Germans to elude the vigilance of the Americans resulted in disaster.

Against their casualties the Americans set a much greater loss inflicted by their bullets on the enemy. They have borne their full part in what a French staff officer well qualified to judge described as one of the finest feats of the war.

The story of the quick advance of the American marines was related in detail by Wilbur Forrest in the *New York Tribune*:

The Quick Advance

It is a narrative that stands for more, perhaps, than most of those written in American history books. It is literally another story of American minute men who abandoned the figurative plowshares of peaceful training camps and rushed to the scene of action. They met the enemy with weapons they knew how to handle…"

On May 30 the enemy reached the Marne east of Château-Thierry and began a forceful advance along the north bank toward the city. The same day American machine gunners received orders 100 kilometers to the rear to jump into auto trucks and hurry into action.

They started almost immediately, and an all-night journey found the battalion at 4 o'clock in the afternoon of the 31st on a hill overlooking Château-Thierry. All around them French batteries were firing full tilt. The enemy was advancing on the city.

Right here those American machine gunners got their first glimpse of real war. German shells crashed into villages within plain view and the little city below them was not being spared. The officers chose a small nearby village as headquarters and the marines waited for darkness before loading little black machine guns on their shoulders and marching into Château-Thierry.

German Shells Rake City

German high explosives and shrapnel were raking the city, but the young Americans under fire for the first time coolly placed their guns in position on the south bank of the river. They saw heavy shells strike the railroad station and they saw it burn. They saw houses fall like packs of cards, and I have the word of a Frenchman, who was present, that they were "cool like American cucumbers."

During the night the Germans gradually filtered into the outskirts on the north side of the town. Roughly speaking, the American guns were so placed between the houses and in the gardens as to enfilade the approaches to the bridge and the streets on the opposite sides. All remained on the south bank with the exception of a Lieutenant, (John T. Bissell,) a youthful Pittsburgher, who was one of West Point's latest graduates.

The Lieutenant with a dozen men and two guns was ordered to cross the river to prevent the enemy's advance along forked roads which merge to the right of the northern approach to the iron bridge. For convenience sake it is permissible to say that A Company was charged with holding the left part of town on the south bank and the approaches to the larger bridges, while B Company's guns swept the opposite approaches to the iron bridge, and therefore, held the right portion of the town.

Several hundred yards separated the two companies. The enemy's shelling was intensified during the night, but no Germans were yet in sight. The machine guns were quiet, although A Company's commander, O. F. Houghton of Portland, Me., was forced to abandon the headquarters he had chosen in a house on the bank of the river and change the position of some guns because of the enemy's precise fire.

It was a waiting game for Company A's guns. In the meantime Company B, at about 5 AM, in broad daylight, saw two columns of the enemy of twelve men each, advancing across an open field toward the river to the right of their position. The Germans carried light machine guns and were blissfully ignorant that our men were here. One American gun swung its shy little nose around toward the Germans and waited. Behind it was an unpoetic youth named Must of Colombia, S. C., a Sergeant, who waited until he saw the whites of their eyes, and then let them have it, as he explained today.

At Close Range

"I got eight out of the bunch by a little surprise shooting," said the Sergeant with a considerable show of pride. "They flopped nicely. Then I turned on the other squad, but they were leery and I got only one. The rest of them got into the ditch and crawled back without showing themselves. Later in the day their Red Cross men came out to pick up the wounded. We've got orders not to fire upon members of the Red Cross, so I let 'em work unmolested. But I kept tally all day when their Red Cross men came out. By my count they carried off nine and they weren't all wounded either."

The Germans during the day of June 1 gained the hills overlooking the north bank of the river. Their machine guns and their artillery observers, therefore, were able to direct a galling fire on the south bank and portions of the north bank which were still held by the French colonials and two machine guns under an American Lieutenant.

Deadly Machine Guns

The enemy's position thus made the north bank untenable and orders were given to retire to the south bank under cover of darkness. At 9:30 PM the French, in accordance with these plans, retired to the south bank and blew up a stone bridge. The American machine gun companies during the retirement poured a galling fire from the flanks into the areas evacuated by the retiring troops.

The enemy was now shelling the south bank more heavily and the enemy machine-gun fire was multiplied. The commander of Company A was forced to change the position of his guns in order to secure a better field of fire. With the light Hotchkiss pieces on their shoulders he led his men into a wood further down the river. Here they were spotted by enemy observers and thirty high explosive shells crashed into the wood. The shelling ceased and the guns went into their positions.

The French were still retiring at 10:30 PM It was pitch dark, except for shell bursts and the streaky flame stabs from the machine guns on both sides—the Americans were in the wood and along the south bank of the river, the Germans on the crest of the hill on the other side.

Suddenly there was an immense detonation. It was the big bridge blowing up. Then there came out of the darkness across the river, as the firing lulled, the ghostly chant of the advancing enemy. It was one of those German mass attacks, where men, shoulder to shoulder, singing in guttural tones the praise of Germany and the Kaiser, blindly walk into death like fanatics.

The sort of creaky, shuffling sound their boots made as they trotted into the open road came across the river like the wailing of lost souls, converged toward the bridge and was heard by these young Americans, who strained their eyes across the river to get what machine-gun men call "the target." But it was in pitch darkness, and there was only the sound to tell them there were plenty of "targets." Every little black devil of a machine gun tore loose with a hellfire. The Americans behind them, who saw their first glimpse of war about thirty hours before, fed in bullets as fast as human hands could work. And the bullets caught their "targets" on the opposite side.

The "target" came on again and again, but nothing could live in that leaden hail. The enemy waves melted back in the darkness.

Now come the even more thrilling experience of the little band of Americans under Lieutenant Bissell who had been cut off and surrounded by the enemy across the river. Even experienced soldiers could not be blamed if they had surrendered there.

At the beginning of the German mass attack a few French colonial soldiers, also cut off by the blown-up bridge, made the Lieutenant understand that then it was every man for himself. The north bank was becoming a seething mass of Germans. All other forces had retired across the river. Bullets were registering on every foot of the space approaching the bridges.

The Germans chant to keep up the courage of the advancing masses. They sometimes yell to disconcert their enemies. With this ghostly chanting drawing nearer to the Lieutenant and his men and the weird yells of the Germans occasionally splitting the night, there was no thought of surrender. Their orders were to retreat by the main bridge, and orders were orders.

Serious Predicament

Picking up both guns, each man carrying his allotted piece in maneuvers, the party of thirteen started along the river for the main bridge. Reaching the vicinity of the approach, they discovered their plight. The enemy was almost upon them. Still carrying their guns, they jumped down, taking cover under the stone parapets at the river's edge. Thus they worked their way down to the iron bridge, though the Germans on the very parapet above were marching into a hail of American machine guns from the south bank.

B company did not know that a detachment had not escaped. The German attack remained at its height, and the enemy, despite its losses, kept sweeping toward the iron bridge. Bissell and his men attempted to cross under their own fire. Three were immediately wounded. They retired, picking up their wounded.

The Lieutenant knew that B Company's guns were across the bridge, and he approached as near as he dared and yelled repeatedly. B Company's officers finished the story, which was narrated and corroborated by the Lieutenant and others at the rest camp today.

The first B Company knew that Americans were opposite them was when they heard a voice calling "Cobbey! Cobbey!" Cobbey was the other Lieutenant.

This time the German attack melted. B Company's guns ceased firing long enough for Cobbey to cross the bridge and lead the Lieutenant and his men to safety. Throughout the remainder of the night the enemy vented his rage by heavy shelling. The next day, June 2, the heavy shelling continued. The enemy had picked up his dead and wounded across the river under cover of darkness and could be seen occasionally flitting from house to house.

Sniping was continuous between the French and the Germans. Machine guns were silent during the day in order not to give away their positions. Nightfall was so quiet that the Americans were not able to understand such warfare. They thought all war was noisy.

However, at 9 o'clock at night the enemy made a fierce rush for the iron bridge. Fifteen minutes of heavy machine-gun firing squelched the attack and the shelling was resumed. The heavy bombardment continued.

"Got" Whole Platoon

On June 3 the Sergeant in charge of one of our platoons at the iron bridge saw the German platoon, of about fifty men forming on top of a hill. They made a beautiful target, according to the Sergeant's story today. He and his companions believe he got them all.

The enemy brought more artillery up by night and began a terrific shelling to culminate in what appeared to be an attempted attack. The French artillery sprinkled the opposite bank of the river with a barrage which the "novice" American fighters called beautiful. They thought it was less than a hundred yards away, and stood up to watch it, and there wasn't any attack.

The French engineers on this night laid a charge under the iron bridge while the American guns laid down a leaden protective barrage. When the charge was detonated the Germans rushed forward from the house to ascertain the cause of the explosion. It was here that a pre-arranged petrol flare lit up the vicinity like day, and again American machine gunners had what they insist on calling "targets."

"I was impressed by many things," a company's captain said. "First of all, the coolness of every man, and especially of a young Georgia theological student who had been drafted, who on the third day complained because the boche shells kept mussing up his gun position. Second, the attitude of those wonderful French colonial troops with us. They gave us inspiration. They said we gave them inspiration; so it was a fifty-fifty exchange. Third, that beautiful French barrage and our wonderful 'targets.'"

Editor's note: There are several errors of historical commission in this article: Firstly, the Germans never crossed the main wagon bridge in Château-Thierry while "chanting and singing" as they were shot down. There is some evidence to the effect that it was the escaping French colonial troops who were shot down on the bridge, and that the entire matter was hushed up. Evidently this July 1918 article may be the origin of this myth which has been perpetuated by several other writers. Second is the use of "marines" in several instances. The marines were never in Château-Thierry, and certainly never fought there. The primary action of the marines was northwest of Château-Thierry and in Belleau Wood.

Watch on the Rhine, the publication of the Society of the Third Infantry Division, issue of February, 2002, carried the following article as part of "Memoirs of World War I," by Sgt. James J. Webster:

Marshal Foch's Address to the American Legion, Kansas City (Extract), November 1, 1921:

It was the spirit of the 3rd American Army Division which took part in the BATTLE OF THE MARNE, and distinguished themselves immediately in the operations around CHATEAU-THIERRY.

A little article appeared in the *Public Ledger*, Tuesday morning, August 19, 1924 from Paris through their special representative, Mr. Raymond G. Carroll.

The general impression in the United States has been that the Marines were rushed to fill a gap in the line at CHATEAU-THIERRY and saved PARIS in May–June 1918. The facts are that the Marines did not fight in CHATEAU-THIERRY. The Second Division in which there were two regiments of the regular army infantry (the 9th and 23rd) was put in on June 1 behind a French division four miles west of CHATEAU-THIERRY. On June 4 the French division retired through the line of the Second Division, which in making a subsequent local advance took the town of VAUX and BELLEAU WOOD.

The first American unit to arrive in the MARNE Sector and which DID fight at CHATEAU-THIERRY was the Seventh Machine Gun Battalion of the 3rd Division, which making a record run overland from Chaumont, a distance of 116 miles beat its own divisions by rail, and on the evening of May 31 from the south side of the MARNE, in the town of CHATEAU-THIERRY, with the French prevented the Germans from crossing the MARNE RIVER. The next morning the Fourth Infantry regiment of the same division arrived there and relieved the French.

This much of history is necessary to explain the erection of a double shaft monument of the Third Division. It should finally silence the oft heard comment, "I saw no monument for the Marines at Château-Thierry."

The Stars & Stripes (official newspaper of the A.E.F.) had this to say:

3rd Meets Shock South of Marne. Crosses in Turn

Every foot of the way contested in 15 kilometer gain. Incessant fighting and maneuvering between infantry and machine gun detachments in broken, obscure country in its two last weeks of battle the 3rd Division had decisively defeated a German offensive and then advanced approximately 15 kilometers (8 miles) through a terribly difficult country, fighting every foot of the way and when it retired from action its losses according to the first tabulated reports had a high amount. This was probably considerably increased by other casualties.

The reason I have quoted the above men and periodical is because there has always been a discussion as to who fought at CHATEAU-THIERRY, and I believe that any division that was within a radius of 15 miles of this town claimed that they fought there. CHATEAU-THIERRY, in the World War is what Gettysburg is to the Civil War and that is a whole lot. So you can imagine that those of the 3rd Division that fought there and are still living are mighty proud of that honor while nothing under the sun can take from and THAT'S THAT!"

Here, in part, is the text of a little booklet evidently published in either 1918 or 1919. This booklet obviously did its part in convincing the American reading public that the American marines fought in Château-Thierry. The envelope in which this booklet was packaged states:

An Appreciation
To Be Sold by
Soldiers and Sailors
Price 25 cents

"America's Army and its Part in the Great War"
Copyright W. C. Both, Chicago

The Marines At Château-Thierry, pages 6 to 8
Château-Thierry: the name of that French town on the Marne lives forever in the memory of Americans.

For there, the United States Marines, whom Berlin has affected to pity as "untrained amateurs," stopped the rush of the famous Prussian Guards and proved that the "amateurs" could shoot straight and didn't know the meaning of the word "retreat." For five days the German masses had been pressing back the French divisions, unbroken but very weary—from the Aisne to the Vesle, to the Ourcq and finally to the Marne. They had taken Château-Thierry and the crest over which the Paris road runs. To the west they had pushed out towards Meaux and Paris. To the east they had crossed the Marne at Dormans. That was on Memorial Day, 1918. Driving in at full speed of its cars, the 7th Machine Gun Battalion had helped to hold the Château-Thierry bridgehead. On the morning of June 2nd Division, and with it the Marine Brigade, was in line across the Paris road down the Marne. Though one of its regiments had been in France nearly a year the Brigade had seen

no hard fighting. It had been 72 hours on the road in motor trucks, coming from the reserve back of Montdidier. Late that afternoon they were attacked by huge masses of Germans advancing across a wheat field. Calmly setting their sights as if they were on the Quantico range the Marines withered the German columns with rifle fire. What proved to be the last drive direct for Paris had been stopped. It was not yet the high tide of the Hun, for after six weeks of beating against the stone wall he was to try one more big attack, up the Marne toward Epernay, in the hope of getting around what he could not break through. Meanwhile the "untrained amateurs" were to prove that they could not only hold but also could strike back. The Germans had filled Belleau Wood, to the west of Château-Thierry, with nests of machine guns. Until they were cleared out the battle of Château-Thierry could not be considered won. On June 6 the Marines went in again to clear them out, with the villages of Torcy and Bouresches as the objectives. Companies that went in 250 strong dwindled to 50 and 60 with a sergeant in command. Lieut. Robertson had only twenty men left of his platoon when he entered Bouresches at 9:45 PM It was fighting from tree to tree, in underbrush so thick that a machine gun 50 yards away could not be seen until it swept the ranks with its fire. Save by long artillery fire that would wipe out the timber the only way was with the bayonet, with perhaps but one man reaching the nest to kill the last of its defenders and turn the gun on the other German positions. That is the way that the Marines and their comrades of the Third Regular Brigade did it. Not until July 6 was Belleau Wood finally cleared. But what the Yanks took they held. And in memory of their valor France has decreed that Belleau Wood, whose taking completed the battle of Château-Thierry, shall be known forever as "The Wood of the United States Marines."

Meanwhile the Third division had been holding the railroad north of the bend of the Marne between the Surmelin mouth and Mezy. "A single regiment," says Gen. Pershing, "wrote one of the most brilliant pages in our military annals. Our men, firing in three directions, met attacks with counterattacks at critical points and threw two German divisions into complete confusion, capturing 600 prisoners." The First, Second and 26th U. S. divisions had joined with the French in the counter-offensive of July 18 toward

Soissons and by reaching Berzy-le-Sec, Tigny and Torcy compelled the Huns to begin a retreat and captured over 7,000 prisoners and 100 guns. The Third division, pushing north from the Marne, had taken Mont-St. Pere, Charteves and Jaulgonne. On July 24 the Rainbow division relieved the 26th, fought its way through the Foret de Fere, and on July 27th had reached the Heights of the Ourcq with the Third and Fourth divisions. On July 29 the 32nd division relieved the Third, and with the Rainbow pushed on to Cierges and Sergy. The 28th and 77th divisions then took up the pursuit of the enemy to the Vesle and the reduction of the Marne salient ended with the capture of Fismes on Aug. 6.

From *The Literary Digest*, 13 September 1919, "Father O'Reilly Tells of the Work of the Third in France":

The 3rd Division, a so-called Regular Army Division in spite of the fact that it was composed almost altogether of the same sort of material which made up the National Army Divisions, got back home the other day, bearing its honors thick upon it. One of the chaplains, the Rev. Father Frank M. O'Reilly, of the 76th Field Artillery, is now in a New York hospital recuperating from wounds and gassing received during the most strenuous days of the war.

The 3rd Division, which played a vital part in the great throw-back around Château-Thierry, has received all too little recognition here at home," said Chaplain O'Reilly, by way of welcoming his old comrades in arms. "The cause is simple, and in memorializing the veterans now returning to their native land with depleted ranks I do not desire to detract any of the hard-won glory from the 1st and 2nd Divisions." To a reporter from the New York Evening Sun, Father O'Reilly gave this account of the history of the 3rd Division in France.

The principal cause for so little information about the fighting of the 3rd Division was that strict censorship maintained by the Army over the naming of units in all cable dispatches home. It was known to all that the first men to get into action, "Pershing's Own," were the doughboys of the 1st Division. Thus, they were identified in a way from the start, first to land and first to fight. Of the 2nd Division little was heard during the fighting except the exploits of the marines, who could be mentioned collectively by name. Thus the story of its exploits passed the censor, and the "devil dogs" received their own due credit.

But the battling 3rd Division had no press representatives with it; it was simply a combat division of the Regular Army, although the replacements from other branches of the Army brought National Guardsmen and National Army (drafted men) into it.

It was the 7th Machine Gun Battalion of the 3rd Division which rode 110 miles on motor trucks and with only 1,000 men held the bridgehead at Château-Thierry for seventy-two hours, preventing the crossing of the Hun. On June 3, 1918, the 3rd Division was rushed into position along the Marne from Château-Thierry eastward for a distance of twelve miles, with the 2nd Division holding the line westward from Château-Thierry for eight miles. Meanwhile the marines were in Belleau Wood, with the 23rd Infantry between them and the town—and the Germans were checked.

The 3rd Division was the only division between Château-Thierry and Reims to feel the shock of the German attack, made by three German divisions, the 10th and 36th Infantry and the 10th Landwehr, who made the assault at Jaulgonne, in a space held by a little more than half of the 3rd Division. The Germans were almost annihilated. When the Germans attempted crossing in boats our doughboys came from No Man's Land to the river, and "playing baseball," hurled showers of hand grenades upon the enemy. Captured maps and plans showed that the Germans had been certain of crossing the river by noon of the first day. The 3rd Division did not budge an inch, and that night no Germans, save dead ones, remained in front of the 3rd Division on the south side of the River Marne. All three Hun divisions were captured or wiped out.

The French on our right fell back, leaving our flank exposed. Our telephone and telegraph wires had been cut by spies, as shown by the scraped insulation observed later, and our division was physically disorganized. The Germans mocked us by sending messages from airplanes, but the 3rd Division never turned back.

This was the occasion of General McAlexander's famous message to the French command: "Unless totally annihilated, I shall not retreat—and then I can't." With rest and replacements the 3rd Division crossed the Marne on July 20, and on July 20 by 4 o'clock in the afternoon was in control of the headwaters of the Ourcq. On August 4 the Vesle was reached and the Château-Thierry salient was history—and the burial place of hundreds of "never-say-die" Yankee boys.

This is the story of the 3rd Division's great contribution to the debacle. Newspapermen were with the National Army divisions and with the Old Guard units. Our battle gave premature birth to the 1st American Army an produced our great American commanders, General Dickman, later commander of the 3rd Army, or Army of Occupation, was placed in command of the 3rd Division shortly after the battle.

The "quick on the trigger" repulse given the Huns by the 3rd Division before the 1st and 2nd (temporarily in reserve) could come up, declares Father O'Reilly, "saved Paris and prevented the ending of the war right there—in July, 1918. Let the American people remember this about the gallant and unsung 3rd Division! He continues:

"In those after-war days, when each nation is claiming the credit of winning the war, it is well to consider the condition of the Allies at the time of the 3rd Division's great stand. I was there and understand intimately the attitude of the various nationalities. A chaplain has more privilege of travel and conversation than either officer or enlisted man.

"The English—and I heard their own feelings expressed by men of all ranks—were indeed, 'with their backs to the wall.' The shibboleth of the French, expressed on all sides and in my hearing was: "The Americans are too late.' Instead of six months' training the men of the 3rd Division were thrown into combat after a few weeks, and, minus their artillery, which had been sent back to America because of an accident at sea, they showed to the surprise of the Germans, and still more astounded Allies, what 'green' troops could do.

The 1st and 26th Divisions had six months' training; the 2nd had three months of it; while the 3rd, facing the first great battle brunt, had a few weeks of infantry work at Chateau-Villain. The artillery had the use of unfamiliar ordnance for six weeks' practice.

A captured German officer said: "The American idiots—shoot at them and they charge you. Kill them—and they keep on coming.

A brief excerpt from H. De Wissen's article, "Seeing Battle-Scarred Europe," appeared in *Forum*, July, 1920. Once again we can readily see how the American public was misled into believing that the Marines fought in Château-Thierry:

The war has overturned all traditions of the tourist. Where Americans used to make pilgrimages to some quaint town where Charles the Bold, or other illustrious bandits of the olden days, used to hold forth, Americans will now swarm over France, seeking out every nook and cranny where Pershing's boys chased the Hun. Places once unheard of, but where American history has been made, places with new and terrible connotations, have relegated old and magic meccas of the tourists into a by-gone Europe, as elusive in our memories as old half-forgotten melodies.

The new tourist map of France divides itself into three great areas. One begins near Paris. Quite nearby is Château-Thierry—a few hours from Paris by rail. Formerly, the only claim of this little town to fame was that La Fontaine, the fabulist, was born there. Charles Martel built a castle at Château-Thierry, and it was he who decisively crushed those other ravagers of civilization, the Saracens, in a battle near Tours more than a thousand years ago. Perhaps his spirit moved with our Marines, as, with the battle swirling around this old château, they broke the shock of the German rush with their flesh, and then went at the Kaiser's picked troops with rifle-butts and bayonets. And it was at Château-Thierry that Major-General Omar Bundy declined to obey the French orders to retreat, and counter-attacked.

Now, from the château, one can follow the line of Bundy's counter-attack up the valley of the Marne and the Ourcq, across the river Vesle, even across the Aisne.

From Thomas Mudd's book, *The Yanks Were There*:

A French report of the work of an American machine gun battalion, which has recently been in action at Château-Thierry, includes the following:

"On May 31 the enemy threatened to take Château-Thierry, attempting to flank the town on our left, and a breach was produced. The blank machine gun battalion, United States Army, was immediately thrown into Château-Thierry simultaneously with a Colonial infantry battalion. Immediately the Americans reinforced the entire defense, especially at the ends of the bridge. Their courage and ability as marksmen evoked the admiration of all.

Crushed by our fire, the enemy hesitated and, as a result of the counterattacks, vigorously supported by the American machine guns, they were thrown beyond the edges of the town. Château-Thierry remained entirely in our hands.

The episode of Château-Thierry will remain one of the most memorable deeds of this war. It is a pleasure for all of us to know that our valiant allies have shared with us there."

From Thomas B. Mudd's book, *The Yanks Were There*:

"American Official Communique, 4 June 1918
OUR MEN DRIVE BACK IN MARNE BATTLE
WITH FRENCH THEY REPULSE FOE REPEATEDLY to the WEST OF CHÂTEAU-THIERRY
Americans Win Praise in Hand-to-Hand Combat and Use of Machine Guns
Smash Up Wave Attacks
Prisoners Have Been Captured by Pershing Troops, Who Lost None Themselves"

Once again from Thomas B. Mudd's book, *The Yanks Were There*:

"WITH THE AMERICAN ARMY IN PICARDY, June 4, (Associated Press.)—American troops cooperating with the French west of Chateau Thierry, north of the Marne, the nearest and most critical point to Paris reached by the enemy, have brilliantly checked the onrushing Germans, beating off repeated attacks and inflicting severe losses, thus adding to the glory of American history.

The American troops fighting near Château-Thierry are part of the reinforcements that have been rushed over since the German High Command determined to force the war to a conclusion in the hope that a decisive victory could be won before the American army arrived in France.

The work of the American 7th Machine Gun Battalion was particularly noteworthy. There was at least one instance where an entire attacking party was wiped out.

The Americans of the 3rd Division who held the south end of the bridge and banks of the river covered the whole operation and protected the French troops while crossing before the explosion.

The French officers fighting with them declared that the Americans displayed wonderful qualities of coolness and courage in the most difficult situation and in the trying struggle in the streets, while afterward they, with their machine guns, prevented all attempts of the enemy to repair the bridge."

Here is an account of the action of the 7th Machine Gun Battalion, U.S. 3rd Division, and its action at Château-Thierry. This article entitled "Sketching Château-Thierry," by Capt Joseph A. Minturn, appeared in the newspaper, *Indianapolis News*, under date of 1 Nov 1919:

Sketching Château-Thierry
By Capt. Joseph A. Minturn, Indianapolis News, Nov. 1,1919
Introduction
Visits Chateau Thierry
Big Battle Discussed
Travel French Roads
Major Tells Story
Ordered to Battle Line
Refugees Block Roads
Traffic Jam Appalling
German Infantry Seen
Hun Airmen Locate Gun
Artillery Fire Increased
Supported by French
Assembled Near Fontenelle
Men Given Credit

Introduction

It was the happy privilege of Capt. Joseph A. Minturn, a lawyer, of Indianapolis, attached during the war to the 309th engineers, to be assigned by general headquarters in France to sketch for the American Government the military lay of the land at Château-Thierry, where the Americans turned the tide of the war and started the Germans homeward. Captain Minturn's sketches are to go into the war archives at Washington. One of them, the large sketch here shown, discloses the terrain of the Château-Thierry country, and Captain Minturn tells the story of Château-Thierry as he heard it from Major John R. Mendenhall, a West Pointer of Hoosier ancestry, who was in the fighting that turned the fortunes of war for the allies. ...and here is Captain Minturn's story, interestingly told:

Visits Château-Thierry

I had been sent to the front several times while stationed at Ft. Plesnoy, near Langres, and one of these trips had extended as far west as Château-Thierry, where I made sketches of the town itself, of Hill 204 and Belleau Wood, which are visible from the old fort hill, below which the town is built.

Big Battle Discussed

I had heard so many discussions by officers at headquarters about the fight at Château-Thierry and vicinity when the German drive had broken through the British lines to the north and had bent the French back within fifty miles of Paris to the point of despair, I confessedly eavesdropped while a young major, with a deep scar from his eyebrow to the hair across the right forehead, described to Colonel Fulmer, my immediate superior, his experience as captain of one of the machine gun companies that saved the day for the Allies and started the Huns back through the Argonne, and to their final defeat. "That youngster's had a great experience, Minturn," he said. "I must get the general to send him with you so you can make drawings of the battle for our manual." A few days later the official order came from General Pershing. We had a chauffeur and a fast motor placed at our disposal. The man was Maj. John R. Mendenhall, then only 25 years old, a graduate of West Point, as his father and grandfather before him had been. It will be of interest to Indianians to know that the grandfather lived at Westfield, Ind., when he received his appointment to West Point, and the family still owns property in that Indiana town.

Travel French Roads

Major Mendenhall and I left Chaumont by the Paris road which winds three times, under the high stone arches of the great railway viaduct, and were kept busy saluting the colored American soldiers who were everywhere, remaking the once beautiful roads now full of chuck holes, developed by the heavy trucking of the war. The easy grades of the highways of France, here winding along and across the high hills and ridges, are splendid examples of engineering developed through centuries, reaching back to Caesar's time, and they can be located as far as the eye can see by double rows of high poplars and other trees, aged, moss-covered and full of mistletoe. The moss, in fact, is everywhere. Its velvet of golden green is a mantle to the ground, to the stone walls and houses, to the tiles on the roofs, and almost to the people who live so slowly and so far behind the times- blending everything into that restful harmony is the special charm of France.

Major Tells Story

"We arrived in France about April 15, 1918," said the major, as we drove along. "I was captain of Company B, 7th Machine Gun Battalion, 3rd Division. The division was billeted in the training area around Château-Villian and our battalion at La Ferte-Sur-Aube. We'll go there first and then follow the same roads we took when ordered to Château-Thierry. Our organization was the machine gun battalion of the division and had two companies with twenty-four active and eight reserve guns; twenty-four officers and 353 men. Our motor equipment was not received until May 20, when we got twenty-four half-ton Ford trucks and two Ford touring cars for each company and six trucks and one touring car for battalion headquarters. We began at once to teach the men how to drive the cars. Our other training schedule called for two months of preliminary, followed by a short period of trench duty in some quiet sector of the front. This should have put us on trench duty about July 1, 1918." Around 10 AM of May 30, Decoration Day at home, an order came to our major, Edward G. Taylor, to go at once on our own transportation to Gonde-en-Brie, and report to the French officer commanding that sector. Speed was urged because the German drive was forcing back the French and the British troops, and all reserves must be thrown in at once to stop the enemy and save Paris." Major Mendenhall and I had now reached La Ferté and were crossing the bridge over a small stream on which was a large mill.

Ordered to Battle Line

"Here is where we started to train," he pointed, "and where we received the hurry-up order to go to the front. When loaded we found that our cars had on three times their capacity, but the battalion left La Ferté at 2:55 PM in good order. Major Taylor went ahead, followed by Company A, and then by Company B, after which came several three-ton trucks with extra ammunition, gasoline and equipment." We had difficulty in making the steep grades on account of unavoidable overloading. In many cases the rear springs touched the axles, and blow-outs were frequent because the tires could not stand the extra pressure and we were soon badly strung out along the road.

Refugees Block Roads

"We made no stop for supper and reached Arces-Sur-Aube by 8:30 PM We were out of gasoline and hoped to get some there, but could not, and had to wait for our three-ton trucks, which came in near midnight. Our route was by Mer-Sur-Seine, Anglure, Sezanne, Montmort and Orbays. We came out of Sezanne on this road we are on now about 5 AM of May 31. It was blocked with refugees with their household goods, babies, old women and little children, crowded and piled on carts, to which cows and donkeys were hitched. Many pulled the carts themselves; and loaded wheelbarrows and dog carts were in the jam. Men and women carried their heavy loads with frightened children clinging to what they could to keep themselves from being trodden down or lost. The expressions on the faces of the refugees were most pitiful, and we began for the first time to realize something of the real meaning of war. Farther on, spaces between cars were forced and filled by small detachments of French and British troops, all looking thoroughly demoralized and discouraged. Following these came artillery, blocking the road entirely at times, the faces of the men showing signs of great fatigue and many sleepless nights. Some of the light batteries were going into position there on the slopes of these hills and were firing vigorously, which added to the confusion and frightfulness. One cannot look at the road now and imagine what I can but faintly describe.

Traffic Jam Appalling

"This appalling jam of terrified traffic made it impossible for us to keep our train intact, and as a result our arrival at Conde-en-Brie was very fragmentary. Great credit is due the individual man, and especially the drivers, for the way they handled the cars and for their untiring efforts to keep them moving and on the proper roads to reach our destination." The major and I reached Conde-en-Brie, built on a hill. Its many shell-shattered buildings told us that we were getting into the battle area. We negotiated the steep hill and reached the center of the town. A shell had demolished all but the sign on the village bookstore, but in a kitchen in the rear we found the proprietor, who sold us out of a scant remainder of her larder.

Gasoline Runs Low

"By 2 PM the entire battalion except the three-ton trucks had arrived here at Conde," the major went on. "We were again almost out of gasoline and our major reported to General Marchand, of the French army, at Janvier Ferme. We were told the enemy was expected to begin shelling Conde at any time, and were ordered to evacuate Janvier Ferme. Our gas tanks were so nearly empty that our Fords would not pull the hill southwest of the town. So, filling a few tanks by emptying gasoline from the others, we moved as many of our companies as we could and the remainder marched on foot, carrying their guns, equipment and packs. They were later picked up by the cars who had filled their tanks upon arrival of the three-ton trucks. "A French courier, greatly excited, met us here. The major pointed to a part of the road by which we were leaving Conde. He urged us to hurry or all would be lost. A full regiment of French cavalry was apparently waiting orders in yonder field, and numberless detachments of French and British soldiers were hurrying across the fields in every direction in what seemed to be the greatest confusion. "We were on a ridge road and approaching Nesles, a suburb of Château-Thierry, when Major Mendenhall stopped the car and we dismounted. "Our Major Taylor, with the two company commanders, preceded the battalion from Conde to this point above Nesles," he continued, "where he reported to a French general commanding a colonial division. This officer, after outlining the scheme of defense, instructed the company commanders to report to a French lieutenant-colonel, then in the town of Château-Thierry, who would indicate the positions we were to occupy. We left instructions for our battalion to rendezvous in Nesles, and, proceeding to Château-Thierry by automobile, found the lieutenant-colonel had crossed to the north side of the River Marne, where he had been captured by a German patrol. The officer, a French captain, who gave us this information, urged us to bring our troops into the town with all speed to prevent the enemy crossing the bridge to the south side of the river. "When we got back to Nesles about half of each company had arrived from Conde-en-Brie, and, assembling gun squads as quickly as possible, we transported them hurriedly in what cars were still in running condition to Château-Thierry, where we reported to Major Taylor in the Place Carnot. By 6 PM about six gun squads from each company were available, and were assigned positions which roughly divided the town into two sectors—Company A on the west toward the cathedral and Hill 204; Company B on the east toward the sugar factory and Brasles—each being responsible for the defense of a bridge, the local river margin and one flank. "Second Lieutenant Cobbey of Company B had a machine gun in a two-story brick house on the bank of the river, ready to fire from a lower window and cover the river bank from the bridge east, and one in a shed on the east of this building with range to the northwest. Second Lieutenant Paul T. Funkhouser had three guns in a wooded peninsula about 600 yards to the east of the bridge we were defending; two guns ranging west along the river, and one east. Two guns, under First Lieutenant Charles Montgomery, were in a sunken garden 200 yards south of the bridge, which also enfiladed it. The other guns of Company B were held at battalion headquarters as a reserve. My post of command was established under the railroad bank, giving me a covered line of communication to all my guns and to the battalion post of command, located in a house facing Place Carnot. This arrangement was completed by 3 PM, June 1.

German Infantrymen Seen

"About 4 AM, just as daylight was getting strong, a column of German infantry was observed marching west of the town of Brasles along the road paralleling the river toward Château-Thierry. They apparently did not know they were in danger. In fact, we afterward learned that they believed the French had abandoned the town and they expected to march through and cross the river, halting for the night at Montmort. The guns under Lieutenants Cobbey and Funkhouser opened fire when the enemy arrived at a slight bend in the road. The German discipline was such that the soldiers continued to advance until our positions were apparently located, when they deployed into the wheat fields between the road and the river. The grain stood waist high and the men were lost to view. However, our men whipped the field continuously with machine gun fire, causing heavy casualties to the enemy. At 5 AM, or within an hour, our guns on the peninsula were located and fired upon by enemy machine guns, wounding a man and forcing the rest to withdraw. Our other guns continued their effective fire. Making a rapid reconnaissance with First Lieutenant J. W. Ransdall, I placed him with two guns near some small buildings where the railroad crosses the Crezancy highway. By this time the enemy machine gun fire was much heavier, coming apparently from the high ridge in the north distance across the Marne from us. A call by phone to the French artillery brought a response within just two minutes, in the form of a '75' barrage on the north, or opposite side of the Marne, and extending from the railroad bridge we were defending, 500 yards east toward Brasles, and creeping north for 500 yards toward the long ridge there. It was the prettiest job you ever saw from our point of view and practically cleared the wheat fields of all Germans. A general artillery duel now commenced, which lasted through the next three days. This shelling made it advisable to move Lieutenants Montgomery and Cobbey's guns.

Artillery Fire Increased

At nightfall of June 2 the enemy machine gun and artillery fire increased tremendously, and we increased ours in the same proportion, keeping at least one gun firing on the bridge at all times. About 11 o'clock that night I heard a terrific explosion, shortly after which all of my guns ceased firing, and in a little while Lieutenant Bissel of Company A came to my post with several wounded men belonging to his company. He said he had taken part in a counter-attack by the French and got left on the north bank of the river; that the French had blown up the west bridge to keep the Germans from following them and this had prevented his retreat, forcing him to make a run for the railroad bridge we were defending. Lieutenant Cobbey controlled the fire of our guns on the railroad bridge but knew the Germans had enfilading fire from their side of the river. He heard Lieutenant Bissel's call for Company B to hold its fire that some of Company A were about to cross. But not being satisfied with holding his fire, Lieutenant Cobbey unhesitatingly crossed the bridge in the face of the enemy fire, found Lieutenant Bissel with his men preparing to swim the river, and dissuading them led them back over the bridge to safety. This act of heroism was characteristic

Lieutenant Paul Taylor Funkhouser
Both Paul and his brother were killed in action.

of all our men. "Fearing that enemy troops had followed Lieutenant Bissel's party across the bridge and were hiding for a surprise attack, Major Taylor sent me four of the battalion reserve guns which I placed as best I could, but, except for heavy gas shelling, nothing further occurred during the night."

Hun Airmen Locate Gun

On the morning of June 2 we dug a pit in an open field as a better position for one of the four extra guns, but the enemy air scouts saw us and we put the gun in a building near the wagon road. Just a few minutes after we abandoned the pit, which we camouflaged before leaving, a German shell was dropped almost into it and would have killed our men had they been there. There was a French passenger coach on a switch in the yard near the bridge under which our men, who were in the open, would duck for cover from aerial observation. During the morning Lieutenant Montgomery, leaving his former guns under Lieutenant Funkhouser, took those having no overhead cover to positions where he covered the railroad track, and to a house, from the second floor of which he did effective long-range firing at the enemy groups on the long ridge across the river. After the slaughter on the level roads near the wheat field the enemy worked toward Château-Thierry on the ridges, where they could be seen by the aid of our field glasses. For several days our men tried out their machine gun theory by practice on human targets.

Supported by French

We were supported by French colonial troops, among them the Senagalese sharpshooters—wild, fierce, dark-skinned, silent fellows, who gave you constant thrills at night by unexpectedly challing at the point of a wicked looking bayonet. By day also their conduct excited my curiosity. A group would be sitting silently under cover, when, without any command, one of them would get up at intervals, face the enemy ridge across the Marne, gaze intently for a minute or two, raise his rifle and fire, then go back and sit down. After some observation with the glasses I learned what they were doing. They could see incredibly far, and when they located a gap in a far-away hedge back of which the Germans were moving, up came a rifle and down dropped a German!

We were relieved at 3 AM on June 4 by Lieutenant Hose and Company A, 9th Machine Gun Battalion, 3rd Division. My company left town for the woods south of Fontenelle in three large trucks over a road being constantly shelled. The firing was so heavy during the early part of the night that it was necessary to change the guns under Lieutenant Cobbey for cool ones and these fresh guns became so hot after a couple of hours of firing that they could not be dismounted and were left with the relieving company.

Assembled Near Fontenelle

Our 7th Machine Gun Battalion was assembled near Fontenelle by 5 AM on June 4, and proceeded to billets at Courbon, where we were met in person and congratulated by Maj. Gen. J. T. Dickman, at that time commanding the 3rd Division. "Our losses throughout the entire engagement were relatively small, being one officer, First Lieutenant Thomas Goddard, Company B, and four enlisted men killed, and thirty-two men wounded, in nearly all cases from shell fire. No American troops except these two machine gun battalions of the 3rd Division were at any time engaged in the town of Château-Thierry itself, this town being in a French sector throughout the second and third battles of the Marne, with the 2nd Division sector on the west, and the sector of the 3rd Division on the east." This is the story of the Battle of Château-Thierry as gathered from the officer in command during the critical hours and at the places where the German pressure was most intense. It was not told at one time, but on several occasions, as we visited the spots referred to.

Men Given Credit

Too much credit cannot be given the men of the battalion; their action throughout was cool and courageous," was the closing declaration by Major Mendenhall to a class of generals and high army officials escorted by General Crookshank, who happened to be at Château-Thierry on a tour of the front when we arrived, and who pressed the major into service to explain what he witnessed here and at Mezy while history was in the making. "Our men did their duty and carried out orders or used their initiative where orders were not at hand, absolutely regardless of personal danger. Coming fresh from the United States, with out the opportunity afforded the earlier arrivals for completing their training, they were rushed practically overnight into a battle upon the outcome of which depended in a great measure the success of the allied cause. Had the enemy succeeded in crossing the Marne at Château-Thierry on that first day of June, there was nothing to hinder its advance to Montmirail and Sezanne, as they had done in 1914, and threatening, if not actually capturing, Paris itself."

From the *Records of the Second Division* (Regular): The following Special Operations Report by LtCol F. L. Davidson, Infantry, relates the actions of the 7th Machine Gun Battalion in Château-Thierry:

7th MACHINE GUN BATTALION, AEF, CHARLY, June 12, 1918

From: Lieut. Col. F. L. Davidson, Infantry
To: The Commanding General, 3d Division (Regular)
Subject: Action of the 7th Machine Gun Battalion at CHATEAU- THIERRY.
[Extract]

1. In compliance with instructions from your office, dated June 10, 1918, I find the action of the 7th Machine Gun Battalion, while at CHÂTEAU-THIERRY, to have been, as follows:

2. The battalion was under the command of Major E. G. Taylor, 7th M.G. Bn., and left La FERTE-sur-AUBE AT 2:55 PM, May 30, 1918, by its own transportation, and was reported to the French General commanding the sector at CONDE-en-BRIE, about 2 PM, May 31, 1918. The battalion was then ordered to proceed at once to CHÂTEAU-THIERRY to assist in the defense of that place.

3. Owing to the fact that the major portion of transportation consisted of light Ford trucks, which were overloaded and driven by inexperienced chauffeurs, and in some cases because of lack of gasoline, the battalion did not all arrive at CONDE-en-BRIE at the time battalion headquarters reported. Up to this time, it had been impossible to assign the fault for this delay to any persons individually. Seventeen squads of the battalion (nine of Company A and eight of Company B) proceeded at once to CHÂTEAU-THIERRY, arriving about 6 PM, same date. A reconnaissance was made by the battalion and company commanders assisted by Lieutenant George Wackernie, the French machine gun officer attached to the battalion. Upon completion of this reconnaissance, the battalion was ordered into position with Company A in protection of buildings on the south bank of the MARNE River, west of southern bridgehead of western bridge of the village. One section of Company A, under 1st Lieutenant J. T. Bissell, 7th M.G. Bn., was sent across the bridge to the north bank of the MARNE River to fire on hostile positions at COURQUEUX and northern

part of CHÂTEAU-THIERRY, with orders to fall back and join Company A across the western bridge if forced out of position. Company B took position in protection of buildings to the right of Company A, with their left about 200 meters east of southern bridgehead of west bridge of village, and their right on CHÂTEAU-THIERRY-CHIERRY Road, about 500 meters west of CHIERRY, each company being ordered to repulse any attempt of the enemy to advance on CHÂTEAU-THIERRY by the bridges entering the village, and to fire on any hostile groups observed. Seventeen guns were in position and firing about 4 AM, June 1, 1918. The battalion P.C. being at office of Zone Major of CHÂTEAU-THIERRY with a reloading station in the open near same place. Shelling of the town by the enemy caused wounding of fourteen enlisted men at this point. A secondary reloading station was established in the park in NESLES.

4. As the belated gun squads arrived they were held by battalion headquarters as a reserve and, as required, were sent into main position.

5. The transportation was ordered back to NESLES, about three kilometers south of CHÂTEAU-THIERRY, and in parking it was obliged to be near active French artillery. This caused them later to be heavily shelled by hostile batteries, resulting in the death of one officer and three enlisted men—two enlisted men being wounded and some transportation damaged.

6. At about 1 AM, June 2, 1918, the detachment on north side of river, under 1st Lieutenant J. T. Bissell, 7th M.G. Bn., together with a French machine-gun unit, were forced from their position on the north side of the river by the enemy, and fell back towards the western bridge. In the meantime, unknown to Lieutenant Bissell, the enemy had formed in considerable strength on the north end of western bridge and attempted to charge into CHÂTEAU-THIERRY. The bridge was blown up by the French at this time, causing the hostile attack to fail. When Lieutenant Bissell, with his detachment, neared the bridge they were subjected to heavy hostile machine-gun fire, and Lieutenant Bissell saw all his men fall, as he thought killed. These men, all but one, later reported to their company. Thinking his detachment was all killed, and that the Germans had possession of the bridge, Lieutenant Bissell proceeded

to the eastern bridge with a group of French and American soldiers. This eastern bridge, being swept by our machine-gun fire, Lieutenant Bissell made an ineffectual attempt to cross the river by swimming, in order to stop the fire. Failing in this, he finally succeeded, while under both hostile and friendly machine-gun fire, in verbally notifying Company B of his predicament, and 2nd Lieutenant E. W. Cobbey, 7th M.G. Bn., caused firing to stop, crossed the bridge and conducted Lieutenant Bissell, who, owing to the darkness, was unacquainted with the bridge, across to the south side of the river, together with a group of about 30 French and American soldiers, four of whom were wounded.

7. Lieutenant Bissell, while on north side of river, having been told by a French officer, that two divisions of the enemy had succeeded in forcing a crossing of the western bridge and had defeated Company A, 7th M.G. Bn., gave this information to Captain Mendenhall, and stated that Company B should get their transportation ready for a withdrawal, if necessary, change their position to a point considerably farther to the rear to meet the probable new attack, if they expected to escape capture.

8. Captain Mendenhall, upon receiving this information, sent a verbal message to his platoon commanders by runner, to withdraw to battalion headquarters and personally reported this action to the battalion commander at the battalion P.C. The battalion commander having knowledge of the destruction of the bridge, and that the information given by Lieutenant Bissell was erroneous, ordered Captain Mendenhall to again take his original position, being given four gun squads of the reserve for that purpose. These instructions were complied with by Captain Mendenhall, personally directing these gun squads into proper position where they again went into action.

9. The order to withdraw, as given by Capt. Mendenhall, seems to have been variously interpreted by members of the company, most of whom interpreted it as delivered by the runner for an order to make a hurried retreat. This seems to have been done by individual groups rather than as an organization. 1st Lieutenants D. S. House and J. H. Ransdell, 7th M.G. Bn., having become separated from the command and lost their way, reported to Headquarters, 3d Division, for instructions as to where their

organization might be found. These officers reported back to their company about 11 PM, June 2, 1918. All members of Company B other than the two officers mentioned above, returned and went into action between the hours of 5 AM and 3 PM, June 2, 1918, where they remained until Company B was relieved at about 2 AM, June 4, 1918, by Company A, 9th Machine Gun Battalion, and Company A was relieved by a French machine gun company. The 7th Machine Gun Battalion, at about 4 AM, same date, proceeded by its own transportation to COURBOIN for billets, arriving there about 11 AM, same date.

10. The final withdrawal from CHÂTEAU-THIERRY was made unmolested by hostile fire. Considerable material was, however, abandoned, the most important being seven machine guns, and three hundred and fifty six ammunition boxes. While this can be accounted for somewhat by the fact that the material of the two companies of the 7th Machine Gun Battalion became unavoidably mixed during the combat, and some ammunition boxes being turned over to relieving the units without taking a receipt, no immediate attempt was made to recover this material when its loss was discovered.

11. Of the seven machine guns and three hundred and fifty-six ammunition boxes abandoned, two guns and fourteen ammunition boxes left by Lieutenant Bissell's detachment on north side of river is believed to have been justifiable. Of the other missing material, three machine guns and one hundred and thirty-six ammunition boxes have since been recovered, leaving at this date, two guns and two hundred and six ammunition boxes that it has been impossible, so far, to locate. A further search for this material is in progress at this time.

12. Owing to the fact that both companies are absent at this time, one of which is actively engaged, it is impossible to give a complete report on transportation abandoned. This will be furnished in a supplementary report that will be rendered as soon as full investigation can be instituted.

13. There seems to have been a lack of positive orders issued by the battalion commander, the companies being too much left to their own initiative. 1st Lieutenant E.J. Hoover, Adjutant, 7th M.G. Bn., was obliged, in many instances, to personally issue orders in the name of the battalion commander in order to get action of some sort.

14. This operation was the initial one made by the battalion, which went into action without having had any sleep for over thirty-six hours, and at the end of a trying trip overland by motor transportation because of overloading, caused breakdowns, thereby taxing their strength in order to complete the journey. Further, the battalion was in action constantly from 6 PM, May 31, 1918, until about 2 AM, June 4, 1918, during most of this time being subjected to heavy hostile fire. Therefore, it is believed that the battalion performed their mission in a creditable manner. The only mistake during the time in action was the temporary withdrawal of Company B to a place other than that desired by their company commander. This was caused through the error of the company commander entrusting the promulgation of his order to the several units of the company verbally by an enlisted man, and the second error of withdrawing because of information that was not verified by reconnaissance. This mistake did not effect the final result, however, for it is believed that the 7th Machine Gun Battalion was to a great degree responsible for the final check of the late German drive. F. L. Davidson"

The following account was written by Maj John R. Mendenhall, commanding officer of Company B, 7th Machine Gun Battalion. From Maj Mendenhall's article, "The Fist in the Dyke," *Infantry Journal*, 43 (Jan–Feb 1936):

THE FIST IN THE DYKE
By Major John R. Mendenhall, Infantry

It appeared to be merely a matter of hours before the Allied dyke crumbled and the grey wave rolled southward over Paris.

At 2:40 AM, May 27, 1918, forty-one German divisions suddenly struck the weakly held Chemin des Dames position. By 8:00 AM that position had been overrun; by noon German battalions were crossing the Aisne; by nightfall the spearhead of the great thrust had reached the Vesle. The road to Paris stood invitingly open. Allied reserves flung against the flanks of this deepening salient crumpled under the German juggernaut. The drive, now almost a triumphal march, continued. On the 29th, Soissons fell and the world learned that Paris was being shelled. By

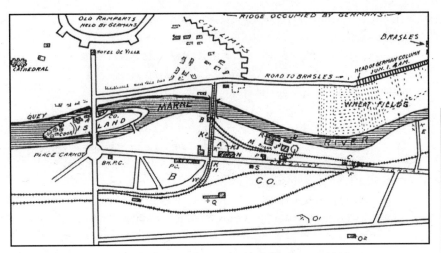

Maj Mendenhall's map of Chateau-Thierry battlefield, June 1, 1918

the 30th, Jaulgonne and Château-Thierry were in German hands and Berlin thrilled to the Crown Prince's laconic communiquè—"We stand along the Marne!"

Hour by hour the German tide rose against the Marne barrier. By the 31st it appeared to be only a matter of hours before the Allied dyke crumbled and the grey wave rolled southward over Paris. It was to dam the threatened torrent at Château-Thierry that the fist of the 7th Machine-Gun Battalion was thrust in the weakened dyke.

The 7th Machine-Gun Battalion, a Regular Army unit, organized in 1917 from trained men of the 4th and 7th Infantry Regiments, consisted of two companies and a headquarters detachment, totaling 20 officers and 375 men. Each company was organized into three four-gun platoons with four reserve guns as replacements. Intensive instruction produced reasonable proficiency with the Hotchkiss guns but the trucks authorized the battalion in December were to be another matter. Not until May 24 did the long awaited motors arrive. Six days later they were used in an urgent tactical mission.

In all, the battalion received 52 Ford Model T trucks of the commercial half-ton variety, 6 small touring cars bearing the same distinguished name, and 24 Indian motorcycles, a few of which boasted side-cars. A canvas of the companies produced only a handful of experienced drivers. As a result our trucks met with many a minor accident. By May 30, hard work, patience, and perseverance brought their own reward—the train could be formed, started and halted with only occasional collisions. Eighteen years ago such a feat fell logically in the class of seven-day wonders.

In summary, then, the 7th Machine-Gun Battalion on the eve of its great adventure enjoyed a superior morale and discipline, and boasted a high state of proficiency in all phases of its training save its work with the newly acquired motors. Its equipment, on the other hand could not be classed as better than fair; its machine guns were old and its trucks were to prove inadequate for the loads required.

Now the 3[d] Division had been scheduled to occupy a quiet sector north of Toul about June 14 for training, but the German break-through along the Chemin des Dames changed all this. On May 30 this division was ordered to join the French XXXVIII Corps that had been flung into the path of the hard-driving German divisions in the vicinity of Château-Thierry.

At 10:00 AM, May 30, the 7th Machine-Gun Battalion received a curt order directing it to proceed at once by its own transportation from La Ferté via Arcis and Sezanne to Conde-en-Brie and report there to the French headquarters. Although rumors of a great disaster along the Chemin des Dames had reached this newly arrived unit, no one dreamed that it would be called on. Therefore the division order struck with the suddenness of a thunderbolt. A battalion warning order was at once issued directing companies to load and to report when ready to move. The men were recalled from drill and essential equipment hastily assembled and checked. Two trucks were assigned to each gun-squad. The first carried half the squad, the gun and some ammunition; the second carried the remainder of the men and additional ammunition. Touring cars were assigned to the personnel of the company and battalion headquarters; runners, scouts and key noncommissioned officers were furnished with motorcycles. Eight heavy duty trucks were secured from the division train for extra ammunition, gasoline and baggage.

At 2:30 PM the column cleared La Ferté led by battalion headquarters. Motorcycle patrols went forward to reconnoiter and mark the route. Company motorcycles were used principally to check the column, to maintain contact, and to carry spare parts to disabled trucks and guide them back to the column. Each truck driver carried an itinerary of the towns he would pass through but only company commanders had maps. Each truck carried a reserve of five gallons of gasoline.

A twenty-mile clip soon overextended the column and a twelve-mile rate was finally selected on as the fastest practical speed. Trucks designed for a half-ton load carried half again that weight and protesting springs bellied down on axles. On steep hills the men were obliged to detruck and walk, sometimes push. The tires of twenty years ago, though out of their infancy, were not yet through adolescence; add to that the fact that the celebrated Model T's had been equipped with deteriorated stock, and the endless tale of punctures need not be elaborated. Delays for minor repairs were frequent.

At 9:00 PM the convoy halted near Sezanne to rest the men and refuel and overhaul the motors. Here the whole battalion bogged down until midnight because the thrifty S.O.S. (no typographical error) at the Sezanne depot would not part with a gallon of gas—a Gallic gesture that Americans came to learn only too well. So there the convoy stood until the trucks loaned by the division train came up with the surplus gasoline. The empty five-gallon cans still carried by each truck expedited the refueling.

On resuming the march, all lights were extinguished. This was a new and somewhat harrowing experience for our half-trained drivers, but the French sun, an early riser in May, soon put in its appearance, to the vast relief of everyone. With daylight came the refugees, a grim reminder of the business ahead. Starting with a few cart-loads, these poor people increased rapidly until they formed a continuous stream, double banked along the narrow road, with every man for himself and all in a hurry. Women and children shared space on large hay wagons, with feather beds, chests of drawers, chicken coops, and chairs, while the men led cattle and horses. Their faces were haggard with weariness, but all could smile and wave encouragement to "les Américains," who alone, were moving north against this current of fear and depression. Meanwhile, it had become virtually impossible to keep the train intact. Toward the end of the march there were seldom as many as ten cars in any group.

As the battalion neared the front, detachments of infantry, heavy siege guns and supply wagons, both French and British,

appeared in the intervals between the refugees, all retreating—the wreck of a defeated army. North of Montmirail there was less confusion. Here artillery was still in firing positions and squadrons of La Tour's 5th Cavalry Division were standing to horse in formation near the road, looking rather medieval with their bannered lances.

At 12:30 PM, May 31, the head of the battalion halted at Conde-en-Brie, having come 110 miles in 22 hours largely over traffic-choked roads. Radiators were steaming and gasoline low when they drew up in the marketplace.

The battalion commander at once reported to General Reynouard, French Army, and was ordered to move his battalion to Château-Thierry without delay. Time, said the General, was all-important. So, trusting to luck that the Model T's would manage the few remaining miles without refueling, the convoy up-anchored and squeaked its way out of Conde-en-Brie. But luck played a dirty trick, for shortly after leaving town the head of the column encountered a steep grade. The gravity feed, coupled with the low gas supply, proved too much for the 1918 Fords; they took a look at the hill, uttered one or two despairing gasps, and died with their boots on. The men detrucked and in approved Doughboy fashion hiked the last four miles carrying their guns and a limited supply of ammunition. Packs and additional ammunition were brought on later in the trucks, a few of which were refueled by draining the tanks of the others before the arrival of the heavy trucks with their reserve drums.

At 3:30 PM, the leading elements of the battalion trudged into Nesles-en-Montagne, the last cover before entering Château-Thierry. Just south of Nesles French batteries were working on the position located on the heights north of Château-Thierry. It was not deemed safe to move the trucks further forward without reconnaissance. Accordingly, a base was established at Nesles and the company commanders went forward to report to Lieutenant Colonel Benezech, commanding the French 33d Colonial Infantry at Les Cheneaux, just north of Château-Thierry.

Upon arriving at the stone bridge over the Marne, in the center of the city, Captain Charles H. Houghton (commanding Company A) accompanies by the battalion liaison officer (French), met a French general to whom he stated his mission. This general

(Marchand, of Fashoda fame, then in command of the French 52[d] Colonial Division) said that Colonel Benezech had either been killed or captured and that he was taking personal command. Thereupon he directed the 7th Machine-Gun Battalion to move up its guns at once and go into positions on the south bank of the Marne with the mission of covering the bridges and protecting the withdrawal of the French to the south bank. The bridges, he stated, were being mined and would be destroyed as soon as the withdrawal had been completed. General Marchand was unequivocally specific—the battalion would remain in position until relieved. Captain Houghton promptly transmitted these orders to Major Taylor, the battalion commander in Nesles.

The city of Château-Thierry straddles the Marne River, the major portion being on the north side where it sprawls about the base of a prominent bluff. A fortified Chateau stands on this bluff and from its walls can be seen not only the entire city, but the level plain between its southern limits and the wooded hills of Nesles. (Map 1). This plain, some 1500 yards wide, affords but little cover. The Marne and a canal form an island within the city. Rue Carnot, the principal north-south street, is almost dead straight and can be easily enfiladed from the Chateau. Starting from the Chateau, this street strides the Marne via a large stone bridge (hereafter referred to as the west bridge), crosses the island and then the canal on a second stone bridge; thence it runs through a square called Place Carnot, crosses a third bridge over the railroad, and finally drives headlong across the plain to Nesles.

A main highway follows the north bank of the Marne. This opens into a long quay-like plaza opposite the west bridge and then continues eastward to the town of Brasles. Another east-west road (referred to as the Crézancy road) passes through Place Carnot on the south bank.

The southern part of the city contains rather extensive railroad yards. A combination wagon and railroad bridge stands just beyond the island on the eastern edge of the city (hereafter referred to as the east bridge). In July, 1918, these two bridges were the only means of crossing the Marne for five miles in either direction; hence the importance of the city.

Except for a short period in 1914, the Marne valley had not been in the war zone. Buildings had not been damaged by shell-fire and the surrounding country was in a high state of cultivation, wheat being the principal crop. Both slopes of the valley are steep and form natural defensive lines. Such, in brief, was the picture that unfolded before the 7th Machine-gun Battalion on that hot May afternoon seventeen years ago.

On receiving General Marchand's orders, the battalion commander directed both companies to send gun-squads to the Place Carnot. Unfortunately, a rapid movement of the gun-squads was not easy to execute. The few trucks that reached Nesles were short of fuel and the gun-squads, all with limited ammunition, were in most cases short of men. Still, by 4:30 PM, each company had at least one platoon assembled in the designated positions and the trucks were shuttling back and forth for others.

The river front was divided between companies: A to the west and B to the east. Each was made responsible for a bridge and a flank. Positions were selected and some guns were sited before dark. Company A, from houses along the river bank, covered the west bridge, with three sections, while Company B covered the east bridge, with two sections. A third section from Company B covered the Crezancy road and the right flank.

During the night, battalion and company commanders made a thorough reconnaissance of the entire front. Based on this reconnaissance, interlocking bands of fire were established from the wooded road east of the town to include the junction of the canal and river on the west. The new gun positions were taken just before daylight on the morning of June 1.

Meanwhile, pursuant to orders from the French, one section of Company A, under Lieutenant John T. Bissell, was sent across the Marne to the northeast exits of the city to cover the withdrawal of the French via the west bridge. They were escorted to their posts at 5:00 PM, by a French rifle platoon.

In crossing the bridge this section received some scattered fire but suffered no casualties. Advancing cautiously to the tower marked **C** on Map 2, one gun was mounted to fire north and east and the other held in reserve pending further reconnaissance. German snipers occupying two Adrian barracks, a gateway at **M**, and some houses in a grove at **N**, were driven back by the French riflemen, and by 7:00 PM a line along a road and wall some 150 yards east of the tower had been established. A French machine gun covered the south flank of this line, so Lieutenant Bissell mounted his second gun near the tower to strengthen the north flank.

The other guns of the battalion were held in company and battalion reserve during the night. Orders emphasized the need for concealment and silence. Guns were to be fired only on the direct orders of an officer (one was posted with practically every section). In Company A, however, the destruction of the west bridge was to be the signal for all guns to open fire immediately on suitable targets.

On June 1 the sun rose at 3:45 AM presaging a clear day.

Lieutenant Cobbey, with four guns in the sugar refinery (**D**) had sited on the bridge and eastern approaches the previous evening, but Lieutenant Funkhouser who during the night had been moved with three guns to the wooded road (**F**) had still to see the terrain to his front. Now, as the light increased, he discerned activity on the road leading from the village of Brasles. German troops, marching in column of squads, were moving along this road toward Château-Thierry. Without hesitation he opened fire; this was immediately taken up by Cobbey's guns at the sugar refinery.

At first the fire was ineffective and the well-disciplined German troops kept on. However, as the light improved the fire was accurately adjusted and great holes were blasted in the columns.

Picture the situation in the eyes of its commander. The defeated Allies were on the run. For several days resistance had been almost negligible. Yesterday afternoon covering troops to his front had occupied Château-Thierry almost without firing a shot, and his battalion, ending a night march, would probably bivouac south of the Marne. Perhaps it had been a longer march than usual; prudence doubtless called for reaching a wooded bivouac before daylight. But wasn't it better to continue a bit further and cross the Marne, the last serious barrier on the road to Paris? The Allies had been so terribly mauled that any serious resistance was virtually out of the question. Spirits ran high. Probably there was singing as the column swung along and perhaps its commander quietly swelled his chest as he contemplated the medal that might soon rest there.

Then, suddenly, the clatter of machine-guns—bullets whining overhead—men dropping—consternation—confusion! Surprise—that principle so often stressed but so seldom employed—and volume of fire on a concentrated target were successfully combined on this clear June morning to bring the triumphal march of a veteran German battalion to an abrupt and bewildered halt.

The Germans deployed in the waist-high wheat growing between the road and the river. Hidden from view, but still under fire, they moved in small groups by short bounds toward the river bank, threatening the east bridge. Soon Funkhouser's guns on the wooded road were located and German machine-gun fire, followed by artillery fire, forced their withdrawal at 7:00 a.m to more protected positions. The section had received six casualties.

Cobbey's guns, safe within the refinery building, remained undisturbed and continued to cover the eastern approaches to the bridge. The Germans, now under the protection of their own machine guns, occupied a group of buildings opposite the factory. Here they massed several times in attempt to reach the bridge, but each time the refinery guns, sweeping the 200 yards of bare flats, drove them back with losses.

German artillery fire now increased steadily. Even though defiladed, machine guns other than those in the lower floors of buildings were maintained in position with difficulty. Command posts were moved into cellars and connected by telephone as the day wore on. Again and again shell fire cut the wires. Reconnaissance groups and runners were forced to keep behind houses; to cross a street was to play tag with a German sniper. Gas, greatly feared at first, proved to be dangerous only in the immediate vicinity of a shell-burst, and such areas could usually be avoided. But it was a different matter indoors; command posts had to resort to double partitions made of wet blankets to avoid the use of gas masks.

There had been no opportunity for sleep since May 29, the last night in La Ferté, and though a system of reliefs enabled men to snatch some rest when off duty, the shell-fire and the general sense of insecurity had worked them into a high state of nervous tension. This was evidenced by sharp commands, impatience bordering on intolerance, and an inability to grasp new situations quickly. Orders were not always carried out as issued. Later this condition jeopardized the battalion's mission.

Ancient tower where Lt Bissell had a machine gun (above)
Lt Bissell's field of fire from his tower (below)

**Ford Model T
Touring Cars**

The supply route, which followed the Rue Carnot, was under enemy observation. Trucks and motorcycle messengers were frequently under fire. Finally, after one officer was killed by a direct hit on a truck in which he was riding, this road was used only at night. On June 1 both rations and ammunition were scarce articles. The food question was solved to some extent by provisions taken from local shops under authority of the French commander, and the ammunition problem was solved by the providential discovery of a dump while moving Company A's command post.

To return to the tactical situation, the French Colonials on the north bank of the river were opposing the Germans in the wooded sections east and north of the city. By noon small French detachments had captured the houses at **N** and one of Lieutenant Bissell's guns had been moved to the gate at **M**. However, German fire of all kinds constantly increased and by 2:00 PM the situation of all French troops north of the river was becoming critical.

Late in the afternoon additional German troops were concentrated in the Bois de Barbillon northeast of Brasle (Map 1). Everything indicated a determined attack against the bridges soon after dark. Meanwhile, the enemy had crossed the Marne at Jaulgonne, some five miles to the east.

Anticipating a possible attack from the east, the battalion commander now ordered Company B to be prepared to cover the remainder of the battalion from positions south of Etampes (Map 1) in case of a withdrawal. Based on these orders second-line positions were selected by the 1st and 3d platoon commanders during the afternoon, although no guns were available to occupy them.

The right flank was also reinforced and the four reserve guns, without crews, were held at the battalion command post in the Place Carnot.

To summarize, on the evening of June 1, just prior to the main German attack, the guns of the battalion were distributed as follows from right to left (Map 2):

Company B
4 guns east of the railroad, the 3d platoon covering the right flank of the battalion (**G**).
4 guns in building of the sugar refinery, the 2d platoon covering the river and the approaches to the east bridge (**D**).
4 guns generally along the Crezancy road, the 1st platoon covering the east bridge (**E**).

Company A
2 guns near the east end of the island crossing fire with the refinery guns.

2 guns in the yard in the center of the company sector, enfilading opposite streets and the square north of the west bridge.

2 guns in the warehouse enfilading the river and square.

2 guns under Lieutenant Bissell north of the river.

4 guns (French) west of the main bridge covering the square (**L**).

4 guns in the park at the west end of the island covering the west flank (**K**).

Company Reserves

Company A: 1 gun near the command post.

Company B: 3 guns near the command post.

Battalion Headquarters: 4 guns, borrowed from companies and without crews, near the Place Carnot.

At dusk on June 1 the German artillery fire which now for the first time included guns of heavy caliber increased still more. The scattered fire of a few exhausted French light batteries was the only Allied response. By 8:40 PM the four French machine guns at **L** (Map 2) had been silenced, and Company A was ordered to replace them. Captain Houghton selected positions for two sections, one firing from a cellar window near the west bridge and one screened by heavy foliage in the park. Since none of his present positions could be abandoned, one gun was taken from each of his three sections east of the bridge and the fourth from company reserve. Their final protective lines crossed in the plaza, blocking the German approach to the bridge.

With the fall of the chateau in the late afternoon a general engagement developed along the entire front north of the river extending from the foot of the bluff to the eastern outskirts of the city. Barricades of furniture and overturned carts had been thrown up in the streets from behind which the French fought desperately with grenades and bayonets, but despite this gallant defense, the battle line was forced back and by 10:00 AM stood at the plaza, in sight of the west bridge.

The French withdrawal starting at first with organized detachments, rapidly degenerated into an out-and-out flight. Individual soldiers broke away from the line of barricades and raced across the bridge. The hand-to-hand mêlée reached the river-bank and surged upon the bridge itself. A German barrage falling upon the houses lining the south bank added to the indescribable confusion. Those squads of Company A that were not sheltered in buildings suffered many casualties in this fire.

Here was the crisis! In another moment the enemy would plunge through the streets of the island, outflanking, surrounding and overcoming the scattered machine-gun squads whose fire was masked by the retreating riflemen. But suddenly there was a tremendous roar. The heavy stonework of the bridge crumbled. The bridge itself was obscured by an enormous cloud of dust while fragments of French and German soldiers hurtled through the air. When the startled spectators on both sides could again see clearly, they saw that one span of the bridge had been completely destroyed and that a fifty-foot gap of deep water separated the opposing forces. General Marchand's mine, planted for just such an emergency, had proved decisive.

Masked as they were by French riflemen, the guns of Company A had not been able to fire. But with the explosion as their signal, they now opened on the Germans still massed in the square north of the river. Confusion and death swept the German ranks as six American machine guns blasted their dense formations at short range. Here was their second surprise in one day, probably even more sanguinary than that of the morning.

Despite their losses, the Germans massed twice more in the plaza. Apparently their higher commanders did not realize the bridge was gone, or perhaps believed that it could still be crossed on the wreckage. Each time, by the light of flares and burning buildings, they were dispersed with great losses.

Let us now return to Lieutenant Bissell. When the fall of the chateau gave the German machine-gunners command of the city the commander of the detachment north of the Marne reported his situation as hopeless and twice requested permission to withdraw. Receiving no reply, he started a withdrawal at 7:30 PM on his own initiative. Lieutenant Bissell, with both his machine guns at the tower **C**, covered the withdrawal, with the assistance of some 20 Senegalese riflemen.

These Senegalese, recruited in the French Congo and speaking an intelligible patois, were little more than savages and had earned a reputation for ruthless cruelty. They were an uncomfortable crew to have around, for one was never sure just what they intended to do.

F Company's view to Brasles. The view is from south to north. The river Marne runs along the line of trees. The town of Brasles is seen just across the river.

At times they seemed to have real difficulty distinguishing between Germans and Americans, and the latter had an uneasy feeling that a few honest mistakes would not lie heavily on the Senegalese conscience. Thus their value at any particular moment was one of those things on which you pay your money and take your choice.

At 9:00 PM the general withdrawal started. Keeping close to the bluffs, Bissell withdrew each gun separately, going himself with the last gun. On approaching the west bridge he observed the great confusion in the square. Wounded French soldiers were everywhere. Rifle fire was continuous. A machine gun suddenly enfiladed the street, where he and most of his platoon had taken refuge, prior to crossing. Then, to cap the climax, he saw the bridge, which he expected to cross, blown into the air!

Hugging the walls of the houses, both French and Americans now worked their way through the streets toward the east bridge. A French officer suggested that, before attempting to cross this bridge, they warn the Americans south of the river not to fire. With a runner, Bissell went to the bridge and called. He was answered by a burst of fire from the guns of Company B. Then a German machine gun to his right rear also opened fire, wounding several of the party.

Cut off by friendly fire and with the enemy closing in, the only apparent avenue of escape lay in swimming the narrow river at this point. However, the Marne was so swift that a swimmer would be carried west to the center of the conflict. Accordingly, Bissell continued his efforts to establish his identity, by shouting his own name and the names of other company officers. At last he received a reply and, in due course, brought his party across the bridge.

The Germans, however, were right on the heels of the retreating Americans, and, before the guns of Company B could again bring fire to bear, they had lodged themselves along the river bank under the protection of some railroad fills. Without rifle support, the position was critical.

As usual, the telephone was out and runners sent to the battalion command post had failed to return. Perhaps the rest of the battalion had been forced to withdraw, in which case my company

Field of fire looking east and toward Crézancy

(Company B) was supposed to cover them. I therefore sent oral messages to my platoon commanders by runner. The message to the 3d platoon directed it to move to the previously selected position south of Etampes where it could still cover the right flank. The orders to the 1st and 2nd platoons were to hold their present positions to limit the movements of the Germans now south of the Marne. They would also cover the bridge to prevent more from crossing.

Since it was only 500 yards to the battalion command post, I decided to go myself and verify the situation. Arriving at headquarters I found there had been no change in the battalion dispositions. There was much concern, however, over the serious threat against the east bridge. Accordingly, I was ordered to clear the Germans from the south bank in my sector, and for this purpose was given the battalion reserve of four gun-squads improvised from battalion and headquarters personnel.

On approaching the cleared area in the vicinity of the east bridge, Germans, recognized by their helmets, could be seen between the Crezancy road and the river. This area, roughly 200 yards square and free from buildings, consisted largely of a depression crossed diagonally by a railroad fill (Figure 1, Company B sector). This fill divided it into two parts, the southern part being a cultivated sunken garden. The area was bounded on the north by the river and on the south by the Crezancy road. The refinery

buildings loomed to the east; to the west stood a large residence, surrounded by a high masonry wall. The 1st platoon had covered this area from positions just south of the Crezancy road and the 2d platoon had covered it from the refinery on the east.

Although the German infantry was massing here, Company B's guns were strangely silent. Something appeared to be wrong. Leaving my reserve platoon with one gun mounted to fire eastward along the Crezancy road and another to enfilade the east bridge, I hurried to the 1st platoon position. There was no trace of the platoon! Had the Germans moved south, overcome them and penetrated into the heart of my sector? Scarcely twenty minutes had elapsed since I left. If this were the case, there should be some sound of fighting to the south, but no sound came from that direction.

How about the 2d platoon? Had it also vanished? It was some distance to the refinery. Possibly the way had been blocked by the enemy. In any event, nothing could be accomplished by going there alone. For the time being, my reserve guns limited the movement of the Germans, but should our real situation become known the result might be disastrous. I returned to my platoon, assembled my section leaders, a corporal and a private, and explained my plan.

Those guns now in position would fire only in case Germans moved south or west of the open ground in force. In any case, all guns would carefully avoid firing toward the refinery. Where necessary, individual Germans would be dealt with by pistols or captured. I would lead the other guns to the refinery, crossing the Crezancy road near the railroad crossing. The Germans in the northern depression could be taken by fire from the refinery. Fire from the refinery would be the signal for the other guns to open up on suitable targets in order to destroy the Germans or drive them back across the bridge.

Preceded at 100 yards by a three-man point, I then led the men out in single file, protected from view by a fence that followed the Crezancy road. Cautiously we approached the refinery. Upon our arrival my worst fear was realized. All was quiet: the 2d platoon had also disappeared. However, we found no Germans in the refinery, which indicated that they were still ignorant of the true state of affairs. We quickly mounted our guns under the long sheds and opened fire on the Germans who could now be seen crouching in the northern depression. Our other guns immediately took up the fire. Unfortunately a line of retreat, hitherto overlooked, still lay open and over this those of the enemy who had escaped our first bursts of fire raced back across the stream. Thereupon all guns were shifted to cover the northern approaches to the bridge and the river bank. At daylight the remainder of Company B was reestablished in its former positions.

It had been a tight squeeze. Had the enemy been aware of our true situation, the result of the engagement might have been reversed in less than a half hour. For our part we thanked God that the "fog of war" was thick. Subsequent inquiry revealed the fact that in the confusion of battle, my runners had delivered my oral messages to all three positions as "Withdraw at once." More through luck than anything else, no harm was done but the value of telephones, or, in their absence, the necessity for written messages was brought home in an unforgettable lesson. In critical situations, when men are under terrific nervous and physical strain, oral messages are utterly unreliable. They are only justified as a last resort.

With one bridge destroyed and troops on either side of the river somewhat demoralized by the night's fighting, both forces rested quietly on their arms during the day of June 2. At 10:00 PM a new attempt was made to cross the east bridge but this was promptly discovered and promptly checked by an intense fire from the guns of both companies.

On June 3 increased enemy activity became evident in the eastern outskirts of the city. Newly placed machine guns enfiladed additional streets south of the river and forced several of our guns to shift position. In general, those shifts were made by moving from one building to another, and the guns continued to cover the same sectors. In all cases the guns were kept well back from the windows to prevent their discovery.

During this day a platoon of Senegalese troops gave a striking example of sniping. Standing behind trees, they fired on the enemy at distances around 800 yards, steadying their long French rifles against the tree trunks. Sometimes they would select a point on a road where men passed frequently. Seeing a German vanish behind some brush they would aim at the point of his reappearance and fire as he emerged. They seldom failed to get their man.

During the afternoon of June 3 we received orders for relief. Meanwhile the threat against the east bridge became more menacing. Therefore, at dusk, under the protection of our machine guns, French engineers placed charges against the abutments at the water's edge, to be fired in case of attack.

German fire and American retaliation increased steadily during the evening. Most of it was ineffective—a mere waste of good ammunition. By 11:00 PM the air-cooled Hotchkiss machine guns of Company B's 2d platoon were cherry red and had to be replaced by cool ones from the company reserve. The relief, late in arriving, was barely completed by dawn. There had been no let-down in the fireworks and some guns, too hot to dismount, were left behind, others from the relieving company being exchanged for them.

Finally in Liberty three-ton trucks instead of Fords, the battalion rumbled past the southern edge of the city, made a dash down the dangerous Rue Carnot, and in short order reached the woods near Nesles. Just as we entered the woods we heard a dull detonation to the north. The east bridge had been destroyed.

At the Marne this battalion was the fist in the Allied dike. Had it engaged in no further combat during the war, this single fight would have amply justified its existence.

From BgGen Charles Crawford's book, *Six Months with the Sixth Brigade*:

The 7th Motorized Machine Gun Battalion (division troops) of two companies, had preceded the other troops and had been put in action at Chateau Thierry where they were fighting to prevent the German crossing of the Marne. Their conduct delighted the French high command and they prevented the pursuit of the broken and disheartened French troops across the river.

From Frederick V. Hemenway's book, *History of the Third Division*:

Commenting upon the action of the 7th Machine Gun Battalion at Château-Thierry, Pétain, the Marshal of France, in an order to his Armies, gave the following citation:

GREAT GENERAL HEADQUARTERS of the French Armies of the East Staff Personnel Bureau (Decorations) Order No. 11.875 "D" (Extract)

With the approbation of the Commander-in-Chief, American E.F., in France, The Marshal of France, Commander-in-Chief of the French Armies of the East, cites in orders of the Army:

THE 7th MACHINE GUN BATTALION (AMERICAN)

Under the command of Major Taylor, barred to the enemy the passage of the Marne. In the course of violent combat, particularly the 31st of May and the 1st of June, 1918, it disputed foot by foot with the Germans the northern outskirts of Château-Thierry, covered itself with incomparable glory, thanks to its valor and skill, costing the enemy sanguinary losses.

THE GREAT GENERAL HEADQUARTERS, 24 Nov 1918.
PÉTAIN,
The Marshal of France,
Commander-in-Chief of the French Armies of the East

In Spaulding and Wright's book, *The Second Division*, Lt Elmer Hess, 15th Field Artillery, moving up in support of the 3rd Brigade noted in his diary:

I went over to Major Bailey's headquarters and was there when he was visited by a French colonel and his adjutant. Through the interpreter, Major Bailey was begged to remove his battalion across the River Marne to the hills overlooking the river on the south bank. This Major Bailey refused to do, stating that his orders were to take these positions, and until his colonel countermanded his orders, he would stay here. The French colonel then informed us that outside of the detachments of French cavalry, there was no infantry in front

of the 1st Battalion; the Germans at any moment might sweep through this sector. He begged us to cross the river immediately as he expected to blow up the bridge which he said was our only avenue of escape. Again Major Bailey refused to withdraw. An hour later we heard a terrific detonation which we knew meant the destruction of the bridge over the Marne and our supposed last avenue of escape. Lieutenant Peabody who was in the kitchen of a farm house, raised a bottle of wine and drank a health to the bridge in which we all joined before the reverberations of the explosion had passed away.

According to MajGen Joseph T. Dickman, commander of the U.S. 3rd Division, and in his memoir entitled, *The Great Crusade*:

The movement of the 7th Machine Gun Battalion from La Ferté-sur-Aube to Nesles, via Condé-en-Brie, presented many evidences of lack of experience and of inefficiency and weakness. However, the intelligence and initiative of the second officer in command, Captain Charles F. Houghton, and the zeal, courage and endurance of the junior officers and men, made good nearly all of the deficiencies and brought about a successful and highly credible outcome of the operation as a whole.

From "Watch on the Rhine," Official Paper of Army of Occupation, Coblenz, Germany:

A French Appreciation
The 7th Machine-Gun Battalion, being motorized, traveled overland in small Ford trucks from its training area in the vicinity of Château-Villian, and reached Château-Thierry late in the afternoon on May 31. Positions were immediately taken up in that historic city, part of which was already occupied by the enemy. After a thorough reconnaissance each company was given a mission. The general mission was to repulse any attempt of the enemy to advance on Château-Thierry by the bridges entering the city. About one o'clock in the morning of June 2 a detachment of this battalion was forced from its position on the north side of the river and fell back across the large bridge. In the meantime the enemy had formed in considerable strength on the north end of the bridge and attempted to enter into Château-Thierry. This bridge was then blown up and caused the immediate failure of the enemy attack.

General Marchand, commanding the 10th French Colonial Division made the following statement after the action:

On May 31, the 7th Machine-Gun Battalion, U.S.A., had just arrived with its automobiles. It installed itself in a cantonment to the south of Château-Thierry. At 3:30 PM the enemy threatened to take Château-Thierry, attempting to flank the town on our left, where an opening had occurred. The unit was immediately thrown into Château-Thierry at the same time as a Colonial Infantry Battalion which was in the same cantonment with it. Immediately the Americans reinforced the entire bridge, especially the approaches of the bridge. Their courage and skill as marksmen evoked the admiration of all.

Crushed by our fire, the enemy hesitated and, as a result of the counter attacks, vigorously supported by the American machine guns, they were thrown beyond the edges of the town. Château-Thierry remained entirely in our hands.

The American machine guns held the south bank. They formed a protection for the withdrawal of the troops retiring from the northern section for the purpose of crossing the bridge prior to its destruction. Here again the courage of the Americans was beyond all praise. The Colonials themselves, though accustomed to acts of bravery, were struck by the wonderful morale in the face of fire, the impossibility and the extraordinary sang-froid of their allies.

In a combat in the street and at night, where coolness is one of the principal military virtues, the Americans could only play their role. Their watchfulness never failed them and with their machine guns playing upon the roads of entrance and the destroyed bridges and foot-bridges, they prevented any repairs by the enemy.

The losses of the 7th Machine-Gun Battalion, U.S.A. had been heavy, but not out of proportion to the great services they rendered nor to the bloody losses which they inflicted upon the Boches.

They will be relieved at the same time as the French troops, at the side of whom they fought (this evening). The French Command, knowing their just pride, feared they would have humiliated these valiant troops if they had offered them rest sooner than their French companions in the fight.

The episode of Château-Thierry will remain one of the very fine deeds of this war. It is a pleasure for all of us to certify that our valiant allies with us participated in this event—our bonds of affection and of confidence will be strengthened by the same pride which we share in common.

At the present time the Germans, without doubt severely tested, dare not remain in the northern part of Château-Thierry, which, however, we no longer occupy. The bullets which the American guns are sending do not give the Boche any taste to take up a residence there.

Here is the complete Chapter III from *Forgotten Fights of the A.E.F.*, by Pugh and Thayer, 1921:

Chapter III—When The Yanks Came

Over There, Over There,
Send the word, send the word over there,
That the Yanks are coming,
The Yanks are coming..............

Those were the words of a rather popular song that came into its own during the infancy of the A.E.F. and was sung up and down the land, from cantonments in the "States" to Seicheprey, away up on that almost forgotten sector "northwest of Toul," where the handful of A.E.F.ers had been first introduced to "friend Jerry."

And it was true, too, for the Yanks were coming with every ship that touched the shores of France, and they were coming with the determination that they wouldn't "come back till it was over, Over There!"

Then came the month of June, 1918, when the whole of the civilized world was scarcely breathing, or rather, seemingly dared not breathe, while the gray-clad hosts of Prussian Autocracy were dashing forward, in an avalanche of brute power and militaristic domination, down through Fere-en-Tardenois to the banks of the already historic Marne. And, following this period of deepest darkness for the allied cause, came the startling and breath-taking news that the full avalanche of the enemy hordes had been met and stopped on the banks of the Marne by a mere handful of Yankees, "With the Help of God and a few Marines!"

Ask those who were there at the bridge-head of Château-Thierry, those weary and bedraggled men of the 7th Machine Gun

Battalion, Third Division, who, with the wear and tear of over a hundred and eighty weary kilometers of hiking behind them, to say nothing of their thirty-six hours or more without sleep, even for a few moments, plodded wearily into the battered little town on the banks of the Marne, in the sunset of that June evening, with the white and gray puffs of the exploding enemy shells dotting the twilight skies of summer. When, on the 27th of May, 1918, the enemy smashed through the thinly-held French positions on the plateau of the Chemin des Dames and dashed forward towards the Marne, only two American divisions were available for Marshal Foch to throw into the breach in a mad attempt to stop or, at least, to stem for the moment, the onrushing enemy tide.

And so it was, that the first to get into the apex of the great battle which was fast developing here, and, according to the official reports of the operations, the only "men who fought in Château-Thierry itself," were the men of the 7th Machine Gun Battalion, of the Third Division. Nevertheless, it stands also as a matter of official history, that the majority of the fighting in this area, that is, the area to the north of the town of Château-Thierry, fell to the men of the Second Division, who were destined to make a name for themselves and for American arms such as has scarcely ever been equaled in our entire history, in their fight in the Bois de Belleau, Torcy, Bussiares, and Bouresches, and in the valley of the little creek, the Ru Gobert.

Perhaps it might be well to quote the words of one of the members of the historical section of the Great Headquarters, A.E.F., staff as setting forth in the fewest and most pointed words, the crux of the whole matter. He says: "The Third Division was the first to reach the banks of the Marne; and those were Third Division machine gunners, who, racing across country in their little Hommes 40, Chevaux 8, reached the river in time to fight for four days and nights that gallant fight at the Château-Thierry bridges, of which the thrill ran around the world."

And, let it here be said that the Third Division was at this time making at Château-Thierry a name that shall stand for all time as equal to any other that has ever been blazoned upon the tablets of America's glorious history.

The Third Division had, as yet, completed only part of its period of training in the vicinity of Chateauvillain and La Ferté sur Aube when it received orders, on May 30th, 1918, to move at once to the front. This order stated that: "The 5th Infantry Brigade, consisting of the 4th and 7th infantries and the 8th Machine Gun Battalion, will be attached to the 6th French Army, under General Degoutte, and assigned to the defense of the passage of the Marne from Château-Thierry to Dormans. That part of the 6th Infantry Brigade, consisting of the 38th Infantry and half of the 9th Machine Gun Battalion, will hold the crossings of the Marne from Dormans eastward to Damery, under direction of the 10th Colonial French Division of the 5th French Army. The remainder of the 6th Infantry Brigade, viz., the 30th Infantry and the remaining half of the 9th Machine Gun Battalion, will be the support of the 5th Brigade. The Divisional Machine Gun Battalion, the 7th—will march at once for Château-Thierry; the remaining troops will go by rail May 31st, for their respective destinations."

Of these various assignments, none proved so urgent as that of the Divisional Machine Gun Battalion, the 7th, which was in the fighting from the first time they entered the little town of Château-Thierry, until its final relief, ninety-six hours later. The remainder of the 3rd Division suffered very slightly, with the exception of some severe fighting in the Jaulgonne Bend of the Marne, where the enemy attempted a crossing, but was halted.

And so it was that, with the horizon-blue-clad poilus of France, worn and weary and mud-bedraggled, and torn and bleeding, fighting a seemingly hopeless battle with the advancing enemy waves in the shell-torn streets ahead of them, the men of the 7th Machine Gun Battalion, hastily getting their guns into position so as to play along the main bridge in the center of the town, and likewise up and down the banks of the Marne on both sides, went into battle which was to continue for ninety-six hours more!

Wave after wave of the enemy hosts swept forward towards the coveted goal, determined to either take the bridge or to make possible a crossing at some other point which would enable them to deploy into the open and almost level country beyond the banks of the Marne. But, across the stream, was the indomitable barrier of Yankee gunners, and "once again, for the second time in four years, they made the Marne the high tide of the Hun invasion!"

Thousands of shells of all calibres flew overhead; some of them with their sinister whistle, many of them seemingly howling, but all of them uniting in one great rising crescendo, and the fortunes of battle ebbed and flowed beneath them. Great enemy shells dropped with crash and roar into the thin line of stubborn American doughboys, throwing debris of every description high into the air, and filling the spaces between the great rising chant and crescendo of battle with the moans and shrieks of the dying and wounded. Beyond, through the battered streets of the town, gray-clad masses began to move forward, down to the banks of the Marne.

It was the enemy infantry, advancing in their packed formation, resembling a great gray monster crawling down to devour the men who were standing their ground at the bridges of Château-Thierry. They soon deploy, fresh troops filling the gaps and then they advance again towards the goal of Prussian ambition: the Marne. Low, sinister shrieks and whistles come from above, and the shells from the allied batteries begin to fall in the midst of the advancing enemy masses. Men, covered with blood and mud, crawling over one another, and rushing about in a dazed state, writhing in agony or pushing doggedly forward, attempt to advance again to the river banks. The ground and streets are dotted with the huddled forms of the dead and dying, but the second wave is already pressing forward, and once again the Yankee machine guns tear great gaping holes in their advancing ranks; and still they hurl themselves against the American positions among the shell-holes and ruins along the river.

All the time, the uncanny whistle of the flying bullets, with their s-s-s-s-s-s! came from the advancing hosts across the river, and then, once again the Yanks turned the muzzles of their deadly guns full on this onward rushing wave of humanity, poured forth a steady stream of steel, as the guns rat-tat-tat their message of death and hate. Shrieks, curses and groans rise from the ranks across the river, which was now running with the blood of the contending hosts, and time and again the whole mad drama of war is deepened by the boom of the batteries in the rear, adding their finishing touch to the ghastliness of the scene.

But the 7th Machine Gun Battalion stuck!—and behind them and the barrier formed by their comrades, clad in the immortal blue of long-suffering France, the allied forces were able to dispose more fresh troops, of the 164th French and 3rd United States

Divisions. These new troops took up strong defensive positions along the Marne on both sides of the town, and effecting, by the 30th Infantry, liaison with the 9th Infantry, of the 2nd Division, on the right of that division, near Mountcourt, west of the river.

Finally, came the morning of the 4th of June, and with it relief for the weary 7th Machine Gun Battalion! But, as they filed out of their positions, and plodded backward from the line of the river, they seemed to wear the faint semblance of a smile of victory, for behind them were the men of two other regiments of their own division, the 3rd, as well as an entire French division. Why did they smile even though those smiles were the smiles of the exhausted and weary men who have stood face to face with death for ninety-six long hours? Because they knew that victory was theirs; that the setting sun of that day should bring into being the birth of that new power which was destined, even then, to spell defeat and ruin for the proud banners of Prussian autocracy! They were supremely confident that the enemy never would break through the line of heroes who they had left in charge of their blood-bought lines along the Marne banks, and in the streets of Château-Thierry.

It is true the operation had been costly, but had it been even more costly, it surely would have been worth the price. When it is considered what effect the fighting of the untried American troops had upon the morale of the allied armies, perhaps never before had any like number of men in so short a time contributed as much to the final victory as did the 2nd and 3rd Divisions at and near Château-Thierry.

As one writer, whose name I have forgotten for the time being, puts it: "The mother of every boy who was killed there can say that no soldier's life ever was given more effectively during the whole war."

How brave and self-sacrificing and altogether noble have been our mothers and all of our noble American women during these stirring times! And still all of their care and devotion had for its ending a grave in France!

There, where poppies bloom, and fields are scarred
With unknown heroes' graves, remorseless, numb,
And swifter than the lightning it may come
From unknown depths where earthly joys are barred,
Where Love is lost, the quickening pulse is still

And Death's rhythmical beat is audible.
Or in the trench where golden hearted Truth,
Clad in the panoply of grace and right,
Sublimely pours the sweet red wine of youth
A surf of blood upon the sea of Might."

And still has there been no agonizing cry of revolt from the mother or wife or sweetheart, no furious imprecations, no bitterness of soul.

And so America stoops and kisses the cold, still lips of her martyred sons, covering them with her starry banner of Liberty; placing them, her supreme sacrifice of honor and love, upon the Altar of God's throne, that Liberty and Justice and Freedom from Oppression may not be forever lost amidst the crushing and brutal blows of the Mailed Fist and Iron Heel of the Autocrat.

Returning to the discussion of the relative importance of the fight at Châteu-Thierry, let us consider for a few moments, what it meant to the allied cause and morale, at this stage of the great game of chess which was being waged on the western frontier of civilization. Perhaps it would be best to quote several noted authorities.

The first one at hand, written by a staff officer of the A.E.F. Headquarters, states:

The effect on the French was immediate, visible and startling. The drooping French morale revived as a midsummer flower lifts its head after a cooling shower." The same authority, later adds: "The American morale had also been sagging. It could not have been otherwise. Our troops had had to wait around too long, and it had taken all the heart out of them. Homesick beyond words, they had to prepare themselves slowly for trench warfare, a deadly thing, the while the world told them that the war would last for years and years. They began to wonder whether they were going to be so darned good after all. Then suddenly the whole face of the matter changed. News came from the Marne valley that Americans were pitching into the fight, that it was old-fashioned, paste-'em-one-in-the-eye fighting of their own sort, that they were getting away with murder. And every American from Camp Lewis to Toul, said: 'Gee, we're pretty good,' and became so by thinking it."

And you can readily see what sort of effect this would have on the troops in France. Of course, every division, either on ship or already landing, began to feel that, after everything was said and done, the stories of enemy prowess were idle tales of the billets, and that there would really be nothing to it, when they would be given the chance to get into the game for good. They began to think that all of these weary months of training was all "bunk" and unnecessary; that all they needed was the chance to take "a paste at that Big German Rifle Range," and they would show what sort of stuff they were made of.

Accordingly, General Pershing became commander of a bunch of real fighting units, scarcely more than raw recruits, of only a few short months' training. Transformed, almost overnight, into units fit to put into immediate use at the fighting lines, should the necessity arise for throwing them into the breach at once.

And, then and there, the policy of sending them into the fight at once was adopted, and, as one of our army men puts it: "All that happened from July 18th to November 11th followed as a natural though unforeseen consequence of what happened in June northwest of Château-Thierry. Just as an electric spark will, in a flash, take a jar of properly proportioned hydrogen and oxygen and turn it into water, so the current which, spitting blue flame and setting the whole world a tingle, ran forth from Belleau Wood in June, 1918, took that miscellaneous assortment of dubious Americans known as the A.E.F. and turned it into an army."

Let us get the true perspective of the fight at the Château-Thierry area and see just what it means and really amounted to, from the purely military standpoint. After all, it was not so much of a miracle as we have been told it was.

It is true that the Americans, with the aid of their almost exhausted allies, the French, did stop the German drive at the banks of the Marne, and, when the lines moved again, their direction was towards Germany. But let us also remember that, when the Germans smashed through the Chemin des Dames plateau area on May 27th, the allied troops had already established a new defensive line and system of well chosen positions, manned by men who were thoroughly schooled in their calling and highly capable of withstanding anything that the enemy would probably bring against them. And this line of defenses was in a position which met and, as history already recounts, turned the tide of German invasion. But that tide of invasion consisted of a German army which was almost already exhausted by its incredibly successful advance—an advance which carried it across the Aisne, through Tardenois and the Ourcq, and down to the very banks of the historic Marne. The enemy troops had already out-run even its own expectations and was tired out by its drive, and almost unsupported, on account of the inability of its supplies and reserves to keep pace with the rapidity of its advance.

There has existed a sort of popular notion in this country, that our valiant allies, the French, were at this time, in full retreat through the advancing lines of American troops, and that our men were therefore forced to stand alone and meet the Hun hordes, bearing the brunt of the fray and finally pushing the invaders backward as their victorious waves swept forward in counter-attack.

This notion is not at all true, and furthermore mightily unfair to our valiant allies and friends, the horizon-blue-clad poilus of France.

From sources that are official, and, therefore, of much more value as authoritative than would be even the works of the most highly credited correspondents or officers, the story of what really took place comes to me in this manner. The Americans were now operating under command of the French General Degoutte, who was commanding the corps in whose sector they were operating. Opposing the German advance were two French divisions, which were already sadly depleted, and weary from their constant fighting of five days' duration, disheartened, and nearly having reached the limit of their physical endurance. Yet they were ordered to hold their ground until the Americans could get into line behind them. And hold they did, as best they could, and with the determination with which only the poilus of France can fight! After the Americans had formed their defensive lines, the French troops were to fall back through these lines and withdrew for a much-needed rest.

Everything that took place after this time was strictly according to orders that had been issued to the commanders of the several divisions engaged, as well as to the corps commander, General Degoutte. Therefore, the withdrawal of the exhausted French was no reflection upon their already proved indomitable spirit and stoicism, for in holding as they did just long enough for the resistance lines to be formed, they had already done their full share.

As these facts were, of course, known to only those of high command or at least to only those who were entitled to know, the troops and also the correspondents, construed it faultily, and we find them continually spreading this false impression abroad throughout the land. Certainly, these men have never lived and fought beside those same French poilus, or else they would never have even so much as dreamed of him yielding a precious inch of his beloved France to the foe.

The spirit of the Yanks, as they advanced to the battlefront, through roads streaming with worn and weary and battered French troops, swarming to the rear in an almost bewildered and dazed sort of way, was little short of wonderful, for they continued their advance with spirits unbroken and nerves unshaken. And to most of them it surely must have seemed as if they alone were holding firm, when all about them was crumbling before the gigantic Hun battering ram. And so the sunset of June 5th, 1918, brought to the battered and shell-torn streets of Château-Thierry, the light of victory and the promise of deliverance, as the rat-tat-tat of the guns resounded through the ruins of what had once been busy streets, and down along the banks of the river that divides the town into sections. The crumbling ruins of the bridges, turned red and dusty yellow in the slanting rays of the setting sun, the red-tiled roofs of the houses across the river, now scarred and torn by the incessant rain of shells and the spatter of shrapnel and machine gun fire, lent a sort of colorful touch to the plaster walls of the houses, whose smoking ruins stood, looking it seemed, with pitying and wistful windows calling to the spitting fire of the guns to win them back again to the folds of the tricolor of France. The bridge of the Marne, a crumpled ruin, a pile of stones, now-with here and there the huddled form of some brave Yank or poilu, locked in death-grip with his opponent, in the blue-gray uniform of the guard, over whose silent forms sang the ominous song of the machine guns and the whine of the shells bursting beyond, in the further end of the town.

And further on, from the Chateau garden, surrounded by its great stone wall, with its massive wooden gates, and with its courtyard and gardens strewn with the bodies of the slain; its flowers and plants trampled under foot of the surging hosts which, only a short time previous had been locked in deadly conflict; its well and lattice porticoes torn and twisted by the bursting shells, looked out and beyond to the tall tower of the cathedral, which now reflected the glory of the sunset, as if a new halo of glory had crowned its lofty spire. All was peaceful now, except for the patter of the distant machine guns, and the great round moon rose over soil redeemed for France! The Yanks had come!"

The following selection, from a work of fiction, is said by the author to follow his own personal experiences as a truck driver during the war. Leslie W. Quick, from his book, *Jimmy Goes to War*:

It was early morning on June 2. The night had been spent inching through ceaseless traffic.

"Woodpeckers," said Al, listening.

Number Four, with its load of ammunition skirted a copse of trees, swung left past picture-book houses on the outskirts of a town, and ground to a halt at the edge of a river.

"Château-Thierry," said Jimmy.

The river was the Marne, which split the town into two portions. From the south bank camouflaged batteries of machine guns, manned by Americans, raked the streets on the far side.

A grizzled old sergeant came forward to the camion and lifted the rear curtain. His movements were slow, unhurried, as if he might have been sauntering into the street back home to examine the vegetables some huckster was offering for sale.

"Phutt-phutt shells," he told himself calmly. "Well, we can use them." Without raising his voice he called, "Detail," and a half-dozen privates jumped to attention. "Unload," said the sergeant.

He came to the front of the camion and put one foot on the running board.

"We're the Seventh Machine Gun Battalion of the Third Division," he said companionably, forestalling their questions, "and our job is to keep the Germans from crossing the Marne here in Château-Thierry. We'll do it."

"Sure?" asked Al.

"Oh, yes." There was a note of calm finality in the voice that made Jimmy believe in spite of himself. The sergeant, eyes partially closed, drawled on reminiscently, "We came in night before last, with Kaiser Bill's heavy artillery trying to convince us this was a king of unhygienic spot to camp." He smiled tolerantly. "But by four in the morning we had seventeen guns in position and firing, and every time yesterday any mob of strangers with green-gray uniforms and round pot-helmets came sight-seeing over the river in Château-Thierry, we waved 'em back by running a few clips through the phutt-phutts. They always took the hint and went away from there."

"But how about night?" Jimmy asked. "You can't see the enemy in the dark, can you?"

The sergeant shifted his leg to find a more comfortable position. "Oh, at night. Well, with the guns set to spray the streets yonder to the north, and doing it sort of regularly, it doesn't make much difference whether we can see the Germans or not. The result is pretty much the same. Of course—" His fingers scrawled circles in the dust on Number Four's panel.

"Yes?"

"Well, up to this morning we were kind of handicapped by having to keep in mind the position of a few men of our own over there. We'd sent a little detachment from Company A across the river on outpost duty. It sort of cramped our firing." His faced cleared. "But that's out now."

"Out?"

"Why, yes. About an hour after midnight the Germans piled in from the northwest and cut between our observers and the west bridge, which they had planned to use if attacked. The detachment made for the east bridge; they would, naturally. But our guns were playing a lullaby over that and they couldn't cross, and we were dimpling the river, too, and they couldn't swim it."

"… Excuse me a minute."

To the north sounded a series of explosions like trench mortars. Across the river, where the streets had been etched by the morning sun, a fog descended. On the south bank the machine guns crackled in sudden fury, all of them joining the chorus.

"Woodpeckers," said Al again.

"A German advance," said Jimmy, sucking in his breath. "That's a smoke screen."

The cloud thickened and spread, rolling closer and closer to the river. Little bursts of flame tore from it, and the air whistled and droned with rifle bullets. All about them the machine guns swung in semi-circles, spitting fire in long staccato bursts.

It was all over in a few minutes. No enemy, Jimmy knew, could advance in the face of that deadly barrage. The smoke screen lifted lazily and dissolved like fog, till the sun shone once more on the empty streets north of the Marne.

The grizzled sergeant strolled to the waiting camion, leisurely wiping his hands. "Detail," he remarked in a conversational tone, "finish unloading." He scratched his head. "Let's see now, what was I saying?"

Jimmy searched his paralyzed mind a long time before the memory came. "Those trapped fellows on outpost duty across the river last night," he reminded, wondering why his voice sounded so hoarse. "Were—were they all killed?"

"They were Americans," said the sergeant in mild reproof, "and Americans know how to take care of themselves. They don't scare worth a cent. Well, their CO yelled at us across the east bridge till we recognized his voice and ceased firing while he brought over his detachment."

The camion was unloaded at last. Al cranked the motor and Jimmy, at the wheel, threw the lever into low. But even with the clutch pedal giving under his yielding foot, Jimmy hesitated. Some elusive question hid in the back of his mind.

"Oh!" he said. "When the Germans cut off the detachment from the west bridge, didn't they come over it themselves to this side?"

The grizzled sergeant answered politely, as one replies to children. "Naturally they didn't. You see, the west bridge was mined, and we just touched her off and blew her to smithereens. No, the Germans didn't cross. They never will cross the Marne in Château-Thierry."

Number Four rolled away from the sibilant chant of the machine guns.

"Woodpeckers," said Al.

"Gibraltar," said Jimmy.

They were thinking of different things.

In Their Own Words—The Americans

Ernest Peixotto, one of the eight official combat artists of the AEF, wrote in his book, *The American Front*:

> Château-Thierry itself was by no means hopelessly ruined; had, in fact, only suffered in spots. Many of its streets were quite intact. Others were but a mass of debris. The church of St. Crepin was filled with plunder, collected by the Germans, ready to be taken but abandoned at the last minute in the hurry of their departure.
>
> The handsome stone bridge across the Marne had been dynamited and the heavy masonry of two of its arches lay blocking the channel, but already blue-coated engineers were swarming over it like ants restoring a trampled ant-hill. Long, serpentine like columns of khaki-clad troops crawled over the two pontoons to the eastward and clattered along the stone-paved quays into the city on their war northward to reinforce the attack.
>
> Château-Thierry, a name that was destined to loom big in the pages of American history! The old town, built, according to tradition, by Charles Martel for the Frankish King, Thierry IV, and, like so many other French towns, repeatedly sacked and pillaged, everywhere showed the effects of the recent heavy fighting. Buildings once stately and beautiful lay in ruins, and debris of all sorts filled the streets. Charles Martel—Charles the Hammer—would have been amazed at what modern weapons of warfare had done to his handiwork, amazed too at the sight of American troops of many divisions in the town where King Thierry had once held his court.

Elmer Ganser, 126th Infantry Regiment, 32nd Division remembers in his book, *History of the 126th Infantry in the War with Germany*:

> The now famous town of Château-Thierry was reached at 7:00 PM, July 27th, where the regiment de-trained in the square on the north side of the Marne River, and marched through Brasles to the Bois de Barbillon, about three kilometers northeast of Château-Thierry, where we rested for the night.
>
> During their short stay in the town, the Germans ransacked every building and house, and everything of value, including priceless art treasures, was either removed or destroyed. The interior of houses, unharmed by shell-fire, were complete wrecks. The Hun

had torn to shreds the bedding, clothing and carpets, and furniture and dishes were broken to bits. The streets were littered with the debris of fallen walls, and the southern arch of the ancient bridge was blown up by the Huns when they evacuated the town as a result of the Allied counter offensive of July 18, 1918.

Here is an excerpt from Captain Alden Brooks' book, *As I Saw It*:

It had been a whole half year since the regiment had passed through the city of Château-Thierry on the way to Soissons and the Chemin des Dames. The men were raw militia then; they were untried and their fighting qualities unknown, but they came back as seasoned veterans, hardened by six-months' active service at the front. Many of the old and well-loved faces were missing; many new ones could be seen, while vacant places in the ranks told of the hard campaign just passed. But it was the same old regiment that weary in mind and body and with thinned ranks, unslung their packs in the battered convent and paused to take breath.

Tired though they were, the men welcomed this opportunity of looking around at the city which bore the name of the great offensive through which they had just passed. The city itself stood on the banks of the Marne River, which flowed westerly through the middle of the town. Along its banks were shops and factories, while on the northern side the pretentious residences of the well-to-do were built upon the slopes of a hill which rose almost from the water's edge. This northern bank had been the apex of that great salient which had been driven straight toward Paris, and had been stopped by the 2nd Division at Belleau Woods and later by the machine gunners of the 2nd Division posted in the buildings along the southern bank of the river.

Undoubtedly Château-Thierry had been one of the most attractive of the smaller cities of France before the German hordes bore down upon it, bringing in their wake ruin and desolation. At first glance the effects from shell fire did not seem to be very impressive, for the regiment had been long accustomed to ruined towns where bits of standing wall were the rule rather than the exception. Almost every building, however, bore evidences of the recent fighting; gaping holes and pock-marked walls showed everywhere, while here and there the crumbling ruins were all that remained on some once attractive home. Now and then houses were

seen half of which had been blown away, for all the world resembling a child's doll house whose front walls have been discarded the better to reveal the interior. They would have seemed ridiculous were it not for the smashed furniture inside, where broken beds or tables hung precariously over the tottering edges of the floors or were piled in jumbled and almost unrecognizable confusion in the corners.

Château-Thierry differed from the usual run of French towns in that the houses were detached, and were surrounded by yards and well-kept flower gardens, much as in our larger suburban communities. A great many of these yards were literally covered with curtains, bedding, clocks, vases, pictures, and all manner of smashed furniture, for, on receiving orders to withdraw, the Germans had apparently thrown everything possible out the windows. Seemingly they took a particular dislike to clocks, vases, and pictures, many of the latter, particularly oil paintings, being slashed with knives and the gilt frames hacked and broken. Nor did the Huns confine themselves to throwing things outside, for the interiors of most homes were knee-deep in wreckage of all sorts, often not a square inch of floor space being visible, while some instances were seen where hand grenades had been exploded, doubtless for want of time to destroy more methodically. Many bundles were found, tied up and addressed to relatives or friends in Germany and containing all manner of clothing, clocks, ornaments, and lingerie, It was all very interesting, but no one was sorry to leave such scenes of vandalism and wanton destruction of civilian property.

In the *New York Times Current History Magazine* of September, 1918, comes the following excerpt from an article by Edwin H. James, "America's Part in a Historic Battle":

The Turning Point

July 22.—Château-Thierry, the nearest German-held point to Paris, was occupied yesterday morning by French and Americans, who established a strong position north of the river preparatory to pushing on. Bridges were thrown across the stream and guns were brought up.

I went into Château-Thierry a short time after the Germans left it—a city which will forever occupy a place in American history. It must always be recalled as marking a region where the American troops stopped the enemy just where his "peace drives" of 1918 took him nearest to Paris and the fruition of his insolent hopes.

Where hundreds on hundreds of shells had screeched overhead that Sunday morning, their roar interrupted by the rat-a-tat of machine gunners, it was peaceful almost, if one discarded the casual shells that the retreating boche sent backward. Up the road moved the graceful French cavalrymen and blue-coated poilus, cracking jokes about the boche going to Paris.

We passed the crest of the hill, and since no one stopped us ran into the city until halted by debris and barricades.

Ruins In Château-Thierry

It was uncanny. But for an occasional shell and the droning of our airplanes overhead, absolute quiet ruled amid the debris where thousands on thousands of shells had put war's mark on the pretty and historic little city. For a moment we stood at Carnot Place looking north into the city. Not a living being was in sight.

The advance troops, which crossed, had moved on and other troops were not yet there. Up the Rue Carnot, paved with a three-foot deep carpet of debris, one saw barricade after barricade raised fifteen feet high, perhaps two to every block. Those on this side of the river were made by the French, and those on the other side by the Germans.

All was quiet now along those grim little forts from behind which machine guns and rifles had spit venom for seven long weeks. To our left lay the railroad station and yards. The station was but an empty shell, and the tracks were torn up in hundreds of places where bottled hate had fallen from Hunward.

There was much wreckage along the Quai de la Poterne and the Promenade de la Levée, marking the business district of the city. The invader had left his characteristic marks. Shop after shop lay in ruins, with shells of walls standing. Pretty little cafés were gone beyond repair.

On the outskirts of the city the residential districts were in much better shape. Here were found perhaps three-score persons who had stayed on through all the hell that had raged there. Among them was Mme. de Prey, 87 years old, to whom home had meant more than life. She had occupied her seven weeks caring for German wounded. A French General, who learned what she had done, kissed her weathered cheeks in homage. There were in the midst of this war wreckage a trio of children, who, left out of doors the first time for so long, made the best of their opportunity.

The magnificent stone bridge over the Marne on the Rue Carnot was blown up for almost its entire length.

In years to come American tourists will go to see Château-Thierry. They will not see the debris and carnage I saw yesterday, but it will be many years before the war marks are wiped away. Remember that on the line of white stone houses on the south bank of the river the American machine gunners, after a thirty-hour ride in camions from another part of France, placed their tools of war and held for thirteen hours against the mad rushes of the oncoming Germans to get across the river seven weeks ago."

From *Combat Engineer! The History of the 107th Engineer Battalion*, by Frederick Stonehouse:

In response to the heavy German offensive at the Marne, the 32nd Division with the 107th was shifted to that sector, arriving on the 25th of July. Arriving in the sector, the 107th was greeted by what seemed like an endless drizzle of cold rain and an unending sea of muck. The first night was spent in the nearly deserted village of Fleurines with troops huddled in rain soaked pup tents.

The following day the Regiment boarded a convoy of trucks and moved through to the front, passing through one shell-torn village after another. The 107th was still a green outfit and at every opportunity many of the men eagerly hunted for souvenirs. By late that night they arrived at the central square of Château-Thierry. The men were billeted everywhere and anywhere. Some ended up in cowsheds, while others enjoyed the comforts of the Hotel DuCygne, with, of all things, clean towels."

From James B. Nolan's book, *The Reading Militia*:

On July 27th Company B marched through Château-Thierry and struck northward in the direction of heavy cannonading. Even the callous boys were struck by the appearance of the shattered town of Château-Thierry.

"We all thought of Reading," wrote one of them to his home newspaper, "and tried to picture Penn street in the condition of these streets here. The ruins were awful and even house corners were shot away. We guessed that the first bombardment must have come about meal time, for we could see the prepared meals still standing on the tables in the ruined houses."

Elmer Sherwood, of the 42nd Division, remembers in his book, *Diary of a Rainbow Veteran*, that:

> We then drove into the city of Château-Thierry, where all of the batteries of our regiment stopped to feed the horses and have mess; this place is not so shot up as those we just passed through but those first towns were right in the middle of 'No Man's Land.' It is bad enough though and all of the bridges are down over the Marne River and the town itself is in a sad plight. American planes are flying all around here and only an occasional shot can be heard. They say the Germans retreated in terrible disorder but with speed. In fact, so much speed, that they left everything, from a ten-inch gun to their helmets behind.

Lt Robert Hoffman, 111th Infantry Regiment, U.S. 28th Division from his book, *I Remember the Last War*:

> This was my first time in Chateau Thierry. I had seen it from a distance from the heights of Hill 204, when it was occupied by the Germans. Now the Germans were many miles away. The people were already coming back into the city. There were a few women and children, a few elderly men, and soldiers in abundance—both from the French and American armies.
>
> I saw something of Chateau Thierry as we drove through it. It must have been a beautiful town before it had been shelled and occupied by the Germans, for even in its partly-shattered state it still showed signs of beauty.

Leo V. Jacks, an artilleryman in the 119th Field Artillery, U.S. 32nd Division, wrote in his book, *Service Record: By an Artilleryman*:

> We descended farther into the valley in a gradually lengthening column and two hours later we were tramping the deserted streets of Château-Thierry. Every house was pock-marked by bullet holes, and many dreadfully shattered by artillery fire. On some doors the Germans had scribbled in chalk *Gute Leute*, but these dwellings seemed as badly damaged as the rest. The pavement was littered with wreckage, as though a tornado had swept by, brass shells glittered in the sunshine, and a few traces of German dead still lay in the alleys.

If the town harbored citizens they, like the famous Toad-in-the-Hole, were not to be found. A hollow rumble echoed continuously as guns and caissons lurched along. Once we passed a house which a large shell had split in two parts, leaving the whole interior visible from the street, and two of our soldiers leaped in and endeavored to play upon the ruin of a piano. But the instrument was damaged and hopelessly out of tune. A clashing jangle of discords followed, succeeded again by a nervous quiet. It is very depressing to walk the streets of a city after a battle, to note everywhere ruin and desolation, and above all that oppressive stillness. Where there should have been many happy people and hastening footfalls, the baking July sun disclosed only silence and death.

American patrols tramped from street to street, and a few French officers in their sky-blue with red trimmings and gold braid were making an inspection tour. The church towers were shattered by shot, windows knocked out everywhere, and barricades of heavy furniture and fragments of stone blocked many side passages, and if the red smears on the walls and floors were any evidence, there had been some savage struggles within doors. It was past noon when we crossed the river, traversed the last suburbs of this terrible city of the dead, and scaled the long heights to the north. It had been hot in the streets, and we were refreshed by a cool breeze that met us in the hills.

From *Iodine and Gasoline, a History of the 117th Sanitary Train*, by Josiah C. Chatfield:

> To those Americans who were there during the stormy days in July and August, Château-Thierry exemplifies one thought, needless, wanton destruction. All through the debris-strewn streets were evidence of the thoroughness with which these master vandals worked in their chosen task of desecration. Every house that had not been ruined by artillery fire had been forced open and ransacked. Nothing seemed too small to escape the marring hands of the invading Huns. Beautiful pieces of ancient furniture, priceless in this age, had their upholstery torn and ripped into tatters, or their polished surfaces defaced by a bayonet. Across the foot of one beautiful bed had been scratched the battle cry, "Gott mit Uns." Every large mirror had been smashed. Mud and filth were everywhere in evidence. Everywhere the Huns had retired to their animal-like slumber amid silken bed clothes without even removing their dirty boots.

GERMAN SOLDIERS MARCHING TO CHÂTEAU-THIERRY

Bottles of ink from a looted stationery store furnished the raiders grenades with which they attacked white walls and costly paintings. Tapestries were in every case cut to ribbons. Even the electric light chandeliers were torn from their fasteners in most instances.

In Harper's *Pictorial Library of the World War, 1920*:

Another canteen girl told the following story: "When Château-Thierry had been cleared of the Germans, we moved there and opened our canteen. The basement we used as a store room was filled with the smell of mustard gas and the walls were streaked with it. The garden had been the scene of some sort of hand-to-hand scrap and there were many new graves under the bushes and many things that ought to have been in graves.

"One of the boys took me out to look at a certain bush. 'What is that hanging up there?' I asked him. Then he wondered why I felt faint and sick when he told me is was bits of a man blown there by a machine gun."

THE FRIENDLY FIRE INCIDENT AT THE WAGON BRIDGE

Many accounts have been written which describe the fighting at the main bridge over the Marne at Château-Thierry, and, with one single exception, all of them make mention of an attack by massed German troops on the night of 1 June 1918. Stories of the Germans "singing gutturally" as they made a suicidal charge into the American machine gun fire are abundant. The accounts given in this chapter on the fighting in Château-Thierry similarly tell of Germans dying by the score on the bridge over the Marne as they "chanted while linked arm in arm, long over-coats swishing." But were they Germans?

The actual truth seems to have been that it was not the Germans who were singing and charging, but the Negroes of the French 10th Colonial (Senegalese) Division, who were trying to get back over the river at night and who were mistaken for Germans and shot down by the Americans. This great tragedy was evidently quickly covered up at the time, and no further official mention of it was made. The event was, however, known among the American and the French troops when it happened and they discussed it among themselves. No one wanted to admit to such a tragic and understandable error made during the heat of combat and in the blackness of night, when American machine gunners unintentionally wiped out many of their French Colonial allies. Those who know the German soldier of World War I and his tactics, can hardly picture him linked arm in arm with his comrades, charging at night while chanting and sing-songing to his death!

German records evidently make no mention of their having made an infantry attack upon the wagon bridge at Château-Thierry. The War Diary of the German 231st Infantry Division states, in part:

A surprise attempt to seize a bridgehead on the south bank had to be renounced. Since this had not been accomplished on the first day, the enemy has now had time to emplace numerous machine guns on the south bank. The buildings of the south part of the village were studded with machine guns, particularly those near the intact bridge which alone was covered by 5 machine guns. The bridgehead was to be forced in 3 or 4 days after thorough preparation by artillery and minenwerfer. However, since this crossing as well as the seizure of the position, immediately in front of the commanding heights occupied by the enemy, would have resulted in heavy losses, the plan was abandoned by corps headquarters.

Alden Brooks, an American who served as an artillery officer in the French Army, and who served close to Belleau Wood in 1918, wrote in his book, *As I Saw It*:

As for the incidents of yesterday and the day before, what had happened was this. On the night of June 1 everything had been prepared to trap the Germans in an ambush on the bridge at Château-Thierry—the bridge had been mined; American gunners placed in houses this side; and as soon as the enemy were well on the bridge, some of them across, the bridge was to have been blown up and those caught on this side shot down where they were. Unfortunately, in the excitement of the firing, the commander of colonial troops defending the place had given the order to blow up the bridge too soon; hence, not only were no Germans killed, but it was Frenchmen and a small band of Americans with them, fighting a rear-guard action the other side, who were caught and divided from their fellows. The Americans, and after them most of the Frenchmen, had managed to cross farther up-stream on a railway bridge that was still intact; but Americans in position on this side by the main bridge had shot, killed in dark mid-stream, some fifty Senegalese trying to swim their way across, whose cries from the opposite bank in broken Senegalese-French had seemed to American ears only so many German voices singing a war- song, or by wile trying to allay the firing. But that was as much as there was to it; never any serious attempt by the Germans to cross; just a hazardous sniping on both sides; and, so far, no artillery daring to fire on the center of the town, so close, down there, were friend and foe together.

During the next week I heard several times the story of the Senegalese being shot in mid-river by the Americans. Whatever head-shaking there was over this, there always followed, none the less, a half-smile and praise of the American gunners."

Editor's comment: What really did happen on that tragic night of 31 May/1 June? Was there an incident of amicide, or friendly fire, which killed and wounded many of our French allies?

In Their Own Words—The Germans

June 1, 1918

The attack on the 31st had placed us in possession of the dominating hills north of the Marne which dominated Château-Thierry.

Patrols and small detachments had penetrated the city at various places, but the city proper was still in the hands of the enemy which held it occupied with numerous machine guns.

At 8:30 the west edge of the city was reached. Shortly before this the enemy had blown up the railway bridge southwest of Château-Thierry.

So the north part of Château-Thierry was in our hands. Our infantry had occupied the west part and the block of houses near the blown up bridge along the bank of the Marne. There 2 companies of the 3rd Bn 443rd Inf were in position who, after having reached the bridge from the west, had advanced to that point coming from the north.

During the very intense street fighting in Château-Thierry the many enemy machine guns firing from the cellars and out of the windows had made it very tough for the infantry and in part cost us severe casualties, and the units had become thoroughly mixed. They could not be reorganized during the day of the 2nd."

Editor's note: "...the railway bridge southwest of Château-Thierry...." would evidently refer to the railroad bridge which crossed the Marne at the same location as does the modern highway bridge in the vicinity of the municipal swimming pool.

Group CCorps Headquarters (183)
Corps Headquarters 4 Res. Corps.   June 1, 1918—8 PM
(1a No 505 Operations. Corps Order
(3,) The regulations governing the visiting of Château-Thierry rests in the hands of the Corps Headquarters and the 231st Inf. Div. Château-Thierry can only be visited on written permission from the Corps Headquarters or the Commanding General of the 231st Inf Div. I emphatically forbid the visiting of Château-Thierry by troops of the neighboring or rearward divisions as well as by columns (supply trains) of attached units.

The Commanding General von Conta

Copies to 10, 22, 28, 36, 197, 231, 237, 5th Guard Inf Div. Corps Distribution B.

"June 1, 1918. 4.00 AM

Reconnaissance Patrol to Marne Bridge in Château-Thierry

The Marne bridge in Château-Thierry is a reinforced concrete bridge with two openings which have a span of 35 meters each. The supporting frame of each opening consists of three arched ribs. In the center part of the roadway rests directly on the ribs, and on the sides on vertical supports which lead to the ribs.

The bridge was blasted about 15 meters from the opposite end, so incompletely, however, that it is immediately passable for the infantry and for light vehicles, but for heavy vehicles only after repairs have been made.

The patrol was fired upon by two MG's which are emplaced on the opposite bank on either side of the bridge. Corporal Zinnow of the patrol was wounded in the right side of the chest and in the upper left thigh.

(Sgd) Kallabis, 1st Vice Sgt Major 354th Pion Co.

Editor's note: it appears that the Sgt Kallabis is describing the railway bridge over the Marne which crossed in the southwestern part of Château-Thierry. Today a modern highway bridge which crosses the Marne in the vicinity of the present day swimming pool has replaced the old railway bridge.

Report from 353rd Res Pion Co to 231st Pion Co
Thru 231st Pion Commander. By Order Coln, 2nd Lt and Adj.
The company is located at the creek 800 meters north of Brasles.
Together with 2nd Lt Nickel and a patrol of eight men I have reconnoitered the bridge at Château-Thierry. The bridge is completely open to traffic of all loads. The enemy attempted to blow up the bridge, but not successfully. The superstructure of the bridge is entirely undamaged. The enemy has placed MG's on the opposite bank in the immediate vicinity of the bridge. To secure the bridge against being blown up I left one squad behind, which is to retire after the arrival of the platoon from the 354th Pion Co.

Editor's note: It appears that this message refers to the railway and vehicle bridge that crossed the Marne River from Brasles to the sugar mill.

June 2, 1918
Scout Section June 3, 1918. 10.00 AM

444th Inf Despatched from Billets in Courpoil 10.30 AM

Mission:

1) It is to be determined which parts of Château-Thierry north of the Marne are still occupied by the enemy, and

2) in what condition the bridges across the Marne are at present.

I approached the city from the northwest in order to be able to leave the horses at a place as free from fire as possible.

On the southern edge of the woods of Peuplier Sal. I met Captain Schafer, Fus. Bn 442nd Inf, who informed me that it was possible to enter only that part of the city which lies west of the main street, since the eastern part, especially the Chateau hill, was still occupied in strength by the enemy.

But almost all the houses which had been indicated to me as being occupied by the enemy proved to be vacant, at least I was not fired upon when approaching them. The chateau and the chateau hill were free of the enemy.

Only immediately north of the blown-up bridge a few members of the enemy force were very cleverly hidden in a cellar, which made it impossible to enter the street (two men were wounded in my presence). Very likely various other such scattered men are located in houses and cellars. However, organized resistance is no longer being offered.

I was prevented from reaching the bridge by the sentry in the cellar who could not be reached with rifle. From here I saw that the two outer piers of the stone bridge were still standing and that only the center one had been blown up, so that the bridge had a gap of from 20 to 25 meters.

The reinforced concrete bridge about 700 meters to the east is still intact.

The railway bridge southwest of the city is completely destroyed.

Neuendorf, 2nd Lt of Res and Scout Off 444th Inf

Editor's note: Notice that this account makes mention of all three bridges crossing the Marne at Château-Thierry. The "two outer piers of the stone bridge...." probably refers to the old stone wagon bridge which went over the Marne in the center of town. "The reinforced concrete bridge about 700 meters to the east...." refers to the railway/vehicle bridge crossing between Brasles and the mill. "The railway bridge southwest of the city...." refers to the railroad bridge which crossed in the same place as does the modern highway bridge adjacent to the municipal swimming pool.

It appears as if the Germans became confused over the presence in Château-Thierry of three bridges over the Marne River. There were evidently one comparatively new concrete railway bridge over the river Marne at Brasle, the old stone wagon bridge in the center of the city, and the stone railroad bridge which crossed the Marne in the southwest part of the city. It would seem that the Germans were not aware of the new and large combination railroad and vehicle bridge which crossed the Marne several hundred yards upstream from the old wagon-bridge in the center of town. The following German report goes far towards explaining some of their confusion:

> June 2, 1918
>
> 6.00 AM. Final report by Brigade, 6.00 AM
>
> Only during the day time was it discovered that in addition to the blown up stone bridge there was a new reinforced concrete bridge still existing in good condition which was not shown on any map, and having been reconnoitered by patrols as early as May 31, had been mistaken for the stone bridge since blown up shown on the map. The enemy, therefore, still had communication with the south bank during the night. When more and more machine gun nests were reported during the afternoon, the 1st Bn 443rd Inf, formed in three large assault sections, was sent in to mop up the city. This was accomplished by nightfall, when the bridge which was still intact was also occupied, so that all traffic across it was prevented.

Editor's note: In 1918 there were three bridges over the Marne river in Château-Thierry: A. The combination railroad, vehicle and pedestrian bridge which crossed from Brasles over to the vicinity of the sugar mill on the opposite bank of the Marne River. B. The old stone wagon bridge in the center of Château-Thierry. C. A stone railroad bridge which crossed the river in the vicinity of the present-day municipal swimming pool at the intersection of the Avenue d'Essomes/Avenue Géneral de Gaulle and the Voie Express. The present-day "Voie Express," the road which bypasses auto traffic around Château-Thierry, was originally the roadbed of the this now defunct Chemin de Fer du Sud de l'Aisne (railroad). It is not known at this date of writing what role, if any, the third bridge **C** played in the defense of Château-Thierry. French Army engineers blew this bridge in 1918. Wartime and post-war accounts confuse the three bridges in both the historical sense and in photographs.

Gen de Mondesir, commander of the French 39th Division says, that the railroad bridge southwest of the city was rebuilt by French engineers on 20 July 1918, to allow troops of the 39th Division to launch an assault on Hill 204 before taking Château-Thierry on 21 July 1918.

On 21 July, after the Germans had evacuated Château-Thierry, the French put a ladder on the ruins of the Brasles bridge, and it was used to cross the river at 8:15 AM, 21 July 1918. On 21 July at midday, French soldiers and American engineers from the 28th Division placed a pontoon footbridge across the Marne. The same day a main bridge was started across the river in the center of Château-Thierry and finished on 22 July, permitting the artillery to cross the river.

There are a number of photographs showing ladders crossing the ruins of the downed bridges in Château-Thierry. The exact number of bridges with ladders and the location of footbridges are confusing. It is known that any and all methods were used to get men, wagons, supplies and artillery across the Marne. At least initially, all of the blown bridges had temporary foot-ladders on the demolished structures.

The Chemin de Fer du Sud de l'Aisne, also known as La Compagnie du Sud de l'Aisne (CSA), was conceived about 1878 to be a railroad line serving the many towns and villages surrounding Château-Thierry. The total length of the railroad line as finally constructed was 82 kilometers. Three lines were built: A. Château-Thierry to Mareuil-sur-Ourcq, 30 kilometers. B. Essomes-sur-Marne to Verdelot, 28 kilometers. C. Gandelu to Neuilly Saint Front, 18 kilometers.

From its completion in 1910, and until 1946, the CSA enabled the farmers and merchants to ship their produce and wares into and out of Château-Thierry and the many surrounding villages and towns. Although badly damaged during World War I, the line and its stations were repaired in post-war years and prospered until 1946, by which time the motor vehicle had supplanted the railroads for shipping agricultural and mercantile products. The lines were finally dismantled in post World War II years. Some of the former stations are now private residences.

From *Records of the Second Division*, [American] is an editorial translation of an entry in the war diary of the German 231st Infantry Division, under date of 1 June 1918:

In the morning of June 1, the situation was as follows. The attack of May 31 had placed us in possession of the heights north of the Marne, controlling Château-Thierry. We had entered the village at several points with patrols and small detachments, but the town itself remained in the hands of the enemy who was holding it with numerous machine guns.

Elements of the 444th Inf. Regt. lying on the east edge, were forced to withdraw during the forenoon under pressure of superior hostile forced advancing to the east.

Major v. Görne was directed to conduct the organized attack on Château-Thierry.

The attack was ordered for 7 PM The 3d Bn., 442d, 2nd Bn., 443d and 1st Bn., 444th Inf. Regts., attacked from the northwest and 3d Bn., 443d Inf. Regt., from the north. 1st Bn., 443d Inf. Regt. and 255th Mountain M.G. Bn., were in reserve. The attack progressed very well from the west, while the 3d Bn., 443d Inf. Regt., encountered strong resistance (many machine guns) in the north part of the village.

At 8:30 PM, the west edge of the village was reached. Shortly before that time, the enemy had blown up the railroad bridge southwest of Château-Thierry.

At 10:15 PM, while our battalion, advancing from the north, was still in the vicinity of Les Chesneaux, white light signals were reported as coming from the village near the chateau.

Since the 444th Inf. Regt., on May 31, had sustained such heavy losses through flanking fire of the hostile batteries, it had been instructed to support the attack from the east during darkness, only in case the forces advancing from the west did not reach the Marne bridges.

At 11 PM, our light signals from the southwest part of the village and along the Marne indicated that the north bank had been reached. The 444th Inf. Regt. therefore, was not sent into action.

The 442d Inf. Regt. had orders to force a crossing and push forward a bridgehead on the south bank to the railroad. Captain Wilhelmi, 2d General Staff officer of the division, who had been sent forward by the division commander with oral instructions for the 442d Inf. Regt., had joined the attack and rushed across the bridge to the south bank of the Marne, where he encountered an occupied barricade. He was barely able to regain the north bank with his men when the bridge blew up.

Thus the north part of Château-Thierry was in our possession.

Our forces had occupied the west part and a block of houses near the blown-up bridge on the bank of the Marne. Here were 2 companies of the 3d Bn., 443d Inf Regt.

The very violent house to house fighting in Château-Thierry, particularly the many hostile machine guns firing [from] cellars and windows, made heavy demands on our infantry and caused severe losses. Units were badly mixed and could not be reorganized until daylight June 2.

Osius, Major, General Staff

In *Records of the Second Division*, [American] Vol. 4, pp. 250–1, is the following entry from the war diary of the German 231st Infantry Division, under date of 2 June 1918:

At 2 AM, it turned out that there were still numerous, hostile machine-gun nests and scattered, small detachments in the north and east parts of the village [Château-Thierry]. This would explain the contradictory reports. While the 442d Inf. Regt reported Château-Thierry in our possession, our patrols approaching the village from the east received violent machine-gun fire as late as the morning of June 2. In the course of the day about 70 prisoners were taken by 3d Bn., 443d Inf. Regt. and 2d Mc., 444th Inf. Regt. One revolving cannon and several machine guns were captured. Event the two pioneer companies which, following the infantry at night, had reached the village and there posted sentinels to keep order, brought in numerous prisoners. Not until daylight was it discovered that, besides the demolished stone bridge, there existed a new, reinforced concrete bridge in good condition which did not appear on any map, had been reconnoitered by our patrols on May 31, but had been mistaken on the map for the now destroyed stone bridge. Thus, the enemy still had connection with the south bank during the night.

When, during the afternoon, more and more hostile machine-gun nests were reported, the 1st Bn., 443d Inf. Regt. was ordered to mop up the village with 3 major assault groups. By the arrival of dusk this task had been accomplished, and the intact bridge occupied, preventing all traffic by this route.

However, isolated Frenchmen, particularly Negroes, were brought in later; they had been found in cellars shooting at individuals.

A surprise attempt to seize a bridgehead on the south bank had to be renounced. Since this had not been accomplished on the first day, the enemy now had time to emplace numerous machine guns on the south bank. The buildings of the south part of the village were studded with machine guns, particularly those near the intact bridge which alone was covered by 5 machine guns. The division, therefore, was issued the order to reconnoiter the crossing possibilities and to make careful preparations. The bridgehead was to be forced in 3 or 4 days after thorough preparation by artillery and minenwerfer. However, since this crossing as well as the seizure of the position, immediately in front of the commanding heights occupied by the enemy, would have resulted in heavy losses, the plan was abandoned by corps headquarters.

Château-Thierry was subjected to heavy hostile machine-gun and artillery harassing fire, particularly at night, this rendered it very difficult, if not impossible, to bring in the valuable stores of food and other supplied captured. Ever since June 2, the French have accurately adjusted their fire on the roads leading to Château-Thierry and were subjecting them to frequent surprise concentrations. During the night June 2/3, the village was systematically bombarded by heavy calibers, destroying many buildings and causing numerous fires. Despite the fact that many inhabitants were still in the village, which could not have been unknown to the enemy, he ruthlessly continued the bombardment of his own village during the succeeding days.

OSSIUS,
Major, General Staff

Group C
Corps Headquarters 4th Reserve Corps
Ia No 516 Operations.
Corps Headquarters (186) June 3/18–12:30 AM
Corps Order.
4. The 231st Inf Div is holding the captured positions and is preparing the river crossing at Château-Thierry. Other than this, preparations for crossing the Marne will be limited to patrols to establish the identity of the enemy.
The Commanding General
Signed von Conta

Group C
Corps Headquarters 4th Reserve Corps (193)
Ia No 518 Operations. Corps Headquarters June 4/1918
Corps Order
1. Corps Conta, which is charged with the protection of the left flank of the 7th Army during the attack of the 7th Army right flank, is compelled to temporarily assume the defensive, after positions most suitable for this purpose are captured. I insist that all commanders inform their troops, leaving no doubt in their minds, that our attack up to this time had passed far beyond the objectives that were first assigned, and had achieved far greater successes than had been anticipated. The offensive spirit must be maintained even though a temporary lull in the attack seems to exist. In the general picture of the operations, no halt or lull exists. We are the victors and will remain on the offensive. The enemy is defeated and the high command will utilize this great success to the fullest extent.

2. Wherever portions of our front must halt and wait before they again advance, the infantry must organize itself in depth and dig in. Likewise reserves in the rear and rest troops must protect themselves against the splintering effect of air bombs.

The Island

A TOUR OF THE GUN POSITIONS OF THE 7TH MOTORIZED MACHINE GUN BATTALION, U.S. 3RD DIVISION

This tour is based on Maj Mendenhall's account entitled "The Fist in the Dyke."

1. To visit the site of Lieutenant Bissell's two machine guns of Company A in the center of Château-Thierry:

Map location **C** on Maj Mendenhall's map is the intersection of Avenue Jaussaume Latour and Place Jeu de Paume in the center of Château-Thierry. To reach the area where Lt Bissell had his guns is but a short walk from the town square and the city hall. Walk down Avenue J. Latour until you see on your left of front the vestige of a very old castle tower. Lt Bissell had one machine gun mounted at the top of this tower and facing out over the park area seen to your right of front. A second gun was placed in reserve adjacent to the tower, and on the right side of the tower so as to protect Bissell's northern flank. It is possible to go up on to the base of the old tower by going through the gate of the "Funarium", the large ex-château seen directly in the rear of the tower. The "Funarium" is open Mon–Thur 8–11:30 AM, and 1:30–5:00 PM Public access to the tower is through the gate of funarium, at which point turn right and walk up onto the tower. Standing on the tower, one can see the field of fire of Bissell's machine gun and read the description of what Lt Bissell saw and did as related in Maj Mendenhall's account.

2. To visit the site of Lt Bissell's four machine guns of Company A on the island between the Marne River and the Fausse Marne (False Marne):

From the town hall and the City Square, drive south on Rue Carnot, and over the main bridge in the center of town. Immediately after crossing the main bridge, turn right on the Quai Couesnon that runs along side of the bank of the Marne River. Continue to the end of the Quai Couesnon where you see a park area at the end of the island. If you miss the right turn at Quai Couesnon, all is not lost—you can also turn right on the Quai Coutelier just before crossing the bridge over the Fausse Marne. Go as far as you can to the end of the island. There is parking at the end of the Rue de l'Isle. The parking area goes along to the end of the island and to the junction of the Fausse Marne and the Marne River. Walk to the pathway that leads into the park area along the riverbank. Looking from your left front to your right front you see the bank along which Lt Bissell placed his machine guns. This is location **K** on Maj Mendenhall's map.

3. To visit the site of Lt Cobbey's four guns sited in the sugar mill and those of Lt Funkhouser along the bank of the Marne River:

The road traveled along the bank of the Marne eventually turns into an unimproved dirt road as it runs alongside of the refining mill. During wet and rainy weather the road can be full of water-filled potholes.

Going south on the Rue Carnot, cross over the Fausse Marne Bridge. Just before reaching the Place Paul Dommer, turn left on the Quai Depuis-Delizy. Reaching a dirt road, continue alongside of the mill and the bank of the river Marne. Cobbey had four guns placed in the old mill building seen to your right. His field of fire was across the Marne and from your right to left.

Your view is across the river to where the RTA bus terminal and parking lot are now located. You can see the former railroad embankment upon which sits the RTA terminal building.

When the water level of the Marne is low, because of drought or for maintenance, the remains of the old bridge can be seen as reinforced concrete debris lying on the riverbank. Several twisted reinforced concrete remains can be seen on the upper part of the bank you are on.

Continue down the dirt road until you arrive at a very large factory building on your right. At the right hand corner of this factory complex you will see a paved road going up hill and to a bridge which crosses the Paris-Metz railroad. There is a line of poles containing electrical and phone lines on both sides of this road. Lt Funkhouser's three guns were sited on the river bank at the base of the paved road. Turn right at this point, go up this road and over the bridge. To view Funkhouser's field of fire, park your vehicle and walk on to the bridge. Facing the Marne River, you can see that Funkhouser's guns could easily fire into the town of Brasles, seen across the river. The Germans were marching down the road from Brasles into Château-Thierry, when Funkhouser's machine guns suddenly interrupted their journey.

4. To visit the site of Company B's three guns along the Crézancy road, the railroad and north of Etampes-sur-Marne:

Going south on Rue Carnot, cross over the main bridge in Château-Thierry, over the Fausse Marne Bridge and on to Place Paul Dommer. Take the Avenue de la République in the direction of Crézancy (east). Park your vehicle at a convenient location between the intersection of Rue Chierry and Avenue de la République. Do not cross over the railroad at this time.

Standing at the intersection of Rue Chierry (which leads into the area of the railroad station) and Avenue de la République, face to your front in the direction of the Marne River. Directly to your rear is a steep embankment. Several guns were evidently sited on this embankment, the gun crews using the slope (military crest) of the bank for cover. This is probably location **E** on Maj Mendenhall's map. To your front, you can see that the Rue Chierry ends in a barrier after it crosses the Rue de la République. Also to your front is seen the sunken area as described in Maj Mendenhall's account. Notice that this area has not substantially changed over the intervening years since the war. The sunken area now contains a new building that was not there in 1918. To your right of front is seen the entrance to the refinery, and further to your right, the Paris-Metz railroad.

One gun was located approximately at the point where the railroad spur going from the mill intersects with the main Paris-Metz line. This is location **G** on Maj Mendenhall's map.

5. To Visit the Site of Company B's two guns sited along the Crézancy Road and north of Etampes-sur-Marne:

Continue along the Avenue de la République and over the main railroad line. At the traffic circle, take the Rue du Chemin de Fer to the right. Turn left on the Chemin de Courboin (leads off of Avenue Ernest Couvrecelle as you are leaving Etampes-sur-Marne). Bissell's two guns would have probably been located out in the field that you see to your front and at the end of the Chemin de Courboin. The two guns faced east and guarded the road coming into Château-Thierry from Crézancy.

The Mill, the field of view of E Company

POST-WAR CHÂTEAU-THIERRY

The following article appeared in the army newspaper, *Stars and Stripes*, in early 1919:

CHÂTEAU-THIERRY ALREADY MECCA FOR SIGHTSEERS

Souvenir Shops Flourish Amid Ruins of Marne City

There is a great clattering of hammers in Château-Thierry today, where in the yesterday of last summer machine guns hammered ear-splitting echoes between the burning buildings and against the hill above the Marne.

The Germans are in Château-Thierry again, but they are nailing boards on the sides of wrecked shop fronts and stringing telephone and electric light wires, under the direction of French guards. The bridgehead of the Marne looks across a new bridge, but is a temporary wooden bridge mounted on scows. The stone buildings at both ends of the bridge are still fresh with the scars of the bridgehead battles—great ragged, gouged places in the walls where shells struck, scarcely a square yard that is not bored and chipped from rifle and machine gun bullets.

Château-Thierry is busy with her resurrection. New glass is taking the place of hastily nailed boards on the shop fronts, the shell holes in the roofs are being spanned with new tile, and weakened walls are being stiffened with concrete and stone. Most of the inhabitants are back, although rows of roofless houses in some streets tell plainly that many have not returned.

Ready for New Invasion

But even in her work of rehabilitation, Château-Thierry is conscious of her place in American history. She knows she will be a center for pilgrims from across the ocean, and the past few weeks she has seen the beginning of that great tide of travelling Americans which will soon be pouring in upon her.

A hotel is already open—you can even find it at night among the wrecked houses, because it stands out whole-walled and roofed. The shops which have scarcely finished removing the wooden barricades and replacing the panes are already full of battle souvenirs intended to appeal to Americans. The name 'Château-Thierry' stamped upon them will make them sell, even though they are new and brassy and obviously the product of some machine. The same souvenirs are probably already on sale back in the five and ten cent stores of New York.

Every train from Paris leaves its band of pilgrim Americans. They arrive by day and night, and the American uniform is always in sight. Scores of sailors on permission from ports make their first stop here on their way to the battlefields.

Old Timers Return

Officers and soldiers on short permissions hurry through the streets out toward Belleau Wood and the scarred country toward Fismes and Soissons. Many of them had been all over that territory when the 2nd and 3rd Divisions were helping to check the last great German drive on Paris. Army nurses, with plenty of spare time while they are waiting for boats to take them back to the States, walk leisurely through Château-Thierry, buying souvenirs and mailing innumerable postcards.

Meanwhile the old residents of the town come out and smile upon all this changing Inprocession. They look forward to the coming of summer and sunshine, and calculate the attraction of each bullet-marked wall. Hotels for tourists will rise upon foundations that once held town houses that kept in aristocratic seclusion behind iron fences and stone walls.

There are plenty of battle marks on Château-Thierry's walls, and Château-Thierry will keep many of them to show what she has suffered—the clock in the railroad station, for instance, pierced by a dozen bullets. The only hotel now open has as attraction beds with bullet-pierced wooden panels, doorknobs gashed with machine gun bullets, rows of holes in door and window casings made when the fighting was from house to house.

Here is an excerpt from Hamilton Holt's article "Where America Turned the Tide," in the 24 May 1919 issue of the periodical *Independent*:

Seicheprey, Cantigny, Château-Thierry, St. Mihiel and the Argonne are the five imperishable French names that must remain forever engraved on the hearts of all true Americans....

We then entered our car and in a few minutes found ourselves in Chateau Thierry. The city still bore many marks of its recent bombardments, but as the inhabitants had returned it seemed a normal French city. Chateau Thierry marks Germany's farthest advance toward Paris. It is only within a two hour automobile run from the capital and is bound to be for all time to come a shrine for American pilgrims. We motored through Château-Thierry and saw shell holes and shrapnel nicks in almost all the houses.

In 1923, John M. Gauss, a Marine serving aboard the U.S.S. Pittsburgh, wrote:

U.S.S. Pittsburgh, Gothenburg, Sweden   July 26, 1923
Dear Ma:
    On the return trip we passed through Château-Thierry. I was surprised to see how little this country and the villages showed the effects of the artillery and some were still in ruins, but most of them have been repaired. In that part of the country, new red-tiled roofs and fresh plastered walls are conspicuous. The fine trees which usually line French roads are missing too. You can see their stumps cut off even with the ground. In Château-Thierry many wooden shutters, gates, etc. show bullet marks. Left there purposely, I suppose. I have seen pictures of the town taken just after the battle, which shows it in ruins, but now it is almost completely restored. It certainly is wonderful!

A view of Château-Thierry and the Marne from upstream. The pontoon bridge crossed in the foreground and between the two sets of stairs on the river bank.

"The famous railroad bridge between Brasles and sugar factory of Château-Thierry, called bridge of the CSA (Compagnie du Sud de L'Aisne), it was the little train which lead from Château-Thierry to Essomes, Vaux, Bouresches, Belleau, Torcy, Bussiares, etc."

On the road to Château-Thierry

The pedestrian bridge across the Fausse (false) Marne.

The utility pipeline across the Fausse Marne.

A WALKING TOUR OF CHÂTEAU-THIERRY

Drive to the municipal parking lot (Place des Etats Unis) of Château-Thierry, location **A** on your map and park your automobile. The entrance to the parking lot (Place des Etats Unis) is on your left and from the Avenue Jules Lefebvre, the road which passes through the city and which runs parallel to the Marne River and on to the suburb of Brasle.

Parking is free in most of the lot except in the area at the head of the lot and close to the Rue Drugeon and the little lunch wagon. In this area the parking stalls are painted blue and a blue parking disk is required for you to park your vehicle on weekdays. The disque bleue can be purchased in any local tabac, (tobacco and sundries store). The blue disk is not evidently required on Saturdays, Sundays, or on holidays. Park in the free parking stalls that are outlined in white. There is plenty of free parking available during the French lunch (dinner) break which is from 12 to 2 PM. At this time many French workers drive to their homes for their large meal of the day.

When exiting this parking lot, *do not attempt to exit in the area of the food stand at the head of the parking lot*, and particularly at the start of the 12 PM lunch break, or at 5 PM, when everyone leaves work. Although there is a traffic light controlling this intersection, there are three merging roads here and only the French seem to understand just who has the right of way. Enter and exit the parking lot from the Avenue Jules Lefebvre, even if you must turn around at some point down the road to come back into town. It is much safer this way.

It would do you, the walking tourist, good to keep your itinerary of Château-Thierry in its proper historical perspective by remembering that several hundred thousand American doughboys have previously trod the roads you will follow in Château-Thierry.

On their respective sides of the river, the Franco-American forces and Germans established better communications between their units by breaking holes through house and garden walls. The machine gun and rifle fire from both sides was so intense that no one could safely expose himself, even briefly. The soldiers established tunnel systems through houses so they could rapidly move around in the city. They barricaded the streets and established machine gun posts everywhere, in basements, in houses and in factories.

Walk up to the head of the Place des Etats Unis (municipal parking lot) and in the direction of the main bridge over the Marne River.

At the entrance to the parking lot, (by the luncheon stand) turn around and look at the parking lot area. You are seeing the same view as in 1918 when the AEF used what is now the parking lot as a staging area for troop movements.

Turn left on the Rue Drugeon-Lecart, which is just a few feet beyond the little fast food stand at the head of and in the right corner of the parking lot. You will see the name of the street just above the "Pharmacie J. Prieur" sign which hangs parallel to the Rue Drugeon.

Walk in the direction of the city hall and the Town Square.

As you come out of the Rue Drugeon you will see in the town square, from left to right: the covered market, the American Memorial church, the tourist office and the Hôtel de Ville (city hall).

Walk to the tourist office **B**.

Your walking tour of the town of Château-Thierry begins and ends at the tourist office (Syndicat de Initiative or Bureau de Tourisme), 12 Place de l'Hôtel de Ville, in the main town square.

The tourist office is no longer in its former location in the small and separate building to the left of the city hall. It is now in the small office on the left outside corner of the city hall, and is titled "Accueil."

The tourist office and Hôtel de Ville (city hall) are given as locations **A** and **B**, respectively, on the map of the center of town. Here, in the tourist office you can obtain free maps and other information regarding Château-Thierry and the surrounding area. The staff is multilingual and there is always someone on duty who speaks English.

Hôtel de Ville as it was for the entering American troops

Champagne Awaits–the 3rd Div band leads the way towards City Hall

Stained glass window at the Methodist Church

Belhan Tower

THE HÔTEL DE VILLE—THE TOWN HALL

Upon leaving the tourist office, turn to your left and go to the Hôtel de Ville, in the main square and marked **B** on your map. There is nothing of real interest to the tourist inside of the Hôtel de Ville. It is, however, open to the general public if you wish to go inside the building.

The Hôtel de Ville, built on the site of the old corn market, consists of two buildings, of which the Palais is Renaissance in origin. The bombardments of 1918 destroyed one of the turrets, while shell splinters scarred the building. The immediate surroundings suffered greatly from shellfire.

Raymond Poincaré (then a minister, and later President of France) inaugurated the Hôtel de Ville in 1893.

During the battle of Château-Thierry in 1918 the Germans had cut a hole in the center of the Hôtel de Ville clock. Inside the clock tower they mounted a machine gun which fired through this hole and at anything moving on the main road, running through the south side of the city.

For your information, "Hôtel de Ville" in French bears no relationship whatsoever with a "hotel" as we know it in English, but is the name for the city (or town) hall in France. To your right front, along the Chemin de Ronde footpath which goes round the walls on the east side of the old castle, is the Jardin Minard (public gardens).

To your right rear is the Rue du Chateau, called "Rue de la Montagne" during the Revolution. From the 17th century until the Revolution it was the only road open to traffic, and led to the manor house. The local officials lived on this road.

On the right side of the Rue du Chateau, and at No. 11, is the Hôtel Dieu. Jeanne de Navarre, the daughter of Blanche d'Artois, founded this hospital in 1304. At her death, Jeanne left 1,200 monetary pounds to cover the cost of ten hospital beds. There is a small plaque on the wall that gives the history and significance of the hospital. The building is not presently used as a hospital, but for municipal offices.

THE AMERICAN METHODIST MEMORIAL CHURCH

Upon leaving the city hall, cross the main plaza in the direction of the tourist office and go to location **C** on your map, the American Memorial Church. Begun in 1922, and inaugurated on 13 July, 1924, this American Protestant Methodist Evangelical Reformed Church is a memorial to the War of 1914–1918.

A placard on the front door tells of its opening and closing hours. It is normally open Sunday from 10:30 AM until 5 PM. There are some very beautiful stained glass windows in this church, the largest one of which, facing the town plaza, depicts scenes of military life during the World War I. Depicted on this window are Lafayette and Generals Foch, Joffre, Pétain, and Nivelle welcoming American General Pershing to France.

Contrary to some of the tourist literature published in the past, the church does not contain a small museum of war relics. There is some amount of historical confusion existing to this day between the American Memorial Church and the "Maison Amitie Franco-Americaine"—The House of French–American Friendship, (M.A.F.A.) around the corner at No. 2, Place des Etats Unis.

At one time the Methodist Church operated the M.A.F.A. and the M.A.F.A. building housed a museum of World War I artifacts. For this reason it was also sometimes called the "American Museum." The church is normally open on Sundays. If the church is not open during your visit, perhaps an inquiry at the Tourist Office will produce someone who can open the church for you.

THE COVERED MARKET OF CHÂTEAU-THIERRY

Adjacent to the American Memorial Church is the old covered market of Château-Thierry. This is normally open for business only on Friday. Friday is also the market day in Château-Thierry, the day on which this town square will be chock-full of vendors of many interesting wares.

There is an interesting *vestige de la guerre* still remaining inside the old market. As you enter the market, look to your left and you will see a now inoperative public toilet door. Above the door is the blue inscription, "W.C. Hommes, Men." This tri-lingual title served the men of three nations in 1918 and in the post-war years: the British, French, and Americans.

THE BELHAN TOWER

Upon leaving the market, look to your right front at approximately two o'clock, in the direction of location **D** on your map.

The tall tower you see is the Belhan Tower (Belfry), in the former Ru du Pont. The tower formed a part of the Belhan Mansion (16th century), the home of a wealthy grain merchant. This tower was originally part of a fort built in the 12th century by the Counts of Champagne. In past years the French called it the Hotel Belhan and later the "Hostellerie du Mouton d'Or" (the Inn of the Golden Sheep). Jean Belhan, a corn chandler, made it his home in the 16th century. There is a curved stair-case and a chapel dedicated to Sainte-Barbe, the patron saint of soldiers. If you wish to visit this ancient tower, please inquire at the tourist office.

THE WATER FOUNTAIN

The little water fountain in the main square was built in 1478 by Antoine known as "Le Grand Batard de Bourgogne," freely translated as, "The Big Bastard of Bourgogne." The water is evidently potable, as it has never harmed your editor during several hot summer visits to the town plaza of Château-Thierry. Photographs on page 153 show American soldiers filling their canteens and water buckets from this fountain.

Above the door is the blue inscription, "W.C. Hommes, Men." This tri-lingual title served the men of three nations in 1918 and in the post-war years: the British, French, and Americans.

The home of Jean de la Fontaine

The Home of Jean de la Fontaine

SHOPPING IN CHÂTEAU-THIERRY

Turn to your right and walk a short distance to the Grand Rue. Turn right on the Grand Rue and you are on one of the main streets of Château-Thierry for shopping. The Grand Rue is closed to motor vehicle traffic and is for pedestrians only.

Walk and observe the stores and markets on the right hand side of the street first, and at the point where the shops diminish and finally disappear altogether, cross over to the other side and continue back to the town square. At top of the Rue, where it begins to turn into the Avenue de Soissons, there is a Choclatier on the right side of the road who has the most delicious liquor-filled chocolate bon bons.

THE HOME OF JEAN DE LA FONTAINE
[MUSÉE JEAN-DE-LA FONTAINE]

Although the fables of Jean de la Fontaine, such as *The Fable of the Fox and the Grapes*, were about life in the great valley stretching from Château-Thierry eastward to Jaulgonne, it is in Château-Thierry itself, eloquent with traditions of him as well as of others as greatly distinguished, that one comes upon the personal glamour of La Fontaine, eccentric child of the Marne.

To visit the quaint, simple house where the master of fables, Jean de la Fontaine (1621–1695) was born, continue on from the Grand Rue and bear to the right, into the Rue Jean de la Fontaine and stop at No. 12, map location **E**, which is on your left. Jean de la Fontaine is the most famous native of Château-Thierry.

Built in 1559 (or 1452 according to another source), the stone-sided house contained a museum before World War I. After the 1918 battle in Château-Thierry, most of the museum's fine relics went to Paris for safekeeping. Today, the house is once again a museum. Although remodeled and having some contemporary paneling, the house retains its original staircase. There is a collection of souvenirs of the writer, paintings, period furniture and illustrations of the fables.

The museum contains a collection of Fontaine's mementos, various editions of his works published over many centuries of French letters, and a trio of rooms outfitted with furniture from the 17th, 18th, and 19th centuries, respectively, each centered around some aspect of the effect of de la Fontaine on those respective centuries. There are temporary exhibits—recent ones included a collection of engravings by Salvador Dali that illustrate aspects of works by de la Fontaine. Copies of his fables (allegorical barnyard stories depicting the foibles of humans) and contes (short stories that are a lot racier than his fables) are for sale in the bookshop. From April to October, the museum is open Wednesday through Monday from 9 AM to NOON, and 2 to 6 PM. From November to March, it's open Wednesday through Monday from 10 AM to NOON and 2 to 5 PM.

Admission costs in early 2006 are €3.16 for adults and €1.58 for students and persons under 12. Admission is free to everyone on Wednesday.

La Rue de la Fontaine was originally called "Rue de Beauvais," then "Rue des Cordeliers" (Cobblers' Street), and during the Revolution "Rue du District." During the 17th century it was the home of the Bourgeoisie and the government officials.

When the Allied troops reentered Château-Thierry, they found La Fontaine's cellar transformed into an elegant German dug-out. The wildly tossed coverlets, the half-drained liqueurs and the abandoned cigars bore witness to the hasty exit of the German colonels, who had been hiding there from the Allied shells.

With that innate intelligence which distinguishes local authorities in all lands, the municipal council of Château-Thierry had already mutilated this relic home for the sake of 'street-improvement.' They did preserve what remained as a museum of the memorials of the immortal writer of fables.

There is no French writer whose expressions and language have to such an extent entered into popular speech and literary diction, so that his position in France and in this respect may be compared almost with that of Shakespeare in England."

Located a few steps from the Place de la Hôtel-de-Ville [City Hall], Fontaine's home is one of France's most visited literary shrines.

ST. CRÉPIN CHURCH

Under the rule of the English and the House of Burgundy, the church was completely destroyed about 1421. The present church, rebuilt in the middle of the 15th century, has a 16th century belfry.

St. Crépin—the poor, battered church, which, when the Germans left town in July, contained a kind of warehouse for stolen goods. Inside the church were mountains of goods from Château-Thierry, including all of the fine cloth and silver and copper of the town, assembled there ready for shipment to the all-absorbing homefolk in Germany.

Be certain to look up at the badly shrapnel-pocked and battered bell tower. The entrance to the church, as you are facing its facade, is to the left and down a small alley alongside of the church building. The church entrance is not through the main doors at the front of the church. You can go inside of the church if you wish to do so. Many American soldiers visited this church in 1918, as did the many veterans who returned to Château-Thierry in the post-war years.

Retrace your route on the Grand Rue until you arrive back at the town square. Walk straight ahead until you come to the Rue du Général de Gaulle. Turn right on the Rue de Général de Gaulle at location **E** on your map.

When you reach the bridge over the Marne River and the Avenue Jules Lefebvre turn around to your rear and look up the Rue de Général de Gaulle. You should be facing in

ST. CRÉPIN CHURCH

To visit the church of Saint Crépin, continue following the Grand Rue as it bears to the left and crosses the Avenue de Soissons and enters the Rue Saint Crépin. A few yards up the Rue Saint Crépin and to your right is Saint Crépin church. See location **S** on the town map.

German loot inside St. Crépin Church

View to St. Crépin Church from Château-Thierry Castle

The Statue of Jean de la Fontaine

the direction from which you came and towards the city hall and the Belhan Tower.

The Rue de Général de Gaulle was formerly known as the Rue du Maréchal Pétain. You are now looking at the scene of the photograph of the street barricade and of the drawing by AEF combat artist William J. Aylward.

The Germans established their first line of resistance on this side of the Marne River at the entrance to this street, in front of No. 27. They raised barricades of paving stones and earth. The largest barricade closed the end of the street, making it possible for the Germans to pass unseen from the Place de l'Hôtel de Ville to the Grand Rue (formerly the Rue du Général Dégoutte).

The Rue de Général de Gaulle (formerly Rue de Maréschal Pétain or Rue du Pont) saw much street fighting and widespread destruction in 1918. Other streets had barricades made up of pianos, tables, beds, sofas, bags stuffed with clothing, and rubbish. Turn around again and face the main bridge over the River Marne.

You are now looking at the scene of the photographs taken of the destroyed bridge over the Marne.

Turn to your right and walk down the Avenue Jules Lefebvre. Continue walking past several small streets on your right until you are standing at the entrance to the municipal parking lot at location **F** on your map. You should be just a few yards in front of the little food stand to your left of front.

Looking to your left rear is the scene of several more of the old photographs (pages 259-261) of the blown bridge over the Marne.

THE STATUE OF JEAN DE LA FONTAINE

To your left front is the statue of Jean de la Fontaine. This statue by Laitié and erected in 1824, is of La Fontaine, the writer of fables. The statue, which shows La Fontaine aged about 30–40 years, and was presented to the village in 1822 by Louis XVIII, a patron of the arts. The lower part of the left leg, broken off by a shell splinter in 1918, was repaired after the war. The repairs are still visible today.

Jean de la Fontaine was born in Château-Thierry and he was baptized on 8 July 1621 in the church of St.Crépin.

The original monument to the U.S 3rd Division had its location where the statue of Jean de la Fontaine now stands. Fontaine's statue was located where the modern-day 3rd Division memorial stands on the right side of Avenue Jules Lefebvre.

It is most difficult to offer an explanation of why the U.S. 3rd Division memorials and the statue of Fontaine have been so frequently shifted from one location to another. Possibly the many movements have been due to changing political climes.

Turn to your front and look down in the direction of locations **G** and **H** on your map.

Here is a partial excerpt from Joseph Hansen's book, *The Marne*:

> At the northern end of the last bridge, facing west along the broad boulevard which borders the right bank of the Marne, stands a statue, by Laitié, of the great fabulist; chipped by German and American machine-gun bullets and with its left leg broken by a shell splinter, but still intact in the main. Set in the pavement almost at La Fontaine's feet is a square stone tablet on which are chiseled the words: "Dedicated to the 3rd Division, U.S.A."

THE PLACE DES ÉTATS-UNIS (SQUARE OF THE UNITED STATES)

You are now looking at the same area as in the photograph (top right) of the 150th Field Artillery, 42nd Division. The municipal parking lot to your front, formerly known as the Champ-de-Mars, is now the Place des Etats-Unis (Square of the United States), in honor of the great stand made in this area by the Americans. At the far end of the parking lot is the Palais de Justice **G**.

THE SITE OF THE ORIGINAL U.S. 3RD DIVISION MEMORIAL

Look to your left of front, just where the center divider in the Avenue Jules Lefebvre begins and where the statue of Jean de la Fontaine stands. This is where the original monument to the U.S. 3rd Division stood before 1940. The monument was badly damaged in 1940, when the bridge across the Marne was blown up by French Army Engineers. During the course of post-war street widening and improvements to the avenues, the remains of the old 3rd Division monument were removed. You will see the new 3rd Division monument during the remainder of your tour.

Concerning the disposition of the original 3rd Division monument, accusations have occasionally been read to the effect that the Germans destroyed the monument, either by aerial bombing in World War Two or deliberately by land forces. Neither case is evidently true. One unit history, published as late as 1965, contains the following statement which is illustrative of how history can be deliberately warped by writers who are ignorant of their history.

> After the war the Third Division Veterans Association erected a monument at Château-Thierry to the memory of those members of the outfit who made the supreme sacrifice. That monument no longer exists. When the Nazis came down to Château-Thierry again last year there were no American soldiers there to deny them passage of the river. As a matter of fact there were no soldiers of any kind there. The young Nazis saw the Third Division monument and made note of it. Later, in their own time, they came back and destroyed the monument. It is to be hoped that one day the Third Division Veterans Association may have the privilege of restoring the monument.

Place des Etats-Unis (Square of the United States)

Site of the original 3rd Division memorial

A wreath is laid at the 3rd Division memorial

Château-Thierry — Methodist Memorial
The Court as it was in 1922
With the Director and Mrs Wadsworth

THE MAISON AMITIÉ FRANCO-AMERICAINE—THE HOUSE OF FRENCH-AMERICAN FRIENDSHIP

The bank on the corner of the Place des États Unis, Societé General, is No. 1. At No. 2, and over the court entrance is a trio of small French flags.

Number 2, Place des États-Unis, is the building that houses the Maison Amitié Franco-Americaine, (The House of French–American Friendship). For some years after the war this was "'The War Memorial' which was in the form of an American Institution established in the old Hotel l'Elephant to give help of every kind to the people of the Town and surrounding villages."

Immediately after the war many efforts were made by Americans to help the French Government with their effort to restore the many towns and villages which found themselves devastated during the war. In particular, the Methodist Episcopal Church of the United States was assigned 32 villages to aid in their reconstruction efforts. The delegates of this church felt the need to erect memorials to honor the soldiers who had fought and died in the Château-Thierry area. "The gift of the Methodist Episcopal Church to Château-Thierry should be more than a passing gift of material relief. It should be an enduring monument of happiness, build out of the desolation of war."

The church purchased the old Hotel de l'Elephant in Château-Thierry and renamed it as the Methodist Memorial, which was to be named The Community House of Friendliness. Its program of events and activities were to include:

1. A Crèche (nursery) for daily care of babies, 3 months to 2 years of age, and from destitute and devastated homes.

2. Educational Classes; classes in English 5 evenings a week, also typewriting, millinery, sewing, drawing, modeling, domestic sciences and gymnastics.

3. A Free Circulating Library and Reading Room with storytelling activities.

4. Boy Scout and Camp Fire Girl troops.

5. Special Meeting Rooms set up for conferences and for a variety of other performances.

6. War Museum, which includes war material from all nations and parts of airplanes including the motor of Quentin Roosevelt's plane (which fell at Chamery).

Editor's comment: I am not quite certain when or how Roosevelt's alleged airplane motor was obtained but the above postwar quotation gives the story of why it is there.

Walk into the interior courtyard, where you will find displayed a number of relics and memorials of World War I. The courtyard contains the motor and propeller which is allegedly from the airplane of U.S. Air Service fighter pilot Lt Quentin Roosevelt, who was shot down in action and killed on 14 July 1918. At the time of his death Roosevelt was serving with the 95th Squadron, 1st Pursuit Group. There is some question as to the originality of the displayed airplane motor. When shot down, Roosevelt flew a Nieuport

28 fighter plane, which type aircraft was equipped with rotary, air-cooled 150 hp. Gnome Monosoupape engine. The airplane engine displayed in the courtyard is a Hispano-Suiza liquid cooled engine, similar to that used in the well-known SPAD 7 fighter plane.

A letter from the United States Air Force Museum states, in part:

> According to information we have here, Quentin Roosevelt was indeed flying a Nieuport 28C.1 aircraft the day he was shot down and killed. No 28C.1 ever used a liquid-cooled engine! At least, no Nieuport assigned to a combat unit ever did. It is possible that one or two were fitted experimentally with liquid cooled engines, but it is not mentioned in the many booklets or articles on the type written over the years. So he folks at MAFA do not have what they think they have. Who is going to tell them? Not us. Am surprised that no French aviation buff/historian has not picked up on this one. Maybe they have but did not want to upset the apple cart?

Another letter, from the American Aviation Historical Society, Santa Ana, California, states:

> Quentin Roosevelt was a member of 95th Squadron, 1st Pursuit Group. As you are aware, he was killed on July 14, 1918 flying his Nieuport 28.
>
> All Nieuports used in combat during World War I were equipped with air-cooled rotary engines. The Nieuport 28 was powered by a 150 hp Gnome Monosoupape 9N rotary engine. It is true that some experimentals or prototypes were powered by liquid cooled engines but they never progressed beyond the prototype model until after the war.
>
> I do not see that it is possible that the Hispano-Suiza engine on display at the M.A.F.A. in Château-Thierry has any connection with Quentin Roosevelt."
> Yours truly
> Byron B. Calomaris

The framed placard which hangs over the airplane engine states, "Glorieux vestiges de l'avion du Lieutenant Quentin Roosevelt, tombé au cours d'un combat trés inégal Coulonges-en-Tardenois l'age de 21 ans le 14 Juillet 1918 pour la liberte de la France." The English translation is: "Glorious remains of the airplane of Lieutenant Quentin Roosevelt, killed in an unequal aerial combat at Coulonges-en-Tardenois at the age of 21 years on 14 July 1918 for the liberty of France."

Unfortunately, the placard is very misleading, as this is not the original engine of Roosevelt's airplane. However, in a general historical context, what real difference does it make? Quite possibly, the original motor of Roosevelt's airplane may have been displayed here, at least until 1940; at this time just about everything made of metal,

"Glorious remains of the airplane of Lieutenant Quentin Roosevelt, killed in an unequal aerial combat at Coulonges-en-Tardenois at the age of 21 years on 14 July 1918 for the liberty of France."

Lieutenant Quentin Roosevelt's airplane engine at the MAFA museum

Palais du Justice, then above and now, below

The 3rd Division Memorial

and particularly old war trophies in the form of cannon, were shipped to Germany to be melted down and used in their war machine. Then again, knowing the mind-set of the Germans, it is quite possible that they left Roosevelt's airplane engine alone, and it met some other fate. The Germans had a great deal of respect for Theodore Roosevelt and his family, respect which may well have existed even up to and including World War II. The Germans took great pains in 1918 to bury young Roosevelt with full military honors, what with hundreds of Germans being present for the burial ceremonies. They also fenced in Quentin's burial plot and left the remains of his aircraft at the site. It wasn't very long at all before souvenir hunters from both armies had picked the aircraft remains down to the bare bones.

We should respect the fact that the French have seen fit to display any type of aircraft engine in honor of Quentin Roosevelt, who gave his life in the cause of preserving freedom. There is also a metal plaque from the Great War Society affixed to the inner wall of the courtyard and above Roosevelt's supposed fighter plane engine.

The plaque was unveiled at 10:30 hours on 14 July 1992 by the mayor of Château-Thierry. Also present were: Mr. Jacques Lesage, President of the France Louisiane Association, and Mr. Phillip de la Mater, Superintendent of the Aisne-Marne American Military Cemetery and Memorial, Belleau, France. The Great War Society is an organization composed of a group of American historians affiliated with Stanford University, Stanford, California. This society devotes itself to the study of the causes and origins of World War I.

At one time the Methodist Church of America ran the M.A.F.A. building. In pre-World War II days the M.A.F.A. building contained a large museum of World War I military artifacts. There were also several large German artillery pieces in front of the building. Unfortunately, in 1940, the Germans confiscated every piece of the weapons collection, including the cannons.

In 1940 the engineers of the French Army blew up the main wagon bridge over the Marne in Château-Thierry. The explosion was so tremendous that the M.A.F.A. building and the 3rd Division Memorial suffered tremendous damage. The two sculptures on the front of the M.A.F.A. building of a French soldier (a *poilu*), the other an American soldier (a "Sammy") fell off and shattered. A local sculptor named Achille Jacopin carved the soldier representations, as seen in the photograph (page 254) of the exterior of the M.A.F.A building.

THE PALAIS DE JUSTICE

Continue down the Avenue Jules Lefebvre until you arrive at the intersection of the Avenue de Soissons. Turn to your right and look up the hill in the direction of Soissons. To your right of front is the Palais de Justice. Shrapnel from aerial bombs and artillery shells had badly pocked this building in 1918. The hundreds of pocks and chips were filled in at some unknown date between 1983 and 1988. In looking closely at the facade of this building you can still see where many holes were.

Why the French found it necessary to institute repairs at such a late date remains a mystery. From the standpoint of historical interest, it may perhaps have been better if they had left the building alone. Note on the face of the building facing the square the remains of the inscription, "Liberty, Equality, Fraternity." This is a vivid reminder of an earlier French Republic.

THE AVENUE DE SOISSONS

In 1918 the Avenue de Soissons was the main route north and from Château-Thierry to Soissons. It seems that few of the thousands of American soldiers entering Château-Thierry had to labor up this very steep hill in the direction of the northward advance of the Allied armies. Military literature makes scant mention of any hot, grueling up-hill climbs out of Château-Thierry by either artillery or infantry troops of the AEF.

Those few American soldiers who did make the difficult climb up the Avenue de Soissons probably did so before the construction of pontoon bridges over the level crossings to the east of the city and where the stone bridges were down. At this time the Avenue de Soissons would have been the only route to the north.

It seems that, because there was only one steep road leading directly north out of Château-Thierry, most of the American troops, particularly the artillery trains with their many heavy artillery pieces and wagons, took a somewhat roundabout route to the east of Château-Thierry and crossed the river on pontoon bridges which were quickly established there. Thus a long uphill climb and the attendant extreme congestion on the Avenue de Soissons was avoided. Most of the written accounts by the American soldiers mention crossing the Marne on pontoon bridges.

If the artillery battalion shown in the photographs (right) had to climb this hill in that hot summer of 1918 it would have been very hard on both the men and the animals.

The express road to Soissons shown on your map as lying to the left of Château-Thierry did not exist in 1918.

In looking at the narrow roadway of the Avenue de Soissons, you can see that it could hardly support two-way military traffic into and out of Château-Thierry.

Here are two brief descriptions of the entry of the 101st Infantry Regiment, U.S 26th Division and of the 112th Infantry Regiment, U.S. 28th Division going into and out of Château-Thierry. Although these descriptions do not specifically mention the Avenue de Soissons, they do seem to correspond exactly in their description with that avenue, its attendant steep hill, and coming out on a plain at the top of the hill:

At the corner where you are standing there is an interesting memorial to the French concentration camp victims during the era of Nazi occupation in World War II.

In 1940 the Germans built a temporary bridge which crossed the Marne River at the point where the Avenue de Soissons intersects with the Avenue Jules Lefebre.

Cross the Avenue de Soissons.

Avenue de Soissons

Memorial to the French concentration camp victims during the era of Nazi occupation in World War II.

Demarcation Stone

You are now at the main post office. This is a very good opportunity for you to mail any postcards or letters that you may have bought while shopping on the Rue Peitonne.

Continue down the Avenue Jules Lefebvre. Adjacent to the post office at location **H** on your map is the monument to the U.S. 3rd Division.

THE U. S. 3RD DIVISION MEMORIAL

Initiative for the erection of the present memorial to the 3rd Division monument properly belongs to the governing body of Château-Thierry. The existing monument, designed by M. Podela of Château-Thierry, had its formal dedication in 1961. The center shaft is 13 feet tall, side panels 7 feet tall, overall length is 47 feet. The cavity forming the front of the monument, now containing bedding plants, had an interesting design feature. It contained a shallow pool of water, a submersible lighting system and a 3rd Infantry Division patch executed in blue and white. Abandonment of these features was a concession to a combination of environmental and economic considerations. The present-day memorial commemorates the services of the 3rd Division in both World Wars.

Continue a few yards beyond the 3rd Division memorial and, using the pedestrian crosswalk, carefully cross to the other side of the Rue Jules Lefebvre. Walk in the direction from which you came and towards the main bridge over the river Marne.

On your right is seen a small memorial to World War II French resistance fighter, Jean Moulin.

THE DEMARCATION STONE

Continue down the Rue Jules Lefebvre until you arrive at location **I** on your town map, below a cluster of road signs and just before the traffic light at the Avenue de Soissons. Here you will see a Demarcation Stone in the form of a small pyramid surmounted by a wreathed French helmet. In the decade following the Armistice, 119 of these small monuments were erected in Belgium and France at intervals along the 960 kilometers of the Western Front, from the Ypres Salient in Belgium to the Swiss border, to mark the limit of German advance in 1918. The Touring Club of France and the Touring Club of Belgium were the prime movers of this scheme that caught the imagination of the public. Of pink granite, the monuments were no more than a meter in height. The sculptor Paul Moreau Vauthier who produced three basic types, differing mainly in the helmet of the capstone designed them. These were either of the British tin helmet or the French and Belgian 'Poilu's' helmet design. On the side of the stones were decorations consisting of a soldier's equipment—gas mask case, water bottle, etc., and each bore the inscription: "Here the Invader was brought to a standstill" in either French, Flemish, or English. On the front face, the name of the place they were to stand in or near was inscribed.

The stones which became known as Demarcation Bornes or Stones were placed in positions where the battle line crossed a road or street, in town or country, at points decided by Marshal Pétain and the General Staffs of France, Belgium and Britain. Funds to help in the erection of the monuments came from many sources beside the two Touring Clubs, which bore the main expenses, and local authorities, ex-servicemen's organizations and private persons all contributed to their cost. The number of stones standing in place today is much depleted as many were destroyed or lost during the Second World War or has become victims of the motor vehicle. Others have been broken up by the explosion of old ammunition which was placed against them by farmers.

The Demarcation Stone you are looking at has the accouterments of the French Army, together with several hand grenades and a water bottle, carved upon it. There is one other such demarcation stone in this area, and it is in an erroneous location just outside of the Aisne-Marne American Military Cemetery at Belleau, France, just a few miles from where this stone is located.

Continue walking down the Rue Jules Lefebvre in the direction of the bridge over the Marne. As you approach the bridge, look to your right. The Germans held the side of the river you are on. The Americans and the French were across the Marne, on the other side of the demolished bridge and the river. Thus as the demarcation stone indicates, the Germans only reached this side of the river at Château-Thierry, and never crossed to the opposite side.

Stop several hundred feet before you reach the bridge, at about location **J** on your map, and look from your front to your right front and across the river.

You are now looking at the scene of the photographs of the stone wagon bridge as shown to the right.

About 100 feet from the bridge, look to your right and across the river. You are looking at the approximate point where another two-way pontoon bridge was constructed across the river by French and American engineer troops. The bridge ran from the road between the end of the buildings and the park-like area of trees on the opposite bank, to the concrete steps and the ramp in the bank below you. Imagine, if you would, how many thousands of American soldiers have walked up the stairway and ramp you see in front of you.

THE MAIN WAGON BRIDGE

Continue walking until you arrive at the corner of the bridge over the Marne at location **K** on your map. Look panoramically from your left to your right.

Lt Bissell and his squad of machine gunners had crossed the bridge you are now on from the other side of the river, and set up their guns to command the intersection of the intersection of the Avenue de Château-Thierry and the Avenue J. Latour, both of which are to your left of front. When the bridge blew up, Lt Bissell, together with his guns and men made their way down the Quai de la Poterne alongside the river (to your front) and to the railway bridge where they were able to cross over to the other side of the river.

Courtesy the Hornby Collection

"Bridge over Marne at Château-Thierry blown up by French to stop German drive." Site of the 3rd Division memorial

Bataille de la Marne 1918
CHÂTEAU-THIERRY — Le Pont sur la Marne

"Bataille de la Marne 1918
CHÂTEAU-THIERRY — Le Pont sur la Marne"

The original three-arch bridge, built by Perronet in 1768, was blown up by the French Army engineers at 10 PM, 1 June 1918, as an obstacle against the German advance when, for the second time, the Germans made their drive to Paris. After three previously futile attempts by army engineers to destroy the bridge with explosive charges, a final explosion of 3500 pounds of dynamite dropped the sturdily-built bridge into the Marne River. After the explosion there remained only a single arch, the others having settled into the riverbed and been later temporarily replaced by a footway as shown to the right.

After the battle had passed, several pontoon bridges were laid across the Marne and parallel to the wagon-bridge by military engineers. But the picture-spot of the city was its blown-up bridge, and so important was this bridge as an artery of traffic in the pursuit of the Germans that, no sooner were the Germans out of town, the work was started on clearing away the fallen masonry and spanning the bridge anew with wooden trestles. A new concrete bridge was built and dedicated on 21 June 1925. This bridge was a gift to the people of Château-Thierry from the people of America.

On 10 June 1940, the rebuilt bridge was blown up by French Army engineers, once again to impede the German advance into France. The bridge that you now see, the Pont Aspirant De Rouge, was rebuilt after World War II. "Aspirant De Rouge" is the name of a French officer-candidate who was killed in June, 1940, at the center of the Rue Carnot when he was defending the south part of Château-Thierry with his men. His armored car was hit by German fire and De Rouge was killed in the street by fire from German machine guns and rifles.

During the fight for the city, the Americans and the French were on the other side of the Marne and had built up a large barricade across the entrance to the Rue Carnot where it entered the bridge. This barricade served the same purpose as did the German barricade on the side of the river where you are sitting, at the entrance to the Rue General de Gaulle—to prevent observation of troop movements. There were apertures for machine guns in the basements of the houses on both sides of the Rue Carnot and American machine gunners occupied many of the houses along the bank of the Marne opposite where you are sitting.

IN THEIR OWN WORDS

From *Leslies Weekly*, September 6, 1919, "Reconstructing a Famous Bridge":

> The old bridge that once spanned the Marne River at Château-Thierry, and but a bullet-scarred portion of which still remains standing, is to be reconstructed. The work, which is now under way, is to be done with funds contributed by citizens of this country. That such should be the case seems fitting, for not only was it either in or near the tiny war-torn French city that many of our soldiers immortalized themselves, but it was actually our own

American troops that destroyed the fine old structure. Just a little more than one year ago—on the night of May 31–June 1, to be exact—the members of the motorized machine gun battalion of our Third Division, operating with their French allies, in a last—and successful endeavor to check the furious German attacks on Château-Thierry, blew up the bridge which they were defending. On Aug. 10, while many French and American notables looked on, Major General Robert L. Howze laid the first stone of the new structure, the cost of which will be met by the American Society for the Relief of Devastated France.

THE RAILROAD BRIDGE AT CHÂTEAU-THIERRY

Start to walk across the bridge and when you are about halfway over, look to your left and in the up-river direction. For some time after the war one could see to the left and right of front and about one-half kilometer upstream, the two square concrete buttresses of the demolished railroad bridge which crossed the Marne at that point, as shown on the old 1918 map of Château-Thierry.

In 1910, and at the insistence of local businessmen and farmers, a railroad line known as the Compagnie des Chemins de Fer Sud de l'Aisne (CSA) was established between Château-Thierry and the surrounding towns. In Château-Thierry the line ran along both quais on the sides of the river, and crossed the Marne on a single track between Brasles and the sugar mill on the opposite river bank on a two-arch reinforced concrete bridge. This bridge was open to railroad traffic, motor vehicles and to pedestrians.

The railroad bridge was blown up by engineers of the French Army at 4:45 PM, 1 June 1918. Old photographs of the demolished railroad bridge show it as an arched concrete span, with superb sculptures of rearing marine horses at each end of the center support. It appears from photograph (lower right) that only the northern span of the bridge was destroyed by the explosive charge.

In 1919, German prisoners of war reconstructed the railroad bridge as a temporary wooden structure. In 1922 the bridge was reconstructed in the same style and structure as the original bridge, except that the new bridge was without the sculptured horses. The photographs show the railroad bridge as it appeared in the 1930s. The railroad bridge was again blown up by engineers of the French Army in 1940. The bridge was never rebuilt and in 1946, because of the increasing popularity of the motor vehicle, the entire railroad line was dismantled.

There is a small concrete buttress on the riverbank just across the road from a modern-day apartment building located to your right of front. This buttress is not one for the railway bridge, which is much farther up-stream. The aerial photograph of Château-Thierry taken in the summer of 1918 shows a two-way pontoon bridge across the Marne a little downstream from where the railway trestle went across from Brasles. The pontoon

Crossing the Marne at Château-Thierry

Destroyed wagon bridge at Château-Thierry

Upstream railroad bridge destroyed, pontoon bridge

German destruction of the railroad tracks and rolling stock at the railroad yards.

Machine gun set up inside a railroad shop. Co A, 9th machine gun battalion, 3rd Division, Château-Thierry, 7 June 1918

bridge spanned from about where the small concrete buttress is located and went on to the other side of the river, where there is still a group of very old wooden pilings which must have been the supports for the temporary pontoon bridge. The location of the pontoon bridge is shown at point **V** of the walking tour map of Château-Thierry and on the 1918 aerial photograph of the city. The railroad bridge was about 400 meters farther upstream. Today, there are very few remnants of the old railroad bridge, with only the graded ramp on the Brasles side of the river, upon which sits the contemporary RTA bus terminal, and the remains of a roadway retaining wall on the mill property on the opposite bank to show that the bridge had ever existed.

When, for reasons of drought or for repair, the water level of the Marne is very low, the remains of the reinforced concrete structure of the railroad bridge can occasionally be seen lying in the mud of the river banks.

Looking from your left front to your right front, the known positions of the 7th Machine Gun Battalion's 24 machine guns is given below. For the locations of the guns from where you are now standing, please consult the map and drawings of the positions of the 7th Machine Gun Battalion's machine guns.

Three guns of Company B were placed in position at the edge of town in a little wooded peninsula **E** on the south bank of the Marne River about 200 meters upstream from the old railway bridge over the Marne. Two guns ranged west along the river and one east. Another two guns were in a sunken garden **A** 200 yards south of the railroad bridge, which also enfiladed it. One gun was in a two-story brick house **D** on the bank of the river, ready to fire from a lower window and cover the river bank from the bridge east, and one in a shed on the east of this building with range to the northwest. The other guns of Company B were held at battalion headquarters as a reserve.

Company A had two guns placed where they commanded the ruins of the lower wagon bridge (the other side of the bridge where you are now). The guns were in a cellar and looked out of vent-holes. Other guns of Company A were and to your right of front and right front along the southern bank of the Marne.

Across the river and a little up-stream is the row of riverbank houses through the chinks and doors and windows of which the American machine guns fired, covering the two bridges for four days and nights.

IN THEIR OWN WORDS

An unnamed German report reads:

> Beyond the bridge with the ladders and up-river from the big bridge was
> a small, narrow arch that crossed to the other side. It was not plain what this

thing was for. Perhaps it carried sewer or gas pipes or a water-main. Anyway, it had not been destroyed, for it was not wide enough for two men to walk abreast, and one man with a rifle could keep the whole German Army from crossing it. On the other side was the parapet of a trench that ran through the back yards of some small houses there. It was but a moment's walk to the south end of the main bridge, where there were many soldiers standing about, several limousines belonging to officers of high rank, motorcycles, bicycles, and horses. They were all there with the same object in view—to find a bridge or discover some method of getting across the river without one.

Editor's note: The "bridge with the ladders" would refer to the main wagon bridge in the center of the city, and the "big bridge" would in turn probably refer to the railroad bridge. Contemporary photographs do show ladders reaching up to the one remaining arch from the wagon bridge roadway, which settled flat into the river when the bridge blew up. Whether or not the "small, narrow arch" farther upstream from the railroad bridge, still exists today, has not been determined at this date of writing. Presumably this was some sort of utilities pipeline that crossed the Marne. Today, there is a small utilities line which crossed the smaller tributary of the Fosse Marne (False Marne) at about location **U** on your walking tour map. It is not known at this date of writing if this might have been the "small, narrow arch" that is referred to.

Looking to your left front is the approximate view of the pontoon bridge (page 267) as shown in the photograph of the bridge and in the aerial photograph of Château-Thierry. The single span pontoon bridge was located about 50 meters downstream from the wagon bridge and is depicted at location **T** on your town map. To your left, and just a few yards down the Quai Couesnon which is on your left, is a **T** intersection. The road leading left, which is the stem of the **T**, was the lead-in road to the pontoon pedestrian bridge that went across the river to the stone steps and ramp area seen directly opposite on the other side of the Marne. Looking just slightly down the Quai Couesnon and across the river will give you the same view of the temporary bridge over the Marne.

In looking at the stone steps leading up to the quay on the down-stream (northern) bank of the Marne, one will notice that these steps are vary much worn down in the center. Such is not the case with the other stone steps leading up to other quays. The worn area is indicative of the passage of many thousands of the hobnailed brogans worn by the American soldiers. Stone could not resist the powerful grinding action of the modern American steel-shod sole. The stone steps here, as in many other places in France, have been hollowed out in the center by doughboy brogans until they are almost worn down in places. Stone vanished beneath the tread of the hobnailed shoe like a horseradish that is rubbed with a rat-tail file. Three hundred and ten thousand

Modern day highway bridge replacing the old railroad bridge

View of Hill 204 and the American Monument from the SW highway bridge

The French War Memorial

doughboys transited through Château-Thierry and many of these thousands walked up the set of steps that you are observing. And, this is not to count the many thousands more who visited this old town after the Armistice and who would have necessarily had to also walk up these steps.

Looking at the bridge from about 50 feet farther down the Rue Carnot duplicates several of the 1918 views of the main wagon bridge as shown in the accompanying photographs in this section.

THE FRENCH WAR MEMORIAL

Continue walking down the Rue Carnot and over the Fausse Marne River to the traffic circle at Place Paul Doumer. Cross the traffic circle on its right side. At location **M** on your map you will see a very distinctive monument to the French soldier dead of the First World War. Instead of the usual depiction of the standing French soldier, this monument shows a fallen soldier, lying on the edge of a German trench, and in the midst of typical battlefield debris.

THE RAILROAD STATION

Cross the traffic circle and the Avenue de Montmirail and continue along the Avenue de la République to the Avenue Wilson where you turn right to the railroad station (la gare) at location **N** on your map. The existent railroad station is the same one that was there in 1918.

The railroad station became the scene of much suffering during the war, as it was one of the main stations for shipping out the wounded of both the French and the American armies. The railroad station as you see it now is the original station. You may, if you wish, walk around the station and on the platforms (quais). Be careful when walking on the train platforms themselves and do not get too close to their edge. Many of the trains that come through here are travelling **very** fast and the suction can easily pull a person off their feet and into the moving train.

IN THEIR OWN WORDS

Lt Robert Hoffman, 111th Infantry, 28th Division, remembers in his book, *I Remember the Last War*:

> There were hundreds of cots lines up on the station platform, chiefly gas patients, waiting their turn to be sent to the base hospitals. They lay there as if dead, with bandages covering their eyes. There were a host of gas casualties on this front.

From Spaulding and Wright's book, *The Second Division*:

> No time was lost for the second trip, which took us to the station of Château-Thierry. Here was our first closeup view of the ravages of war—the shell holes, shattered wheat fields, houses flattened and some partly damaged by shells. In the station and surrounding it were litters bearing our brave boys— mud spattered and with torn uniforms. They were waiting patiently to be taken some place where they could get proper attention.

Helen T. Burrey, reserve nurse, Army Nurse Corps, a graduate of St. Francis Hospital, Pittsburgh, Pa., and a member of the nursing staff of U.S. Army Base Hospital No. 27, was one of the first three nurses to be assigned to hospital trains of the AEF. During the drives which centered in the Château-Thierry sector, work on all hospital trains of the AEF was heavy. Helen Burrey's account, taken from Spaulding & Wright's book, *The Second Division*, states:

> During the drive at Château-Thierry a great number of hospital trains were mobilized at Pantin, a suburb of Paris, for duty into Château-Thierry. From Paris to Château-Thierry was about three hours train ride and 27 was ordered to make the trip. The train was sent to evacuate patients from hospital No. 7, a mobile unit. These patients had received First Aid; major operations were cared for. Some had hardly reacted from their anesthetic and most of them were in a pitiable state.

> In the station and surrounding it were litters covered with boys; mud-splattered and torn were the uniforms they wore. They were patiently waiting to be taken, they did not care where but some place where they could be given proper care. After we received our train load, about 400 patients, one of the things that bothered both patients and nurses most were the countless numbers of flies that infested our train. The odors from the wounds that had no care cannot be described but shall live in the memory of the nurses and orderlies. We made three trips to Château-Thierry. The third one was to a small town outside of Château-Thierry. It was after dark when we got there and we immediately started to load our train with patients that had been gassed. At the height of our work we had an alarm of enemy airplanes which meant lights out and we had to work in the dark getting as many patients under shelter as possible. We loaded our train without keeping count of the patients that could walk. After the train pulled out and we got to a place of safety, the lights were turned on and we found we had patients everywhere, in the berths, on the seats and crowded in the aisle.

Retrace your route back on Avenue Wilson and Avenue de la République to the traffic circle at Place Paul Doumer.

Carrying wounded men to the railroad station for transfer to base hospital, members of the 28th and 77th Divisions, Aug 5, 1918

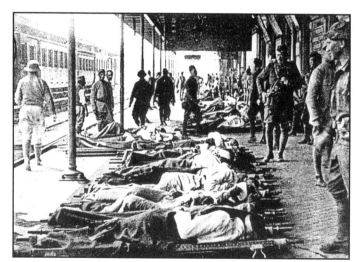

Wounded of the 28th and 77th Divisions at Château-Thierry, August 15, 1918
These men are at the station to be transferred to a base hospital. The greater part of these men received their wounds at Fismes, August 13, 1918, from mustard gas. –*From U.S. Movie*

"Kenneth Ritchie. World War II 1945."

Photo taken on the sugar mill property and showing the terminus of the railroad track which crossed the river on the upstream bridge

Photo taken from the south bank of the river showing the temporary bridge replacing the destroyed main wagon bridge

To the left of Place Paul Doumer are several large markets and stores: E. Leclerc, which has a cafeteria, and Intermarché, which, among others in the same area, sells gasoline. See the town maps obtained at the tourist office for the exact locations of the businesses in this area.

Return by the same route, up the Rue Carnot, over the bridge and to the highway bridge over the Marne River.

THE UPSTREAM PONTOON BRIDGE

To visit the site of the upstream pontoon bridge over the Marne River, turn right at the Quai Couesnon just before crossing the wagon bridge. Go several hundred yards down this road until you come to the old concrete buttress in front of a large, modern, and somewhat long apartment building. To the front of the buttress and across the Marne is the anchoring point of the pontoon bridge. To your right rear are the same two little buildings a shown in some of the photographs in this section.

Return to the wagon bridge and walk along the Quai Couesnon, which is straight ahead of you. At location **W**, shortly past the bridge and cemented into the quai wall as it runs alongside of the river, is a small metal strip about two feet in length and about two inches in width. It seems that a World War II American soldier named Kenneth Ritchie, who perhaps was working on the reconstruction of Château-Thierry, placed the metal strip where you see it today. The inscription reads, "Kenneth Ritchie. World War II 1945."

Cross over the main wagon bridge.

To visit the site of this same pontoon bridge on the other side of the river, cross the bridge and turn to your right on the Rue de Brasles (D-3), which runs parallel to the river. Go a few hundred feet along the Rue de Brasles until you come to the "Brasles" sign. At this point you will see a small dirt path branching off to your right of front. Go down this path about fifty feet, passing over a large concrete culvert. After the culvert, look for a small group of old wooden pilings just at the river bank. Directly opposite these pilings and on the far bank of the river will be seen the corner of the apartment building, the old concrete buttress, and the two small, white buildings.

THE CASTLE OF CHÂTEAU-THIERRY

Return to the main town square in the Place de l'Hôtel de Ville. Directly ahead of you at the end of the bridge are the ramparts of the castle terrace. To the left of the Hôtel de Ville can be seen steps leading to the top of the ramparts. The most troublesome German machine guns had their locations in the grounds of the old château seen above you.

The origin of the castle, known as the "Castle of Thierry," begins in about the year 721. At this time Charles Martel, the victor of the battle of Poitiers against the Arabs, thought of having a strategically placed fortress built on the land belonging to his own castle. The castle was built on a butte called "Mont Blanc." Martel sought out a young prince, Thierry, the son of Dagobert III, from the Abbey of Chelles. He was crowned and became Thierry II. Not wanting this young prince to become involved in the government of the kingdom, Charles Martel confined him to the fortress, hence, the castle's name.

The château or castle has been added to over the many centuries by the different rulers who occupied it: Thibaud, Count of Champagne and of Brie, lord of Château-Thierry, completed the castle's defenses. Henry II, Catherine de Medicis, Richelieu and others stayed at the castle. Napoleon presented the castle to the town on 10 April 1813. The castle, or château, has been besieged on various occasions.

On the site of the castle there is a promenade with a fine view of the surrounding area. There has been at various times an open-air theater and a restaurant, which can be reached by the Rue du Château and by the steps leading up from the Place de l'Hôtel de Ville.

Go up the rampart steps to the top of the ramparts at location **O** on your map. A cautionary note here—the climb to the top is not for the faint hearted or the aged. You can drive an automobile onto the château grounds from the eastern side of the château and as far as the restaurant. Do not attempt to go past the area of the restaurant as there is no vehicle exit in that direction, the way is narrow and it is very difficult to turn a motor vehicle around.

From the ruins of the old château one can see a beautiful panoramic view of the town and the Marne valley. To your immediate right as you emerge from the tunnel in the rampart walls, is a panoramic view table which gives the locations and directions to various points and places on the compass.

Turn around and look out over the city. The panoramic view you see is the same as those taken in 1918 and shown in the accompanying photographs.

To your front and in the foreground you see the Hôtel de Ville, the town square (where the weekly market is held), the Belhan Belfry, and the Rue de Général de Gaulle.

In the distance, and ranging from your left and to left of front, you see the Valley of the Surmelin River, including the towns of Fossoy, Mézy, and Crézancy. On the hill seen in the far distance beyond these towns, the 38th Infantry Regiment, U.S. 3rd Division fought the Germans to a virtual standstill. For its heroic actions on July 15, 1918, the 38th Infantry earned the immortal name of "Rock of the Marne."

Looking up the valley to the east you can see Fossoy and the railroad embankment where the U.S. 3rd Division made its heroic defense against the last great German offensive on 15 July 1918. This was the only part of the allied line that did not give an inch on that day. Despite being exposed on both flanks, the 38th Infantry held on to their positions and drove the Germans back across the river. This defense and the subsequent advance north to the Vesle River cost the 3rd Division 8,000 casualties.

To your right front, immediately west of the town and frowning down upon it, you see Hill 204, which commands the town and the surrounding country. In 1918 this hill

Pontoon bridge at Château-Thierry, 11 Aug 1918

Looking upstream from the main wagon bridge. In the distance is the modern-day sugar mill.

View from the north bank of the Marne showing where the temporary pontoon bridge crossed the river

Pontoon bridge at Château-Thierry, 21 July 1918.

Looking downstream from the main wagon bridge.

marked the right of the sector held by the 2nd Division. From your vantage point the American Memorial on Hill 204 is easily seen.

Hill 204 was the dominating geographical feature in the theater of battle and the Germans held it in force. The hill gave the Germans command of a wide circle of the battlefield, enabling them to sweep their fire up and down both banks of the Marne and to concentrate artillery and machine guns upon the hills and ridges flanking the river on the south, held by the French and Americans.

At the top of the steps, turn to the right and follow the ramparts past the restaurant and as far as the entrance to the park (location **P** on your map). Pass through the portal seen ahead of you and after going ahead a few yards, turn around and look at the portal. This is the Porte St. Jean, built in the 13th Century. Consisting of a pointed arch flanked by two large circular towers, this is the last remaining vestige of the principal entry to the château. The Porte St. Jean leads to the small public park that now occupies the area within the enclosure of the old stronghold. Compare your view with shown in the 1918 photographs. Due to construction at the time the 'now' photographs were taken, it was not possible to obtain a precise comparison photograph.

After passing through the Porte St. Jean, which occupies the entire site of the old castle, walk around it to get a general view of the town and its outskirts. On leaving the park turn to the left to get a view of the old entrance to the castle at location **Q** on your map and as shown in the photographs.

This is the Porte St. Pierre, the last remaining of four such gates or portals added to the castle as fortifications during the Middle Ages. Through this, the only gate still standing in the historic pile which rises on the hillside, rode Jeanne d'Arc (Joan of Arc) and King Charles VII upon their return from the latter's coronation in Reims in 1429.

Facing the Porte St. Pierre you have the option of returning to the town plaza via the dirt path to your right, which parallels the castle ramparts, or walking down the Chemin de Ronde, the paved road going to your right. The dirt path of the Chemin de Ronde encircles the Chateau and is for pedestrians only. The Chemin de Ronde will exit on to Rue Jean de la Fontaine and thence on to Grand Rue and into the town plaza.

The Rue du Château, the paved road to your left, will take you through a very old part of own, around the castle ramparts and the old hospital and into the town plaza. This route will take you past the Hôtel Dieu on your left. Jeanne de Navarre, the daughter of Blanche d'Artois, founded this Catholic hospital in 1304. Although having been in 1876, the building still retains a 17th century chapel.

In 1918 the U.S. Army Medical Corps used the hospital to treat a great number of Americans who were wounded in the fighting near Château-Thierry. AEF Field Hospital No. 168 moved into the old convent building on 29 July 1918, taking over from the Germans who had used it as a hospital capable of accommodating five hundred patients. Within four hours the building had been cleaned and equipped, three hundred and fifty patients had been admitted, and five operating teams were at work. Within twelve hours the hospital was crowded to the limit of its capacity. When the fighting moved northward, the army medical facility moved on to Cohan, a little village about 11 kilometers south of Fismes (on the Vesle).

Evacuation Hospital No. 6 moved to Chierry near Château-Thierry, 29 July, where it combined with Mobile Hospital No. 1. Here it treated over 3,500 patients, evacuating them to Paris by train and barge. Evacuation Hospital No. 5 arrived in Château-Thierry on 2 August. It mainly cared for the seriously wounded, and received augmentation with surgical teams. Evacuation Hospital No. 4 moved to Ecury-sur-Coole where it operated steadily for seventy-two hours with no rest for its surgical teams. It then moved to Chateau Peruse where it remained until 6 August, caring for 1,427 patients.

By 29 July, Evacuation Hospital No. 3 had started work at La Ferte-Milon. Evacuation Hospital No. 5 arrived at Château-Thierry on 2 August. These hospitals greatly increased the capability in the region greatly. Problems continued to arise in moving the hospitals closer to the front, because the destruction from the offensive ruined buildings that the evacuation hospitals could set up in and destroyed the railheads necessary to evacuate from.

IN THEIR OWN WORDS

From *History of Base Hospital No. 18, A.E.F.*:

> The team [a medical shock team] arrived at Château-Thierry July 27, 1918. It was installed in the Hotel Dieu, a Catholic hospital, which had been used by German troops during their stay in the city. From garret to cellar the place had been ransacked; the beds were stacked or broken, mattresses torn open, linen scattered everywhere, and the floors littered with hospital material of every sort. Almost every window pane was broken and several shells had made holes through the brick walls.
>
> The hospital was a very busy place, and for many days over five hundred gassed or wounded passed through in each twenty-four hours. Only the non-transportable wounded were held and treated and it was a depressing experience for all of us to see, day after day, terribly wounded men, many of whom died in spite of all treatment.
>
> The city was bombed several nights, but no serious damage resulted and none of the bombs fell near the hospital.

From *Iodine and Gasoline, a History of the 117th Sanitary Train*, by Josiah C. Chatfield:

> The Château-Thierry Hospital was situated in the former Jeanne Macy school. The building was three stories high and built around a rectangular

Porte St. Jean

Battlefield Taxi

"Château-Thierry. Tablet in honor 3rd Div. Maj. Gen. Howze"

courtyard filled with trees. The French had formerly used it as one section of a large H.O.E. and had left an abundance of medical supplies which subsequently were put to good use.

During the German occupation of the building, the rooms had been used as latrines. Portions of unfinished meals were still upon the dining tables and half-cooked food had deteriorated in the kitchen. The basement was full of German ammunition.

In addition to the rooms available for wards in the school building, Nebraska [the origin state of the hospital unit] erected four large ward tents to be used for gas patients. The hospital was to be an extensive one, equipped with X-ray room, large operating room, and bath.

There is a Franco-British military cemetery at location **R** on your map, on the Rue Léon l'Hermitte. This cemetery is better visited by automobile. The war memorial there was made by sculptor Achille Jacopin, who was born in Château-Thierry.

In 1918 there was a small American military cemetery included within the confines of the larger French cemetery.

Return to the Place de l'Hôtel de Ville

This concludes your tour of Château-Thierry. There are many more places of possible interest to the tourist visiting Château-Thierry, but only those which are considered to be of the most interest to the battleground pilgrim or tourist have been given here. The other additional places of interest are shown on your town maps which were obtained at the tourist office.

CHÂTEAU-THIERRY'S GRATITUDE TO AMERICA

Let us pause for a moment, and listen to the voice of Château-Thierry, speaking through her new Municipal Council at their first session, December 10, 1919:

> The newly-elected Municipal Council of Château-Thierry, at the moment of sitting in the city still in ruins, addresses to the American people the testimony of its gratitude and fraternal sympathy, and assures it that Château-Thierry will faithfully preserve the remembrance of the bravery with which the soldiers of the Great Republic fought for the victory which delivered their city.
>
> A large number of those heroes were killed in the liberating battle and now lie in this little corner of the land of France.
>
> Neither their memory nor their tombs will be forgotten, and the population

of Château-Thierry, itself so sorely tried, will always reserve the most pressing and cordial welcome for the American families which may come here to accomplish their pious pilgrimage: some to render the supreme homage to their loved dead, others to visit the scene on which the events of the World War I took place in 1918.

From Spaulding & Wright's book, *The Second Division*:

French inhabitants of the region where the 2ᵈ Division operated expressed their gratitude. On July 10 the Mayor of the Meaux District (Arrondissement) sent to the Division a resolution passed by all the mayors of the District. It reads:
"Voted in the Congress of the Mayors of the Meaux District who were eye-witnesses on the 25th of June, 1918.
"The Mayors of the Meaux District who were eye-witnesses of the generous and effacious deeds of the American Army in the stopping of the enemy advance send to this Army the heartfelt expression of their admiration and gratefulness.
Meaux, June 25th, 1918
The President of the Committee,
G. LUGOL."

An unnumbered German order issued on 4 June, 1918, immediately after the battle at Château-Thierry reads as follows:

Corps Conta, which is charged with the protection of the left flank of the 7th Army...is compelled to temporarily assume the defensive, after positions most suitable for this purpose are captured. The offensive spirit must be maintained even though a temporary lull exists. We are the victors and will remain on the offensive. The enemy is defeated.

In Joseph Hansen's book, *The Marne*, is the following official American communiqué dated 4 June, 1918:

In the fighting northwest of Château-Thierry our troops broke up an attempt of the enemy to advance to the south through Neuilly Woods and by a counterattack drove him back to the north of the woods. On the Marne front a German battalion which had crossed the river at Jaulgonne was counterattacked by French and American troops and forced to retreat to the right bank. It sustained severe losses in killed and prisoners.

APRIL AT CHATEAU-THIERRY
Tread lightly, April, this is hallowed ground;
Tread lightly as your lyric feet can pass,

Destruction along the Rue Drugeon le Cart

Two bridges across the Marne between World Wars

Today—the bridge across the Marne. Looking north toward the city hall and the Belhan tower

And sprinkle, with no shadow of sound,
Bright crocuses along the tender grass.
Let lilacs softly burst in bloom again,
And spread a carpeting of violets
For silver sandals of the quiet rain
That glitters like the flash of bayonets.
Light up the hills with tulips', wind-blown flame
As acolytes would light the altar-stone;
Twine poppies far to lovely for a name
Around the lonely crosses, one by one.
Tread lightly, April, soft and crystal-clear…
[A generation's April slumbers here.]

—Daniel Whitehead Hicky

CONCLUSION

The defense of Château-Thierry by the 7th Motorized Machine Gun Battalion, U. S. 3rd Division, from the end of May to early June of 1918, although it is not now recognized as such, marks the true turning point of World War I. That it was a pivot point in the War was well recognized at the time, particularly judging from the reactions of our Allies and the world press.

The German Army had surprised the Allies, stormed down from the Chemin des Dames and had reached the Marne River at Château-Thierry, all within the span of one week. The speed of their movement surprised even the Germans. German infantry reached Château-Thierry, with little in the way of logistical support and were packing into the town. There was but a single railroad line running from Soissons to Château-Thierry. It was not a question of if the Germans would cross the Marne and begin to move westward toward Paris, it was merely a question of when they would do so. Militarily, Château-Thierry had become a vacuum—there was no one there to defend the city.

In the words of Major John Mendenhall, commander of Company B, 7th Motorized Machine Gun Battalion, "It appeared to be merely a matter of hours before the Allied dyke crumbled and the grey wave rolled southward over Paris."

At this time Allied morale, and particularly that of the French civilian and military, was at an all-time low. The army of France, having suffered severe mutinies, would no longer fight offensively, and could barely even defend what it held. The French Army was in a pell-mell retreat, a retreat that was beginning to become panicky. The civil government of Paris was being evacuated to Bordeaux. Civilians were leaving the city in droves. The hue and cry of the moment was one of, *La guerre est fini!* The tempered steel blade of the French sword was bent almost double. A little more stress and it would snap!

Had the Germans been able to move long-range artillery to the Château-Thierry area, they could have then proceeded to bring down the bricks of Paris. France would never have suffered the loss of her beloved capitol and would have sued for peace. The British, no longer supported by the French Army, would have had to give up the Channel ports and retreat back to the British Isles.

General Foch had no forces immediately at hand to send to defend Château-Thierry, and even if he had, they would most likely be unreliable and would promptly retreat before the Germans. The only viable military unit available to the General was one of the machine gun battalions of the U.S. 3rd Division, a battalion that had its own Ford trucks, and which was about 150 miles distant from the town itself. Off they went to Château-Thierry in a non-stop, hell-bent-for-leather two-day race to get to Château-Thierry before the Germans crossed the Marne River. Once there they proceeded to set up their 36 French Hotchkiss machine guns in strategic locations. The rest is history.

CHÂTEAU-THIERRY DURING WORLD WAR II

From the U.S. 3rd Armored Division History Website:

> Combat Command Hickey led the advance with Boudinot on the left. After crossing the river, the command moved to Chousse en Brie, in two columns, driving through the German 48th Inf. Div. On the following day, closely pursuing the retreating enemy and overrunning several rearguards, the command passed through Coulommiers and crossed the Marne, halting for the night just north of that historic river. A detachment was sent to Château-Thierry, and the controversy as to who was the first to enter the town began. The commander of the division's CIC detachment and the photo detachment commander believe the honor is theirs. They had entered the town about 1500 hours on Aug. 28, and obtained from the Mayor a statement reading, "Second taking of Château-Thierry by the Americans; all our gratitude." On their way into town, the two officers passed the 4th Cav. Gp., and later met soldiers of the 7th Rcn. Sq.

The next volume in this series of AEF battlefield guidebooks produced by Battleground Productions will continue the tour of the AEF battlefields in the Marne salient of 1918. To be thoroughly covered in succeeding volumes are the battlegrounds of the U.S. 2nd and 26th Divisions northwest of Château-Thierry and across the Paris-Metz Road, including Hill 142, Belleau Wood, Belleau, Bouresches, Vaux and the occupation of the Pas Fini Sector.

THE END

In World War II, the same bridge was blown up again. Here are WWII German soldiers driving by the bridge.

Appendix

Travel Tips

What's Inside this Section

American World War I Memorials

Unlike World War I memorials in the United States, American memorials in Europe are strictly shrines. They are mostly in open countryside rather than in the cities. The reasoning for this is perfectly logical—most of the fighting of the AEF was in the open countryside and no large cities in France were conquered by the American soldiers. For diplomatic and political reasons, the AEF generally deferred to the French in taking the larger towns and cities, e.g., Château-Thierry and Sedan. Out in the country few constraints existed, and there were no reasons to make the memorials utilitarian. These European memorials are considered by critics to be some of America's finest monuments. The use of site planning to make symbolic connections between the cemeteries and the monuments commemorating those who died is seen as an American hallmark. These memorials set the precedent for how American overseas memorials would be designed in the future.

American World War I memorials overseas commemorate those who gave their lives in the war. With so many American killed, remembering the sacrifice through war memorials was indeed a large task. With the addition of the American memorials and monuments, the number of war memorials on foreign soil was significantly increased. In building memorials and cemeteries for World War I, the American Battle Monuments Commission erred in the placement of memorials in association with the cemeteries which commemorated the campaigns of the AEF. After World War I, some of the major memorials were not located near cemeteries, while others were nearby but were not part of the cemetery's design. Additionally, there were particular problems with memorials voluntarily built by military units. These troop memorials dotted the battlefields and had often been found to be poorly designed, poorly constructed, and lacking provision for maintenance. Many memorials of this type were later ordered destroyed.

Time Necessary To See The Battlefields

Americans visiting Europe often assign only a limited time to the American battle-grounds on the Western Front. About three weeks would ideally be necessary for even a quick tour. Several months could be consumed for an in-depth study tour. Realistically, most tourists can devote a maximum of a week to the American battlefields. Many allot only a few days, then find that the battlefields are much more interesting than they expected, and wish that they could reshape their itinerary.

From one day to one month may be spent seeing the American battlefields in the Marne salient, depending upon the care, detail and thoroughness with which the visitor desires to go over the ground.

It is not mandatory that tourists visit all the battlegrounds and places described in this book. For many people this book may contain too much information. The required information is there for those who wish to do a very simple tour or for those who want to do a very detailed tour.

WHEN TO SEE THE BATTLEFIELDS

Most of the important sites and monuments are accessible at any time of the year. From November to March the weather is often wet, rainy and cold. In winter, daylight hours are short and even the most beautiful garden cemetery is not as attractive then as in spring, summer or autumn. Many sites are snowbound or obscured by fog or rain, while others are difficult to reach because of muddy roads and tracks. Tramping over battlefields—that is, farm fields—is difficult because of the mud. Paths in the woods are also muddy. The best time to visit the battlefields is summer, effectively June to September, but May and October can also be good months. August, usually a very hot month in France, is the month when everyone in France goes on their vacation; many establishments close for the entire month.

The appearance of the battlefields is greatly affected by the season of the year. In the winter, early spring and late autumn, it is easier to see the lay of the land; in summer (when the AEF fought most of its battles), foliage obscures the line of sight.

Sunset in northern France during the months of May through September is about 9:30 PM. The dedicated battlefield visitor will perhaps wish to devote the daylight hours to travelling, and return to his place of lodging and a late snack or meal upon arrival around sunset.

A TRAFFIC SAFETY REMINDER

In this battlefield tour, when you stop in order to observe a panoramic view, or for any other purpose, do so very carefully. The stopping points given in the text are the same as those which were given in the old battlefield guidebooks published between fifty and seventy or more years ago, when the automobile was not nearly so prevalent nor as high speed a vehicle as it is today.

When advised to pull off the road for purposes of viewing the battlefield, be sure there is no traffic behind you and then slowly pull off onto the shoulder of the road, but only if the shoulder appears strong enough to support the weight of your vehicle. If the shoulder is muddy and you might become stuck there, find another location to pull over, and walk back to the desired viewpoint. Be very careful when opening the doors and alighting from the vehicle. On the driver's side you could lose the door and suffer injury if struck by another vehicle. On the passenger side you could very easily step out into the roadside drainage ditch!

If the issue of safety is really in doubt, drive on to a safe place, park and lock your car, (taking your camera and other valuables with you) and walk back to the location recommended for seeing a particular view.

MAPS

Although this book contains an adequate selection of travel and town maps, the selection is necessarily limited to the specific battlefield areas to be visited. If you wish visit optional and somewhat out-of-the-way sites or to have the entire battlefield map handy as a one-piece entity, then the prospective battlefield visitor should have at least several of the *Séries Bleue* 1:25,000 (1cm = 250 meters) series of maps as published by the *Institute Géographique Nationale* (IGN) in France. Most of the larger American map companies have these maps in stock, and they are commonly available in the *libraries* (book stores) in France. Not all the book stores in France will have all the IGN maps. Local stores usually only carry the maps for their immediate geographic area. Château-Thierry has at least one large *librarie* (book store) which has the appropriate maps for that area of France.

For coverage of all the American battlefields mentioned in this book, get from an American or French map dealer the French *Institut Geographique National, Series Bleue* 1:25,000; 1cm = 250m maps. There is a free catalog of these series of maps, *Catalogue, Serie Bleue & Top 25*. The catalog should also be available from your map dealer.

The designation "E" stands for "East," "W" represents "West." The two maps listed below are the maps in 1:25,000 scale which best accompany this book.

2513E – Saacy-sur-Marne
2613W – Château-Thierry

A very good general and overall map of the Marne salient is the IGN *Series Verte* (Series Green) Map No. 9, 1:100,000 (1cm = 1 km), Paris-Laon map.

Information For The Described Tours

Many statements made in the original 1920 text of the old Michelin guidebook and in the ABMC guidebooks of 1927 and 1938, concern conditions or things which have changed radically with the passage of time. In the interest of maintaining the historical context of this battlefield guidebook, very few changes have been made to the original texts except to substitute, at least in certain cases, the past tense for their original present tense, and to explain where necessary, when present day battlefield conditions differ radically from those of yesteryear.

Road directions on the described tours are given where there is a possibility that you might go astray. All road directions are in bold and underlined text so that you may quickly and easily recognize them. At junctions where there are no given motoring instructions, you should continue straight ahead. Easy to read maps are frequently placed where they will aid the motorist.

No mileage is given from point-to-point in the text because of the inherent difficulty in maintaining precise calculations of the mileage. The speedometer or odometer distances recorded by automobiles vary somewhat, and those recorded by the same car under different conditions, such as wet or dry weather, are not the same. Many tourists do not want to be bothered with following miles/kilometer indications. Drivers get lost, the French make a habit of taking drivers on long deviations and detours, and many motorists are forgetful of maintaining the distance calculations between points of interest. Anyway, what useful purpose does such information really serve, except to add to an already somewhat confusing travelling scenario? Let's do it the easier way, and forget about such precise calculations.

For these reasons no odometer or speedometer distances from point to point are given. Some distances are given for general reference and are not essential for following this tour. In the few instances where such distances are helpful or necessary, they are given in kilometers—this is the system used in Europe and in your rental car. For descriptive purposes only, some general distances are given in miles.

At the places where you are told to face in a certain direction, the account of the operations is given with respect to that facing. The meanings of the various expressions used to indicate the different directions are illustrated by the sketch.

Points of interest not included in the battlefield tour itinerary are given as close as possible to a corresponding location on the given tour.

The diagram graphically displays in which direction events occurred on the battlefield in relation to the direction the viewer is facing. Many events

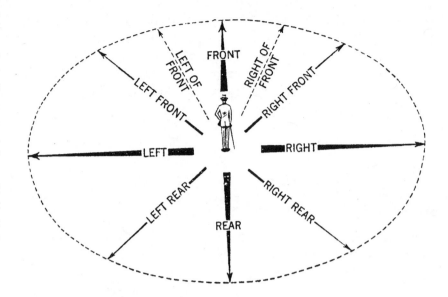

will be described to you using these designations, e.g., to your left front, to your right rear, etc.

To determine directions, carry a compass on the tours.

When determining direction using a magnetic compass, be certain that you are well away from the metal body of your automobile and metallic objects which may be on your person, as they will influence your readings.

To determine compass directions with a round faced watch when the sun is shining, place the watch flat in your hand and face the sun. Point the hour hand in direction you are facing. The point on the rim of the watch halfway between the end of the hour hand and the figure 12 on the dial will be the southernmost point of the watch face.

When facing south, the right side of a person is west and the left side east (the sun rises in the east and sets in the west).

Conversion of meters and kilometers:
1 kilometer = 0.62137 mile
1 mile = 1.6093 kilometers
1 meter = 39.37 inches = 1.09 yards
1 yard = 0.9144 meter

A simple rule for roughly converting kilometers to miles is to multiply the number of kilometers by 0.6. To change from miles to kilometers do the opposite and divide the number of miles by 0.6.

Beware of the Danger

The colossal expenditure in shell and ammunition during the First World War left a dangerous legacy for the visitor of today. Often, small piles of rusting shells are seen on the roadside. These neat piles of ammunition are usually the result of being ploughed up—the "Iron Harvest," as it is called. To this day the French military authorities make regular collections to take these very dangerous objects away for safe demolition.

Eighty years after the guns stopped speaking, hundreds of tons of barbed wire, artillery shells, grenades, and mortar bombs still remain on the surface and underneath the land on which the war was fought. Every year, farmers, forestry and road workers, and unwary, unexpecting tourists stumble across, or dig up, ammunition or battle debris.

Tourists who get a little off the beaten track still find unexploded hand-grenades and fulminate of mercury fuses lying about. For souvenir hunters the first tendency may be to put a few of these into their pockets. *The firing pins of the grenades have rusted through in most cases and need but a touch to explode them.* The sight of such things seems to turn many visitors into collectors, and with little thought of the danger of these seemingly inoffensive objects, they are bundled into the car and in many cases brought home on board airplanes! *Do not jeopardize your vacation by trying to pass any of these items through airport security systems. Please leave them where you see them!*

Do not touch them with your hand or foot. Warn others and stop them if they attempt it. Explosives do not improve with age, in fact, they seem to become progressively more unstable as they get older. Many French and Belgian civilians, adults and children, and occasionally even the military still are maimed and killed by the old munitions. In the last year or so just under 40 people have been killed by old munitions in France.

WARNING!

Death still lurks upon the battlefields—beware of shells, grenades, cartridges, fuses, etc., anything you don't recognize. *They may be deadly!*

If You Don't Know What It Is—Don't Touch It

Even the apparently innocent rusty bayonet or length of barbed wire may possibly carry with it the danger of tetanus if carelessly handled. The French medical authorities have been investigating some of the untouched regions of the battlefields and have found evidence that careless wandering through dirty infectious ground can be dangerous.

Western Front battlefield visitors are cautioned to walk carefully, stay on marked trails or roads, and respect private property.

For the benefit of those persons who may think that an old hand grenade or artillery shell is harmless—read on. The following article, from the 13 September 1993 edition of *Le Monde*, a French newspaper, is typical of the many which appear in European newspapers every year:

In Montauville, a small village near Pont-a-Mousson, [Meurthe-et-Moselle], a stroller, hearing a report that sounded like a plane breaking the sound barrier, discovered the horribly mutilated bodies of Stefen Budde, 24, and Johannes Schulien, 29, two young German workmen from Sarrebruck who came to Lorraine looking for WWI souvenirs.

While loading a shell into their car trunk, it exploded, killing the two young men and leaving a 3-ft. wide crater just behind the car. In the vehicle, the police found metal detectors, pliers, drills and rust removing agents.

The Germans, amateur collectors of war relics, were killed by a WWI shell. They had a passion for relics, especially those of the First World War. Their search for shells, grenades, and bullets was their favorite hobby. They died last week on a dirt road in Lorraine.

The message is clear; when the advice is that one should leave these things well alone, then curiosity should be overcome and a wide berth be given to things which were designed for the purpose of causing injury and death. Do not be foolish enough to add your name or those of your family to the long list of those who have been accidently killed or mutilated on the Western Front by the old munitions of World War I.

What To Wear And Take On The Battlefields

The following items will be beneficial when travelling on the battlefields.

* rain coat or waterproof poncho
* umbrella
* small flashlight
* field glasses
* compass
* small backpack
* toilet paper
* snack rations (cookies, apples, etc.)
* small can opener and a set of travel-type eating utensils
* water bottle, or small canteen
* plastic or cloth shopping bag
* small packages of sealed hand wipes
* thermos bottle
* rubber boots or slip-on rubber shoes
* hat or soft cap
* hiking shoes or an older pair of shoes
* small first aid kit
* sun glasses
* camera
* extra film
* notebook, pen, pencil
* Swiss army knife
* whistle
* survival blanket

Personal Guides On The Battlefields

A noted English historian declared some eighty years ago that, "the skilled game of identifying positions on a battlefield innocent of guides, where one must make out everything for one's self—best of all if no one has ever done it properly before—is almost the greatest of outdoor intellectual pleasures." I might add that it is also one of the most difficult.

For those battlefield visitors who wish to have a French historian guide you around the American battlefields, I would strongly recommend the services of Gilles Lagin, of Marigny-en-Orxois, France, just a few miles west of Château-Thierry. Gilles is a young man, he speaks English, and he knows most of the battlefields in the Marne salient of 1918 very well indeed. *Monsieur* Lagin and his service as a battlefield guide are of particular value to historians of the U.S. Marine Corps (USMC) and U.S. Army, as well as to active duty military personnel and any other persons who wish to visit the battlefields of the AEF. *Monsieur* Lagin is especially recommended for seeing the battlefields of the USMC in his area: Bouresches, on the right-flank of Belleau Wood, Hill 142, on the left flank of the Wood, and Belleau Wood itself. M. Lagin can also take people to the battle sites east of Château-Thierry where the U.S. 3rd Division made its heroic stand on the banks of the Marne River on 15 July 1918, and on northward into the American battlefields in the regions of the Ourcq and Vesle Rivers and Soissons.

Many of the places and scenes of American battles in World War I are either private property or are normally inaccessible to tourists, except in a four-wheel drive vehicle, which M. Lagin posesses. M. Lagin has access to these private properties.

Gilles Lagin
24 Place de la Halle
02810 Marigny-en-Orxois
France

Tel. 01.33.323.70.46.54 (from the USA)
In France dial: 0323.70.46.54
Fax. 011.33.323.70.46.5
Email: gilles.lagin@wanadoo.fr

NOTES ABOUT STYLE

Inasmuch as this book is primarily a guidebook and not a formal battle or military history, it has very few scholarly trappings. Having no desire to clutter the narrative with endnotes, sources and reference numbers that might distract the reader or to attempt to give the manuscript a veneer of polished scholarship which it cannot justly claim, I have largely refrained from such scholarly documentation. This was a decision made after careful deliberation. Listing every individual source and annotating each chapter with quotes and references is cumbersome and would probably make the text unreadable. The comments of your author/editor are compatible with the verbiage and are in the narrative. Let the simple but direct words of the soldiers tell their own true story without surrounding them with a barbed-wire entanglement of technical bric-a-brac. To make this book a fluid read, and as far as it was possible to do so, the designation "[sic]" has been eliminated and obvious spelling errors have been corrected.

This book includes some selections from works of fiction because they best portray the voices and emotions of Americans in combat. Where selections from fictional works have been used, the reader is notified. In the interest of smoother reading, spelling and punctuation are modernized except where a certain echo from the past seemed appropriate.

Let this then be my apology for the style in which this book is written. I have endeavored to write from the viewpoint of the soldier. I believe the average soldier's unvarnished account of his experiences and the reactions to them will bring his hearers much closer to war as he felt it than any description could do, however finely written.

To save space in the text, military ranks have been abbreviated as follows:

General – Gen	Sergeant Major – SgtMaj
Major General – MajGen First	Sergeant – 1stSgt
Lieutenant General – LtGen	Master Sergeant – M/Sgt
Brigadier General – BgGen	Gunnery Sergeant – GySgt
Colonel – Col	Sergeant – Sgt
Lieutenant Colonel – LtCol	Corporal – Cpl
Major – Maj	Private First Class – Pfc
Captain – Capt	Private – Pvt
First Lieutenant – 1stLt	Second Lieutenant – 2ndLt

Other abbreviations of common usage are explained after their first usage in the text, e.g., American Expeditionary Forces (AEF)

When there is any element of doubt as to the identity of Allied or German military units, the Allied units are in bold text and the German units are italicized.

Editor's note: Much has been included in this appendix in the way of miscellaneous facts, charts and other types of statistical tabulations. Inasmuch as this material has been gathered from many sources, most of which never gave the original source of their information, the precise accuracy of some of the figures cannot be vouchsafed. Some of the total casualty statistics for the AEF and its divisions differ, according to the source. I leave it up to the reader to reach some reasonable conclusion where the issue is in doubt.

LIST OF ORGANIZATIONS DEDICATED TO THE STUDY OF AND PERPETUATION OF THE MEMORY OF WORLD WAR I

Editor's note: The names of organization officers, residence addresses, email addresses, telephone numbers, etc., change over time. The information listed is current as of January, 2006.

AMERICAN OVERSEAS MEMORIAL DAY ASSOCIATION

"TO ALL WHO REMEMBER:

"LEST WE FORGET" that we live, work and travel in Europe today because THEY made the ultimate sacrifice to re-open the way of freedom, the American Overseas Memorial Day Association (AOMDA) is dedicated to remember and honor the memory of those who gave their lives in World War I and World War II and whose final resting places are in American Military Cemeteries or in isolated graves in local cemeteries in Europe. "LEST WE FORGET" has been adopted as the Association Motto.

The Association was founded in 1920 and incorporated in 1952 under the laws of Washington, D.C. Article 3(a) of the Certificate of Incorporation gives the AOMDA purpose, which reads in part, "To decorate on the National Memorial Day, and such other public and patriotic holidays as may be appropriate, the graves, tombs and monuments of all American servicemen and servicewomen of the Army, Navy, Air Force and Auxiliary Services buried overseas.

In keeping with this article, the Association is annually responsible for the placing of American (and often local National) flags on all known graves of American servicemen and servicewomen. Both the Paris Office and the AOMDA Committee in Brussels, Belgium, work to accomplish the Association's purpose.

* The placing of flags in the American Military Cemeteries is done through the efforts of the American Battle Monuments Commission.

* For the 183 isolated graves in 123 localities in France, the Association contacts local officials, civic groups and veteran's organizations or individuals (sometimes next-of-kin) to arrange for the placing of flags. The flags are annually mailed by the Association to the persons assuming responsibility for decoration of the grave.

* For the location in Denmark (120 graves), Norway (120 graves), Sweden (12 graves), the American Embassies are sent flags by AOMDA for placement on Memorial Day. The embassies in Denmark and Norway accomplish the flag placement, while in Sweden, the local American Legion Post accomplishes the flag placement.
* In Germany, the various local American Legion posts obtain the flags required for the graves of U.S. service veterans and place the flags on the graves.
* In addition, the Association finances purchases of wreaths for the Memorial Day ceremonies at the World War I and World War II cemeteries in England, France, Italy, Luxembourg, the Netherlands and Tunisia. The AOMDA Committee in Brussels furnishes wreaths for the ceremonies in Belgium.

The Association also coordinates the annual actions for Memorial Day ceremonies in American Military Cemeteries in France and Belgium, with the active support of the Embassies and the American Battle Monuments Commission. Other Memorial Day ceremonies are organized by embassies, consulates, American Legion posts and local groups. These ceremonies include the participation of American and national military units, American and national government and local officials. The ceremonies have become important national events in the lives of many communities and their residents. In effect, the ceremonies are today international testimonies of remembrance and gratitude for the supreme sacrifice made by American soldiers in World War I and World War II.

With the passing of time, expenses increase while revenue decreases as people disappear or forget. WE NEED YOUR HELP! New sources of funding must be found if the AOMDA is to continue its efforts on behalf of those who gave all that they had to give. Will you join us in preserving the memory of those who gave all?

Contributions to the AOMDA are exempt from the US Federal income tax as provided in Section 170 of the Internal Revenue Code, and as provided in French Tax regulations pertaining to Not-for-Profit Associations under the law of 1901.

Funding for support of the Association's Memorial Day activities is provided annually by a grant from American Legion National Headquarters, donations from civic organizations, American commercial firms and individuals, and by payment of Association dues, both lifetime (€460 or equivalent), Active Member annual ($100), or Associate Member annual ($50). As the World War II population base has decreased through mortality, the number of members has correspondingly decreased. Information on memberships and details on providing donations, grants and bequests may be obtained by contacting the Association Office at 34, Avenue de New York, 75016 Paris. (President, Mr. Russell M. Porter, telephone 33-1-42.61.55.77.

THE DOUGHBOY HISTORICAL SOCIETY

The primary activity of the DHS is publication of *The Doughboy*, the Society's quarterly journal. The mission statement indicates that the Doughboy Historical Society is a non-profit organization dedicated to the preservation of the American World War One Heritage. Membership is $15 per year, July 1–July 1. The Doughboy Historical Society publishes a quarterly newsletter which contains articles written by the membership and which also contains a listing of "Wants–Disposals." Their quarterly publication, *The Doughboy*, does have a heavy emphasis on soldier's uniforms, personal gear and equipment. Other articles cover specific events, unit histories, etc., and they tend to be more narrative than analytical. The format may be somewhat disappointing to many subscribers. Journals are only 16–20 pages in length and are produced on a photocopy machine. There are also many 'typos' and spelling errors. However, the very active wants-and-disposals column reinforces the emphasis on militaria and suggests that this Society is especially suited for the collector.

Doughboy Historical Society,
P.O. Box 3912,
Missoula, Montana 59806.

THE GREAT WAR ASSOCIATION

Those persons wanting to develop a true feeling of trench life are advised to join this society of about 600 re-enactors. There are numerous reenactment units, each representing a specific historical regiment or division, representing either the Allied or Central Powers. Members are encouraged to join one of the units, but presently no aviation detachment exists. The membership is dedicated to preserving the memory of all the combatants in the Great War and presenting an accurate portrayal of the war experience to today's generation. They accomplish their goals through public "living history" and interactive displays. They hold two National reenactment events each Spring and Fall at their recreated World War I trench system in Pennsylvania, where members engage in a weekend of "living history" recreating life on the Western Front circa 1914–1918 (time frame will vary each event).

Realism and safety are both heavily emphasized at these reenactments, what with period uniforms, firearms firing blank ammunition, trenches, barbed wire, mortar fire, night raids, etc. Members are required to outfit themselves with original and reproduction equipment, the cost of which can run to many hundreds of dollars. However, reenacting is one of the more unique ways to experience the Great War of 1914–1918.

The Great War Association strives to preserve the oral and written history of the World War and appreciates any opportunity to gain such material. "On the Wire," the official newsletter of the Great War Association, is published three times a year in the Spring, Summer and Fall and informs the membership of upcoming activities.

For further information contact:
Werner Gruhl
5990 Jacobs Ladder
Columbia, MD 21045
(301) 596-5460

THE GREAT WAR FOUNDATION

"Dedicated to Preserving the Memory of Those Who Fought in 'The War to End All Wars' Through Living History, Education, and Commemoration."

"The Great War Foundation, Inc., is a not-for-profit organization established to fill a gap between the scholarly World War I organizations and the historical reenactment societies. Although these groups have widely differing presentations and approaches to history, the general public is not their main audience. The primary mission of the GWF is to present the story of World War I to the public in a manner that is both informative and interesting through publications and presentations including the use of original artifacts, photos and documents."

"The GWF is also actively engaged in developing a location for its living history activities. The **Caesar Krauss Great War Memorial Site** currently features a network of trenches, barbed-wire entanglements, and underground bunkers. GWF members plan to utilize a small portion of this site to construct a mock French village that will include a canteen to host period entertainment. Members will also assist the Great War Aeroplanes Association in building a reproduction of a WWI airfield on part of the site."

"A memorial park will occupy part of the site. Already in place is an obelisk that commemorates Caesar Krauss, for whom the site is named. The park will consist of white memorial crosses, which will form a pattern 240 feet wide and 360 feet long with a six-foot-wide central walkway. These crosses may be purchased from the GWF to honor a World War I soldier, unit, or organization of any nationality. Proceeds from the sale of the crosses will be used to develop the site.

It is the purpose of the Great War Foundation to preserve, honor, and remember the men and women who served their countries in a myriad of ways during World War I. Through fundraising, donations, grants, and endowments, this not-for-profit organization hopes to further develop the Caesar Krauss Great War Memorial Site in Newville, Pennsylvania. Immediate goals include the construction of a memorial garden and a visitor's center.

Caesar Krauss was born in Germany in 1889. He served for a time with a Russian Hussar regiment before coming to America in 1911 or 1912.

Krauss began his U.S. military service on 30 September 1917 in the 313th Infantry Regiment ("Baltimore's Own"), 79th Division. Arriving in France on 14 July 1918, the green troops trained with experienced veterans for several more weeks, and finally headed for the front at the beginning of September. As member of the 79th Division, Corporal Krauss took part in the first phase of the Meuse–Argonne offensive, aiding in the capture of the towns of Montfaucon and Nantillois.

Caesar Krauss died in 1947 at the age of 58 years. His grandson, Mark Anderson, purchased 153 acres of land near Newville, Pennsylvania, for the purpose of memorializing Corporal Krauss, his comrades-in-arms, and all who served in World War I. The development of the memorial site as a living history area is the primary goal of the Great War Foundation.

The Great War Foundation, Inc.
PO Box 19
Chambersburg, PA 17201

GREAT WAR MILITARIA

Great War Militaria, founded in 1989, is the largest business in the world which specializes in the memorabilia and artifacts of World War I. It provides both reproduction and original uniforms, weapons, and equipment to museums, movie companies, collectors, investors, and reenactors. It addition, Great War Militaria maintains one of the largest private museums in the world dedicated to WWI, which is available to research and study to writers and historians. Great War Militaria also has access to a fifty-five acre plot of land which has been recreated in the form of a World War I battlefield complete with full-scale bunkers and trenches. This battlefield has been used in motion-picture productions and documentaries about World War I.

Write Great War Militaria at Box 552 H, Chambersburg, Pennsylvania 17201 for a free catalog of their line of reproduction WWI goods. You can also visit the GWM website at www.greatwar.com.

THE GREAT WAR SOCIETY

THE GREAT WAR SOCIETY (GWS) was founded in 1987 by a group of scholars at the Hoover Institution of War, Revolution and Peace, Stanford University, Palo Alto, California to promote a greater understanding on one of the most critical events in modern history, World War I. No other event has had such a profound and lasting effect on the twentieth and current centuries. The Great War Society is committed to the study of all aspects of the First World War and subsequent world events associated with that tragedy and their *relevance* to our lives today.

When one looks at the history of the twentieth century the effects of World War I are manifest in the rise of Communism, Fascism, Nazism, the Great Depression, World War II, the end of colonialism, the Korean and Vietnam Wars, the continuing crisis in the Middle East, the Balkans, and now the insidious effects of 9/11/2001. One cannot escape the impact World War I has had on our lives.

Its quarterly journal, *Relevance*, mirrors this philosophy and is published quarterly by and for the members of The Great War Society. *Relevance* provides a forum to examine all aspects of the World War I era. Members and non-members alike, are encouraged to submit appropriate articles for publication in *Relevance*. Articles may be submitted to the Editor at the address given below. The GWS has three active chapters located in the San Francisco Bay Area. The national membership has grown considerably as has the world-wide membership primarily because of their having an internet web site. Annual seminars, held at various locations throughout the country, bringing together members, guests, and renowned scholars to discuss the events of the Great War in more depth. Information about the annual seminar will be available on the website, announced in the journal, and advertised in separate mailings to members. The analytical emphasis of the GWS makes it a unique organization.

In addition to receiving *Relevance*, members also receive a membership directory.

The Great War Society is a California non-profit corporation. Dues and contributions have been determined by the IRS to be tax-deductible.

Annual membership: Individual (U.S) $42.50; Individual (Overseas) $47.50; Individual (S.F. Bay Area) $47.50; Family (Parents & Children) $50; Student (U.S.) $25; Student (Overseas) $25.

For further information, contact:

The Great War Society
PO Box18585
Stanford, CA 94309

Internet: www.mcs.net/~mikei/tgws or www.worldwar1.com/tgws/
President: Sal Compagno. Tel. 1-800-966-1216. E-mail: greatwa@ earthlink.net
Editorial Office: Michael Huebner, 953 East F Street, Moscow, ID 83843-3259. Tel. (208) 882-1246.

THE LEAGUE OF WORLD WAR I AVIATION HISTORIANS

Are you interested in World War I air combat? If so, the League of World War I Aviation Historians invites you to become a member of the nonprofit organization dedicated to studying all aspects of war in the air from 1914 through 1918.

With your annually renewable League membership, you will receive their quarterly journal *Over the Front*. Each issue contains articles, columns and illustrative material on airmen, squadrons and a wide variety of events. Articles and features are contributed by some of the most prominent aviation historians in the U.S. and abroad.

The League of World War I Aviation Historians is a nonprofit organization, approved by the U.S. Internal Revenue Service, and devoted entirely to serving its members' interests in studying and preserving information about early military operations in the air.

The League's growing number of regional chapters and biennial national seminars will put you in touch with like-minded colleagues. The League of World War I Aviation Historians is a growing, thriving organization.

If early military aviation is your interest, come and develop it with the League of World War I Aviation Historians.

Annual dues are $37 in the U.S. and Canada, including 4th class postage. (Dues are higher in other countries, due to mailing costs; please write for 1st class mail service and prices in other countries).

Please make all checks payable in U.S. funds to the League of World War I Aviation Historians and list the address to which the journals should be sent. For further information, contact:

Membership Secretary
The League of World War I Aviation Historians
P.O. Box 2475
Rockford, IL 61132-0475, USA

THE LIBERTY MEMORIAL MUSEUM AND ARCHIVES

By the end of World War One, more than four hundred individuals from Kansas City, Missouri, had given their lives in service to their country. Almost immediately after the war, the community joined together to create the Liberty Memorial. The Memorial was conceived as a monument to peace and to commemorate not only the sacrifice of the Kansas Citians, but all those people from around the world who had served on the battlefront and the home-front.

At the Third Annual Convention of the American Legion in Kansas City, Missouri, held 31 October to 2 November 1921, the participants first learned of the plans for the Liberty Memorial. Bold words expressed that "this noble Memorial will be an enduring symbol of the lofty spirit of self-sacrifice that inspired the men who gave their all in the world struggle for liberty - a perpetual challenge to loyalty and devotion."

The original fund raising for the Liberty Memorial began in 1919, with over two million dollars being donated by the citizens of Kansas City for the memorial's construction. Dedication of the site was on November 1, 1921, during the American Legion's national convention. France's Marshal Foch, General Jacques of Belgium, General Diaz of Italy, Admiral Lord Earl Beatty of Great Britain and General of the Armies John J. Pershing were present. President Calvin Coolidge and Queen Marie of Romania delivered the main addresses to a crowd of over 150,000 people at the Memorial's official opening on November 11, 1926.

With its enormous tower, temple-like buildings, enormous carved stone sphinxes, Memory and Future, and pyramidical stairways and massive courtyards, the Liberty Memorial was described as a "vision of patriotism to hail the future with loyal confidence in American Institutions."

Work continued on the memorial following the dedication. By the 1930's, the Great Frieze depicting the progress from war to peace was completed by the famed sculptor Edmond Amatieis. In the 1940's, the now venerable avenue of trees leading up to the memorial was planted by the Navy War Mothers and Army Mothers Club to memorialize their sons. The memorial area became a gathering place where families enjoyed a sense of community.

In 1941, Lord Halifax of Great Britain wrote that the Liberty Memorial "is the most impressive war memorial I've ever seen in any country. I'm glad I had the opportunity to see it."

From the courtyard of the concrete deck, already many feet above the street, rises the 217 foot Memorial Tower. The stone statues atop the memorial tower known as the Guardian Spirits still stand representing those high ideals of Courage, Honor, Patriotism and Sacrifice, but those same qualities are in demand today as well as to preserve the Liberty Memorial.

The famous mural, "Pantheon de la Guerre", is housed in the Museum along with others by Daniel Mac Morris and Jules Guerin.

Flanking the tower are two buildings: the East Museum Building (Memory Hall) and the West Museum Building. The Great Frieze, a stone sculpture by Edmond Amateius, extends 148 feet along the north terrace wall and represents the progress of man from war to peace.

The Liberty Memorial is the only public military museum in the United States specializing in World War One.

The museum normally presents educational exhibits tracing the history of the war and the role played by the United States. Exhibits contain objects and archival materials from the Allied and Central Powers. The museum archives, because of the extensive collection, is world known for its research opportunities.

The archives and research library holds materials related to the World War I period including a wonderful collection of posters, many diaries and journals, letters, personal papers, postcards written by soldiers from camp and overseas, manuscripts, over ten-thousand photographs, sound recordings, motion picture films of troops, original prints, drawings, and technical publications, official correspondence, and over a thousand records of various divisions and organizations. The archives also house major collections of posters and sheet music. Each belligerent country and almost every American division and service organization is represented in the archival collection. The archives and research library are open by appointment.

The museum is recognized as an adjunct to the U.S. Army Museum System and as a branch repository for the Rainbow (42nd) Division. The museum and archives continue to acquire World War I materials of great scope and variety. While its renowned historical collection started in 1920, the museum remains very active today in seeking out and receiving objects from World War One. Each week, new archival items and artifacts associated with World War I and its participants are given by donors from all over the nation and the world. Each piece is carefully preserved and maintained so that researchers and historians can gather information about all aspects of World War I.

The artillery, poster and uniform collection areas are especially important. Thousands of original documents, photographs, ephemera and books make up the museum's archives and library. In short, the archives and museum at the Liberty Memorial will insure that those who served in World War I will not be forgotten.

The West Museum Building has a life-sized replica of a trench and dugout, complete with lighting and sound effects, all of which give visitors a glimpse of what life on the Western Front could have been like.

The East Museum Building (Memory Hall), beside exhibits, holds the plaques with the names of those Kansas Citians who died in the war, illustrative maps of the war and famous murals.

Exhibits in the Museum illustrate all aspects of the war. Large objects include several artillery pieces, a British deck gun and a horse drawn ambulance.

The museum collection is owned by the Liberty Memorial Association, a not-for-profit organization founded in 1919. Its trustees throughout the years have included many veterans, including Captain Harry S. Truman and Medal of Honor recipient John Lewis Barkley.

Students by the thousands have visited the Liberty Memorial Museum. Hannah Farman, an eighth grade student, wrote just a short while ago:

"I am a student from St Francis Xavier whose class visited the museum last Friday. I had a great time. Some of the artifacts were very overwhelming. Those things were actually touched and worn by WWI soldiers! The trench was really fascinating. The guide was very helpful, he answered a lot of questions that furthered my knowledge of WWI."

Unfortunately, the only memorial museum complex in the United States devoted solely to the remembrance of WWI was closed from 1994 until the year 2001. In early November of 1994, the Kansas City, Missouri, Board of Parks and Recreation Commissioners was obliged to close the Liberty Memorial to the general public because of reasons of safety.

At the time of its closing, the memorial awaited extensive restoration and if it were possible for Lord Halifax to return, he and millions of others could not visit the memorial. Its massive courtyards and stairways could not be walked on due to the deterioration of the support system which holds the main courtyard 40 feet above the ground. The problem was as follows: serious deterioration of a concrete deck that is a major feature of the memorial complex plus other physical problems. The Memorial Tower and Museum Buildings remained structurally sound. In October, 1977 the estimated cost of renovation and expansion was $60 million.

The fund-raising campaign was underway for several years and local, state, national and international support were called upon. Individual donations have ranged from $1 to $2,000,000. Legislation was introduced in the Missouri House of Representatives and Senate for potentially $5 million to $7 million in state funds. The voters passed a referendum in 1997 imposing a 0.5cent sales tax on the citizens to pay for restoring the memorial. The restoration work was begun in 1999 and, except for building out a new museum, has been completed.

Even though the main museum was closed to the general public, all other museum operations continued. These included the acquisition and preservation of all types of WWI artifacts and historical materials, research, outreach educational programs, lending to special exhibits at other institutions and restoration of large objects. Restoration has replaced these and addressed a number of other physical issues of the memorial structure. An architectural/engineering firm is worked on the restoration project which included an expansion of the museum facilities, with a potential for a tenfold increase in exhibit, storage, library and educational space. The restoration project allowed for a long-awaited expansion of the museum facility and increased the exhibit space from 5,000 to 42,000 square feet. Previous space limitations allowed only about ten percent of the museum collection to be on exhibit at any one time.

The museum has provided technical support for the HBO production on the life of Harry S. Truman (Captain, 129th Field Artillery) and for KCET-TV in Los Angeles and ABC News on series productions.

The Library and Museum are still available to outside researchers by appointment. The Museum is operating two off-site museum annexes, available to the general public six days a week, at the Town Pavilion, 12 and Main, and at the Ward Parkway Center, 8600 Ward Parkway, both in Kansas City, Missouri.

The Liberty Memorial Association, a non-profit organization and long standing member of the Western Front Association, has established a restoration fund. The Liberty Memorial Museum very much appreciates financial donations, as well as gifts of archival materials and artifacts associated with World War I.

The importance of the restoration of the Liberty Memorial was perhaps best expressed by General John J. Pershing, Commander of the American Expeditionary Forces in World War One:

"This memorial also symbolizes the obligation that rests upon present and future generations to preserve that for which those men and women offered their all, and from many of whom the supreme sacrifice was accepted. May their memory live on, and may every American who looks upon this noble edifice be inspired by their devotion."

The Liberty Memorial is located on Memorial Drive, in Kansas City, Missouri by Penn Valley Park, south of Pershing, west of Crown Center, between Main and Kessler Boulevard.

Persons wishing to learn more about the museum or contribute historical objects, photographs, artwork and the like can write or forward their materials to:

> The Liberty Memorial Museum of World War One
> 100 W. 26th Street
> Kansas City, MO 64108-4616 U.S.A.
> (816) 221-1918

Monetary donations for the Liberty Memorial Restoration and Museum Expansion may be sent to:

> The Liberty Memorial Fund
> Citizens to Save Liberty Memorial
> 6601 Swope Parkway
> Kansas City, Missouri 64132 USA
> **(703) 780-5660**

The Liberty Memorial was rededicated and reopened on Memorial Day weekend in 2002. Thousands of people, largely from the local area, participated in the weekend activities which began Friday night and ended Monday.

In 2004, the Liberty Memorial Museum was designated by the United States Congress as being the official American World War I Museum.

THE WESTERN FRONT ASSOCIATION

"The Western Front Association (WFA) was originally founded in 1980 with the aim of furthering interest in World War I, and to perpetuate the memory, courage and comradeship of both sides who served their countries on both sides of the battlefront and at home. The Association is non-political and does not seek to glorify war, only learn from it. The Association is not a re-enactment society nor is it commercially motivated. Application for membership will be welcomed from anyone with like mind." (WFA Constitution).

Membership of the WFA is approximately 9,000 worldwide, with most members living in the UK. Because of this concentration the WFA has a very strong chapter network. Currently, there are 33 branches in the United Kingdom, as well as branches in the Republic of Ireland, France, Germany, Luxembourg, the United States of America, Canada and Australia and associations affiliated with the WFA in The Netherlands and Belgium. The U.S. Branch offers two types of membership: (1) Membership in the WFA and (2) Friends of the WFA. Most members in the U.S. hold both types of membership.

(1) Membership in the WFA entitles you to three issues of *Stand To!* and three issues of the WFA Bulletin each year. *Stand To!*, the well-respected British journal of the WFA, is devoted solely to WWI materials. It contains articles, photographs submitted by Association members and outside WWI authorities, as well as firsthand accounts, photographs, and previously unpublished materials written during the war, the 1920 era, and just recently. The WFA Bulletin, also a British publication, contains reports of WFA Branch activities worldwide as well as articles and photos on WWI and the Western Front battlefields today. For both publications, the large number of British members results in a heavy British emphasis. Both publications recognize this fact, and are welcoming articles that deal with participation in the Great War by belligerents other than England and other UK members.

U.S. members also receive a journal, *Camaraderie*, with articles on WWI-era history, and a newsletter, *The Field Memo*, with news of Association and other programs related to the study of WWI.

Members are invited to contribute articles, poetry and photographs to all these publications.

Many members of the WFA are historians and researchers with a great knowledge of the larger issues of the war.

Members are also eligible to purchase trench and aerial maps and other commodities from the WFA and to participate in elections as prescribed by the WFA Constitution. There is an annual membership fee of $40.00 ($60.00 for air mail delivery). This money does not support the U.S. Branch. The entire amount is forwarded to the WFA in the United Kingdom.

The U.S. Branch of the WFA was founded in 1990, chartered as a non-profit, membership corporation in 1991, and recognized by the IRS as a tax-exempt 501(c)(3) educational organization in 1992. The U.S. Branch has no paid employees and is administered by a volunteer Board of Directors. It has grown very quickly with members residing in 43 states. It has a schedule of regional conferences on the East Coast, its own newsletter, and annual weekend seminars. Three day conferences have been held in Stanford and San Francisco, CA; Arlington, VA; and near Chicago, IL.

The United States Branch sponsors an annual weekend seminar at major American museum or university. Previous national seminars have been held at West Point and the U.S. Air Force Museum. Regional chapters in various parts of the country offer shorter seminars throughout the year. Seminars feature knowledgeable speakers on various aspects of WWI including diplomacy, tactics, weapons and strategy, battlefield commanders, social, spiritual, political and literary matters, as well as tours of museums and WWI exhibits, documentary and feature films about World War I.

(2) Friends of the WFA receive three editions of the U.S. Branch newsletter Camaraderie, which describes the activities of the U.S. Branch and its Chapters and contains other WFA-WWI material. Members also receive a Membership Directory and advance notices announcing regional Chapter meetings and the Annual Seminar. There are currently five chapters in the U.S.A.; the New England/New York Chapter, which meets periodically at various locations, the East Coast Chapter (although membership in the U.S. Branch is spread throughout the country), which meets regularly at Aberdeen, Maryland, Florida, the Midwest and Tennessee-Kentucky.

(3) Tours. Our branches and affiliates in the U.S., England and Europe sponsor several Western and Italian Front excursions, as well as tours to Gallipoli each year.

A yearly $10 fee (to cover publication and mailing of U.S. Branch materials) will insure that Friends of the WFA receive Camaraderie and all other publications of the U.S. Branch.

Memberships are due by November 11 and extend to November 10 of the following year. Memberships initiated after May 1 and 1/2 of the yearly amounts. For further information, contact:

The Western Front Association
P.O. Box 367
Fruitland, Maryland 21826

President: Thomas J. Johnson, 2213 W. Admiral Drive, Virginia Beach, VA 23451. Tel. (757) – 496-9614. E-mail: tjjohnson59@aol.com

Secretary-Treasurer: Dr. Joseph Liggera, 96 College Avenue, Poughkeepsie, New York, 12603, USA. e-mail: gagin1@aol.com

United States, East Coast Chapter: Chairman: Paul Cora, 204 East Joppa Rd., Apt. 916, Towson, MD 21286-3133. E-mail: pbcora@earthlink.net

United States, New York/New England Chapter: Chairman: Mrs. Lanayre D. Liggera, 96 College Avenue, Poughkeepsie, New York 12603, USA

United States, Pacific Coasts Branch (Canada-United States): Chairman: L. Jack Patten, 2-6325 Metral Drive, Nanaimo BC V9T 2L9 Canada. E-mail: c-s-r@shaw.ca

United States, Florida-Gulf Coast Chapter: Chairman: Hon. Leonard Shurtleff, 6915 NW 49th Street, Gainsville, FL 32653-1152. E-mail: lshurtleff@aol.com

Visit the Association website at: www.wfa-usa.org for up-to-date program information.

AEF FACTS AND FIGURES TO ACCOMPANY THIS BOOK

WAR CASUALTIES

The number of combat deaths in World War I exceeded by far those of any other war before World War II, in which ten million men of the armed forces perished on the battlefields. Of the major combatants, Russia lost two million, Austria-Hungary and France lost 1.4 million each, Germany 1.7 million, and the British Empire one million. That is seven and a half million. The remainder of the dead were primarily from the Ottoman Empire, Serbia, Italy, Romania, and Bulgaria. Civilian deaths from military action, massacre, starvation, and exposure in the war from 1914 to 1918 are estimated at 12,618,000.

WORLD WAR I—American War Casualties by States and Territories

State or Territory	Total Casualties	Killed or Died
Alabama	5,160	1,251
Alaska	15	6
Arizona	557	150
Arkansas	2,658	883
California	6,650	1,747
Canal Zone	3	2
Colorado	1,759	537
Connecticut	6,625	1,265
Delaware	303	87
District of Columbia	773	202
Florida	1,171	467
Georgia	4,425	1,530
Hawaii	13	4
Idaho	1,351	409
Illinois	18,264	4,260
Indiana	5,766	1,510
Iowa	7,311	2,161
Kansas	5,182	1,270
Kentucky	5,380	1,436
Louisiana	2,160	823
Maine	2,090	518
Maryland	3,812	975
Massachusetts	13,505	2,955
Michigan	10,369	2,751
Minnesota	7,323	2,133
Mississippi	2,303	904
Missouri	10,385	2,562
Montana	3,433	934
Nebraska	3,041	855
Nevada	250	71
New Hampshire	1,535	358
New Jersey	10,166	2,367
New Mexico	860	228
New York	40,222	9,196
North Carolina	5,799	1,610
North Dakota	2,560	700
Ohio	16,007	4,082
Oklahoma	6,358	1,471
Oregon	1,577	512
Pennsylvania	35,042	7,898
Philippines	7	3
Puerto Rico	11	1
Rhode Island	1,562	355
South Carolina	3,919	1,138
South Dakota	1,867	554
Tennessee	6,190	1,836
Texas	10,133	2,722
Utah	1,006	302
Vermont	1,170	300
Virginia	6,130	1,635
Washington	3,070	877
West Virginia	4,018	1,063
Wisconsin	9,813	2,649
Wyoming		233

AMERICAN ARMY CASUALTIES IN WORLD WAR I

Cause of Death	Overseas	Domestic	Total
Killed in action	36,926	5	36,931
Died of wounds received in action	13,628	45	13,673
Died of disease	23,853	38,815	62,668
Died of accident	2,557	1,946	4,503
Drowned	328	399	727

Committed suicide	296	671	967
Murdered	159	159	318
Executed	11	25	36
Died of other causes	131	190	321
Total	77,889	42,255	120,144
Total wounded	198,059		
Grand total, died and wounded	275,948	42,255	318,203

The number of Americans who died in World War I is over 100,0000 only if you count those who died of disease and other non-combat related caused in the United States, as well as in Europe.

MISCELLANEOUS FACTS CONCERNING THE AMERICAN EXPEDITIONARY FORCES

Of a total of 43 divisions, 29 saw combat.

Two out of every three American soldiers who reached France took part in battle. Of the 2,084,000 soldiers who went to France, 1,390,000 saw front line service.

Of the 43 AEF divisions which reached France, twenty-nine of them saw combat service. Seven were Regular Army divisions, eleven were National Guard divisions, and eleven were National Army (drafted) divisions.

American divisions were in battle for 200 days and they engaged in thirteen major operations.

From mid-August until the end of the war the American divisions held during the greater period of time a front line longer than that held by the British Army.

In October of 1918 the American divisions held 101 miles of front line or 23% of the entire Western Front.

On 1 April 1918 Germany had a superiority of 324,000 in rifle strength. Due to American arrivals, the allied strength exceeded that of the Germans in June and was more than 600,000 above it in November of 1918.

In the St. Mihiel battle, 550,000 Americans were engaged as compared with 100,000 on the Northern (Union) side in the Battle of Gettysburg. At St. Mihiel the artillery fired more than one million shells in four hours, which was the most intense concentration of artillery fire recorded in history up to that time.

1,200,000 American troops were engaged in the 47-day Meuse–Argonne campaign.

World War I cost the United States more than one million dollars an hour for over two years.

The direct cost of the war to the United States was $22 billion, or enough to pay the entire cost of running the American government from 1791 up to the outbreak of World War II.

American financial expenditure was enough to have conducted the War of the American Revolution continuously for one thousand years.

The first three months of the war cost $2 million a day. The next year of the war cost $22 million a day. The last ten months of the war (April 1916–1919) cost $44 million per day.

MILES OF WESTERN FRONT OCCUPIED BY AMERICAN AND ALLIED FORCES IN 1918

Date (1918)	American	British	French[1]	Belgian	Total
Jan. 31	6	116	323	23	468
Mar. 20	17	116	312	23	468
Mar. 30	19	92	353	23	487
Apr. 10	31	92	348	23	494
Apr. 30	34	83	358	23	498
May 30	23	83	393	23	522
June 10	36	83	389	23	531
June 20	65	83	360	23	531
July 10	62	92	354	23	531
July 20	55	92	362	23	532
July 30	68	92	318	23	501
Aug. 10	79	93	276	23	477
Aug. 30	90	87	262	23	462
Sept. 10	98	87	241	23	449
Sept. 30	82	83	258	28	451
Oct. 10	101	83	244	15	443
Oct. 30	79	68	248	15	410
Nov. 11	83	70	214	25	392

[1] The section of the front which were held by Italian and Portuguese divisions are included with French.

Maximum number of miles of front line held at one time by American units: 101 miles on October 10, 1918.

Total length of the Western Front:

Oct. 1917	468 miles.
July 17, 1918	532 miles.

Maximum number of American divisions that saw action during any one week: 29 during second week of October 1918.

Approximate average actual strength of the various combat divisions on the Western Front During year 1918:

American.......................... 25,000
British.......................... 11,800
French.......................... 11,400
German.......................... 12,300

Greatest number of Americans who arrived in Europe during any single month: 313,410 during the month of July, 1918.

Cumulative arrivals in Europe of American military personnel for the A.E.F.:

By May 31, 1917.................... 1,308
By June 30, 1917.................... 16,220
By July 31, 1917.................... 20,120
By Aug. 31, 1917.................... 39,383
By Sept. 30, 1917.................... 61,927
By Oct. 31, 1917.................... 92,265
By Nov. 30, 1917.................... 129,623
By Dec. 31, 1917.................... 183,896
By Jan. 31, 1918.................... 224,655
By Feb. 28, 1918.................... 254,378
By Mar. 31, 1918.................... 329,005
By Apr. 30, 1918.................... 434,081
By May 31, 1918.................... 667,119
By June 30, 1918.................... 897,293
By July 31, 1918.................... 1,210,703
By Aug. 31, 1918.................... 1,473,190
By Sept. 30, 1918.................... 1,783,955
By Oct. 30, 1918.................... 1,986,618
By Nov. 11, 1918.................... 2,057,675

Actual combat strength of the A.E.F.:

Mar. 21, 1918.................... 162,482
May 27, 1918.................... 406,844
Aug. 10, 1918.................... 822,358
Sept. 12, 1918.................... 999,602
Oct. 12, 1918.................... 1,078,190
Nov. 11, 1918.................... 1,078,222

These figures include only combat troops and exclude the troops in the S.O.S., headquarters, schools, hospitals, liaison service and other special services.

Combat strength of the A.E.F. by branch of service at the time of the Armistice:

Infantry and M.G. Battalions....................................... 646,000
Engineers.. 81,600
Signal Corps.. 21,300
Air Service... 34,800
Artillery.. 278,500
Tank Corps... 10,200
Amm. Trains, Q.M., etc... 70,800
Medical Department[1] 152,300
Cavalry... 6,000
Ordnance[1].. 22,900

[1] Including those on duty in the Services of Supply

Total Strength of the A.E.F. on Nov. 11:
Its total strength was 1,981,701 in which were included 32,835 marines.

Number of civilians employed by the A.E.F.:
42,644 at the time of the Armistice.

Greatest number of American soldiers in hospitals in Europe at any one time: 190,564 men on November 7, 1918.

Percentage of total strength in various branches of the A.E.F., Nov. 1918:

	Officers % of total	Enlisted men % of total
Infantry	21.83	32.4
Engineers	8.69	12.68
Field Artillery	10.91	11.18
Casuals (all branches	3.39	10.81
Medical Dept. (Army)	18.46	7.26
Quartermaster Corps	6.33	7.16
Coast Artillery Corps	4.00	3.78
Air Service	7.30	3.11
Ammunition Trains	1.47	2.48

Signal Corps	1.63	1.83
Supply Trains	1.02	1.61
Ordnance Department	1.53	1.16
Marines	0.75	0.96
Headquarters Troops	0.21	0.78
Military Police	0.49	0.67
Hdqrs. Detachments	0.00	0.55
Tank Corps	0.91	0.50
Cavalry	0.25	0.29
Postal Express Service	0.15	0.15
Medical Dept. (Navy	0.07	0.02
G.H.Q. and General Staff	8.49	0.00

Provisions for hospitalization in A.E.F.:

On November 11, 1918, there were 192,844 normal beds, which could have been increased in an emergency to 276,547. There were 153 base hospitals, 66 camp hospitals, 12 convalescent camps, 21 hospital trains and 6,875 ambulances.

A BRIEF NOTE ON MILITARY TERMS

Squad (American) A basic unit of organization, consisting normally of a corporal and seven privates. A general term for various small groups.

Platoon (Ameican) One of the elements of a company. A platoon is a unit of about 40 soldiers and is commanded by a lieutenant, either a second lieutenant (who wears a gold bar) or a first lieutenant (silver bar). World War strength about 50 men.

Company (Infantry, American) A company—called a troop in the cavalry—consists of four platoons and is usually commanded by a captain (two silver bars). World War strength 256 officers and men.

Battalion (Infantry, American) A tactical unit consisting of a headquarters and four rifle companies. A battalion—called a squadron in the cavalry—consists of four companies (or troops), and is under the command of a major (who wears a gold leaf) or a lieutenant colonel (silver leaf). Total World War strength 1,027 officers and men.

Regiment (Infantry, American) An organization, composed, during the World War, of a headquarters, three battalions (or squadrons), a headquarters company, a supply company, and a machine gun company. A regiment is commanded by a lieutenant colonel or a colonel (silver eagle). Strength 3,770 combatants.

Brigade (Infantry, American) An organization consisting of a headquarters, two infantry regiments and a machine gun battalion. A brigade is commanded by a colonel or a brigadier general (whose insignia of rank is one star). World War strength 8,324 combatants; 6459 rifles.

Brigade (Field Artillery, American) An organization comprising a headquarters, two regiments of 75-mm. guns, one regiment of 155-mm. howitzers, and one six inch trench mortar battery. Under the normal command of a brigadier general. World War strength 4,908 combatants and 48 guns, 24 howitzers and 12 trench mortars.

Division (Infantry, American) Two brigades of infantry and one brigade of artillery. It contained also engineer, machine gun, signal, medical and transportation units and a headquarters. World War strength 28,105 officers and men; 16,193 rifles. A division commander is usually a major general (two stars).

Corps (American) A tactical unit normally made up of a headquarters, two or more divisions and auxiliary troops. A corps is commanded by a major general or a lieutenant general (three stars).

Army (American) An army, sometimes called a field army, contains two or more corps and is under a lieutenant general or a general (four stars).

In the early part of the 20th century, the U.S. Army was headed by the Secretary of War who was a member of the President's cabinet and who advised the President on military matters. The War Department, located in Washington, D.C., consisted of civilians and military men who assisted the Secretary. The top man in uniform was the Army Chief of Staff, who was the principal military adviser of the Secretary of War.

The Chief of Staff presided over the General and Special Staff Sections, each of which was headed by an officer who was responsible for a specific function, for example, Personnel, Intelligence, Plans and Operations, Supplies, Ordnance, and the like.

Third Regulars. Actions: Chateau-Thierry, Marne defense, Marne-Vesle offensive, Cunel and the Meuse. Casualties 18,154. Captured 2,240 infantry and 51 pieces of artillery. Advanced 41 kilometers under fire.

The 3rd Inf. Div. (RA) was organized November 1917 at Camp Greene, S.C. Cited for the Battle of the Marne for stopping the last German offensive near Paris, the Division suffered 7,000 battle casualties in three days on the Marne River. The Division participated in six campaigns in WW I, and sustained 16,856 battle casualties in a little over six months of combat.

THE U.S. THIRD DIVISION

U. S. THIRD DIVISION CASUALTIES

In its four battle campaigns during World War I (Aisne; Aisne–Marne, St. Mihiel, Meuse–Argonne), the U. S. Third Division suffered 3,401 soldiers killed in action, 12,000 soldiers wounded in action, for a total of 15,401 battle casualties.

3ᴰ DIVISION, A.E.F.

May 30–June 5, 1918

DIVISION HEADQUARTERS

Division Commander – Maj. Gen. Joseph T. Dickman
Chief of Staff – Lt. Col. Raymond Shelton, Jr.

5ᵗʰ INFANTRY BRIGADE	6ᵗʰ INFANTRY BRIGADE
Brig. Gen. Fred W. Sladen	Brig. Gen. Charles Crawford
4ᵗʰ Infantry	*30ᵗʰ Infantry*
Col. Halstead Dorey	Col. Edmund L. Butts
7ᵗʰ Infantry	*38ᵗʰ Infantry*
Col. Thomas M. Anderson, Jr.	Col. Ulysses G. McAlexander
8ᵗʰ Machine Gun Battalion	*9ᵗʰ Machine Gun Battalion*
Maj. L. W. T. Waller, U.S.M.C.	Maj. David H. Scott

ORGANIZATIONS

5ᵗʰ Infantry Brigade–4ᵗʰ and 7ᵗʰ Regiments
6ᵗʰ Infantry Brigade–30ᵗʰ and 38ᵗʰ Regiments
7ᵗʰ, 8ᵗʰ and 9ᵗʰ Machine-Gun Battalions
3ʳᵈ Field Artillery Brigade–10ᵗʰ, 76ᵗʰ, 18ᵗʰ Artillery Regiments.
3ʳᵈ Trench Mortar Battery.
6ᵗʰ Engineer Regiment and Train.
5ᵗʰ Field Signal Battalion.
3ʳᵈ Train Headquarters and Military Police
3ʳᵈ Ammunition Train.
3ʳᵈ Supply Train
3ʳᵈ Sanitary Train–5ᵗʰ, 7ᵗʰ, 26ᵗʰ and 27ᵗʰ Ambulance Companies and Field Hospitals.

COMBAT AWARDS

Units	Battle Credits (Casualties)	Individual Awards
4ᵗʰ Inf	Aisne, Champagne (16,450)	Medal of Honor–2
7ᵗʰ Inf	Champagne–Marne	Distinguished Service Medal–3
30ᵗʰ Inf	Aisne-Marne,	Distinguished Service Cross–266
38ᵗʰ Inf	St. Mihiel,	French Croix de Guerre–143
10ᵗʰ FA	Meuse-Argonne	
18ᵗʰ FA		
76ᵗʰ FA		
8ᵗʰ MG Bn		
9ᵗʰ MG Bn		
7ᵗʰ MG Bn		
6ᵗʰ Eng		

The 3ᵈ Division participated in the Champagne–Marne defensive and the Aisne–Marne, St. Mihiel, and Meuse–Argonne offensives. After the armistice on November 11, 1918, the Division undertook occupation duty in the vicinity of Coblenz, along the Rhine River, where it remained until August 1919.

Roster Of Officers

May 1918–November 1918

7ᵗʰ Machine Gun Battalion, 3ʳᵈ Division, AEF
AISNE–MARNE DEFENSIVE

31ˢᵗ May to 4ᵗʰ June, 1918

Major Edward G. Taylor	1ˢᵗ Lt. Erskine J. Hoover
Captain John O. Mendenhall	1ˢᵗ Lt. Ray W. Vail
Captain Lloyd H. Cook	1ˢᵗ Lt. Arthur B. McCormack
Captain Charles F. Houghton	2ⁿᵈ Lt. Frank Cagle
Captain James F. Arthur	2ⁿᵈ Lt. Herbert D. Bowman
1ˢᵗ Lt. Francis F. Patton	2ⁿᵈ Lt. Elias Lyman, Jr.
1ˢᵗ Lt. John T. Bissell	2ⁿᵈ Lt. Paul T. Funkhouser
1ˢᵗ Lt. DeWitt S. Hose	2ⁿᵈ Lt. Luther W. Cobbey
1ˢᵗ Lt. John H. Ransdell	2ⁿᵈ Lt. Selden K. Griffin
1ˢᵗ Lt. Chas. Montgomery, Jr.	2ⁿᵈ Lt. Joseph G. Hanus
***1ˢᵗ Lt. Thomas W. Goddard	2ⁿᵈ Lt. Oliver H. Dickerhoof

GERMAN UNITS OPPOSING U. S. 3RD DIVISION, A.E.F.

(May 30–June 5).

The German Units Concerned: 28th Infantry Division occupies north bank of the Marne between Barzy and Dormans. 231st Infantry Division attacks Château-Thierry and Height 204, capturing Château-Thierry. 36th Infantry Division takes over sector of 28th Infantry Division from Barzy to Tréloupe. Bridgehead at Jaulgonne captured by Americans and French. IV Reserve Corps suspends execution of general attack and organizes for defense.

IV RESERVE CORPS (Seventh Army)

Commander:	Richard v. Conta, General of Infantry
Chief of Staff:	Mooyer, Major, G.S.
Composition:	5th Guard Inf. Div. and 197th, 237th, 10th, 28th, 87th, 231st, 201st, and 36th Infantry Divisions

DIVISIONS IN CONTACT WITH 3D DIVISION, A.E.F.:

28th Infantry Division (relieved June 3, by 36th Infantry Division):

Commander:	v. Arnim, Lieut. General, to June 3.
	Böhm, Major General, from June 4.
1st Gen. Staff Off.:	Schmidt, Captain, G.S.
55th Inf. Brig.:	Böhm, Major General, comdg. to June 3.
	v. Selle, Colonel, comdg. from June 4.
40th Fusilier Regt.:	Girschner, Major, comdg.
109th Body Gren. Regt.:	Baron v. Forstner, Lieut. Col, comdg.

Order Of Battle

July 15, 1918

(from west to east)

FRENCH SIXTH ARMY:

Commander	General Degoutte
Chief of Staff	Colonel Brion
French II Corps: Commander	General Philipot

Fr. 33d Div.–Fr. 2d Div.–Fr. 168th Div.

French VII Corps: Commander	General Massenet

Fr. 47th Div.–Fr. 164th Div.–Fr. 4th Div.

American I Corps: Commander	General Ligget

Fr. 167th Div.–Amer. 26th Div.–Amer. 2d Div.

French XXXVIII Corps: Commander General Debene

Fr. 39th Div.–Amer. 3d Div.–½ Amer. 28th Div., French 73d Div

French III Corps: Commander	General Lebrun

Fr. 125th Div.–Fr. 51st Div.–½ Amer. 28th Div.–Fr. 20th Div.

FRENCH FIFTH ARMY:

Commander–General Berthelot

Chief of Staff–Colonel Bellague

(Since no American units were assigned to the Fifth Army, its composition is omitted here)

FRENCH FOURTH ARMY:

Commander–General Gourand

Chief of Staff–Lieutenant Colonel Pettelot

French IV Corps: Commander–General Pont

Fr. 163d Div.–Fr. 124th Div.–Fr. 132d Div.–Fr. 71st Div.–Fr. 27th Div.

French XXI Corps: Commander–General Naulin

Fr. 170th Div.–Fr. 13th Div.–Fr. 43d Div.–Amer. 42d Div.–Fr. 46th Div.

French VIII Corps: Commander–General Hély d' Oissel

Fr. 161st Div.–Fr. 16th Div.–Fr. 1st D. C. P.–Fr. 4th Algerian Regt.–Fr. 2d Moroccan Regt.–Amer. 369th Regt.

GERMAN ORDER OF BATTLE

German Ninth Army: Commander–F. von Below

German First Army: Commander–von Mudra

German Third Army: Commander–von Euiem

THE 3RD DIVISION INSIGNIA

Description of Insignia. The Division insignia consists of three diagonal stripes 5/16" wide and 5/16" apart, superimposed diagonally upon a dark blue field 2¼" square. When sewed on the left shoulder even with the seam, as prescribed in General Orders from G.H.Q., the three stripes should run from the upper rear corner downward to the front lower corner.

The clear field of blue stands for the loyalty, steadfastness and undying devotion to the principles of right and justice by the American soldier. The three clear cut white stripes stand dually, for the three operations up to the signing of the Armistice, of which the 3rd Division took part (Marne, St. Mihiel, and Meuse–Argonne), and for the numerical designation of the Division. One of the basic facts considered in the designing of the insignia was the striking appearance of any design that embodied the use of equal stripes as shown to the world by the flag of our country. The extreme simplicity of the design was a strong point in its favor, as it can be easily and correctly made by any member of the division, whereas a complicated design invariably deteriorates into caricature.

The idea of the insignia originated with Brigadier General Preston Brown, who was then in command of the Division while the division was in action in the Meuse–Argonne operation.

WHAT A DIVISION IS

There are undoubtedly many readers unfamiliar with military organization who will read this book. To help them understand just what a Division is, even a very brief description may be of value.

A full American World War I Infantry Division was, roughly speaking, composed of 28,000 men and was commanded by a Major-General. Included in this organization were two Infantry Brigades of two Infantry Regiments and one Machine Gun Battalion each, and an Artillery Brigade of three regiments, two lights (75's) and one heavy (6" Howitzer). Then there were, for their respective special duties, a regiment of Engineers, a battalion of Signal Troops, and a Divisional Machine Gun Battalion (motorized). Each brigade had its headquarters, consisting of the Brigadier-General commanding, and the personnel of his staff and assistants. The Division Headquarters Staff numbered about 50 officers and 126 men. To complete the division, add the Headquarters Troop, Train Headquarters, Military Police Company, Supply, Sanitary, Engineer and Ammunition Trains, the Mobile Ordnance Repair Shops, Mobile Veterinary Section, Division Salvage Squad, Railhead Unit, Clothing and Bathing Unit, Mobile Field Laboratory, Sales Commissary, Machine Shop Truck Units, a Bakery Company, and a Laundry Company.

Each and every unit, whether combatant, or otherwise, had its own particular function and duties and its efficient operation and performance of duty was essential to the success of the Division as a whole.

The full strength of the American Infantry division varied between 27,000 and 28,256 officers and men, depending upon various changes made from time to time in the Table of Organization. Due to casualties and the failure to send sufficient replacements promptly to the Divisions at the front the average strength of these American Infantry Divisions from the beginning of the July 18 attack to the armistice was 23,709 men and officers. For this same time period the average strength of the French Division was 10,300, the average British division, except some of the Colonial ones which were maintained at a greater strength, was 10,500, while he average German one was 10,000. Towards the last, German divisions had to be broken up to maintain this strength in the remaining divisions. Even then in the last stage of the war some of them fell well below this average.

The American division had 12 Infantry Rifle Battalions, the French 9, the average British 9 and the German 9. The American had 3 Machine Gun Battalions plus 4 Regimental Machine Gun Companies, the French 9 Machine Gun Companies, the average British 1 Machine Gun Battalion, and the German 9 Machine Gun Companies. The American had 48–75 mm. guns, the French 36, the average British 36–18 pounders, and the Germans 24–77 mm. The Americans had 24–155 mm., the French 12, the average British 12–4.5 inch, and the German 12–105 mm.

The American Infantry Armament included 960 automatic rifles, as against 400 for the division of each of the other countries.

DISCUSSION OF A SALIENT

In Herbert H. Sargent's book, *The Strategy on the Western Front (1914–1918)*, Chicago: McClurg, 1920, pp. 51–5, is the following discussion of a salient:

"A salient is vulnerable; its weak points strategically are the sectors on each side of it near its base; because an attack in force there by threatening the communications of the occupying troops, would, if successful, force their retreat.

Then, too, any advantage of a central position—of interior lines—that may be possessed by troops occupying a salient, is overbalanced by the advantage which the enemy has of interior lines within the angular fronts on each side of the salient. To illustrate: Let the line ABCDE represent the front between the two opposing armies. Now if on account of their central position the troops occupying the salient BCD have an advantage of interior lines, it must be evident that such an advantage is more than counterbalanced by the advantage of interior lines possessed by the opposing troops occupying the angles or counter-salients ABC and CDE.

<pre>
                    C
    French   French

    A   B...........D   E
            Germans
</pre>

But as a matter of fact, where a salient is small, or is well-filled with troops, there is no strategical advantage for troops occupying it; on the contrary, there is a great strategical disadvantage, first, because they have a too-limited space to maneuver in; and secondly, because they are subject to a converging fire from the enemy occupying the counter-salients. Troops within a salient are not infrequently so situated that long-range guns from one or the other side of it can enfilade or take them in reverse.

Then, too, the numerous roads and railways within a salient, though absolutely necessary for the movement of men and supplies, are strategically a source of weakness to the occupying troops, principally because they can be fired upon from many angles and often be enfiladed throughout long stretches by the guns of the troops occupying the counter-salients or by the guns at the nose of the salient. And the nature of the terrain, and position of the roads within a salient, of course, influence greatly the strategical situation of the occupying troops, but these are special cases which would call for a special analysis.

Then again, a salient is *per se* not only weak, but it weakens the whole front by greatly lengthening it, making it necessary, of course, to use many more troops to defend it. Thus the sides BC and CD would require more than twice the number of troops to defend them than would the base BD, which was the line of the original front. And of course when these salients are multiplied the strength of the front becomes much weakened since its length becomes proportionately greatly increased. But on the other hand, it should of course be borne in mind that the weakening is not confined to one side, since the front of the opposing army is correspondingly lengthened and likewise weakened.

It should, perhaps, be remarked here that the foregoing discussion of a salient has reference more particularly to what may be termed a strategical salient; that is to say, a salient large enough to include within it, roads, railways, and other means of communication, thus making it possible, and often practicable, for outside troops to make strategical and combinations against the troops occupying it. It is only in World War I that such salients were first developed; for the reason that it was the first war in which battle lines extended to such great lengths as to permit development of great salients. In former wars the salients have been small and, consequently, their weakness has been due almost solely to tactical considerations. Tactically, other things being equal, the weakness of the salient to troops occupying it is in the main part due to the mathematical fact that you can put more men and guns on the outside of an angle to shoot into it than you can put on the inside to fire out. This is the chief reason why the "Peach Orchard" salient at Gettysburg was a weak point in the Federal line; the "Bloody Angle" at Spottsylvania a weak point in the Confederate line; and the nose of the great strategical salient of Château-Thierry a weak point in the German line. Tactically, each of the great German salients was weak at its nose; strategically, each was weak at its bases.

Having pointed out the weakness of a salient to the troops occupying it, mention is made of the fact that the great attacks made by the Germans in March [1918] and subsequently, created three salients, known as the Amiens, Château-Thierry, and Ypres salients, which placed the Germans occupying them in precarious situations and gave to their adversaries an immense strategical advantage, which General (now Marshal) Foch had been taking full advantage of since he began his great counter-offensive against the Château-Thierry salient on July 18. And, mainly because of this advantage, the Allies have been, and still are, forcing back the Germans toward their original position, generally known as the Hindenburg Line.

But it should be evident to anyone that when they are driven back to that line and the salients ironed out, much greater difficulties will be encountered in forcing the Germans still farther back; and if the Allies should be successful in their great attack towards Amiens in March, 1918, a salient would be created which would place their troops occupying it in a very vulnerable and precarious situation and give to the Germans a great strategical advantage."

SELECT BIBLIOGRAPHY

The bibliography that follows is selective and reflects only those books and periodicals that contributed to the making of this one.

American Battlefields in France, First Section, General Staff (Visitor's Bureau) Headquarters, AEF, American Forces in France, 1918.

The Americans in the Great War, Michelin Illustrated Guides to the Battlefields (1914–1918), Volume I. The Second Battle of the Marne (Chateau-Thierry, Soissons, Fismes), 3 Volumes, (Michelin and Company, Clermond-Ferrand, France, 1920)

Berry, Henry. *Make the Kaiser Dance*. Garden City, NY: Doubleday & Co., 1978. Permission sought..

Both, W. C. *America's Army and its Part in the Great War.* Chicago: 1918

Boyd, Thomas, *Through the Wheat*, NY.: Scribner's, 1927, pp. 64 to 67. Paperback edition by Award Books, 1964. Reprinted 1978 by Southern University Press, Carbondale, ILL. Permission sought.

Brooks, Alden. *As I Saw It.* NY: 1929.

Bullard, Robert L., and Earl Reeves, *American Soldiers Also Fought*, NY.: Longmans, Green, 1936.

Carter, William A. *The Tale of a Devildog, by William A. Carter, One of Them.* Washington, DC: The Canteen Press, 1920. [2nd Division, AEF]

Catlin, Albertus Wright., and Dyer,Walter A. *With The Help of God and a Few Marines.* Garden City, NY: Doubleday, Page, 1919. [2nd Division, AEF].

Chatfield, Josiah C., et al. *Iodine and Gasoline, a History of the 117th Sanitary Train*, Kingsport, Tennessee: Kingsport Press, 1919.

Cobb, Irvin S. *Thte Glory of the Coming: What Mine Eyes Have Seen of Americans in Action.* NY: Doran, 1919.

Crawford, Charles. *Six Months with the Sixth Brigade.* Kansas City, MO: E. B. Barnett, 1928. Hereafter, Crawford, *Six Months with the Sixth Brigade.*

Derby, Richard. *Wade In Sanitary! The Story of a Division Surgeon in France.* NY: Putnam's, 1919.

Dickman, Joseph T., *The Great Crusade: A Narrative of the World War*, NY: D. Appleton Co., 1927

Evans, Frank E., *Daddy Pat of the Marines: Being His Letters from France to His Son Townie*, NY: Stokes,1919.

Ford, George B. *Out of the Ruins*, New York, The Century Co., 1919.

Forrest, Wilbur. *Behind the Front Page: Stories of Newspaper Stories in the Making.* NY: D. Appleton-Century Co., 1934

Gaines, Ruth L., *Helping France The Red Cross in the Devastated Area*, NY.: E.P. Dutton, 1919

Ganser, Elmer B., *History of the 126th Infantry in the War with Germany.* Grand Rapids, MI.: Dean Hicks, 1920

Gibbons, Floyd. *And They Thought We Wouldn't Fight!* NY: Doran, 1918.

Gulberg, Martin Gus. *A War Diary.* Chicago, ILL: Drake Press, 1927.

Harbord, James G. *A Month In Belleau Wood in 1918.* Detroit, MI: N.p.: 8 cols., 1928. Also in *Leatherneck*, v. 11, no 6 (Jun 1928): pp. 10–12, 54.

Hansen, Joseph Mills. *The Marne, Historic and Picturesque.* A. C. McClurg & Co., 1922.

Harbord, James G. Address by MajGen James G. Harbord before the Detroit Bond Club, February 22nd, 1928.

Harbord, James G., *Leaves From a War Diary*, NY: Dodd Mead and Co., 1925

Harbord, James G., *The American Army in France*, Boston: Little, Brown, 1936

Harper's Pictorial Library of the World War, Vol. X, "Deeds of Heroism and Darin," 1920.

Havlin, Arthur C. *The History of Company A, 102nd Machine Gun Battalion, 26th Division, A.E.F.* Boston, MA: H.C. Rodd, 1928.

Hemenway, Frederick V. *History of the Third Division, United States Army in the World War for the Period Dec. 1, 1917 to Jan. 1, 1919.* Third Division, U.S. Army. Germany: Andernach-on-Rhine, 1919. Printed in Cologne, Germany by M. Dumont Schauberg, 1919.

Hendricks, Charles, *Combat and Construction: U.S. Army Engineers in World War I*, U.S. Army Corps of Engineers, 1993.

History of Base Hospital No. 18, A.E.F. (Johns Hopkins Unit), Baltimore, MD: Base Hospital 18 Association, 1919. Thomas Ellis Co.

Hoffman, Robert C. *I Remember the Last War.* [111th Infantry Regiment, 28th Division, AEF]. York, PA: Strength & Health Publishing Co., 1940.

Hungerford, Edward. *With the Doughboys in France: A Few Chapters of the American Effort.* NY: Macmillan, 1920.

Jaffin, Jonathan H. *Medical Support for the American Expeditionary Forces in France During the First World War.* Fort Leavenworth, Kansas, 1990.

Kay, Ross. *With Pershing at the Front: American Soldiers in the Trenches.* NY: Barse & Hopkins, 1918.

Lavine, A. Lincoln., *Circuits of Victory*, NY.: Country Life Press, Doubleday Page & Co., Garden City, NY., 1921.

Lejeune, John A. *The Reminiscences of a Marine.* Philadelphia, PA: Dorrance, 1930.

Long, H. R. A letter describing the battle for Belleau Wood by Lieutenant H. R. Long, USMC, 6th Machine Gun Battalion, as originally published in the newspaper, "The Adirondack Enterprise," edition of 23 August 1918.

Mackin, Elton. *And Suddenly We Didn't Want To Die.* Novato, CA: Presidio Press, 1993. Used with permission.

Mitchell, Gen William A., *Memoirs of World War I: From Start to Finish of Our Greatest War*, Westport, CT.: Greenwood, 1975.

Morgan, Daniel E. *When the World Went Mad*. Boston: The Christopher Publishing House, 1922. 2nd Copyright by The Brass Hat, Pike, NH, 1993.

Morrey, Willard R. *The Ninth U.S. Infantry in the World War*. Germany: n. p., 1918.

Mudd, Thomas b.r. *The Yanks Were There: A Chronological and Documentary Review of World War One*. NY: Vantage, 1958.

Nolan, James B. *The Reading Militia in the Great War.* Reading, PA: F. A. Woerner, 1921. Palmer, Frederick. *Our Gallant Madness*. Garden City, NY: Doubleday, Doran, 1937.

Pattullo, George. *Horrors of Moonlight*. Allston & Depew, 1939.

Pierrefeu, Jean de. *French Headquarters 1915–1918*, Geoffrey Bles, Ltd., 1929.

Peixotto, Ernest. *The American Front*. Scribner's, 1919.

Pottle, Frederick A. *Strecchers: The Story of a Hospital Unit on The Western Front*. New Haven, CT: 1929.

Pottle, Frederick A. Per. *Outlook and Independent*, 9 Oct 1929, pp. 125, 196–7, "The Backwash of Battle."

Powis, Albert, Sr., "The Trenches at Verdun Through Belleau Woods," *The Torch*, September–October 1993. Permission sought.

Pugh, Irving E., & William F. Thayer. *Forgotten Fights of the A.E.F.* Boston: Roxborough Publishing Company, 1921

Richmond, Clarence L., *The War Diary of Clarence Richmond*, n.p., n.d. Used with permission of the diary owner and grandson of Clarence Richmond, Clarence Richmond, Jr. A copy of the original diary is at the Cleveland Public Library, Cleveland, Tennessee. The diary of Clarence Richmond was also serialized by his local newspaper, *The Cleveland Daily Banner*, in 1979.

Rickenbacker, Edward V. *Fighting the Flying Circus*, 1919, and Doubleday & Co., Garden City, NY: 1965

Robertson, Dean L., 79th Co., 6th Marines, MS diary of, typescript, unpublished, n.p., n.d., pp. 3, 4.

Scanlon, William. *God Have Mercy on Us: A Story Of 1918*. Boston, Houghton-Mifflin, 1929.

Sherwood, Elmer W., *Diary of a Rainbow Veteran: Written at the Front*, Terre-Haute, IN.: Moore-Langen, 1929.

Sinclair, Upton., *Jimmie Higgins: A Story*, NY.: Boni & Liveright, 1919.

Silverthorn, LtGen Merwin H., USMC (Ret), "A Brigade of Marines," *Marine Corps Gazette*, 55 (Nov 1971. Courtesy of *Marine Corps Gazette Magazine*.

Spaulding, Oliver Lyman., and Wright, John Womack. *The Second Division American Expeditionary Force in France: 1917–1918*. NY: Historical Committee of the Second Division Association: Hillman Press, 1937.

The Stars and Stripes; The Complete File of the Official Newspaper of the A.E.F., 1918–1919. NY: Arno, 1971.

Stonehouse, Frederick. "*Combat Engineer! The History of the 107th Engineer Battalion (1881–1961)*.

Story, Sommerville. *Present Day Paris and the Battlefields*. NY: D. Appleton & Co., 1920.

Strickland, Daniel W. *Connecticut Fights The Story of the 102nd Regiment, 26th Division*. New Haven, CT: Quinnipiack Press, 1930.

Strott, George George. *The Medical Department of the U.S. Navy with the Army and Marine Corps in France in World War I*. Navmed 1197. Washington, DC: U.S. Navy Department, Bureau of Medicine and Surgery, 1947.

Thomason, John W., Jr. *The Second Division Northwest of Château-Thierry, 1 June–10 July, 1918*. Washington, DC: National War College, 1928. Unpublished manuscript.

Townsend, Harry Everett, *War Diary of a Combat Artist: Captain Harry E. Townsend*, Alfred E. Cornebise, ed., University Press of Colorado. Hereafter, Townsend, *War Diary*.

U.S. Army. General Service Schools, Fort Leavenworth. *The German Offensive of July 15, 1918 (Marne Source Book)*. Fort Leavenworth, KS: The General Service Schools Press, 1923.

U.S. Army. 2nd Infantry Division. *Records of the Second Division (Regular)*. U.S. War Department. Army War College Historical Section, Washington, D.C., & Ft. Sam Houston, Texas. 1924–1928. Ten volumes(some in several parts). About 200 pages in each part. Also microfilm 05–2 1924/* 10 reels.

United States Surgeon General's Office, *The Medical Department of the United States Army in the World War*, 17 vols. USGPO, 1921–1929. Vol. VIII, Field Operations

Van Every, Dale. *The A.E.F. in Battle*. NY: Appleton, 1918.

The War Diary of the German 231st Infantry Division.

War Diary of the 94th Pursuit Squadron entitled, "The Hat in the Ring Gang.

Weaver, W.G. *History of the 8th Machine Gun Battalion*. Ann Arbor: Edwards Bros., 1965. [3rd Division, A.E.F.]

Wharton, James B. *Squad*. NY: Coward-McCann, 1928.

Wise, Frederick M., and Frost, Meigs O. *A Marine Tells It to You*. NY: J.H. Sears, 1929. Reprinted by The Marine Corps Assoc., Quantico, Va., 1981.

Wood, Peter P. *Diary of Lt. Peter P. Wood, USMC, 6th Machine Gun Battalion, 1917–1919*." Compiled and edited by David Sleeper, 2001. Used with permission.

Woolcott, Alexander. *A Friendly Guide for American Pilgrims to the Shrines Between the Marne and the Vesle*, Lafayette Publishing Company, Paris, 1919.

Woolcott, Alexander. *THE COMMAND is FORWARD–TALES of the A.E.F. BATTLEFIELDS as THEY APPEARED in the STARS and STRIPES*. NY: Century, 1919.

Wunderlich, Raymond. *From Trench and Dugout*. Stockton, CA: 1919.

PERIODICALS

Alphaud, Gabriel, *New York Times Current History Magazine,* "The Desecrated Birthplace of La Fontaine," Vol. 5, Oct 1916, pp. 54–6.

Canfield, Dorothy, *Harper's Monthly Magazine,* "Khaki Confidences at Château-Thierry," Vol. 137, No. 822, pp. 777 to 784.

Derby, Richard, "Wade in Sanitary!" *Scribner's Magazine,* September, 1919, Vol. 66, p. 342.

De Wissen, H., *Forum,* "Seeing Battle-Scarred Europe," Vol. 64, July 1920, page 43.

Indianapolis News, "Funkhouser Memorial," Nov 1, 1919 pp. 138–146.

Gibbons, H. A., *Harper's Magazine,* "An Ancient Village on the Marne," Vol. 132, April 1916, pp. 674–84.

Gibbs, Lacey, Excerpt from the diary of Lacey Gibbs, *The Doughboy,* Fall, 1981, Vol. 4, No. 2., as submitted by Denis Gordon. Used with permission.

Holt, Hamilton. *Independent,* "Where America Turned the Tide," issue of 24 May 1919.

James, Edwin L. *The New York Times Current History Magazine,* "America's Part in a Historic Battle," Vol. 8, pt. 2, September, 1918, pp. 402–3, and 492–3.

Kelton, Col. Robert H. C., *Century Magazine,* "The Miracle of Chateau-Thierry," May, 1919, page 99.

Krulewitch, MajGen M. L., "Belleau Wood," *Marine Corps Gazette,* Vol. 55 (Nov 1971). Used with permission.

Odell, Joseph H. *The Outlook,* "The Battle of Château-Thierry and Beyond," Sep. 11, 1918, Vol. 120, pp. 51–2.

Pottle, Frederick A., *Outlook and Independent,* "The Backwash of Battle," 9 Oct 1929, pp. 125, 196–7.

Scidmore, Eliza R., *The Outlook,* "In the War-Swept Marne Country," Wednesday, 26 June, 1918, pp. 342–3.

Silverthorn, LtGen Merwin H., USMC (Ret), "A Brigade of Marines," *Marine Corps Gazette,* Vol. 55 (Nov 1971). Used with permission.

Webster, James J. *The Watch on the Rhine,* publication of the Society of the Third Infantry Division, issue of February, 2002, under "Memoirs of World War I," page 23.

The Literary Digest, "Château-Thierry Now Has a Place in American History," Vol. 58, August 10, 1918, pp. 49, 50.

The Literary Digest, Vol. 58, Sept. 14, 1918, p. 29, "The American Chateau-Thierry."

Collier's, "Emptying the Bag: Part III of "On the German Heels," 30 November 1918, pp. 9,10.

Literary Digest, "The Festive Rubberneck Wagon in France's Battle-Fields." Vol. 67, Nov 27, 1920, p.65.

Literary Digest, "They Used to Call It the Front," Vol. 69, April 23, 1921, pp. 45–6.

Literary Digest, Vol. 72, Feb 11, 1922, p. 38, "France's Devastated Areas, Yesterday and To-Day." See also: Ford, George B. *Out of the Ruins,* New York, Century Co., 1919, pp. 29–30, 32.

New York Times Current History Magazine, "American Defense of Château-Thierry," Vol. 8, pt. 2, July, 1918, pp. 62 to 65.

Literary Digest, "Father O'Reilly Tells of the Work of the Third in France." Sept. 13, 1919, page 93.

AFTERWORD

The author appeals to all readers of this book to propose any constructive suggestions, or to provide additional materials that will help to make this a more useful and better guidebook for battlefield travelers. Such suggestions should be addressed in care of the publisher.

INDEX

NOTES TO SECTION TWO

1. Pottle, Frederick A. *Stretchers: The Story of a Hospital Unit on The Western Front:* New Haven, CT: 1929. Hereafter, Pottle, *Stretchers.*
2. Derby, Richard. *Wade in Sanitary! The Story of a Division Surgeon in France,* NY.: Putnam's, 1919, p.p. 50 and 73. Hereafter, Derby, *Wade in Sanitary!*
3. Jaffin, Jonathan H. Maj., USA, *Medical Support for the American Expeditionary Forces in France During the First World War,* Ft. Leavenworth, KS: 1990, p.113.
4. Per. Derby, Richard. "Wade in Sanitary!" *Scribner's Magazine,* September, 1919, Vol. 66, Sept., 1919, p. 342:
5. Scanlon, William, *God Have Mercy on Us: A Story of 1918,* Boston: Houghton Mifflin, 1929, pp. 4, 5. Hereafter, Scanlon, *God Have Mercy on Us.*
6. Cooke, Elliot D., "We Can Take It" *Infantry Journal,* May–Dec 1937, pp. 86, 87. Hereafter, Cooke, *We Can Take It.*
7. Mackin, Elton E., *Suddenly We Didn't Want To Die,* Novato, CA.: Presidio Press, 1993, pp. 24, 25. Hereafter, Mackin, *And Suddenly We Didn't Want to Die.*
8. Wood, Peter P. *Diary of Lt. Peter P. Wood, USMC, 6ᵗʰ Machine Gun Battalion, 1917–1919."* Compiled and edited by David Sleeper, 2001. Used with permission.
9. Richmond, Clarence L., *The War Diary of Clarence Richmond,* n. p., n. d. Used with permission of the diary owner and grandson of Clarence Richmond, Clarence Richmond, Jr. A copy of the original diary is at the Cleveland Public Library, Cleveland, Tennesee. The diary of Clarence Richmond was also serialized by his local newspaper, "The Cleveland Daily Banner," in 1979. Hereafter, Richmond, *War Diary.*
10. Thomason, John W., Jr. *The Second Division Northwest of Château-Thierry, 1 June–10 July 1918.* Washington, DC: National War College, 1928. Unpublished manuscript, pp.18, 19, 27. Hereafter, Thomason, *The Second Division Northwest of Château-Thierry.*
11. *Memoirs of an Ambulance Company Officer,* by Harry L. Smith, M.D., The Doomsday Press, Rochester, Minnesota, 1940. Privately printed.
12. Wise, Frederic M., and Frost, Meigs O., *A Marine Tells It to You,* NY.: J.H. Sears, 1929, pp. 193, 194. Reprinted by The Marine Corps Assoc., Quantico, Va., 1981, Hereafter, Wise, *A Marine Tells It to You.*
13. Morrey, Willard R. *The Ninth U.S. Infantry in the World War.* Germany: n.p., pp. 6, 7. Hereafter, Morrey, *The Ninth U.S. Infantry.*
14. Cooke, *We Can Take It,* pp. 87 to 89.
15. Derby, Richard. "Wade In Sanitary!, *Scribner's Magazine,* September, 1919.
16. Hansen, *The Marne,* p. 277.
17. Hansen, *The Marne* p.p. 274–5.
18. Spaulding, Col Oliver L., USA and Col John W. Wright, USA, *The Second Division, American Expeditionary Force in France: 1917–1918,* NY: Historical Committee of the Second Division Association, Hillman Press, 1937, p. 249. Hereafter, Spaulding & Wright, *The Second Division.*
19. Hansen, *The Marne,* pp. 272–274.
20. *History of Base Hospital No. 18, A.E.F. (Johns Hopkins Unit),* Baltimore, MD: Base Hospital 18 Association, 1919. Thomas Ellis Co., pp. 87, 88.
21. Story, Sommerville. *Present Day Paris and the Battlefields....* NY: D. Appleton & Co., 1920, page 168.
22. Hansen, *The Marne,* pp. 261 to 267.
23. Bailey, *Diary.*
24. Townsend, Harry Everett, *War Diary of a Combat Artist: Captain Harry E. Townsend,* Alfred E. Cornebise, ed., University Press of Colorado. Hereafter, Townsend, *War Diary.*
25. Havlin, Arthur C., *The History of Company A, 102ⁿᵈ Machine Gun Battalion, 26ᵗʰ Division, A.E.F,* Boston, H.C. Rodd, 1928, pp. 97, 98, 99. Hereafter, Havlin, *History of Company A.* Havlin, *History of Company A.,*
26. Pottle, Frederick A. *Stretchers: The Story of a Hospital Unit on The Western Front:* New Haven, CT: 1929.
27. Rickenbacker, Edward V. *Fighting the Flying Circus,* 1919, and Doubleday & Co., Garden City, NY: 1965, page 141.
28. War Diary of the 94ᵗʰ Pursuit Squadron entitled, "The Hat in the Ring Gang."
29. *The Stars and Stripes; The Complete File of the Official Newspaper of the A.E.F, 1918–1919,* NY: Arno, 1971.
30. Ford, George B. *Out of the Ruins,* New York, The Century Co., 1919.
31. Mitchell, Gen William A., *Memoirs of World War I: From Start to Finish of Our Greatest War,* Westport, CT.: Greenwood, 1975.
32. Harbord, Gen James G., *Leaves From a War Diary,* NY: Dodd Mead and Co., 1925, pp. 127 to 129. Hereafter, Harbord, *Leaves from a War Diary.*
33. Harbord, Gen James G., *The American Army in France,* Boston: Little, Brown, 1936, pp. 268, 269, 279 to 281. Hereafter, Harbord, *The American Army in France.*
34. Pierrefeu, Jean de. *French Headquarters 1915–1918,* Geoffrey Bles, Ltd., 1929. Hereafter, Pierrefeu, *French Headquarters.*
35. Brooks, Alden, *As I Saw It,* NY.; Alfred A. Knopf, 1929, 1930. Hereafter, Brooks, *As I Saw It.*
36. Hansen, Joseph Mills, *The Marne, Historic and Picturesque,* A.C. McClurg & Co., 1922, pp. 103, 109–10. Hereafter, Hansen, *The Marne.*
37. Cobb, Irvin S. *The Glory of the Coming: What Mine Eyes Have Seen of Americans in Action.* Doran, 1919, pp. 86–7.

38. Harbord, Gen James G., *A Month in Belleau Wood in 1918*, Detroit, MI.: N.p.: 8 cols., 1928. Also in *Leatherneck*, v. 11, no 6 (Jun 1928): pp.10–12, 54.

39. Hungerford, Edward, *With the Doughboys in France: A Few Chapters of the American Effort*, NY: Macmillan, 1920, pp.145, 146.

40. Thomason, *The Second Division*, pp. 16, 20, 21.

41. Berry, Henry. *Make the Kaiser Dance*, Doubleday & Co., Garden City, NY.: 1978, pp. 78, Permission sought. Hereafter, Berry, *Make the Kaiser Dance*.

42. A letter describing the battle for Belleau Wood by Lieutenant H. R. Long, USMC, 6th Machine Gun Battalion, as originally published in the newspaper,"The Adirondack Enterprise", edition of 23 August 1918.

43. Cooke, *We Can Take It*, pp. 83 to 86.

44. Gulberg, Martin Gus., *A War Diary*, Chicago: Drake Press,1927, p. 22. Hereafter, Gulberg, *A War Diary*.

45. Scanlon, *God Have Mercy on Us!*, pp. 3, 4.

46. Cowing, Kemper Frey, comp. "*Dear Folks at Home…The Glorious Story of the United States Marines in France As Told by Their Letters from the Battlefields*," edited by Courtney R. Cooper. Boston: Houghton Mifflin, 1919, pp.147 to 149. Hereafter, Cowing, *Dear Folks at Home*.

47. Boyd, Thomas, *Through the Wheat*, NY: Scribner's, 1927, pp.63, 64. Paperback edition by Award Books, 1964. Reprinted 1978 by Southern University Press, Carbondale, ILL. Permission sought. Hereafter, Boyd, *Through the Wheat*.

48. Cowing, *Dear Folks at Home*, pp. 50, 151.

49. Evans, Frank E., *Daddy Pat of the Marines: Being His Letters from France to His Son Townie*, NY: Stokes,1919, pp. 111 to 118. Hereafter, Evans, *Daddy Pat of the Marines*.

50. Bullard, Robert L., and Earl Reeves, *American Soldiers Also Fought*, NY: Longmans, Green, 1936, pp. 35 to 37.

51. Morgan, Daniel E., *When the World Went Mad*, Boston: Christopher Publishing House, 1922, pp. 27, 28. Hereafter, Morgan, *When the World Went Mad*.

52. Cowing, *Dear Folks at Home*, pp.140, 141.

53. Spaulding and Wright, *The Second Division*, pp. 248, 249.

54. Spaulding and Wright, *The Second Division*, p. 250.

55. Hendricks, Charles, *Combat and Construction: U.S. Army Engineers in World War I*, U.S. Army Corps of Engineers, 1993.

56. Thomason, *The Second Division*, p. 38.

57. Sinclair, Upton, *Jimmie Higgins: A Story*, NY.: Boni & Liveright, 1919, pp. 218, 220, 232, 233.

58. Kay, Ross, *With Pershing at the Front: American Soldiers in the Trenches*, NY.: Barse & Hopkins, 1918, pp.146, 147, 153. Hereafter, *With Pershing at the Front*.

59. Per. Krulewitch, MajGen M. L. "Belleau Wood," *Marine Corps Gazette*, 55 (Nov 1971), pp.19, 20. Courtesy of *Marine Corps Gazette Magazine*.

60. Spaulding and Wright, *The Second Division*, p. 44.

61. Excerpt from the diary of Lacey Gibbs, *The Doughboy*, Fall, 1981, Vol. 4, No. 2., as submitted by Denis Gordon. Used with permission. Hereafter, Gibbs, *Diary*.

62. Per. Silverthorn, LtGen Merwin H., USMC (Ret), "A Brigade of Marines," *Marine Corps Gazette*, 55 (Nov 1971), pp. 23 to 26. Courtesy of *Marine Corps Gazette Magazine*.

63. Frederick Palmer. *Our Gallant Madness*, Garden City, NY.: Doubleday, Doran, 1937, pp.239 to 241, 243. Hereafter, Palmer, *Our Gallant Madness*.

64. U.S. Army. General Service Schools, Fort Leavenworth. *The German Offensive of July 15, 1918 (Marne Source Book)*, Fort Leavenworth, KS: The General Service Schools Press, 1923, p. 716. Hereafter, *Marne Source Book*.

65. Van Every, Dale. *The A.E.F. in Battle*, NY.: D. Appleton and Company, 1928, pp. 77 to 80. Hereafter, Van Every, *The A.E.F. in Battle*.

66. Gaines, Ruth L., *Helping France—The Red Cross in the Devastated Area*, NY.: E.P. Dutton, 1919, pp. 58, 69, 70, 76, 77.

67. Lejeune, John A., *The Reminiscences of a Marine*, Philadelphia: Dorrance, 1930, p. 292. Hereafter, Lejeune, *Reminiscences of a Marine*.

68. Townsend, *War Diary*. pp. 28, 29.

69. Wharton, James B., *Squad*, NY. Coward-McCann, 1928, pp. 24 to 29.

70. Lavine, A. Lincoln., *Circuits of Victory*, NY.: Country Life Press, Doubleday Page & Co., Garden City, NY., 1921, p. 369. Hereafter, Lavine, *Circuits of Victory*.

71. Strickland, Daniel W., *Connecticut Fights, The Story of the 102nd Regiment, 26th Division*, New Haven: Quinnipiack Press, 1930, pp. 170 to 172. Hereafter, Strickland, *Connecticut Fights*.

72. Pattullo, George. *Horrors of Moonlight*, 1939, Allston & Depew, pp. 55 to 60. Hereafter, Pattullo, *Horrors of Moonlight*.

73. Derby, Richard., *Wade in Sanitary! The Story of a Division Surgeon in France*, NY: Putnam's, 1919, p.p. 50 and 73. Hereafter, Derby, *Wade in Sanitary!*

74. Per. *Outlook and Independent*, 9 Oct 1929, pp. 125, 196–7, "The Backwash of Battle," by Frederick A. Pottle.

75. Pottle, *Stretchers*.

76. Richmond, *War Diary*.

77. Robertson, Dean L., 79th Co., 6th Marines, MS diary of, typescript, unpublished, n.p., n.d., p. 6. Hereafter, Robertson, *Manuscript*.

78. Scanlon, *God Have Mercy on Us!*, p. 111.

79. Gulberg, *A War Diary*, pp. 26, 27.

80. U.S. Army. 2nd Infantry Division. *Records of the Second Division (Regular)*. U.S. War Department. Army War College Historical Section, Washington, D.C., & Ft. Sam Houston, Texas. 1924–1928. Ten volumes (some in several parts). About 200 pages in each part. Also microfilm 05–2 1924/* 10 reels. Vol 4, p. 232. Hereafter, *Records*.

81. Robertson, *Manuscript*, p. 79.

82. Cooke, *We Can Take It*, pp. 89, 90.

83. Strott, George George., *The Medical Department of the U.S. Navy with the Army and MarineCorps in France in World War I*, Washington: U.S. Navy Department, Bureau of Medicine and Surgery, 1947. Navmed 1197, "Excerpts from Log of a Battalion Surgeon," p. 45. Hereafter, Strott, *Medical Department, U.S. Navy*.

84. Bailey, *Diary*.

85. Gulbert, *A War Diary*, pp. 22, 23.

86. Scanlon, *God Have Mercy on Us!*, pp. 5 to 8.

87. Townsend, *War Diary*, p. 36.

88. Scanlon, *God Have Mercy on Us!*.

89. Woolcott, Alexander. *A Friendly Guide for American Pilgrims to the Shrines Between the Marne and the Vesle*, Lafayette Publishing Company, Paris, 1919, p. 11. Hereafter, Woolcott, *A Friendly Guide*.

90. Derby, *Wade in Sanitary!*

91. Chatfield, Josiah C., et al. *Iodine and Gasoline, a History of the 117th Sanitary Train*, Kingsport, Tennessee: Kingsport Press, 1919. Hereafter, *Iodine and Gasoline*.

92. Gibbons, Floyd. *"And They Thought We Wouldn't Fight,"* NY: George H. Doran Company, 1918.

93. Woolcott, *A Friendly Guide*, page 11.

94. Woolcott, Alexander. *The Command Is Forward—Tales of the A.E.F. Battlefields As They Appeared in the Stars and Stripes*. NY: Century, 1919, page 282.

95. Lavine, *Circuits of Victory*, p. 454.

96. Woolcott, *A Friendly Guide*, p. 10, 11.

97. Address by MajGen James G. Harbord before the Detroit Bond Club, February 22nd, 1928. Hereafter, Harbord, *Address*.

98. Harbord, *The American Army in France*, pp. 287, 288, 295.

99. Harbord, *Address*.

100. Wunderlich, Raymond., *From Trench and Dugout*, Stockton, CA.: 1919, pp. 56, 57. Hereafter, Wunderlich, *From Trench and Dugout*.

101. Lavine, *Circuits of Victory*, p. 368.

102. Catlin, Albertus Wright, and Dyer, Walter A, *With the Help of God and a Few Marines*, Garden City, NY.: Doubleday, Page, 1919, pp. 91, 103. Hereafter, Catlin, *With the Help of God*.

103. Carter, William A, *The Tale of a Devildog, by William A. Carter, One of Them*, Washington, DC.: The Canteen Press, 1920. Hereafter, Carter, *The Tale of a Devildog*.

NOTES TO SECTION THREE

1. Per. Kelton, Robert H. C., "The Miracle of Chateau-Thierry," *Century Magazine*, May, 1919, page 99.

2. Per. Alphaud, Gabriel. "The Desecrated Birthplace of La Fontaine," *New York Times Current History Magazine*, Vol. 5, Oct 1916, pp. 54–6.

3. Per. Gibbons, H. A., "An Ancient Village on the Marne," *Harper's Magazine*, Vol. 132, April 1916, pp. 674–84.

4. Per. Canfield, Dorothy. "Khaki Confidences at Château-Thierry," *Harper's Monthly Magazine*, Vol. 137, No. 822, pp. 777 to 784.

5 Per. "Château-Thierry Now Has a Place in American History." *The Literary Digest*, Vol, 58, August 10, 1918, pp. 49, 50.

6. Per. Hopper, James. "The American Chateau-Thierry." *The Literary Digest*, Vol. 58, Sept. 14, 1918, p. 29. Also: Hopper, James. "Emptying the Bag": Part III of "On the German Heels."

7. Per. Hansen, Joseph. "The Marne," *Collier's*, 30 November 1918, pp. 9,10, 243 to 251.

7. Woolcott, *The Command is Forward*, p. 282.

8. *American Battlefields in France*, First Section, General Staff (Visitor's Bureau) Headquarters, Headquarters, AEF, American Forces in France, 1918.

9. Per. "The Festive Rubberneck Wagon in France's Battle-Fields." *Literary Digest*, Vol. 67, Nov 27, 1920, p. 65.

11. Story, Sommerville. *Present Day Paris and the Battlefields…*. NY: D. Appleton & Co., 1920, pp. 143–4.

12. Per. "They Used to Call It the Front." *Literary Digest*, Vol. 69, April 23, 1921, pp. 45–6.

13. *The Americans in the Great War*, Michelin Illustrated Guides to the Battlefields (1914–1918), Volume I. The Second Battle of the Marne (Chateau-Thierry, Soissons, Fismes), 3 Volumes, (Michelin and Company, Clermond-Ferrand, France, 1920), pp. 41–42, Hereafter, Michelin, *The Americans in the Great War*. Used with permission of Michelin and Company.

14. Per. Ford, George B. "France's Devastated Areas, Yesterday and To-Day." *Literary Digest*, Vol. 72, Feb 11, 1922, p. 38, See also: *Out of the Ruins*, New York, Century Co., 1919, pp. 29–30, 32.

15. Per. Scidmore, Eliza R. "In the War-Swept Marne Country," *The Outlook*, Wednesday, 26 June, 1918, pp. 342–3.

16. Per. Odell, Joseph H. "The Battle of Château-Thierry and Beyond," *The Outlook*, Sep. 11, 1918, Vol. 120, pp. 51–2.

17. McClure Newspaper Syndicate, July, 1919.

18. Harper's Pictorial Record of the World War, 1920.

19. United States Surgeon General's Office, *The Medical Department of the United States Army in the World War*, 17 vols. USGPO, 1921–1929. Vol. VIII, Field Op-

erations, p.313. Hereafter, Surgeon General, *Medical Department, U.S. Army.*

20. Source unknown, but probably from one of the 1919 editions of the newspaper, *Indianapolis News*

21. Forrest, Wilbur. *Behind the Front Page: Stories of Newspaper Stories in the Making.* NY: D. Appleton-Century Co., 1934, pp. 114 to 122.

22. Per. "American Defense of Château-Thierry," *New York Times Current History Magazine*, Vol. 8, pt. 2, July, 1918, pp. 62 to 65.

23. *The Watch on the Rhine*, publication of the Society of the Third Infantry Division, issue of February, 2002, under "Memoirs of World War I, by Sgt.James J. Webster, page 23.

25. Both, W. C. *America's Army and its Part in the Great War.* Chicago: 1918

26. Per. "Father O'Reilly Tells of the Work of the Third in France." *Literary Digest*, Sept. 13, 1919, page 93.

27. Per. De Wissen, H. "Seeing Battle-Scarred Europe," *Forum*, Vol. 64, July 1920, page 43.

28. Mudd, Thomas B. R., *The Yanks Were There: A Chronological and Documentary Review of World War One*, NY.: Vantage, 1958, pp. 159, 160. Hereafter, Mudd, *The Yanks Were There.*

29. *Indianapolis News*, Nov 1, 1919, "Funkhouser Memorial, pp. 138–146.

30. *Records*, pp. 211–12.

31. Mendenhall, John R., "The First in the Dyke," *Infantry Journal* 43 (Jan-Feb. 1936), pp. 13-23.

32. Crawford, *Six Months with the Sixth Brigade.* Kansas City, MO: E. B. Barnett, 1928, p. 44. 33. Hemenway, Frederick V, *History of the Third Division, United States Army in the World War for the Period Dec. 1, 1917 to Jan. 1, 1919*, Third Division, U.S. Army, Germany: Andernach-on-Rhine, 1919. Printed in Cologne, Germany by M. Dumont Schauberg, 1919, pp. 269, 270.

33. Hereafter, Hemenway, *History of the Third Division.*

34. Spaulding & Wright, *The Second Division*, pp. 249, 250.

35. Dickman, Joseph T., *The Great Crusade: A Narrative of the World War*, NY.: D. Appleton

Co., 1927, p. 53. Hereafter, Dickman, *The Great Crusade.*

36. "*Watch on the Rhine*," Official paper of the Army of Occupation, Coblenz, Germany, date and issue unknown.

37. Pugh, Irving E., & William F. Thayer. *Forgotten Fights of the A.E.F.* Boston: Roxborough Publishing Company, 1921.

38. Peixotto, Ernest, *The American Front*, Scribner's, 1919, pp. 91, 92. Hereafter, Peixotto, *The American Front.*

39. Ganser, Elmer B., *History of the 126th Infantry in the War with Germany*, Grand Rapids, MI.: Dean Hicks, 1920, pp. 91, 92. Hereafter, Ganser, *History of the 126th Infantry.*

40. Brooks, *As I Saw It*, pp. 150 to 163.

41. Per. James, Edwin L., America's Part in a Historic Battle," *The New York Times Current History Magazine*, Vol. 8, pt. 2, September, 1918, pp. 402–3, and 492–3.

42. Stonehouse, Frederick. "*Combat Engineer! The History of the 107th Engineer Battalion (1881–1961).*"

43. Nolan, James B., *The Reading Militia in the Great War*, Reading, PA.: F. A. Woerner, 1921, p. 131.

44. Sherwood, Elmer W., *Diary of a Rainbow Veteran: Written at the Front*, Terre-Haute, IN.: Moore-Langen, 1929. Hereafter, Sherwood, *Diary of a Rainbow Veteran.*

45. Hoffman, Robert C., *I Remember the Last War*. York, PA.: Strength & Health Publishing Co., 1940, p. 155. Hereafter, Hoffman, *I Remember the Last War.*

46. Jacks, Leo V., *Service Record: By an Artilleryman*, Scribner's, 1928, pp. 16, 17. Hereafter, Jacks, *Service Record.*

47. Chatfield, Josiah C., et al. *Iodine and Gasoline, a History of the 117th Sanitary Train*, Kingsport, Tennessee: Kingsport Press, 1919.

48. *Harper's Pictorial Library of the World War*, 1920.

49. *The War Diary of the German 231st Infantry Division.*

50. Brooks, *As I Saw It*, p. 154.

51. Per. Holt, Hamilton. "Where America Turned the Tide," *Independent*, issue of 24 May 1919, p. 301.

52. The letters of John Montgomery Gauss, as seen on the website: http://homepages.rootsweb.com/~schmblss/home/Letters/Gauss/1923-07-26.htm

53. Hansen, *The Marne.*

54. Weaver, MajGen W. G., USA Ret., *History of the 8th Machine Gun Battalion, 5th Brigade, 3rd Infantry Division*, Edwards Brothers, Inc., Ann Arbor, Michigan, 1965, p. 100.

55. Letter dated 20 April 1999 from D. Menard, Curate, Department of the Air Force, United States Air Force Museum, 1100 Spatz Street, Wright-Patterson Air Force Base, Ohio 45433-7102, to the editor.

56. Per. *Leslie's Weekly*, September 6, 1919.

57. Hoffman, *I Remember the Last War.*

58. Spaulding & Wright, *The Second Division*, p. 95.

59. Spaulding & Wright, *The Second Division.*

60. *History of Base Hospital No. 18, A.E.F. (Johns Hopkins Unit)*, Baltimore, MD: Base Hospital 18 Association, 1919. Thomas Ellis Co., pp. 87, 88.

61. *Iodine and Gasoline.*

62. Spaulding & Wright, *The Second Division.*

63. Hansen, *The Marne.*

About The Author

David Homsher, a veteran of U.S. Army service during the Korean War, and now retired, is an amateur historian-author who has dedicated himself to perpetuating the memory of the American World War I "Doughboy"and the battlefields on which he fought. An avid researcher, he has made many trips to France, walking the battlefields, seeking out battle sites, and tracing the actions of the AEF units involved.

David has spent many hours in research in the National Archives and other major libraries and has an extensive collection of books, diaries and articles about the "War to End all Wars."

David has had a life-long interest in World War I, has had many articles published in periodicals and historical journals. His desire to publicize the achievments of the AEF and his personal familiarity with the battle sites has led him to decide to write a series of guidebooks to the World War I battlefields of the AEF in 1918.

David Homsher retired from a major domestic airline in 1990 in order to become totally immersed in writing his battlefield guidebooks. Homsher has spent almost two decades researching and writing his series of self-published guidebooks to the AEF battlefields in and near Château-Thierry, France, of which this is the first volume to be published.

Born in Pennsylvania but living for many years in California, Homsher has also committed his love of American World War I history to paper by having had many articles printed in World War I historical journals and periodicals.

Homsher, 74, now lives in San Mateo, California, where he has his own publishing company, Battleground Productions. Homsher is a long-time member of the following organizations and societies: Western Front Association, Great War Society, Doughboy Historical Society, Society for Military History, Company of Military Historians, Army Historical Foundation.

This And Future AEF Battlefield Guidebooks

This book, *American Battlefields of World War I: Château-Thierry—Then and Now*, is the first of a number of proposed guidebooks to the AEF battlefields in France and Belgium. As originally written, this book covered the three AEF battle areas at the tip of the Marne Salient: Château-Thierry, northwest of Château-Thierry and east of Château-Thierry. In its original form the book was enormous, some 1,200 pages in length, without photographs—much too large for a battlefield guidebook. The editorial decision was then made to chop this monster of a book into three logical segments, one for each of the mentioned battle areas.

This book takes the traveler through the geographic area of the Aisne-Marne Defensive campaign of 27 May to 5 June, 1918, including the Château-Thierry Operation. Beginning at the Charles de Gaulle International Airport and continuing east to Château-Thierry, the traveler will see the sites of military interest that relate to our Allies and to units of the AEF, as well as the battle-sites of the U. S. 3rd Division in the town of Château-Thierry.

The experience of the AEF in the summer of 1918 and the emergency at the Marne is perhaps the most confusing and complicated of the war, with multiple units and portions of units moving back and forth from one sector to another, leading up to and including separate battles at Cantigny, Soissons, the Marne, Belleau Wood, Château-Thierry, etc.

This is primarily a *geographic* guidebook. It is not a chronological or organizational guidebook. Due to the extreme emergency of the situation at Château-Thierry in late May of 1918, French and American units were rushing all over the area. Thus, for any particular town or village, one may find a number of military units having been there, either individually or together. If the reader occasionally gets the impression of, 'What is going on here?' can you imagine the thoughts of the military commanders at this time? You thought that you were confused! Read on and you will find out that you are not the only one. Château-Thierry was the 'Chinese fire drill' of 1918.

This destroys any appearance of a continuous narrative. The reader will sometimes find it confusing. But it serves very well to show how much military events are really the sum total of a complicated series of actions and decisions, often none too well coordinated, all interacting upon each other in a confused way to produce the final situation. This approach makes the reader aware of all that is going on without letting him lose sight of the fact that the participants in this action were very ignorant of much that was happening. It is also clear that there were considerable periods when nothing was happening, punctuated by sudden battle events lasting with great intensity for a short time and then stopping as suddenly as they began. The contrast between the attitude of mind at headquarters and the actual state of affairs at the fighting front will be apparent to an entirely inexperienced reader.

The second volume in this series will tour the battlefields of the AEF in and around Belleau Wood and the *Pas Fini* sector, the area northwest of Château-Thierry during the months of May, June, July of 1918.

The third volume will tour the AEF battlefields along the Marne River and east of Château-Thierry.

Additional AEF battlefield guidebooks are planned and will be announced at a future date.

YOU ARE NOT FORGOTTEN